Fodor's 94 Cape Cod, Martha's Vineyard, Nantucket

Candice Gianetti

Fodor's Travel Publications, Inc.
New York • Toronto • London • Sydney • Auckland

Fodor's Cape Cod, Martha's Vineyard, Nantucket

Editor: Scott McNeely
Editorial Contributors: Phil Joseph, Marcy Pritchard
Creative Director: Fabrizio La Rocca
Cartographer: David Lindroth
Illustrator: Karl Tanner
Cover Photograph: Catherine Karnow/Woodfin Camp

Design: Vignelli Associates

About the Author

Candice Gianetti is a freelance writer and editor who lives on Martha's Vineyard.

Special Sales

Contents

Maps

Foreword

For their help in putting together this guide, the author wishes especially to thank Frank Ackerman at the Cape Cod National Seashore, Michael Frucci at the Cape Cod Chamber of Commerce, Randi Vega at the Martha's Vineyard Chamber of Commerce, and Maurene Campbell at the Nantucket Chamber of Commerce.

While every care has been taken to ensure the accuracy of the information in this guide, the passage of time will always bring change, and consequently the publisher cannot accept responsibility for errors that may occur.

All prices and opening times quoted here are based on information supplied to us at press time. Hours and admission fees may change, however, and the prudent traveler will avoid inconvenience by calling ahead.

Fodor's wants to hear about your travel experiences, both pleasant and unpleasant. When a hotel or restaurant fails to live up to its billing, let us know and we will investigate the complaint and revise our entries where the facts warrant it. Send your letters to the editors of Fodor's Travel Publications, 201 E. 50th Street, New York, NY 10022.

Highlights '94
and
Fodor's Choice

Highlights '94

Amtrak ended direct summer service to the Cape from Washington, DC, requiring travelers to transfer in New York, but the actions of other area transportation outfits seem to indicate confidence in the Cape and islands' prospects. **USAir Express** came to Martha's Vineyard in 1993, offering summer service from New York in 36-seat Shorts 360 and 37-seat Dash 8-100 aircraft. **Cape Air** continues to increase its service, including additional joint-fare and ticketing-and-baggage arrangements with major airlines and a new **Vineyard Shuttle** running hourly each way in season between the Vineyard and Boston. And while we're on the subject of shuttles, Nantucket got a new **Madaket Beach shuttle bus** and Falmouth got a new **Woods Hole–Shore Drive Beach shuttle** last year.

The **Steamship Authority** is in the midst of some massive projects. In addition to building a new ferry and rehabbing another, it is building two new terminals. Hyannis's 9,000-square-foot terminal, scheduled for construction between 1994 and 1995, is expected to cost $4 million (on top of the $4.5 million purchase of additional land). A new, more attractive terminal will be built at Vineyard Haven—Martha's Vineyard's main gateway, serving 1.4 million passengers a year or 6,500 a day in summer—at a cost of $2 million. It will be built in the area now occupied by the present terminal and the hot dog stand, rest rooms, and former Seaman's Bethel across the street.

As usual, there continues to be plenty of winter weather on the Cape and islands. On the Cape, storms wiped out the last unexcavated bits of the **archaeological dig** at Coast Guard Beach. On Nantucket's south shore, storms have claimed most of the homes at **Cisco** (along with the land beneath them); the rest have been declared unsafe. In April 1993 one house was moved off a bluff that had receded 75 feet inland since the previous October. In 'Sconset, several houses at **Codfish Park** were lost to erosion in the winter of 1992–93.

On the Vineyard, the Trustees of Reservations also report an increased rate of erosion on south-facing beaches (75 feet in some spots). While 60–75 acres of beach were created at **Wasque** over the past 20 years, the current cycle of erosion reclaims an average of 17 feet annually. In Oak Bluffs, the battle continues among town, state, and the Army Corps of Engineers to save **Beach Road,** a view-rich narrow strip between the ocean and Sengekontacket Pond. On Chappaquiddick, **Mytoi**'s Japanese gardens, devastated by Hurricane Bob and the winter nor'easter of 1991, are slowly being restored as funds are available.

There was actually a lot of good news on the little island of Martha's Vineyard in 1993. Historian and longtime West Tisbury resident **David McCullough** won the Pulitzer Prize for *Truman* (joining the ranks of summer residents and fellow Pulitzer winners William Styron and Anthony Lewis). After years of uncertainty over the future of the beloved West Tisbury general store, the Martha's Vineyard Preservation Trust—to the joy of all concerned—bought **Alley's** to keep it open as a year-round meeting place and postal outlet for the community. It cost $300,000; a massive capital campaign raised an additional $300,000 for major renovations, expected to be completed by Memorial Day 1994.

At the Land Bank's **Sepiessa Point Reservation,** a 20-year process of gaining public access to Tisbury Great Pond—fought by riparian owners of the pond—was settled in June 1993. There is now parking space, a road to the pond, and public access for motorboating, oystering by boat, blue-crab hunting along the shore, fishing, swimming, or just walking around the lovely property. The Trustees' **Long Point** reserve has acquired an additional 500 feet of beach frontage for public use.

There have been a lot of changes in Edgartown: The **Charlotte Inn's gift shop** has moved across the street to free up its former space for guests' use as an English-style club room. **Bickerton & Ripley** took over an adjacent shop to expand its downstairs and make more room for author's parties. Edgartown's financially troubled **Katama Farms** dairy bit the dust, as did the **South Pole Slush Company** of Oak Bluffs. **Larry's Tackle Shop,** a fixture on Edgartown harbor for 45 years, moved to larger quarters on Main Street, adding a saltwater flyfishing department (with clinics) and stocking bait and chum for offshore fishermen. Speaking of fish, after an eight-year absence while they were being restocked all over the East Coast, striped bass were returned to the **Martha's Vineyard Striped Bass and Bluefish Derby** in a limited way for the 1993 season.

While Hyannis's prestigious **Richard A. Bourne** auction house called it quits, Provincetown welcomed two new art galleries with offbeat themes: **Star Gallery,** offering signed, limited-edition lithographs by John Lennon and Jerry Garcia, as well as original rock-theme artworks by gallery owner Doug Johnson; and **Animated Classics,** featuring the originals of art used in the making of cartoons by Hanna Barbera and other major studios. Hyannis Public Library got a new **multicultural center** with books, videos, tapes, puzzles, dolls, games, and programs that introduce children to the diversity of world cultures.

Cape Cod Scenic Railroad's new **Ecology Discovery Tour** out of Hyannis features commentary by a naturalist on the construction of the railroad and its effect on the ecosystem, as well as a guided walk at a nature preserve. The **Cape Cod Chamber of Commerce** is trying to get state funding to

build a visitor center on Route 25 in Wareham by 1994 to
reduce congestion at the Route 28 center in Bourne.

Throughout the area, there's news in museumland. The
John F. Kennedy Hyannis Museum appears to be fixed in
its place at the Old Town Hall on Main Street and gearing
up to add a video and more photographs to its small collection. The **Cape Cod Children's Museum,** opened in 1993 in
the Falmouth Mall, offers interactive exhibits, learning-
play space, and educational programs for children 1–10.
The Wellfleet Historical Society's **Samuel Rider House** has
been closed indefinitely due to structural deterioration; furniture and paintings from its collection have been trans-
ferred to the Main Street museum. Three Martha's
Vineyard Preservation Trust properties in Edgartown—
the **Old Whaling Church,** the **Dr. Daniel Fisher House,** and
the **Vincent House**—are now open only to participants in a
historical walking tour (the Whaling Church continues to
be open for cultural events). The Dukes County Historical
Society's museum changed its name to **The Vineyard Museum.** (Another name change: **Chilmark Chamber Players**
became the Martha's Vineyard Chamber Music Society.)

Fundraising continues by Boston's Museum of Afro-Ameri-
can History to turn the 19th-century **African Meeting
House** on Nantucket into a staffed exhibit space documenting the African-American experience on the island. The island's public library, the **Atheneum,** is busy raising $2.8
million for structural work and modernizing, including
building a new children's wing that will spill over into the
adjacent park.

The **Nantucket Historical Association** celebrates its centennial in 1994 with major exhibits, parties, and other
events throughout the summer. A photographic exhibit upstairs at the Thomas Macy Warehouse will tell the history
of the association. The **China Trade show** at the Peter
Foulger Museum will exhibit 200 objects (paintings, porcelains, other decorative items from Nantucket's China
trade) from private homes and the NHA collection. The
Fair Street Museum will host an exhibit of antique **Nantucket lightship baskets** from NHA and private collections.
The NHA's **Greater Light** and **1800 House** museums will
remain closed for the 1994 season, but if you've been to the
Hadwen House, you should have a look at its transforma-
tion after a two-year redecoration, finished in summer 1993,
that returned it to its mid-19th-century appearance. Antique gas chandeliers have been installed throughout, along
with reproduction wallpapers, window treatments, and
even a specially commissioned reproduction Brussels carpet. Gone are the Empire and Regency furnishings, replaced by pieces from the NHA collection that reflect the
house's 1845–46 origins.

The harbor's importance to the island is marked in the new,
three-day **Nantucket Harborfest.** Events include a blessing

of the fleet, a clambake, kayak and windsurfing races, a children's pirate parade, shop window displays, and chowder and bluefish cooking contests. Along with regular visits by **cruise ships,** Martha's Vineyard's harbors have begun to enjoy the sight of **tall ships** anchoring offshore for a few days of R&R throughout the summer (ship visits are sometimes allowed). At press time, a day of tall ships was being planned as a new annual September event: Three Class B tall ships will anchor in different down-Island ports and offer cruises and ship visits.

Cape Cod's history, culture, and ecology are celebrated in another event new in 1993, **Cape Heritage Week,** created through the joint efforts of museums, historical societies, theater groups, libraries, and the Cape Cod National Seashore. Dozens of events are scheduled throughout the week, ranging from parades to storytelling and plays to nature and historical tours to special exhibits and lectures.

On the food and entertainment scene: Chatham's **Wayside Inn** was sold and closed for complete retooling by the new owners (plans for its entertainment offerings when it reopens for the 1994 season were uncertain at press time). Hyannis's **Asa Bearse House,** after long troubles including a bankruptcy, is once again a hot year-round night spot, offering live music and dancing nightly in season. **Christine's,** a major concert venue in West Dennis, has built a 300-seat addition to its nightclub. **Coconuts Comedy Club** is now part of Hyannis's Holiday Inn. In Provincetown, the **Mews** has moved down the street to quarters once occupied by Franco's; renovations to the fire-damaged downstairs have resulted in a beautiful dining room with the beach right outside a wall of floor-to-ceiling windows.

On the Vineyard, **Sandcastles** replaced the beleaguered **Martha's** in Edgartown, the **Roadhouse** is gone, and the venerable **Black Dog** restaurant has gone nonsmoking. The island got two new barbecue places where once there were none, plus a new **Dairy Queen** and **Dunkin' Doughnuts** (can the golden arches be far behind?).

Visitors will be pleased to know that the first **Lyme disease vaccine** for humans is being tested on Nantucket. Developed at the Harvard School of Public Health and 95% effective on mice, the vaccine may be available within five years. Nature lovers will and four-wheel-drivers won't be so pleased about new federal and state mandates enlarging protection areas around piping plover nesting sites, which have meant sporadic **beach closings** to four-wheel-drive vehicles on many area beaches from mid-March to mid-August.

Fodor's Choice

No two people will agree on what makes a perfect vacation, but it's fun and helpful to know what others think. We hope you'll have a chance to experience some of Fodor's Choices yourself on Cape Cod, Martha's Vineyard, and Nantucket. For detailed information about each entry, refer to the appropriate chapter.

Special Moments

Sunset Jeep or horseback rides through the Provincetown dunes

Watching fireworks from the Oak Bluffs green, Martha's Vineyard

A community sing at the Oak Bluffs Camp Ground, Martha's Vineyard

Glimpsing Nantucket town as you approach by ferry

Lunch in the rose garden of Chanticleer, Nantucket

Stargazing from Nantucket's Loines Observatory

Sights

Bright purple cranberries floating on the flooded bogs just before harvest, Cape Cod and Nantucket

The old New England scene of the waterwheel-powered Dexter Gristmill on Shawme Pond in Sandwich

Hallet's Store, a century-old drugstore in Yarmouth Port

The marsh life at Bass Hole Boardwalk, Yarmouth Port

Harbor seals off Race Point in winter, Provincetown

Whales breaching alongside your whale-watch boat

The candy-colored Victorian cottages of the Oak Bluffs Camp Ground, Martha's Vineyard

Nantucket's cobblestone streets and historic architecture

The moors of Nantucket in fall

Museums

Heritage Plantation, Sandwich

Julia Wood House, Falmouth

Old Atwood House and Museums, Chatham

The Vineyard Museum, Edgartown, Martha's Vineyard

Whaling Museum, Nantucket

Viewpoints

From the Pilgrim Monument, Provincetown, of the town and surrounding waters

From the Province Lands Visitor Center observation deck, for a 360° panorama of duneland and ocean

From Nobska Light, Woods Hole, of the Elizabeth Islands and Martha's Vineyard across the sound

From Chatham Light, of the "Chatham Break"

From Scargo Hill, Dennis, of the lake and town below and of ocean and bay beyond

From Gay Head Cliffs, Martha's Vineyard, of the cliff striations and the Elizabeth Islands across the sound

From First Congregational Church, Nantucket, for the best view of Nantucket's moors, ponds, streets, and lighthouses

Nature Areas

Cape Cod National Seashore

Monomoy Wildlife Refuge, off Chatham

Nickerson State Park, Brewster

Wellfleet Bay Wildlife Sanctuary, South Wellfleet

Felix Neck, Martha's Vineyard

Long Point, Martha's Vineyard

Wasque, Chappaquiddick Island

Coatue–Coskata–Great Point, Nantucket

Eel Point, Nantucket

Beaches

Nauset Light, Coast Guard, and Race Point beaches on the Cape Cod National Seashore

Sandy Neck Beach, West Barnstable

Old Silver Beach, North Falmouth

West Dennis Beach

Lucy Vincent Beach, Chilmark, Martha's Vineyard

South Beach, Martha's Vineyard

Wasque Beach, Chappaquiddick

Surfside Beach, Nantucket

Eel Point, Nantucket

Shopping

The weekly flea market at the Wellfleet Drive-In Theatre

Farmer's markets on Martha's Vineyard

Farm stands everywhere

Route 6A on Cape Cod for crafts and antiques

Provincetown, Wellfleet, and Nantucket for art

Cape Cod Mall, Hyannis

Eldred's auction house, East Dennis

Rafael Osona auction house, Nantucket

Tree's Place, Orleans, for crafts and art

Scargo Pottery, Dennis

Janis Aldridge, Nantucket, for beautifully framed antique prints

Lightship baskets and scrimshaw on Nantucket

Nantucket-theme rugs by Claire Murray, Nantucket

Art Galleries

Long Point, Provincetown

Provincetown Art Association and Museum

Blue Heron Gallery, Wellfleet

Granary Gallery, West Tisbury, Martha's Vineyard

Robert Wilson Galleries, Nantucket

Taste Treats

Clam chowder at The Flume, Mashpee

Fried clams at Baxter's, Hyannis

Cioppino at Roadhouse Cafe, Hyannis

Portuguese kale soup at Land Ho! or Kadee's, both in Orleans

Ice cream at Four Seas, Centerville

Fresh, sweet bay scallops in fall and winter

Dining

Chillingsworth, Brewster (*Very Expensive*)

Regatta of Falmouth-by-the-Sea (*Expensive*)

The Paddock, Hyannis (*Moderate–Expensive*)

Nauset Beach Club, Orleans (*Moderate*)

Up the Creek, Hyannis (*Moderate*)

L'étoile, Edgartown, Martha's Vineyard (*Very Expensive*)

Lambert's Cove Country Inn, West Tisbury, Martha's Vineyard (*Expensive*)

Jimmy Seas Pan Pasta, Oak Bluffs, Martha's Vineyard (*Moderate–Expensive*)

Topper's, Nantucket (*Very Expensive*)

Club Car, Nantucket (*Expensive–Very Expensive*)

American Seasons, Nantucket (*Moderate–Expensive*)

Le Languedoc bistro, Nantucket (*Inexpensive–Moderate*)

Lodging

Chatham Bars Inn, Chatham (*Very Expensive*)

Inn at West Falmouth (*Very Expensive*)

Captain's House Inn, Chatham (*Expensive*)

Wedgewood Inn, Yarmouth Port (*Expensive*)

Captain Freeman Inn, Brewster (*Moderate–Expensive*)

Inn on Sea Street, Hyannis (*Moderate*)

Charlotte Inn, Edgartown, Martha's Vineyard (*Very Expensive*)

Lambert's Cove Country Inn, West Tisbury, Martha's Vineyard (*Moderate*)

Sea Spray Inn, Oak Bluffs, Martha's Vineyard (*Inexpensive–Moderate*)

Wauwinet, Nantucket (*Very Expensive*)

White Elephant, Nantucket (*Very Expensive*)

Harbor House, Nantucket (*Expensive*)

Cliff Lodge, Nantucket (*Moderate*)

Corner House, Nantucket (*Inexpensive–Moderate*)

Children's Activities

Aqua Circus of Cape Cod, West Yarmouth

Bassett Wild Animal Farm, Brewster

Heritage Plantation, Sandwich

Plimoth Plantation, Plymouth

Pirate's Cove minigolf, South Yarmouth

Water Wizz Water Park, Wareham

Flying Horses Carousel, Martha's Vineyard

Vineyard Playhouse and Actors Theater of Nantucket children's events

Cape Cod, Martha's Vineyard, and Nantucket

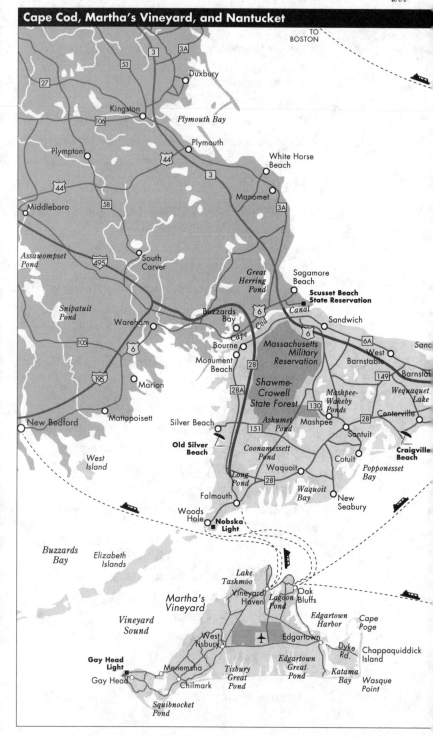

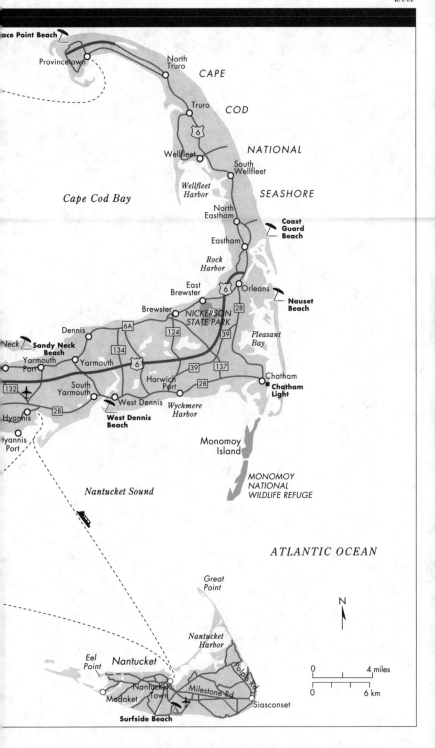

ace Point Beach

Provincetown

North
Truro

CAPE

Truro

COD

U.S. 6

NATIONAL

Wellfleet

South
Wellfleet

SEASHORE

Cape Cod Bay

*Wellfleet
Harbor*

North
Eastham

Coast
Guard
Beach

Eastham

*Rock
Harbor*

East
Brewster

Orleans

Nauset
Beach

Brewster

U.S. 6

NICKERSON
STATE PARK

28

124

39

*Pleasant
Bay*

Neck

Sandy Neck
Beach

Dennis

6A

134

Yarmouth
Port

Yarmouth

U.S. 6

39

137

132

South
Yarmouth

Harwich
Port

28

Chatham

Chatham
Light

Hyannis

28

West Dennis

*Wychmere
Harbor*

West Dennis
Beach

lyannis
Port

Monomoy
Island

Nantucket Sound

MONOMOY
NATIONAL
WILDLIFE REFUGE

ATLANTIC OCEAN

*Great
Point*

N

*Nantucket
Harbor*

*Eel
Point*

Nantucket

Polpis Rd

0   4 miles

Madaket

Nantucket
Town

Milestone Rd

Siasconset

0   6 km

Surfside Beach

World Time Zones

Numbers below vertical bands relate each zone to Greenwich Mean Time (0 hrs.).
Local times frequently differ from these general indications,
as indicated by light-face numbers on map.

Algiers, **29**

Anchorage, **3**

Athens, **41**

Auckland, **1**

Baghdad, **46**

Bangkok, **50**

Beijing, **54**

Berlin, **34**

Bogotá, **19**

Budapest, **37**

Buenos Aires, **24**

Caracas, **22**

Chicago, **9**

Copenhagen, **33**

Dallas, **10**

Delhi, **48**

Denver, **8**

Djakarta, **53**

Dublin, **26**

Edmonton, **7**

Hong Kong, **56**

Honolulu, **2**

Istanbul, **40**

Jerusalem, **42**

Johannesburg, **44**

Lima, **20**

Lisbon, **28**

London (Greenwich), **27**

Los Angeles, **6**

Madrid, **38**

Manila, **57**

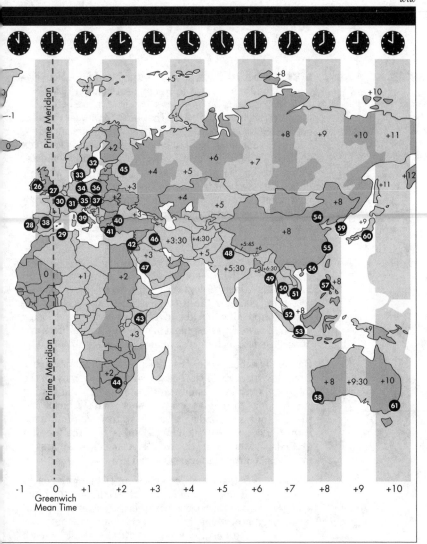

Introduction

The world to-day is sick to its thin blood for lack of elemental things," wrote Henry Beston in his 1928 Cape Cod classic *The Outermost House*, "for fire before the hands, for water welling from the earth, for air, for the dear earth itself underfoot." It is this that the Cape and its neighboring islands most have to offer an increasingly complex and artificial world: the chance to reconnect with elemental things. Walking along the shore, poking among the washed-up sea life or watching birds fish in the surf, listening to the rhythm of the waves, experiencing the mystery and tranquillity of night on the beach or the power of a storm on water—all this is somehow strengthening and life-affirming and utterly, satisfyingly real.

Cape Cod—a craggy arm of a peninsula 50 miles southeast of Boston— and the islands of Martha's Vineyard and Nantucket share their geologic origins as debris deposited by a retreating glacier in the last ice age. They also share a moderate coastal climate and a diversity of terrain that foster an equally diverse assortment of plant and animal life, some of which exist nowhere else in northern climes.

Barrier beaches (sandbars that protect an inner harbor from the battering of the ocean), such as Monomoy on the Cape and Coatue on Nantucket, are breeding and resting grounds for a stunning variety of shore and sea birds, and the marshes and ponds are rich in waterfowl. Stellwagen Bank, just north of Provincetown, is a prime feeding grounds for whales and dolphins, and shallow sandbars are favorite playgrounds for harbor and gray seals.

Among the flotsam and jetsam along the shores beachcombers find horseshoe crabs, starfish, sea urchins, sponges, jellyfish, coral, and a plethora of shells: white quahogs, elegant scallops, blue mussels, long straight razor clams, spiraling periwinkles, pointy turret shells, smooth round moon snails, conical whelks, rough-ridged oysters.

Much of the land, including a third of Nantucket's acreage and a quarter of the Vineyard's, is protected from development. Nature preserves encompassing pine forests, marshes, swamps, cranberry bogs, and many other varieties of terrain are laced with well-marked walking and bicycling trails. On Nantucket, acres of moorland are spread with a rough tapestry of gnarled scrub oaks, low-lying blueberry bushes, fragrant bayberry, bearberry, and heather (the last originally brought to Nantucket from Scotland by accident in a shipment of pine trees).

Thanks to the establishment of the Cape Cod National Seashore in 1961, one can walk for almost 30 miles along the

Atlantic beach virtually without seeing a trace of human habitation—besides a few historic shacks in the dunes of Provincetown, or the lighthouses that stand watch over the Cape's dangerous shoals. Across dunes anchored by hearty poverty grass sprawl beach plums, pink salt-spray roses, and purple beach peas.

Through the creation of many National Historic Districts—in which change is kept to a minimum to preserve the historical integrity of the area—similar protection has been extended to the Cape and islands' oldest and loveliest manmade landscapes. One of the most important, as well as most visually harmonious, is along the Old King's Highway, where the Cape's first towns—Sandwich, Barnstable, and Yarmouth—were incorporated in 1639. Lining this tree-shaded country road are simple saltboxes from the earliest days, fancier houses built later by prosperous sea captains, and the traditional Cape cottages, shingles weathered to a silvery gray, with soft pink roses spilling across them or massed over low split-rail fences. Here, too, are the white-steepled churches, taverns, and village greens that savor of old New England, as well as some of the Cape's many windmills.

Practically the entire island of Nantucket is part of its historic district. A rigid enforcement of district guidelines has created a town architecturally almost frozen in time, and one of the world's great treasures. Among the neat clapboard and weathered-shingle houses that line its cobblestone streets and narrow lanes are former warehouses, factories, and mansions dating back to the golden age of whaling.

Most recently, Provincetown was designated a historic district, preserving for posterity its cheerful mix of tiny waterfront shops (former fish shacks) and everything from a 1746 Cape house to a mansarded French Second Empire to an octagonal house.

Besides the districts, the Cape and islands preserve their past in a wealth of small museums—nearly every town has one—that document local history, often back to Indian days. (In 1620, when the Pilgrims first anchored at Provincetown, exploring the Cape before heading on to Plymouth, an estimated 30,000 Wampanoags lived on Cape Cod.) Often set in houses that are themselves historic, these museums provide a visual history of the lives of the English settlers and their descendants, including their economic pursuits: from farming, to the harvesting of salt, salt hay, and cranberries (still an important local crop), to fishing and whaling, to tourism, which began as far back as the late 19th century.

The importance of whaling to the area—Nantucket was the world's premier whaling port in the early to mid-19th century, and it was a Yarmouth man who taught Nantucketers how—is reflected in the historical museums. The travels of the area's whaling and packet-schooner seamen and captains are illustrated with such items as antique nautical equipment, harpoons, charts, maps, journals, scrimshaw created during the often years-long whaling voyages, and gifts brought back from exotic ports for wives who had waited so patiently (those who *had* waited, that is—some women chose to go along with their husbands for the ride).

The economies of the Cape and the islands are extremely dependent on tourism, and most options in tourist facilities can be found. Lodgings range from no-frills guest houses and motels to antiques-and-lace bed-and-breakfasts to full-service resort hotels on the beach; families can opt for waterfront condominiums, minimalist cottages in the woods, or ultraluxurious summer homes with breathtaking ocean views. Restaurants include rustic, nautical-motif fish houses as well as elegant gourmet restaurants (a specialty of Nantucket) and everything in between. Dining can be a romantic experience, with views of dramatic sunsets over water, or a gathering of family and friends at wharfside picnic tables to devour fried clams.

All three areas are noted for interesting shopping (for crafts, art, and antiques especially); for lots of theater, both small community groups and professional summer stock; and for plenty of recreational offerings that take advantage of the marine environment, including water sports, fishing charters, and even Jeep safaris to isolated beaches for surfcasting. All are also family oriented—especially the Cape, which has endless amusements to offer children beyond the ever-beckoning beach. There are also such typical New England entertainments as chowder suppers and clambakes.

Cape Cod is the area most suffering from overdevelopment. Massive growth in tourism in years past led to construction of tacky roadside motels, nightmare stretches of wall-to-wall tourist magnets along Route 28, and the megabuildup of Hyannis. Also, getting over the bridges that join the Cape to the mainland can be misery at peak weekend times in summer. But wise planners can avoid that problem, as they can avoid the built-up areas and stick to the many still-charming areas if they choose. Within its 70-mile span, the Cape offers a broad spectrum of vacation experiences: picturesque old New England towns, an extraordinary scientific community at Woods Hole, the frenetic shopping and people-watching former art colony of Provincetown, the tamer art-gallery town of Wellfleet, and quiet cottage communities with little more than a clam shack and a general store to divert one's attention from the beach.

Nantucket, about 12 miles by 3, is reached by plane or a two-hour ferry ride, and its remoteness appeals to those seeking escape. It has just the one town, plus a small beachside village of rose-covered cottages that once housed an actors' colony. Large tracts of undeveloped moorland and nature preserves give the island an open, breezy feel. It has long been a summer bastion of the quietly wealthy, who are likely to be seen dressed down to the hilt and tooling around on beat-up bicycles.

Martha's Vineyard, on the other hand, is known as the celebrity island, for its star summer residents in the arts and entertainment who participate in the annual Celebrity Hat Auction and other high-visibility charitable events. Nantucketers tend to think of their sister island as glitzy, which it could be called only in comparison. About 20 miles by 10, the Vineyard offers more variety than Nantucket: Its six towns range from a young and rowdy seaside town of Victorian cottages to a rural New England village to an elegant, well-manicured town of sea captains' homes and flower gardens. The landscape, too, is more varied, including a 4,000-acre pine forest, rolling farmland enclosed by dry stone walls, and dramatic clay cliffs.

Both islands are ringed with beautiful wide, sandy beaches, some backed with high or low dunes, others with moorland, others bordering marshes. Either Martha's Vineyard or Nantucket can be profitably visited in a day trip from a Cape Cod base but will well repay a longer stay.

The "season" used to be strictly from Memorial Day to Labor Day, but the boundaries have blurred; many places now open in April or earlier and close as late as November, and a core remain open year-round. Unfortunately, most of the historic sites and museums, largely staffed by volunteers, still adhere to the traditional dates and so are inaccessible in the off-season.

Each of the seasons invites a different kind of visit. In summer, you have your choice of plunking down somewhere near a beach and never moving, filling your schedule with museums and activities, or combining the two in whatever mix suits you. In fall, the water may be warm enough for swimming as late as October, crowds are gone, and prices are lower. Turning foliage, though nothing like the dramatic displays found elsewhere in New England, is still an enjoyable addition to a fall visit; it reaches its peak around the end of October. Moors turn purple and gold and rust; burning bush along roadsides flames a brilliant red. Cranberries ripen to a bright burgundy color and are harvested by a method fascinating to watch. Trees around freshwater marshes, ponds, and swamps tend to color earlier and brighter; the red maple swamps, Beech Forest in Provincetown, and Route 6A from Sandwich to Orleans are particularly colorful spots.

Fall and winter are oyster and scallop season, and the restaurants that remain open feature a wide selection of dishes made with the freshly caught delicacies. Winter is a quiet time, when many tourist-oriented activities and facilities shut down, but prices are low and you can walk the beaches in often total solitude. For a quiet or romantic weekend getaway, country inns offer cozy rooms with canopy beds, where you can curl up before the fireplace after returning from a leisurely, candlelit dinner. The Chatham Bars Inn in Chatham offers theme weekends, such as wine tasting or swing dancing, that can make for a festive winter break. On Martha's Vineyard, the Harbor View Hotel also offers winter mystery and other theme weekends in attractive transportation-plus packages.

As for spring, it gets a wee wet, and on Nantucket expect a good dose of fog. Still, the daffodils come bursting up from roadsides, especially on Nantucket, and everything begins to turn green. By April, seasonal shops and restaurants begin to open, and locals prepare for yet another summer.

1 Essential Information

Before You Go

Visitor Information

For more information on the Cape and the islands, contact the **Cape Cod Chamber of Commerce** (junction of Rtes. 6 and 132, Hyannis 02601, tel. 508/362–3225), **Martha's Vineyard Chamber of Commerce** (Box 1698, Vineyard Haven 02568, tel. 508/693–0085), and the **Nantucket Chamber of Commerce** (15 Main St., Nantucket 02554, tel. 508/228–1700). The latter two charge $3 and $3.50, respectively, to mail out guidebooks listing services and events. For a list of local Cape Cod chambers of commerce, which can also provide information, *see* Essential Information in Chapter 3, Cape Cod.

Other information sources include the **Department of Environmental Management** (Division of Forests and Parks, 100 Cambridge St., Room 1905, Boston 02202, tel. 617/727–3180), which offers brochures and maps on state forests and parks and a leaflet on camping; the **Department of Food and Agriculture** (100 Cambridge St., 21st Floor, Boston 02202, tel. 617/727–3018), offering information on fairs, farmer's markets, and pick-your-own apple, strawberry, and vegetable farms; and the **Division of Fisheries and Wildlife** (Field Headquarters, Westboro 01581, tel. 508/792–7270) for information on fish and wildlife laws (supply a stamped, self-addressed business-size envelope).

Massachusetts Office of Travel & Tourism (100 Cambridge St., 13th Floor, Boston 02202, tel. 617/727–3201 or 800/447–6277) puts out a summer guidebook, calendars of events, a fall foliage guide, bed-and-breakfast and general lodgings guides, campground listings, and a road map.

Tours and Packages

Should you buy your travel arrangements to Cape Cod packaged or do it yourself? There are advantages either way. Buying packaged arrangements saves you money, particularly if you can find a program that includes exactly the features you want. You also get a pretty good idea of what your trip will cost from the outset. Generally, you have two options: fully escorted tours and independent packages. Escorted tours are most often via motorcoach, with a tour director in charge. They're ideal if you don't mind having limited free time and traveling with strangers. Your baggage is handled, your time is rigorously scheduled, and most meals are planned. Such tours are therefore the most hassle-free way to see a destination, as well as generally the least expensive. Independent packages allow plenty of flexibility. They generally include airline travel and hotels, with certain options available, such as sightseeing, car rental, and excursions. Such packages are usually more expensive than escorted tours, but your time is your own.

While you can book directly through tour operators, you will pay no more to go through a travel agent, who will be able to tell you about tours and packages from a number of operators. Whatever program you ultimately choose, be sure to find out exactly what is included: taxes, tips, transfers, meals, baggage handling, ground transportation, entertainment, excursions, sports or recreation (and rental equipment if necessary). Ask about the quality/grade of hotel used, its location, the size of its rooms, the kind of beds, and its amenities, such as pool, room service, or programs for children, if they're important to you. Find out the operator's cancellation penalties; nearly everyone charges them, and the only way to avoid them is to buy trip-cancellation insurance (*see* Trip Insurance, *below*). Also ask about the single supplement, a surcharge assessed to solo travelers; some operators do not make you pay it if you agree to be matched up with a roommate of the same sex, even if one is not found by departure time. Remember that a program that has features you won't use may not be the most cost-wise choice for you.

Fully Escorted Tours Escorted tours are usually sold in three categories: deluxe, first-class, and tourist or budget class. The most important differences are the price, of course, and the level of accommodations. Some operators specialize in one category, while others offer a range.

Contact **Maupintour** (Box 807, Lawrence, KS 66044, tel. 913/843–1211 or 800/255–4266) and **Tauck Tours** (11 Wilton Rd., Westport, CT 06681, tel. 203/226–6911 or 800/468–2825) in the deluxe category; or **Country Squire Tours** (668 Main St., Hyannis, MA 02601, tel. 508/771–6441 or 800/225–8051), **Domenico Tours** (751 Broadway, Bayonne, NJ 07002, tel. 201/823–8687 or 800/554–8687), **Gadabout Tours** (700 E. Tahquitz-Canyon Way, Palm Springs, CA 92262, tel. 619/325–5556 or 800/952–5068), and **Mayflower Tours** (Box 490, Downer's Grove, IL 60515, tel. 708/960–3430 or tel. 800/323–7604).

Most itineraries are jam-packed with sightseeing, so you see a lot in a short amount of time (usually one place per day). To judge just how fast-paced the tour is, review the itinerary carefully. If you are in a different hotel each night, you will be getting up early each day to head out, travel to your next destination, do some sightseeing, have dinner, and go to bed; then you'll start all over again. If you want some free time, make sure it's mentioned in the tour brochure; if you want to be escorted to every meal, confirm that any tour you consider does that. Also, when comparing programs, be sure to find out if the motorcoach is air-conditioned and has a rest room on board. Make your selection based on price and stops on the itinerary.

Independent Packages Independent packages are usually offered by airlines, tour operators who may also do escorted programs, and any number of other companies from large, established firms to small, new entrepreneurs. However, there are few independent packages to Cape Cod. Most independent travelers to the Cape come on their own (via private car or recreational vehicle), and since large hotels are virtually nonexistent on the Cape, airlines don't get involved in hotel accommodations. Airlines that fly to Boston do offer rental-car packages (it takes less than an hour to drive to the Cape), and **Amtrak** (tel. 800/321–8684) offers packages that combine train fare and hotel accommodations on the Cape.

Special-Interest Travel Special-interest programs may be fully escorted or independent. Some require a certain amount of expertise, but most are for the average traveler and are usually hosted by experts in the subject matter. When the program is escorted, it enjoys the advantages and disadvantages of all escorted programs; because your fellow travelers are apt to be passionate or knowledgeable about the subject, they can prove as enjoyable a part of your travel experience as the destination itself. The price range is wide, but the cost is usually higher—sometimes a lot higher—than for ordinary escorted tours and packages, because of the expert guiding and special activities.

Sailing and **Oceanic Society Expeditions** (Fort Mason Center, Bldg. E, San *Whale-watching* Francisco, CA 94123, tel. 415/441–1106 or 800/326–7491) offers sailing adventures aboard a 95-foot schooner that combine sailing and whale watching along the Massachusetts coast.

Tips for British Travelers

Government Contact the **United States Travel and Tourism Administration** **Tourist Office** (Box 1EN, London W1A 1EN, tel. 071/495–4466).

Passports British subjects need a valid 10-year passport. A visa is not **and Visas** necessary unless (1) you are planning to stay more than 90 days; (2) your trip is for purposes other than vacation; (3) you have at some time been refused a visa, or refused admission to, the United States, or have been required to leave by the U.S. Immigration and Naturalization Service; or (4) you do not have a return or onward ticket. You will need to fill out the Visa Waiver Form 1–94W, supplied by the airline.

To apply for a visa or for more information, call the U.S. Embassy's Visa Information Line (tel. 0891/200–290; calls cost 48p per minute or 36p per minute cheap rate). If you qualify for visa-free travel but want a visa anyway, you must apply in writing, enclosing an SAE, to the U.S. Embassy's Visa Branch (5 Upper Grosvenor St., London W1A 2JB), or, for residents of Northern Ireland, to the U.S. Consulate General (Queen's House, Queen St., Belfast BT1 6EO). Submit a completed Nonimmigrant Visa Application (Form 156), a valid passport, a photograph, and evidence of your intended departure from the United States after a temporary visit. If you require a visa, call 0891/234–224 to schedule an interview.

Customs British visitors aged 21 or over may import the following into the United States: 200 cigarettes or 50 cigars or 2 kilograms of tobacco; one U.S. liter of alcohol; gifts to the value of $100. Restricted items include meat products, seeds, plants, and fruits. Never carry illegal drugs.

Airports Boston has the nearest international airport. To get from Bos-**and Airlines** ton to the Cape and the islands, *see* Arriving and Departing, *below.*

Flying time to Boston from all British airports is more than six hours on most flights.

Three airlines fly to Boston from London Heathrow: **British Airways** (tel. 081/897–4000), **Northwest** (tel. 0345/747800), and **TWA** (tel. 071/439–0707). Northwest also has four flights a week to Boston from Prestwick, near Glasgow in Scotland. There are no flights to Boston from London's Gatwick airport.

British travelers combining a trip to New England with a visit to New York should consider flying into New York's JFK airport or the Newark airport, both of which offer more flights from Britain than Boston does. Four airlines fly to New York from London Heathrow: British Airways, TWA, **American** (tel. 0800/010151), and **United** (tel. 0800/888555). British Airways has as many as six flights a day, two on the Concorde. Three airlines fly to New York from London Gatwick: **British Airways, Continental** (tel. 0293/776464), and **Virgin Atlantic** (tel. 0293/562000); British Airways also flies to New York from Manchester, England.

Insurance Most tour operators, travel agents, and insurance agents sell specialized policies covering accident, medical expenses, personal liability, trip cancellation, and loss or theft of personal property. Some policies include coverage for delayed departure and legal expenses, winter-sports, accidents, or motoring abroad. You can also purchase an annual travel-insurance policy valid for every trip you make during the year in which it's purchased (usually only trips of less than 90 days). Before you leave, make sure you will be covered if you have a preexisting medical condition or are pregnant; your insurers may not pay for routine or continuing treatment, or may require a note from your doctor certifying your fitness to travel.

The **Association of British Insurers**, a trade association representing 450 insurance companies, advises extra medical coverage for visitors to the United States.

For advice by phone or a free booklet, "Holiday Insurance," that sets out what to expect from a holiday-insurance policy and gives price guidelines, contact the Association of British Insurers (51 Gresham St., London EC2V 7HQ, tel. 071/600–3333; 30 Gordon St., Glasgow G1 3PU, tel. 041/226–3905; Scottish Provincial Bldg., Donegall Sq. W, Belfast BT1 6JE, tel. 0232/249176; call for other locations).

Tour Operators Tour operators offering packages to Cape Cod include **British Airways Holidays** (Atlantic House, Hazelwick Avenue, Three Bridges, Crawley, West Sussex RH10 1NP, tel. 0293/518022), **Cosmosair** (Ground Floor, Dale House, Tiviot Dale, Stockport, Cheshire SK1 1TB, tel. 061/480–5799), **Jetsave Travel Ltd.** (Sussex House, London Rd., East Grinstead, W. Sussex RH19 1LD, tel. 0342/312033), **Kuoni Travel** (Kuoni House, Dorking, Surrey RH5 4AZ, tel. 0306/742222), and **North American Vacations** (Acorn House, 172/174 Albert Road, Jarrow, Tyne & Wear NE32 5JA, tel. 091/483–6226).

Hints for Travelers with Disabilites Main information sources include the **Royal Association for Disability and Rehabilitation** (RADAR, 25 Mortimer St., London W1N 8AB, tel. 071/637–5400), which publishes travel information for the disabled in Britain, and **Mobility International** (228 Borough High St., London SE1 1JX, tel. 071/403–5688), the headquarters of an international membership organization that serves as a clearinghouse of travel information for people with disabilities.

When to Go

Memorial Day through Labor Day (in some cases, Columbus Day) is high season on Cape Cod, Martha's Vineyard, and Nantucket. This is summer with a capital *S*, a time for barbecues, beach bumming, water sports, and swimming. During summer everything is open for business on the Cape, but you can also expect high-season evils: high prices, crowds, and traffic.

Spring and fall are the times to enjoy bird walks, nature hikes, and country drives, along with lower inn and restaurant prices. Evergreens and scrub make up a good part of the area's ground cover, so the display of autumn colors is not as striking as that in other parts of New England. Still, under crisp blue skies in the clear autumn light, the lower Cape and islands' cover of heather, gorse, blueberry, bayberry, boxberry, and beach plum resembles, in Thoreau's words, "the richest rug imaginable spread over an uneven surface." Spring, too, can be beautiful, bursting with wildflowers and greening grasses, though it does arrive late and is unpredictable—on Nantucket especially, spring is often damp and foggy.

In winter, many museums, shops, restaurants, and lodgings close, especially on the islands. The Cape's community theater network continues throughout the year, and many golf courses remain open, except when it snows (some then open their courses to cross-country skiers). A number of intimate bed-and-breakfasts and inns—some with fireplaces, canopy beds, and well-stocked libraries and board-game collections—also remain open, and for as much as 50% off high-season rates, they make romantic retreats after a day of ice fishing, pond skating, or otherwise enjoying winter in the country. On the islands especially, though, don't come in winter looking for action.

Many towns on the Cape and islands celebrate Christmas in an old-fashioned way, with wandering carolers and bands, theatrical performances, crafts sales, and holiday house tours. Nantucket's Christmas Stroll is the best-known event (*see* Festivals and Seasonal Events, *below*). The Cape extends the season to six weeks, from Thanksgiving to New Year's, offering special packages, inn and restaurant discounts, and a full program of activities (including First Night celebrations in many towns).

Lodging reservations are tight in summer in the whole area. The most intense tourist time is the last two weeks in July and most of August; if you come then without a hotel or inn reservation, you'll still find accommodations, but be prepared to settle for less than your first choice. Also book several months in advance for a visit to Nantucket during the Daffodil Festival in late April, or the Christmas Stroll on the first weekend in December; many people return every year for these events, which are worth planning a trip around.

Climate Though its beaches rival the best the Caribbean has to offer, this area is not the Caribbean and does not come with a guarantee of sun-filled days. While there are plenty of idyllic beach days to go around, rain or fog is not an uncommon part of even an August vacation here. Visitors who do not learn to appreciate the beauty of the land and sea in mist and rain may find themselves mighty cranky.

Temperatures in winter and summer are milder on the Cape and islands than on the mainland, due in part to the warming influence of the Gulf Stream and the moderating ocean breezes. As a rule (and there have been dramatically anomalous years), the Cape and islands get much less snow than the mainland, and what falls generally does not last. Still, winter can bring bone-chilling dampness, especially on the windswept islands.

The following are average daily maximum and minimum temperatures for Hyannis; it's likely to be two or three degrees cooler on the coast and on the islands.

Jan.	40F	4C	May	62F	17C	Sept.	70F	21C
	25	− 4		48	9		56	13
Feb.	41F	5C	June	71F	22C	Oct.	59F	15C
	26	− 3		56	13		47	8
Mar.	42F	6C	July	78F	26C	Nov.	49F	9C
	28	− 2		63	17		37	3
Apr.	53F	12C	Aug.	76F	24C	Dec.	40F	4C
	40	4		61	16		26	− 3

Information Sources For tide information and weather and coastal marine forecasts, call 508/771–5522 or 508/790–1061.

For current weather conditions for cities in the United States and abroad, plus the local time and helpful travel tips, call the **Weather Channel Connection** (tel. 900/932–8437; 95¢ per minute) from a touch-tone phone.

Festivals and Seasonal Events

The Massachusetts Office of Travel & Tourism (*see* Visitor Information, *above*) offers events listings and a whale-watch guide for the entire state. Also see the events calendar in *Cape Cod Life* magazine (*see* Further Reading, *below*).

Late Apr.: Nantucket's four-day **Daffodil Festival** (tel. 508/228–1700) celebrates spring with a flower show, shop-window displays, and a procession of antique cars adorned with daffodils that ends in picnics at Siasconset. For about five weeks from mid-April to mid-May, 2 million daffodils bloom along Nantucket roadsides and in private gardens.

Summer: From June through August, the area is busy with **summer theater, town band concerts,** and **arts and crafts fairs.**

Early June: Hyannis Harbor Festival (tel. 508/775–2201) is a two-day celebration that includes the blessing of the fleet, boat races, entertainment, and food. **Cape Cod Antique Dealers Association Annual Antiques Show** at Sandwich's Heritage Plantation (tel. 508/888–3300) is attended by 50 dealers in fine 18th- and 19th-century English and American furniture, folk art, Sandwich glass, jewelry, and more.

Mid- to late June: Cape Heritage '94 (tel. 508/362–3225) is a weeklong celebration of the Cape's history and culture hosted by museums, historical societies, theater groups, libraries, and the Cape Cod National Seashore. In Edgartown's **A Taste of the Vineyard** (tel. 508/627–4440), ticket holders wander among tents set up downtown as they sample treats provided by local restaurants, caterers, and wine sellers. It's a formal evening, with dancing and an auction. **Nantucket Harborfest** (tel. 508/228–1700) is three days of boat and children's parades, a blessing of the fleet, a clambake, and culinary and water-sports competitions.

Last Sun. in June: The Blessing of the Fleet (tel. 508/487–3424) in Provincetown is the culmination of a weekend of festivities, including a banquet and dance. On Sunday, a parade ends at the wharf, where fishermen and their families and friends pile onto their boats and form a procession. The bishop stands on the dock and blesses the boats with holy water as they pass by.

July 4 weekend: The Mashpee Powwow (tel. 508/477–0208) brings together Wampanoag Indians from North and South America for three days of dance contests, drumming, a fireball game, a road race, and a clambake, plus the crowning of the Mashpee Wampanoag Indian princess on the final night. Visitors are welcome and Native American foods and crafts are sold. **Fireworks displays** are still a part of Fourth of July celebrations in several Cape towns and on Nantucket.

Mid-July: Edgartown Regatta (tel. 508/627–4361), started in 1923, is three days of yacht racing around Martha's Vineyard. In East Sandwich, the **Cape Cod Antiquarian Book Fair** (tel. 508/888–2331), sponsored by the Burgess Society, features the offerings of more than 60 dealers in old and rare books.

Late July: The Barnstable County Fair (Rte. 151, East Falmouth, tel. 508/563–3200), begun in 1844, is Cape Cod's biggest event. The seven-day affair features livestock and food judgings; horse, pony, and oxen pulls and shows; arts and crafts demonstrations; musical and stage entertainment; carnival rides; and lots of food.

Aug.: On Nantucket, an **Annual House Tour** is held by the garden club, and a **Sandcastle Contest** at Jetties Beach results in some amazing sculptures (tel. 508/228–1700 for both events). On Martha's Vineyard, **fireworks** (tel. 508/693–0085) explode over the ocean while the town watches from the Oak Bluffs village green and the town band plays on the gazebo.

Early Aug.: At the Vineyard's benefit **Possible Dreams Auction** (tel. 508/693–7900), held the first Monday of August, Art Buchwald auctions off such starry prizes as a sailboat ride with Walter Cronkite.

Mid-Aug.: Martha's Vineyard Agricultural Fair (tel. 508/693–4343) is pure Americana, with livestock and food judging, animal shows, a carnival, plus evening musical entertainment, over three days. The **Falmouth Road Race** (Box 732, Falmouth 02541, tel. 508/540–7000) is a world-class race covering 7.1 miles of coast from Woods Hole to Falmouth Heights; apply the previous fall or winter.

Late Aug.: Sails Around Cape Cod (tel. 508/430–1111) is a 155-nautical-mile race to Harwich Port and back via Provincetown and the canal. The two-day race for yachts 28 feet or larger is accompanied by an awards banquet and other activities.

Sept.: The Bourne Scallopfest (tel. 508/759–3122), the weekend after Labor Day, attracts thousands of people to Buzzards Bay for three days of fried scallops (and barbecued chicken, hot dogs, and burgers) served under a tent, plus rafts and food booths and entertainment. **The Harwich Cranberry Harvest Festival** (tel. 508/430–2811) is 10 days of festivities, including a country-western jamboree, an arts and crafts show, fireworks, pancake breakfasts, an antique-car show, and much more.

Mid-Sept.: Tivoli Day (tel. 508/693–0085), an end-of-summer celebration in Oak Bluffs on Martha's Vineyard, features a street fair with live entertainment and crafts, plus a world-class 60-mile bike race, the **Tour of Martha's Vineyard** (tel. 508/693–1656).

Mid-Sept.–mid-Oct.: The month-long **Martha's Vineyard Striped Bass and Bluefish Derby** (Box 2101, Edgartown 02539, tel. 508/627–8342) is one of the East Coast's premier fishing contests, offering more than $100,000 in prizes for albacore, bluefish, striped bass, and bonito catches.

Late Sept.: Bird Carvers' Exhibit and Auction (tel. 508/896–3867) at the Cape Cod Museum of Natural History in Brewster showcases local and regional bird carvers' art over three days.

Oct.: Nantucket Cranberry Harvest Festival (tel. 508/228–1700) is a three-day celebration, including bog tours, a cookery contest, and a crafts exhibition.

Thanksgiving Eve: Provincetown Festival of Lights (tel. 508/487–3424), commemorating the Pilgrims' landing, begins with the lighting of 5,000 white and gold bulbs draped over the Pilgrim Monument. The lights are lit nightly until Little Christmas (Jan. 7). A performance of the "Hallelujah Chorus" accompanies the lighting, and the monument museum offers an open house and tours.

Early Dec.: Many Cape and island towns do up the Christmas season in grand style. The best-known celebration is the Nantucket **Christmas Stroll** (tel. 508/228–1700), which takes place the first Saturday of the month. Carolers and musicians entertain strollers as they walk the festive cobblestone streets and sample shops' wares and seasonal refreshments. Activities include theatrical performances, art exhibitions, crafts sales, and a tour of historic homes. This old-time celebration is magical. To avoid the throngs, visit on one of the surrounding weekends (festivities begin the day after Thanksgiving).

On Martha's Vineyard, **Christmas in Edgartown** (tel. 508/627–4711), the second weekend of the month, includes tours of historic homes, teas, carriage rides, a parade, caroling, and other entertainment. Vineyard Haven packs a chowder contest, church bazaars, plays, and concerts into its **Twelve Days of Christmas** (tel. 508/693–2725).

Falmouth's **Christmas by the Sea** (tel. 508/548–8500), the first full weekend of December, includes lighting ceremonies at the Village Green, caroling at Nobska Light in Woods Hole, an antiques show, a house tour, church fairs, and a parade.

Chatham's **Main Street Open House** (tel. 508/945–0342) takes place the following weekend, with hayrides, caroling, a book-and-author tea, and more, culminating in a dinner dance at the grand Chatham Bars Inn. The open house is part of a month-long celebration beginning just after Thanksgiving and ending with a lavish **First Night** celebration including fireworks over Oyster Pond, on New Year's Eve.

What to Pack

Clothing Only a few restaurants on Cape Cod, Martha's Vineyard, and Nantucket require formal dress; the area prides itself on informality. Do pack a sweater or jacket, even in summer, for the nights can be cool. Also, *see* clothing suggestions in Staying Healthy, *below*, regarding Lyme disease.

Miscellaneous Sunscreen, sunglasses, hats, and insect repellent are important in summer, and rain gear is a year-round necessity. Bring an extra pair of eyeglasses or contact lenses. If you have a health problem that may require you to purchase a prescription drug, pack enough to last the duration of the trip. And don't forget to pack a list of the addresses of offices that supply refunds for lost or stolen traveler's checks.

Luggage Regulations Free baggage allowances on an airline depend on the airline, the route, and the class of your ticket. In general, on domestic flights you are entitled to check two bags—neither exceeding 62 inches, or 158 centimeters (length + width + height), or weighing more than 70 pounds (32 kilograms). A third piece may be brought aboard as a carryon; its total dimensions are generally limited to less than 45 inches (114 centimeters), so it will fit easily under the seat in front of you or in the overhead compartment. There are variations, so ask in advance. The single rule, a Federal Aviation Administration safety regulation that pertains to carry-on baggage on U.S. airlines, requires that carryons be properly stowed and allows the airline to limit allowances and tailor them to different aircraft and operational conditions. Charges for excess, oversize, or overweight pieces vary, so inquire before you pack.

Safeguarding Your Luggage Before leaving home, itemize your bags' contents and their worth; this list will help you estimate the extent of your loss if your bags go astray. To minimize that risk, tag them inside and out with your name, address, and phone number. (If you use your home address, cover it so that potential thieves can't see it.) At check-in, make sure that the tag attached by baggage handlers bears the correct three-letter code for your destination. If your bags do not arrive with you, or if you detect damage, do not leave the airport until you've filed a written report with the airline.

Insurance In the event of loss, damage, or theft on domestic flights, airlines limit their liability to $1,250 per passenger. Excess-valuation insurance can be bought directly from the airline at check-in but leaves your bags vulnerable on the ground. Your own homeowner's policy may fill the gap; or you may want special luggage insurance. Sources include **The Travelers Companies** (1 Tower Sq., Hartford, CT 06183, tel. 203/277–0111 or 800/243–3174) and **Wallach and Company, Inc.** (107 W. Federal St., Box 480, Middleburg, VA 22117, tel. 703/687–3166 or 800/237–6615), underwritten by Lloyds, London.

Traveler's Checks

Although you will want plenty of cash when visiting small cities or rural areas, traveler's checks are usually preferable. The most widely recognized are **American Express, Barclay's, Thomas Cook,** and those issued by major commercial banks such as **Citibank** and **Bank of America.** American Express also issues *Traveler's Cheques for Two,* which can be countersigned and used by you or your traveling companion. Some checks are free; usually the issuing company or the bank at which you make your purchase charges 1% of the checks' face value as a fee. Be sure to buy a few checks in small denominations to cash toward the end of your trip, when you don't want to be left with more foreign currency than you can spend. Always record the numbers of checks as you spend them, and keep this list separate from the checks.

Getting Money from Home

Cash Machines Automated-teller machines (ATMs) are proliferating; many are tied to international networks such as **Cirrus** and **Plus.** You can use your bank card at ATMs away from home to withdraw money from an account and get cash advances on a credit-card account (providing your card has been programmed with a personal identification number, or PIN). Check in advance on limits on withdrawals and cash advances within specified periods. Remember that on cash advances you are charged interest from the day you get the money from ATMs as well as from tellers. And note that transaction fees for ATM withdrawals outside your home turf will probably be higher than for withdrawals at home.

For specific Cirrus locations in the United States and Canada, call 800/424-7787 (for U.S. Plus locations, 800/843-7587), and press the area code and first three digits of the number you're calling from (or the calling area where you want an ATM).

American Express The company's **Express Cash** system lets you withdraw cash
Cardholder and/or traveler's checks from a worldwide network of 57,000
Services American Express dispensers and participating bank ATMs. You must *enroll first* (call 800/227-4669 for a form and allow two weeks for processing). Withdrawals are charged not to your card but to a designated bank account. You can withdraw up to $1,000 per seven-day period on the basic card, more if your card is gold or platinum. There is a 2% fee (minimum $2.50, maximum $10) for each cash transaction, and a 1% fee for traveler's checks (except for the platinum card), which are available only from American Express dispensers.

At AmEx offices, cardholders can also cash personal checks for up to $1,000 in any seven-day period; of this $200 can be in cash, more if available, with the balance paid in traveler's checks, for which all but platinum cardholders pay a 1% fee. Higher limits apply to the gold and platinum cards.

Wiring Money You don't have to be a cardholder to send or receive an American Express MoneyGram for up to $10,000. To send one, go to an American Express MoneyGram agent, pay up to $1,000 with a credit card and anything over that in cash, and phone a transaction reference number to your intended recipient, who needs only present identification and the reference number to the nearest MoneyGram agent to pick up the cash. There are MoneyGram agents in more than 60 countries (call 800/543-4080 for locations). Fees range from 5% to 10%, depending on the amount and how you pay. You can't use American Express, which is really a convenience card—only Discover, Master-Card, and Visa credit cards.

You can also use **Western Union**. To wire money, take either cash or a check to the nearest office. (Or you can call and use a credit card.) Fees are roughly 5%–10%. Money sent from the United States or Canada will be available for pick up at agent locations in Cape Cod within minutes. Note that once the money is in the system it can be picked up at *any* location. There are approximately 20,000 agents worldwide (call 800/325-6000 for locations).

Traveling with Cameras, Camcorders, and Laptops

About Film and Cameras If your camera is new or if you haven't used it for a while, shoot and develop a few rolls of film before leaving home. Pack some lens tissue and an extra battery for your built-in light meter, and invest in an inexpensive skylight filter, to both protect your lens and provide some definition in hazy shots. Store film in a cool, dry place—never in the car's glove compartment or on the shelf under the rear window.

Films above ISO 400 are more sensitive to damage from airport security X-rays than others; very high speed films, ISO 1,000 and above, are exceedingly vulnerable. To protect your film, don't put it in checked luggage; carry it with you in a plastic bag and ask for a hand inspection. Such requests are honored at American airports. Don't depend on a lead-lined bag to protect film in checked luggage—the airline may very well turn up the dosage of radiation to see what you've got in there. Airport metal detectors do not harm film, although you'll set off the alarm if you walk through one with a roll in your pocket. Call the Kodak Information Center (tel. 800/242–2424) for details.

About Camcorders Before your trip, put new or long-unused camcorders through their paces, and practice panning and zooming. Invest in a skylight filter to protect the lens, and check the lithium battery that lights up the LCD (liquid crystal display) modes. As for the rechargeable nickel-cadmium batteries that are the camera's power source, take along an extra pair, so while you're using your camcorder you'll have one battery ready and another recharging.

About Videotape Unlike still-camera film, videotape is not damaged by X-rays. However, it may well be harmed by the magnetic field of a walk-through metal detector. Airport security personnel may want you to turn the camcorder on to prove that that's what it is, so make sure the battery is charged when you get to the airport.

About Laptops Security X-rays do not harm hard-disk or floppy-disk storage. Most airlines allow you to use your laptop aloft but request that you turn it off during takeoff and landing so as not to interfere with navigation equipment. Make sure the battery is charged when you arrive at the airport, because you may be asked to turn on the computer at security checkpoints to prove that it is what it appears to be. If you're a heavy computer user, consider traveling with a backup battery.

Staying Healthy

A problem common on the East Coast is Lyme disease (named after Lyme, Connecticut, where it was first diagnosed). This bacterial infection is transmitted by deer ticks and can be very serious, leading to chronic arthritis and worse if left untreated, which it often is because it is difficult to diagnose. Pregnant women are advised to avoid areas of possible infestation; if contracted during early pregnancy, the disease can harm a fetus.

Deer ticks are most prevalent April–October but can be found year-round. They are about the size of a pinhead; wearing light-colored clothing makes it easier to spot any ticks that might have attached themselves to you. Anyone planning to explore wooded areas or places with tall grasses (including dunes) should wear long pants, socks drawn up over pant cuffs, and a long-sleeve shirt with a close-fitting collar; boots are also recommended. The National Centers for Disease Control recommends that DEET repellent be applied to skin (not face!) and that permethrin be applied to clothing directly before entering infested areas; these repellents should be used very carefully and conservatively with small children.

Avoid walking in pathless brush areas and dune grasses, or brushing against low foliage. On returning from an outing, check your clothes and body for ticks (they also attach themselves to pets). To remove a tick, apply a tweezers to where it is attached to the skin and pull without squeezing the body of the tick—if the tick is squeezed, the body fluids containing the bacteria will be released and spread. Disinfect the bite with alcohol and save the tick in a closed jar in case symptoms of the disease develop.

The first symptom may be a ringlike rash, or flulike symptoms, such as malaise, fever, chills, and joint or facial pains. If diagnosed early, Lyme disease can be treated with antibiotics. If you suspect your symptoms may be due to a tick bite, inform your doctor and ask to be tested for the disease. For more information, contact the Centers for Disease Control (tel. 404/332–4555) or the Massachusetts Department of Public Health (Southeast Office, c/o Joan Tompson Allen, 109 Rhode Island Rd., Lakeville, MA 02347, tel. 508/947–1231). Brochures on the disease are available at many tourist information areas.

Car Rentals

Most major car-rental companies are represented in New England including **Avis** (tel. 800/331–1212, 800/879–2847 in Canada), **Budget** (tel. 800/527–0700), **Dollar** (tel. 800/800–4000), **Hertz** (tel. 800/654–3131, 800/263-0600 in Canada), and **National** (tel. 800/227–7368). **Thrifty** (tel. 800/367–2277) is also active in the region. In cities, unlimited-mileage rates range from about $35 per day for an economy car to $48 for a large car; weekly unlimited-mileage rates range from $135 to $250. This does not include sales tax, which in Massachusetts is 5% on car rentals.

Extra Charges Picking up the car in one city or country and leaving it in another may entail drop-off charges or one-way service fees, which can be substantial. The cost of a collision or loss damage waiver (*see below*) can be high also.

Cutting Costs If you know you will want a car for more than a day or two, you can save by planning ahead. Major international companies have programs that discount their standard rates by 15%–30% if you make the reservation before departure (anywhere from two to 14 days), rent for a minimum number of days (typically three or four), and prepay the rental. Ask about these advance-purchase schemes when you call for information. More economical rentals are those that come as part of fly/drive or other packages, even those as bare-bones as the rental plus an airline ticket (*see* Tours and Packages, *above*).

Other sources of savings are the companies that operate as wholesalers—companies that do not own their own fleets but rent in bulk from those that do and offer advantageous rates to their customers. Rentals through such companies must be arranged and paid for in advance. Among them is **Auto Europe** (Box 1097, Camden, ME 04843, tel. 207/236–8235 or 800/223–5555, 800/458–9503 in Canada). You won't see these deals advertised; they're even better in summer, when business travel is down. Always ask if unlimited mileage is available. Find out about any required deposits, cancellation penalties, and drop-off charges, and confirm the cost of the collision damage waiver (CDW).

One last tip: Remember to fill the tank when you turn in the vehicle, to avoid being charged for refueling at what you'll swear is the most expensive pump in town.

Insurance and Collision Damage Waiver The standard rental contract includes liability coverage (for damage to public property, injury to pedestrians, etc.) and coverage for the car against fire, theft (not included in certain countries), and collision damage with a deductible—most commonly $2,000–$3,000, occasionally more. In the case of an accident, you are responsible for the deductible amount unless you've purchased the CDW, which costs an average $12 a day, although this varies depending on what you've rented, where, and from whom.

Because this adds up quickly, you may be inclined to say "no thanks"—and that's certainly your option, although the rental agent may not tell you so. Note before you decline that deductibles are occasionally high enough that totaling a car would make you responsible for its full value. Planning ahead will help you make the right decision. By all means, find out if your own insurance covers damage to a rental car while traveling (not simply a car to drive when yours is in for repairs). And check whether charging car rentals to any of your credit cards will get you a CDW at no charge. In many states, laws mandate that renters be told what the CDW costs, that it's optional, and that their own auto insurance may provide the same protection.

Traveling with Children

Cape Cod is very family oriented and provides every imaginable diversion for kids, plus plenty of lodgings and restaurants that cater to them and that are affordable for families on a budget. Cottages and condominiums are popular with families, offering privacy, room, kitchens, and sometimes laundry facilities; often cottage or condo communities have play yards and pools, sometimes even full children's programs.

Publications *Local Guides* The Bristol County Convention & Visitors Bureau (Box 976, New Bedford, MA 02741, tel. 508/997–1250 or 800/288–6263) has a calendar of family-oriented events along south-coastal New England in its "Southern Coastal New England Guide."

Just for Kids: The New England Guide and Activity Book for Young Travelers, by Ed and Roon Frost (Glove Compartment Books, Box 1602, Portsmouth, NH 03802), is available by mail for $7.95 plus $3 shipping and handling.

Newsletter ***Family Travel Times,*** published 10 times a year by **Travel With Your Children** (TWYCH, 45 W. 18th St., 7th Floor Tower, New York, NY 10011, tel. 212/206–0688; annual subscription $55), covers destinations, types of vacations, and modes of travel.

Books *Great Vacations with Your Kids,* by Dorothy Jordon and Marjorie Cohen ($13; Penguin USA, 120 Woodbine St., Bergenfield,

NJ 07621, tel. 800/253–6476) and *Traveling with Children—And Enjoying It,* by Arlene K. Butler ($11.95 plus $3 shipping per book; Globe Pequot Press, Box 833, Old Saybrook, CT 06475, tel. 800/243–0495, or 800/962–0973 in CT) help plan your trip with children, from toddlers to teens. From the same publisher is *Recommended Family Resorts in the United States, Canada, and the Caribbean,* by Jane Wilford with Janet Tice ($12.95).

Tour Operators **GrandTravel** (6900 Wisconsin Ave., Suite 706, Chevy Chase, MD 20815, tel. 301/986–0790 or 800/247–7651) offers international and domestic tours for grandparents traveling with their grandchildren. The catalogue, as charmingly written and illustrated as a children's book, positively invites armchair traveling with lap-sitters aboard. **Rascals in Paradise** (650 5th St., Suite 505, San Francisco, CA 94107, tel. 415/978–9800 or 800/872–7225) specializes in programs for families.

Getting There On domestic flights, children under 2 not occupying a seat
Airfares travel free, and older children currently travel on the "lowest applicable" adult fare.

Baggage The adult baggage allowance applies for children paying half or more of the adult fare. Check with the airline for particulars.

Safety Seats The FAA recommends the use of safety seats aloft and details approved models in the free leaflet "**Child/Infant Safety Seats Recommended for Use in Aircraft**" (available from the Federal Aviation Administration, APA–200, 800 Independence Ave. SW, Washington, DC 20591, tel. 202/267–3479). Airline policy varies. U.S. carriers must allow FAA-approved models, but because these seats are strapped into a regular passenger seat, they may require that parents buy a ticket even for an infant under 2 who would otherwise ride free.

Facilities Aloft Airlines do provide other facilities and services for children, such as children's meals and freestanding bassinets (to those sitting in seats on the bulkhead, where there's enough legroom to accommodate them). Make your request when reserving. The annual February/March issue of *Family Travel Times* gives details of the children's services of dozens of airlines ($10; *see above*). "Kids and Teens in Flight" (free from the U.S. Department of Transportation, tel. 202/366–2220) offers tips for children flying alone.

Lodging **Best Western Chateau Motor Inn** in Provincetown, **Hampton Inn Cape Cod** in Hyannis, **Quality Inn** in Falmouth, and **Sheraton Ocean Park Inn** in Eastham allow children under age 18 to share their parents' room for free. In season, the oceanfront **New Seabury Resort** offers summer day programs for children 4–14 at a local camp (sports, nature studies, arts and crafts classes, games, overnights), plus tennis and golf clinics, minigolf, and activities like puppet shows and bands. West Dennis's **Lighthouse Inn** offers an extensive summer program of supervised activities daily 9:30–3 and children's dinners and entertainment 5:30–8:30, including Saturday night pizza-and-movie parties; it also has a private beach, a game room, a playground, and minigolf. **Chatham Bars Inn, Ocean Edge** in Brewster, and **Tara Hyannis Hotel** offer summer programs for kids, with arts and crafts, outdoor activities, and games; the Tara's program includes pajama parties, supper parties, tennis and golf clinics, and swimming lessons. **Sea Crest** in North Falmouth offers a children's day camp. *See* Lodging in Chapter 3, Cape Cod, for more information.

On Martha's Vineyard (*see* Lodging in Chapter 4, Martha's Vineyard), the **Mattakesett** condominium community has a full children's program and plenty of amenities for kids. At the **Colonial Inn** in Edgartown, children under 16 stay free.

On Nantucket, at **Beachside Resort** (*see* Lodging in Chapter 5, Nantucket), children under 16 stay free. At the **Harbor House,** children under 13 dine free with their parents between 5 and 6:30 PM.

Hints for Travelers with Disabilities

The Cape's accessibility for the disabled, already above average, was strengthened by new laws in 1992. Lift-van service is available on the Cape and islands, and all Cape public buses are accessible (*see* Getting Around *in individual chapters*).

Cape Organization for Rights of the Disabled (CORD; tel. 508/775–8300) will supply information on accessibility of restaurants, hotels, beaches, and other tourist facilities on Cape Cod. **Sight Loss Services** (tel. 508/394–3904 or 800/427–6842 in MA) provides accessibility and other information and referrals for the visually impaired.

The **Cape Cod National Seashore** (South Wellfleet 02663, tel. 508/349–3785) has many facilities, services, and programs accessible to disabled visitors. Write for information on what is available, or ask at the Seashore visitor centers (Eastham, tel. 508/255–3421; Provincetown, tel. 508/487–1256).

Organizations Several organizations provide travel information for people with disabilities, usually for a membership fee, and some publish newsletters and bulletins. Among them are the **Information Center for Individuals with Disabilities** (Fort Point Pl., 27–43 Wormwood St., Boston, MA 02210, tel. 617/727–5540 or 800/462–5015 in MA between 11 and 4, or leave message; TDD/TTY tel. 617/345–9743); **Mobility International USA** (Box 3551, Eugene, OR 97403, voice and TDD tel. 503/343–1284), the U.S. branch of an international organization based in Britain (*see below*) and present in 30 countries; **MossRehab Hospital Travel Information Service** (1200 W. Tabor Rd., Philadelphia, PA 19141, tel. 215/456–9603, TDD tel. 215/456–9602); the **Society for the Advancement of Travel for the Handicapped** (SATH, 347 5th Ave., Suite 610, New York, NY 10016, tel. 212/447–7284, fax 212/725–8253); the **Travel Industry and Disabled Exchange** (TIDE, 5435 Donna Ave., Tarzana, CA 91356, tel. 818/368–5648); and **Travelin' Talk** (Box 3534, Clarksville, TN 37043, tel. 615/552–6670).

Travel Agencies and Tour Operators **Directions Unlimited** (720 N. Bedford Rd., Bedford Hills, NY 10507, tel. 914/241–1700), a travel agency, has expertise in tours and cruises for the disabled. **Evergreen Travel Service** (4114 198th St. SW, Suite 13, Lynnwood, WA 98036, tel. 206/776–1184 or 800/435–2288) operates Wings on Wheels Tours for those in wheelchairs, White Cane Tours for the blind, and tours for the deaf and makes group and independent arrangements for travelers with any disability. **Flying Wheels Travel** (143 W. Bridge St., Box 382, Owatonna, MN 55060, tel. 800/535–6790 or 800/722–9351 in MN), a tour operator and travel agency, arranges international tours, cruises, and independent travel itineraries for people with mobility disabilities. **Nautilus**, at the same address as TIDE (*see above*), packages tours for the disabled internationally.

Publications In addition to the fact sheets, newsletters, and books mentioned above are several free publications available from the Consumer Information Center (Pueblo, CO 81009): "New Horizons for the Air Traveler with a Disability," a U.S. Department of Transportation booklet describing changes resulting from the 1986 Air Carrier Access Act and those still to come from the 1990 Americans with Disabilities Act (include Department 608Y in the address), and the Airport Operators Council's *Access Travel: Airports* (Dept. 5804), which describes facilities and services for the disabled at more than 500 airports worldwide.

Twin Peaks Press (Box 129, Vancouver, WA 98666, tel. 206/694–2462 or 800/637–2256) publishes the *Directory of Travel Agencies for the Disabled* ($19.95), listing more than 370 agencies worldwide; *Travel for the Disabled* ($19.95), listing some 500 access guides and accessible places worldwide; the *Directory of Accessible Van Rentals* ($9.95) for campers and RV travelers worldwide; and *Wheelchair Vagabond* ($14.95), a collection of personal travel tips. Add $2 per book for shipping. The Sierra Club publishes *Easy Access to National Parks* ($16 plus $3 shipping; 730 Polk St., San Francisco, CA 94109, tel. 415/776–2211).

Hints for Older Travelers

More than half of Cape Cod's year-round population is made up of retirees, so the area caters to older people in many ways; discounts for senior citizens are widely available, many restaurants offer early-bird specials from around 4 to 7 PM, and wheelchair-access ramps are common. Many inns will accommodate requests for rooms on the ground floor if notified when reservations are made. Older travelers may want to request a room with a shower or ask that they not be put in a room with a Victorian clawfoot tub that requires the bather to climb in and out.

Elder Services of Cape Cod and the Islands (68 Rte. 134, South Dennis 02660, tel. 508/394–4630 or 800/244–4630 in MA; on Martha's Vineyard, Box 2337, Oak Bluffs 02557, tel. 508/693–4393; on Nantucket, 144 Orange St., Nantucket 02554, tel. 508/228–4647) offers information and referrals.

Organizations The **American Association of Retired Persons** (AARP, 601 E St. NW, Washington, DC 20049, tel. 202/434–2277) provides independent travelers the Purchase Privilege Program, which offers discounts on hotels, car rentals, and sightseeing, and the AARP Motoring Plan, provided by Amoco, which furnishes domestic trip-routing information and emergency road-service aid for an annual fee of $39.95 per person or couple ($59.95 for a premium version). AARP also arranges group tours, cruises, and apartment living through AARP Travel Experience from American Express (400 Pinnacle Way, Suite 450, Norcross, GA 30071, tel. 800/927–0111); these can be booked through travel agents, except for the cruises, which must be booked directly (tel. 800/745–4567). AARP membership is open to those 50 and over; annual dues are $8 per person or couple.

Two other membership organizations offer discounts on lodgings, car rentals, and other travel products, along with such nontravel perks as magazines and newsletters. The **National Council of Senior Citizens** (1331 F St. NW, Washington, DC 20004, tel. 202/347–8800) is a nonprofit advocacy group with some 5,000 local clubs across the United States; membership costs $12 per person or couple annually. **Mature Outlook** (6001 N. Clark St., Chicago, IL 60660, tel. 800/336–6330), a Sears Roebuck & Co. subsidiary with 800,000 members, charges $9.95 for an annual membership.

Note: When using any senior-citizen identification card for reduced hotel rates, mention it when booking, not when checking out. At restaurants, show your card before you're seated; discounts may be limited to certain menus, days, or hours. If you are renting a car, ask about promotional rates that might improve on your senior-citizen discount.

Educational Travel **Elderhostel** (75 Federal St., 3rd floor, Boston, MA 02110, tel. 617/426–7788) is a nonprofit organization that has offered inexpensive study programs for people 60 and older since 1975. Programs are held at more than 1,800 educational institutions in the United States, Canada, and 45 other countries; courses cover everything from marine science to Greek myths and cowboy poetry. Participants generally attend lectures in the morning and spend the afternoon sightseeing or on field trips; they live in dorms on the host campuses. Fees for programs in the United States and Canada, which usually last one week, run about $300, not including transportation.

Tour Operators **Saga International Holidays** (222 Berkeley St., Boston, MA 02116, tel. 800/343–0273), which specializes in group travel for people over 60, offers a selection of variously priced tours and cruises covering five continents. If you want to take your grandchildren, look into **GrandTravel** (*see* Traveling with Children, *above*).

Further Reading

General The classic works on Cape Cod are Henry David Thoreau's
Cape Cod *Cape Cod*, an account of his walking tours in the mid-1800s, and Henry Beston's 1928 *The Outermost House*, which chronicles the seasons during a solitary year in a cabin at ocean's edge. Both reveal the character of Cape Codders and are rich in tales and local lore, as well as observations on nature and its processes. *Cape Cod: Henry David Thoreau's Complete Text with the Journey Recreated in Pictures*, by William F. Robinson, is a handsome New York Graphics Society edition, illustrated with prints from the period and current photographs. *Cape Cod Pilot*, by Josef Berger (alias Jeremiah Digges), is a WPA guidebook from 1937 that is filled with "whacking good yarns" about everything from religion to fishing, as well as a lot of still useful information.

Martha's Vineyard *On the Vineyard II*, with 38 essays by island authors (including Walter Cronkite, William Styron, and Carly Simon) and more than 200 photographs by islander Peter Simon, captures the Vineyard's many moods.

Nantucket *Nantucket Style*, by Leslie Linsley and Jon Aron (published by Rizzoli), is a look at 25 houses, from 18th-century mansions to rustic seaside cottages, with 300 illustrations. Recently reprinted is Henry Chandler Forman's architectural classic *Early Nantucket and Its Whale Houses.*

History Cape Cod *Cape Cod, Its People & Their History,* by Henry C. Kittredge (first published in 1930), is the standard history of the area, told with anecdotes and style as well as scholarship. *Sand in Their Shoes,* compiled by Edith and Frank Shay, is a compendium of writings on Cape Cod life throughout history. *Of Plimoth Plantation* is Governor William Bradford's description of the Pilgrims' voyage to and early years in the New World. *Art in Narrow Streets,* by Ross Moffett, and *Time and the Town: A Provincetown Chronicle,* by Provincetown Playhouse founder Mary Heaton Vorse, paint the social landscape of Provincetown in the first half of this century. A new illustrated history for children, *The Story of Cape Cod,* by Kevin Shortsleeve (available through *Cape Cod Life,* tel. 800/645–4482), is written in rhyming verse and sure to entertain.

Martha's Vineyard The many books written by Henry Beetle Hough, the Pulitzer Prize–winning editor of the *Vineyard Gazette* for 60 years, include his 1970 *Martha's Vineyard* and his 1936 *Martha's Vineyard, Summer Resort.*

Nantucket Alexander Starbuck's 1924 *History of Nantucket,* now out of print, is the most comprehensive work on early Nantucket. *Nantucket: The Life of an Island,* by Edwin P. Hoyt, is a lively and fascinating popular history.

Fiction Herman Melville's *Moby-Dick,* set on a 19th-century Nantucket whaling ship, captures the spirit of the whaling era. *Cape Cod,* by William Martin, is a historical novel and mystery following two families from the *Mayflower* voyage to the present, with lots of Cape history and flavor along the way. *Murder on Martha's Vineyard,* by David Osborn, and Alice Hoffman's lovely *Illumination Night* are set on the island. *Dark Nantucket Noon,* by Jane Langton, is a novel full of island atmosphere. *Nantucket Daybreak* is set in off-season Nantucket and portrays the life of scallopers in a story of love and betrayal.

Photography *A Summer's Day* (winner of the 1985 Ansel Adams Award for Best Photography Book) and *Cape Light* present color landscapes, still lifes, and portraits by Provincetown-associated photographer Joel Meyerowitz. *Martha's Vineyard* and *Eisenstaedt: Martha's Vineyard* are explorations of the island by *Life* magazine photographer Alfred Eisenstaedt, a summer resident for decades.

Periodicals Glossy magazines on the area include *Cape Cod Life* (Box 767, Cataumet 02534, tel. 508/564–4466), *Provincetown Arts* (Box 35, Provincetown 02657, tel. 508/487–3167), *Martha's Vineyard Magazine* (Box 66, Edgartown 02539, tel. 508/627–4311), and *Nantucket Journal* (tel. 800/825–0061).

Arriving and Departing

By Plane

Flights are either nonstop, direct, or connecting. A **nonstop** flight requires no change of plane and makes no stops. A **direct** flight stops at least once and can involve a change of plane, although the flight number remains the same; if the first leg is late, the second waits. This is not the case with a **connecting** flight, which involves a different plane and a different flight number.

Airports and Airlines Most flights to Cape Cod land in Hyannis; regular flights are also scheduled year-round between Boston and Provincetown. Service to Martha's Vineyard and Nantucket is available out of Boston, Hyannis, and New Bedford airports, as well as through nationwide connections; air service also connects the islands. For details, *see* individual chapters.

Many travelers fly into Boston's **Logan International Airport** (tel. 617/567–5400) and drive to the Cape and the islands; for routes to Cape Cod, *see* Arriving and Departing by Car in Chapter 3, Cape Cod.

Cutting Flight Costs The Sunday travel section of most newspapers is a good source of deals. When booking, particularly through an unfamiliar company, call the Better Business Bureau to find out whether any complaints have been registered against the company, pay with a credit card if you can, and consider trip-cancellation and default insurance.

Promotional Airfares All the less expensive fares, called promotional or discount fares, are round-trip and involve restrictions. The exact nature of the restrictions depends on the airline, the route, and the season and on whether travel is domestic or international, but you must usually buy the ticket—commonly called an APEX (advance purchase excursion) when it's for international travel—in advance (seven, 14, or 21 days are usual). You must also respect certain minimum- and maximum-stay requirements (for instance, over a Saturday night or at least seven and no more than 30, 45, or 90 days), and you must be willing to pay penalties for changes. Airlines generally allow some changes for a fee. But the cheaper the fare, the more likely the ticket is to be nonrefundable; it would take a death in the family for the airline to give you any of your money back if you had to cancel. The lowest fares are also subject to availability; because only a certain percentage of the plane's total seats will be sold at that price, they may go quickly.

Consolidators Consolidators or bulk-fare operators—also known as bucket shops—buy blocks of seats on scheduled flights that airlines anticipate they won't be able to sell. They pay wholesale prices, add a markup, and resell the seats to travel agents or directly to the public at prices that still undercut the airline's promotional or discount fares. You pay more than on a charter but ordinarily less than for an APEX ticket, and, even when there is not much of a price difference, the ticket usually comes without the advance-purchase restriction. Moreover, although tickets are marked nonrefundable so you can't turn them in to the airline for a full-fare refund, some consolidators sometimes give you your money back. Carefully read the fine print detailing penalties for changes and cancellations. If you doubt the reliability of a company, call the airline once you've made your booking and confirm that you do, indeed, have a reservation on the flight. The biggest U.S. consolidator, C.L. Thomson Express, sells only to travel agents. Well-established consolidators selling to the public include **UniTravel** (Box 12485, St. Louis, MO 63132, tel. 314/569–0900 or 800/325–2222); **Council Charter** (205 E. 42nd St., New York, NY 10017, tel. 212/661–0311 or 800/800–8222), a division of the Council on International Educational Exchange and a longtime charter operator now functioning more as a consolidator; and **Travac** (989 6th Ave., New York, NY 10018, tel. 212/563–3303 or 800/872–8800), also a former charterer.

Charter Flights Charters usually have the lowest fares and the most restrictions. Departures are limited and seldom on time, and you can lose all or most of your money if you cancel. (Generally, the closer to departure you cancel, the more you lose, although sometimes you will be charged only a small fee if you supply a substitute passenger.) The charterer, on the other hand, may legally cancel the flight for any reason up to 10 days before departure; within 10 days of departure, the flight may be canceled only if it becomes physically impossible to operate it. The charterer may also revise the itinerary or increase the price after you have bought the ticket, but if the new arrangement constitutes a "major change," you have the right to a refund. Before buying a charter ticket, read the fine print for the company's refund policy and details on major changes. Money for charter flights is usually paid into a bank escrow account, the name of which should be on the contract. If you don't pay by credit card, make your check payable to the escrow account (unless you're dealing with a travel agent, in which case, his or her check should be payable to the escrow account). The Department of Transportation's Consumer Affairs Office (I–25, Washington, DC 20590, tel. 202/366–2220) can answer questions on charters and send you its "Plane Talk: Public Charter Flights" information sheet.

Charter operators may offer flights alone or with ground arrangements that constitute a charter package. Well-established charter operators include **Council Charter** (205 E. 42nd St., New York, NY 10017, tel. 212/661–0311 or 800/800–8222), now largely a consolidator, despite its name, and **Travel Charter** (1120 E. Long Lake Rd., Troy, MI 48098, tel. 313/528–3500 or 800/521–5267), with Midwestern departures. **DER Tours** (Box 1606, Des Plains, IL 60017, tel. 800/782–2424), a charterer and consolidator, sells through travel agents.

Discount Travel Travel clubs offer their members unsold space on airplanes,
Clubs cruise ships, and package tours at nearly the last minute and at well below the original cost. Suppliers thus receive some revenue for their "leftovers," and members get a bargain. Membership generally includes a regular bulletin or access to a toll-free telephone hot line giving details of available trips departing anywhere from three or four days to several months in the future. Packages tend to be more common than flights alone, so if airfares are your only interest, read the literature before joining. Reductions on hotels are also available. Clubs include **Discount Travel International** (114 Forrest Ave., Suite 203, Narberth, PA 19072, tel. 215/668–7184; $45 annually, single or family), **Moment's Notice** (425 Madison Ave., New York, NY 10017, tel. 212/486–0503; $45 annually, single or family), **Travelers Advantage** (CUC Travel Service, 49 Music Sq. W, Nashville, TN 37203, tel. 800/548–1116; $49 annually, single or family), and **Worldwide Discount Travel Club** (1674 Meridian Ave., Miami Beach, FL 33139, tel. 305/534–2082; $50 annually for family, $40 single).

Smoking Since February 1990, smoking has been banned on all domestic flights of less than six hours duration; the ban also applies to domestic segments of international flights aboard U.S. and foreign carriers. On U.S. carriers flying to New England, a seat in a no-smoking section must be provided for every passenger who requests one, and the section must be enlarged to accommodate such passengers if necessary as long as they have complied with the airline's deadline for check-in and seat assignment. If smoking bothers you, request a seat far from the smoking section.

By Car

The speed limit in Massachusetts is 55 mph, though, except on Cape Cod's Route 6, you'll find little opportunity to reach it on the Cape and islands. For driving routes to Cape Cod, *see* Arriving and Departing by Car in Chapter 3, Cape Cod. To get to Martha's Vineyard with your car, you'll have to take a ferry from Woods Hole; to reach Nantucket, a ferry from Hyannis (*see* Arriving and Departing by Ferry in Chapter 4, Martha's Vineyard, and Chapter 5, Nantucket).

By Train

Amtrak (tel. 800/872–7245) has limited service to Cape Cod in season; in the off-season, trains to Boston connect with bus service to the Cape. For more details, *see* Arriving and Departing by Train in Chapter 3, Cape Cod.

By Bus

Bus service is available to Cape Cod, with stops at many towns and some connecting service to the islands by ferry; express buses run from Logan Airport in Boston to Hyannis (*see* Arriving and Departing by Bus in Chapter 3, Cape Cod).

By Boat

Provincetown is reached by ferry from Boston and Plymouth in season; Martha's Vineyard, from Woods Hole year-round and from Falmouth, Hyannis, and New Bedford in season; Nantucket, from Hyannis year-round. In season, a passenger ferry connects the islands, and a cruise out of Hyannis makes a one-day round-trip with stops at both islands. *See* Arriving and Departing by Ferry in Chapter 3, Cape Cod; Chapter 4, Martha's Vineyard; and Chapter 5, Nantucket.

Staying on Cape Cod, Martha's Vineyard, and Nantucket

Shopping

Art galleries and crafts shops abound on Cape Cod, Martha's Vineyard, and Nantucket, a reflection of the long attraction the area has held for artists and craftsmen. The region is also a popular antiquing spot. For a directory of area antiques dealers and auctions, contact the Cape Cod Antique Dealers Association (send business-size, stamped, self-addressed envelope to Box 196, Harwich 02645). On the Cape, Provincetown and

Wellfleet are the main centers for art. Both the Provincetown Gallery Guild (Box 242, Provincetown 02657) and the Wellfleet Art Galleries Association (Box 916, Wellfleet 02667) issue pamphlets on local galleries. For a listing of crafts shops on the Cape, write to the Society of Cape Cod Craftsmen (Box 791, Sandwich 02563), the Artisans' Guild of Cape Cod (send business-size, self-addressed, stamped envelope to Box 1, East Sandwich 02537), or Cape Cod Potters (Box 76, Chatham 02633).

Coastal environments and a seafaring past account for the proliferation of sea-related crafts on the Cape and the islands (as well as of marine-antiques dealers). A craft form that originated on the years-long voyages to whaling grounds is scrimshaw, the etching of finely detailed designs of sailing ships and sea creatures onto a hard surface. In the beginning, the bones or teeth of whales were used; today's ecologically minded (and legally constrained) scrimshanders use a synthetic substitute like Corian, a DuPont material for countertops.

Another whalers' pastime was the sailor's valentine: a glass-enclosed wood box, often in an octagonal shape (derived from the shape of the compass boxes that were originally used), containing an intricate arrangement of often tiny seashells. The shells were collected on stopovers in the West Indies and elsewhere, sorted by color, size, and shape, and then glued into elaborate patterns during the long hours aboard ship. Exquisite examples can be seen at a Nantucket gallery, the Sailor's Valentine (*see* Chapter 5, Nantucket).

The Nantucket lightship basket was developed in the mid-19th century on a lightship off the island's coast. In good weather there was little to do, and so (the story goes) crew members began weaving intricately patterned baskets of cane, a trade some continued onshore and passed on. Later a woven lid and decoration were added, and the utilitarian baskets were on their way to becoming the handbags that today cost hundreds of dollars. While Nantucket is still the locus of the craft, with a dozen active basket makers, antique and new baskets can be found on the Cape and the Vineyard as well.

Cranberry glass, a light ruby glass made by fusing gold with glass or crystal, is sold in gift shops all over the Cape. It was once made by the Sandwich Glass company (among others) but now retains only the association with Cape Cod, as it is made elsewhere in the United States and in Europe.

On the islands the majority of shops close down in winter; because of the Cape's large year-round population, its shops tend to remain open, though most Provincetown and Wellfleet shops and galleries shut down. Throughout the Cape and islands, shop owners respond to the flow of tourists as well as to their own inclinations; it's best to phone a shop before going out of your way to visit it.

Shop hours are generally 9 or 10 to 5, though in high season many tourist-oriented stores stay open until 10 PM or later. Except in the main tourist areas, shops are often closed on Sunday. The Massachusetts sales tax is 5%.

Sports and the Outdoors

The Cape and the islands are top spots for swimming, surfing, windsurfing, sailing, and virtually all water sports. Shipwrecks make for interesting dive sites, but don't expect a tropical underwater landscape. Golfers have many excellent courses to choose from, including championship layouts, and most remain open nearly year-round. Bicycling is a joy on the mostly level roads, along paved and scenic bike paths, and through the many nature preserves. (Massachusetts law requires a headlight after dark, a red rear reflector, and reflectors visible from either side of the bike.) Bird-watchers have an endless variety of habitats to choose from, often in a single nature preserve.

Fishing is extremely popular, especially for bluefish and striped bass, and the area is the site of some major derbies. A license (available at tackle shops) is required for persons age 15 or over for fishing in inland waters. The Cape Cod Chamber of Commerce (*see* Visitor Information, *above*) puts out a "Sportsman's Guide to Cape Cod," with a map pinpointing boat-launching facilities, surf-fishing locations, and fishing ponds and streams. The guide also contains information on charter, party, and whale-watch boats; game, bottom, and freshwater fishing; and hunting and fishing regulations.

Spectators can choose from a plethora of bike and running races, golf competitions, horse shows, sailboat races, and the well-attended Cape Cod Baseball League, breeding ground of champions.

Beaches

Cape Cod, Martha's Vineyard, and Nantucket are known for long, dune-backed sand beaches, both surf and calm. Swimming season is approximately mid-June–September (sometimes into October). The Cape Cod National Seashore has the Cape's best beaches, with high dunes, wide strands of sand, and no development on the shores. The islands have miles of beautiful, protected coastline as well.

National and State Parks

For further information on the parks mentioned here, as well as on nature and wildlife preserves, see the relevant chapters.

National Parks The **Cape Cod National Seashore** is a 30-mile stretch of the Cape between Eastham and Provincetown that is protected from development. It includes spectacular beaches, dunes, and many other habitats, making for excellent swimming, fishing, bike riding, bird-watching, and nature walks.

State Parks **Manuel F. Corellus State Forest** is 4,000 acres on Martha's Vineyard, laced with hiking, biking, and horse trails.

Nickerson State Park, more than 2,000 acres of forest in Brewster, is a popular camping, biking, boating, fishing, hiking, swimming, and cross-country skiing area.

Scusset Beach State Reservation in Sandwich is 450 acres with camping, biking, ocean swimming, fishing, and walking trails.

Shawme-Crowell State Forest in Sandwich is 742 acres with camping and walking trails.

Dining

Cape, Vineyard, and Nantucket restaurants offer an endless variety of fresh fish and shellfish. Each restaurant has its version of New England clam chowder, a rich milk- (and sometimes cream-) based dish usually made with the large clams called quahogs (pronounced "KO-hawgs"), chunks of potato, and salt pork. Clams are served in a variety of other ways as well—on the half shell, fried, or baked into a splendid concoction of clams, butter, and bread crumbs called seaclam pie. Clam shacks everywhere serve tasty fried fish and shellfish, accompanied by crisp onion rings—a nice, greasy meal to be savored when you're in a hurry or just on strike against sensible eating.

Other area specialties are the much-prized Wellfleet oysters and the tiny, delicate, buttery-sweet bay scallops (pronounced "SKAWL-lops" here), available fresh from the sea in late fall and winter. The ubiquity of Portuguese dishes—such as kale soup or *linguiça* (a spicy sausage)—on Cape and islands menus is due to a long history of Portuguese immigration; since whaling days, Portuguese have made their living from these seas, particularly around Provincetown. While bastions of haute cuisine can be found on the Cape, most restaurants feature traditional New England family fare—pot roast, baked scrod (codfish), chicken pot pie, mashed potatoes and gravy, soups, and stews. Nantucket has spawned a number of first-rate gourmet restaurants, with price tags to match—though most have added lower-priced café or prix-fixe menus in acknowledgment of hard times. Consistency from year to year is a problem, because there is a high turnover among chefs. Because of the short high season and the generally conservative year-round population, in the off-season even adventurous restaurants retreat to more traditional fare, early-bird specials, and buffets in order to survive.

Dress Dress advice in this book's listings refers to dinner only; almost without exception, casual dress is in order at lunch. At establishments where "come as you are" does not always apply, the most that is usually expected is "smart casual," meaning just a neat, minimally dressy look—no shorts, T-shirts, or ripped jeans.

Ratings Throughout this book, restaurant price ranges are based on the regular dinner menu and include one appetizer, one entrée, and one dessert, without wine, tax, or service. Highly recommended restaurants are indicated by a star ★.

Lodging

Bed-and-breakfasts are popular on Cape Cod, Martha's Vineyard, and Nantucket. Many are housed in old sea captains' homes and other 17th-, 18th-, and 19th- century buildings. In most cases, B&Bs are not appropriate for families, because noise travels easily, rooms are often small, and the furnishings are too fragile to withstand normal children's abuse. Usually a B&B will not offer a phone or TV in guest rooms; also, more and more B&Bs do not allow smoking. The Massachusetts Office of Travel and Tourism (*see* Visitor Information, *above*) offers a free guide to B&Bs and reservation services, and another on non-B&B lodgings.

Besides B&Bs, this highly developed tourist region has a wide range of lodging options. Luxurious self-contained resorts, beachfront and otherwise, offer all kinds of sporting facilities, restaurants, entertainment, services (including business services and children's programs), and all the assistance one could ever need in making vacation arrangements. Single-night lodgings for those just passing through can be found at countless tacky but cheap and conveniently located little roadside motels, as well as at others that are spotless and cheery yet still inexpensive, or at chain hotels at all price levels; these places often have a pool, TVs, or other amenities to keep children entertained in the evening. Families may want to consider condominiums, cottages, and efficiencies, which offer more space, living areas, kitchens, and sometimes laundry facilities, children's play areas, or children's programs.

Youth Hostels There are AYH hostels on Martha's Vineyard and Nantucket, as well as in Hyannis, Eastham, and Truro on Cape Cod (*see* Lodging *in relevant chapters*). Accommodations are simple, dormitories are segregated for men and women, common rooms and kitchens are shared, and everyone helps with the cleanup. Usually it's lights out at 11 PM. The price can't be beat—about $10 a night.

Camping Camping is not allowed on Nantucket, but there are many private and state-park camping areas on Cape Cod and Martha's Vineyard. Write to the Massachusetts Office of Travel & Tourism (*see* Visitor Information, *above*). For state-park campgrounds, see individual chapters.

Home Exchange This is obviously an inexpensive solution to the lodging problem, because house-swapping means living rent-free. You find a house, apartment, or other vacation property to exchange for your own by becoming a member of a home-exchange organization, which then sends you its annual directories listing available exchanges and includes your own listing in at least one of them. Arrangements for the actual exchange are made by the two parties to it, not by the organization. Principal clearinghouses include **Intervac U.S./International Home Exchange** (Box 590504, San Francisco, CA 94159, tel. 415/435–3497), the oldest, with thousands of foreign and domestic homes for exchange in its three annual directories; membership is $62, or $72 if you want to receive the directories but remain unlisted. The **Vacation Exchange Club** (Box 650, Key West, FL 33041, tel. 800/638–3841), also with thousands of foreign and domestic listings, publishes four annual directories plus updates; the $50 membership includes your listing in one book. **Loan-a-Home** (2 Park La., Apt. 6E, Mount Vernon, NY 10552, tel. 914/664–7640) specializes in long-term exchanges; there is no charge to list your home, but the directories cost $35 or $45 depending on the number you receive.

Apartment and Villa Rentals If you want a home base that's roomy enough for a family and comes with cooking facilities, a furnished rental may be the solution. It's generally cost-wise, too, although not always—some rentals are luxury properties (economical only when your party is large). Home-exchange directories do list rentals—often second homes owned by prospective house swappers—and there are services that can not only look for a house or apartment for you (even a castle if that's your fancy) but also handle the paperwork. Some send an illustrated catalogue and others send photographs of specific properties, sometimes at a charge; up-front registration fees may apply.

Among the companies is **Rent a Home International** (7200 34th Ave. NW, Seattle, WA 98117, tel. 206/789–9377 or 800/488–7368). **Hideaways International** (767 Islington St., Box 4433, Portsmouth, NH 03802, tel. 603/430–4433 or 800/843–4433) functions as a travel club. Membership ($79 yearly per person or family at the same address) includes two annual guides plus quarterly newsletters; rentals are arranged directly between members, not by the club staff.

Ratings Throughout this book, lodging prices are based on a standard double room (double occupancy) in high season. Unless otherwise noted, a listed establishment's rooms have private baths. Suites are defined here as bedrooms with *separate* sitting rooms; be aware that establishments sometimes label an especially large or nice room a suite. Also, note that "Continental breakfast" can mean anything from coffee and muffins to elaborate spreads with various fresh-squeezed juices, fresh fruit, homemade granola, and home-baked breads and muffins. If this sort of thing matters to you, be sure to inquire what breakfast includes when making your reservation. Highly recommended lodgings are indicated by a star ★.

Credit Cards

The following credit-card abbreviations are used in this book: AE, American Express; D, Discover; DC, Diners Club; MC, MasterCard; V, Visa.

2 Portraits of Cape Cod, Martha's Vineyard, and Nantucket

A Brief History

The fortunes of Cape Cod have always been linked to the sea. For centuries, fishermen in search of a livelihood, explorers in search of new worlds, and pilgrims of one sort or another in search of a new life—down to the beach-bound tourists of today—all have turned to the waters around this narrow peninsula arcing into the Atlantic to fulfill their needs and ambitions.

While some maintain that the Viking Thorwald from Iceland broke his keel on the shoals here in 1004, European exploration of Cape Cod most likely dates to 1602, when Bartholomew Gosnold sailed from Falmouth, England, to investigate the American coast for trade opportunities. He first anchored off what is now Provincetown and named the cape for the great quantities of cod his crew managed to catch. He then moved on to Cuttyhunk in the Elizabeth Islands (which he named for the queen); on leaving after a few weeks, he noted that the crew were "much fatter and in better health than when we went out of England." Samuel de Champlain, explorer and geographer for the king of France, visited in 1605 and 1606; his encounter with the resident Wampanoag tribe in the Chatham area resulted in deaths on both sides.

None of these visits, however, led to settlement; that began only with the chance landing of the Pilgrims, some of whom were Separatists rebelling from enforced membership in the Church of England, others merchants looking for economic opportunity. On September 16, 1620, the *Mayflower*, with 101 passengers, set out from Plymouth, England, for an area of land granted them by the Virginia Company (Jamestown had been settled in 1607). After more than two months at sea in the crowded boat they saw land; it was far north of their intended destination, but after the stormy passage and considering the approach of winter, they put in at Provincetown Harbor on November 21. Before going ashore they drew up the Mayflower Compact, America's first document establishing self-governance, because they were in an area under no official jurisdiction and dissension had already begun to surface.

Setting off in a small boat, a party led by Captain Myles Standish made a number of expeditions over several weeks, seeking a suitable site for a settlement in the wilderness of woods and scrub. Finally they chose Plymouth, and there they established the colony, governed by William Bradford, that is today re-created at Plimoth Plantation.

Over the next 20 years, settlers spread north and south from Plymouth. The first parts of Cape Cod to be settled were the bayside sections of Sandwich, Barnstable, and

Yarmouth (all incorporated in 1639), along an old Indian trail that is now Route 6A. (Martha's Vineyard was first settled in 1642, and Nantucket in 1659.) Most of the newcomers hunted, farmed, and fished; salt hay from the marshes was used to feed cattle and roof houses.

The first homes built by the English settlers on Cape Cod were wigwams built of twigs, bark, hides, cornstalks, and grasses, which they copied from those of the local Wampanoag Indians who had lived here for thousands of years before the Europeans arrived. Eventually, the settlers stripped the land of its forests to make farmland, graze sheep, and build more European-style homes, though with a New World look all their own. The steep-roofed saltbox and the Cape Cod cottage—still the most popular style of house on the Cape, and copied all over the country—were designed to accommodate growing families.

A newly married couple might begin by building a one- or two-room half-Cape, a rather lopsided 1½-story building with a door on one side of the facade and two windows on the other; a single chimney rose up on the wall behind the door. As the family grew, an addition might be built on the other side of the door large enough for a single window, turning the half-Cape into a three-quarter-Cape; a two-window addition would make it a symmetrical full Cape. Additions built onto the sides and back were called warts. An interesting feature of some Cape houses is the graceful bow roof, slightly curved like the bottom of a boat (not surprising, since ship's carpenters did much of the house-building as well). More noticeable, often in the older houses, is a profusion of small, irregularly shaped and located windows in the gable ends; Thoreau wrote of one such house that it looked as if each of the various occupants "had punched a hole where his necessities required it." Many ancient houses have been turned into historical museums. In some, docents take you on a tour of the times as you pass from the keeping room—the heart of the house, where meals were cooked at a great hearth before which the family gathered for warmth—to the nearby borning room, in whose warmth babies were born and the sick were tended, to the "showy" front parlors where company was entertained. Summer and winter kitchens, backyard pumps, beehive ovens, elaborate raised wall paneling, wide-board pine flooring, wainscoting, a doll made of corn husks, a spinning wheel, a stereopticon, a hand-stitched sampler or glove—each of these historic remnants gives a glimpse into the daily life of another age.

The Wampanoags taught the settlers what they knew of the land and how to live off it. Early on they showed them how to strip and process blubber from whales that became stranded on the beaches. To coax more whales onto the beach, men would sometimes surround them in small boats and make a commotion in the water with their oars until the whales swam to their doom in the only direction left open to them. By the mid-18th century, as the supply of near-shore whales thinned out, the hunt for the far-flung sperm whale began, growing into a major New England industry and making many a sea captain's fortune. Wellfleet, Truro, and Provincetown were the only ports on the Cape that could support deep-water distance whaling (and these were overtaken by Nantucket and New Bedford), but ports along the bay conducted active trade with packet ships carrying goods and passengers to and from Boston. Cape seamen were in great demand for ships sailing from Boston, New York, and other deep-water ports. In the mid-19th century, the Cape saw its most prosperous days, thanks largely to the whaling industry.

The decline in whaling hit the economies of Martha's Vineyard and Nantucket first and hardest, and both islands began cultivating tourism in the 19th century. Martha's Vineyard had played host to annual Methodist Camp Meetings since 1835, and Siasconset, on Nantucket, became a summer haven for New York theater folk when train service reached that remote end of the island in 1884. Whereas previously people traveled from Boston to and along the Cape only by stagecoach or packet boat, in 1848 the first train service from Boston began, reaching to Sandwich; by 1873 it had been extended little by little to Provincetown. In the 1890s, President Grover Cleveland made his Bourne residence (now gone) the Cape's first "summer White House" (to be followed in the 1960s by JFK). Grand seaside resorts grew up for summering families, and Cape Cod began to actively court visitors.

Artists were drawn to Provincetown starting in the early part of the century with the establishment of several art schools. Writers (including John Reed and the young Eugene O'Neill) started the Provincetown Players, which would be the germ of Cape community theater and professional summer-stock companies. The Barnstable Comedy Club, founded in 1922 and still going strong, is the most notable of the area's many amateur groups; novelist Kurt Vonnegut acted in its productions in the 1950s and 1960s, and had some of his early plays produced by the group. Professional summer stock began with the still-healthy Cape Playhouse in Dennis in 1927, and its early years featured the likes of Bette Davis (who was first an usher there), Henry Fonda, Ruth Gordon, Humphrey Bogart, and Gertrude Lawrence. In 1928, the University Players Guild (today called Falmouth Playhouse) opened in Falmouth, attracting the likes of James Cagney, Orson Welles, Josh Logan, Tallulah Bankhead, and Jimmy Stewart (who, while on summer vacation from Princeton, had his first bit part during Falmouth's first season).

The idea of a Cape Cod canal, linking the bay to the sound, was studied as early as the 17th century, but not until 1914 did the privately built canal merge the waters of the two bays. It was not, however, a thunderous success; too narrow and winding, the canal allowed only one-way traffic and created dangerous currents. The federal government bought it in 1928 and had the U.S. Army Corps of Engineers rebuild it. In the 1930s three bridges—two traffic and one railroad—went up, and the rest is the latter-day history of tourism on Cape Cod.

The building of the Mid-Cape Highway (Route 6) in the 1950s marked the great boom in the Cape's growth, and the presidency of John F. Kennedy, who summered in Hyannis Port, certainly added to the area's allure. Today the Cape's summer population is over 500,000, 2½ times the year-round population.

Though tourism, construction, and light industry are the mainstays of the Cape's economy these days, the earliest inhabitants' occupations have not disappeared. There are still more than 100 farms on the Cape, and the fishing industry—including lobstering, scalloping, and oyster aquaculture, as well as the fruits of fishing fleets such as those in Provincetown and Chatham—brings in $2 million a month.

Visitors are still drawn here by the sea: Scientists come to delve into the mysteries of the deep, artists come for the light, and everyone comes for the charm of the beach towns, the beauty of the white sand, the soft breezes, and the roaring surf.

The Outermost House

By Henry Beston

The sand bar of Eastham is the sea wall of the inlet. Its crest overhangs the beach, and from the high, wind-trampled rim, a long slope well overgrown with dune grass descends to the meadows on the west. Seen from the tower at Nauset, the land has an air of geographical simplicity; as a matter of fact, it is full of hollows, blind passages, and amphitheatres in which the roaring of the sea changes into the far roar of a cataract. I often wander into these curious pits. On their floors of sand, on their slopes, I find patterns made by the feet of visiting birds. Here, in a little disturbed and claw-marked space of sand, a flock of larks has alighted; here one of the birds has wandered off by himself; here are the deeper tracks of hungry crows; here the webbed impressions of a gull. There is always something poetic and mysterious to me about these tracks in the pits of the dunes; they begin at nowhere, sometimes with the faint impression of an alighting wing, and vanish as suddenly into the trackless nowhere of the sky.

Below the eastern rim the dunes fall in steeps of sand to the beach. Walking the beach close in along these steeps, one walks in the afternoon shade of a kind of sand escarpment, now seven or eight feet high and reasonably level, now 15 or 20 feet high to the top of a dome or mound. In four or five places storms have washed gullies or "cuts" clean through the wall. Dune plants grow in these dry beds, rooting themselves in under old, half-buried wreckage, clumps of dusty miller, Artemisia stelleriana, being the most familiar green. The plant flourishes in the most exposed situations, it jumps from the dune rim to the naked slopes, it even tries to find a permanent station on the beach. Silvery gray-green all summer long, in autumn it puts on gold and russet-golden colourings of singular delicacy and beauty.

The grass grows thickest on the slopes and shoulders of the mounds, its tall leaves inclosing intrusive heads and clumps of the thick-fleshed dune goldenrod. Still lower down the slope, where the sands open and the spears rise thin, the beach pea catches the eye with its familiar leaf and faded topmost bloom; lower still, on desert-like floors, are tussock mats of poverty grass and the flat green stars of innumerable spurges. The only real bushes of the region are beach plum thickets, and these are few and far between.

This essay is excerpted from Henry Beston's 1928 book *The Outermost House*, which chronicles a year spent in a solitary cottage at Coast Guard Beach, near Eastham, on Cape Cod.

All these plants have enormously long taproots which bury themselves deep in the moist core of the sands. The greater part of the year I have two beaches, one above, one below. The lower or tidal beach begins at mean low water and climbs a clean slope to the high-water mark of the average low-course tide; the upper beach, more of a plateau in form, occupies the space between high water and the dunes. The width of these beaches changes with every storm and every tide, but I shall not be far out if I call them both an average 75 feet wide. Unseasonable storm tides and high-course tides make of the beach one vast new floor. Winter tides narrow the winter's upper beach and often sweep across it to the dunes. The whole beach builds up in summer as if each tide pushed more and more sand against it out of the sea. Perhaps currents wash in sand from the outer bars.

It is no easy task to find a name or a phrase for the color of Eastham sand. Its tone, moreover, varies with the hour and the seasons. One friend says yellow on its way to brown, another speaks of the colour of raw silk. Whatever color images these hints may offer to a reader's mind, the color of the sand here on a June day is as warm and rich a tone as one may find. Late in the afternoon, there descends upon the beach and the bordering sea a delicate overtone of faintest violet. There is no harshness here in the landscape line, no hard northern brightness or brusque revelation; there is always reserve and mystery, always something beyond, on earth and sea something which nature, honouring, conceals.

The sand here has a life of its own, even if it is only a life borrowed from the wind. One pleasant summer afternoon, while a high, gusty westerly was blowing, I saw a little "wind devil," a miniature tornado six feet high, rush at full speed out of a cut, whirl itself full of sand upon the beach, and spin off breakerward. As it crossed the beach, the "devil" caught the sun, and there burst out of the sand smoke a brownish prism of burning, spinning, and fantastic color. South of me, the dune I call "big dune" now and then goes through a curious performance. Seen lengthwise, the giant has the shape of a wave, its slope to the beach being a magnificent fan of purest wind-blown sand, its westward slope a descent to a sandy amphitheatre. During a recent winter, a coast guard key post was erected on the peak of the dune; the feet of the night patrols trod down and nicked the crest, and presently this insignificant notch began to "work" and deepen. It is now eight or nine feet wide and as many deep. From across the marshes, it might be a kind of great, roundish bite out of the crest. On windy autumn days, when the sand is still dry and alive, and westerly gusts and currents take on a genuine violence, the loose sand behind the dune is whirled up by the wind and poured eastward through this funnel. At such times the peak "smokes" like a volcano. The smoke is now a streaming blackish plume, now a thin old-ivory wraith, and it billows, eddies, and pours out as from a sea Vesuvius.

Between the dunes and the marshes, an irregular width of salt-hay land extends from the sand slopes to the marshier widths of tidal land along the creeks. Each region has its own grasses, the meadows being almost a patchwork of competing growths. In the late summer and the autumn the marsh lavender, thin-strewn but straying everywhere, lifts its cloud of tiny sun-faded flowers above the tawny, almost deer-coloured grasses. The marsh islands beyond are but great masses of thatch grass rising from floors of sodded mud and sand; there are hidden pools in these unvisited acres which only sunset reveals. The wild ducks know them well and take refuge in them when stalked by gunners.

How singular it is that so little has been written about the birds of Cape Cod! The peninsula, from an ornithologist's point of view, is one of the most interesting in the world. The interest does not centre on the resident birds, for they are no more numerous here than they are in various other pleasant places; it lies in the fact that living here, one may see more kinds and varieties of birds than it would seem possible to discover in any one small region. At Eastham, for instance, among visitors and migrants, residents and casuals, I had land birds and moor birds, marsh birds and beach birds, sea birds and coastal birds, even birds of the outer ocean. West Indian hurricanes, moreover, often catch up and fling ashore here curious tropical and semitropical forms, a glossy ibis in one storm, a frigate bird in another. When living on the beach, I kept a particularly careful lookout during gales.

Eastham bar is only 3 miles long and scarce a quarter of a mile wide across its sands. Yet in this little world nature has already given her humbler creatures a protective coloration. Stop at the coast guard station and catch a locust on the station lawn—we have the maritime locust here, *Trimerotropsis maritima harris*—and, having caught him, study him well; you will find him tinted with green. Go 50 feet into the dunes and catch another, and you shall see an insect made of sand. The spiders, too, are made of sand— the phrase is none too strong—and so are the toads that go beach combing on moonlit summer nights. One may stand at the breakers' edge and study a whole world in one's hand.

They say here that great waves reach this coast in threes. Three great waves, then an indeterminate run of lesser rhythms, then three great waves again. On Celtic coasts it is the seventh wave that is seen coming like a king out of the grey, cold sea. The Cape tradition, however, is no half-real, half-mystical fancy, but the truth itself. Great waves do indeed approach this beach by threes. Again and again have I watched three giants roll in one after the other out of the Atlantic, cross the outer bar, break, form again, and follow each other in to fulfillment and destruction on this solitary beach. Coast guard crews are all well aware of this triple rhythm and take advantage of the lull that follows the last wave to launch their boats.

It is true that there are single giants as well. I have been roused by them in the night. Waked by their tremendous and unexpected crash, I have sometimes heard the last of the heavy overspill, sometimes only the loud, withdrawing roar. After the roar came a briefest pause, and after the pause the return of ocean to the night's long cadences. Such solitary titans, flinging their green tons down upon a quiet world, shake beach and dune. Late one September night, as I sat reading, the very father of all waves must have flung himself down before the house, for the quiet of the night was suddenly overturned by a gigantic, tumbling crash and an earthquake rumbling; the beach trembled beneath the avalanche, the dune shook, and my house so shook in its dune that the flame of a lamp quivered and pictures jarred on the wall.

The three great elemental sounds in nature are the sound of rain, the sound of wind in a primeval wood, and the sound of outer ocean on a beach. I have heard them all, and of the three elemental voices, that of ocean is the most awesome, beautiful, and varied. For it is a mistake to talk of the monotone of ocean or of the monotonous nature of its sound. The sea has many voices. Listen to the surf, really lend it your ears, and you will hear in it a world of sounds: hollow boomings and heavy roarings, great watery tumblings and tramplings, long hissing seethes, sharp, rifle-shot reports, splashes, whispers, the grinding undertone of stones, and sometimes vocal sounds that might be the half-heard talk of people in the sea. And not only is the great sound varied in the manner of its making, it is also constantly changing its tempo, its pitch, its accent, and its rhythm, being now loud and thundering, now almost placid, now furious, now grave and solemn-slow, now a simple measure, now a rhythm monstrous with a sense of purpose and elemental will.

Every mood of the wind, every change in the day's weather, every phase of the tide—all these have subtle sea musics all their own. Surf of the ebb, for instance, is one music, surf of the flood another, the change in the two musics being most clearly marked during the first hour of a rising tide. With the renewal of the tidal energy, the sound of the surf grows louder, the fury of battle returns to it as it turns again on the land, and beat and sound change with the renewal of the war.

Sound of surf in these autumnal dunes—the continuousness of it, sound of endless charging, endless incoming and gathering, endless fulfillment and dissolution, endless fecundity, and endless death. I have been trying to study out the mechanics of that mighty resonance. The dominant note is the great spilling crash made by each arriving wave. It may be hollow and booming, it may be heavy and churning, it may be a tumbling roar. The second fundamental sound is the wild seething cataract roar of the wave's dissolution and the rush of its foaming waters up the beach—this second sound *diminuendo.* The third fundamental sound is the endless dissolving hiss of the inmost slides of foam. The first two sounds reach the ear as a unisonance—the booming impact of the tons of water and the wild roar of the up-rush blending—and this mingled sound dissolves into the foam-bubble hissing of the third. Above the tumult, like birds, fly wisps of watery noise, splashes and counter splashes, whispers, seething, slaps, and chucklings. An overtone sound of other breakers, mingled with a general rumbling, fells earth and sea and air.

Here do I pause to warn my reader that although I have recounted the history of a breaker—an ideal breaker—the surf process must be understood as mingled and continuous, waves hurrying after waves, interrupting waves, washing back on waves, overwhelming waves. Moreover, I have described the sound of a high surf in fair weather. A storm surf is mechanically the same thing, but it *grinds,* and this same long, sepulchral grinding—sound of utter terror to all mariners—is a development of the second fundamental sound; it is the cry of the breaker water roaring its way ashore and dragging at the sand. A strange underbody of sound when heard through the high, wild screaming of a gale.

Breaking waves that have to run up a steep tilt of the beach are often followed by a dragging, grinding sound—the note of the baffled water running downhill again to the sea. It is loudest when the tide is low and breakers are rolling beach stones up and down a slope of the lower beach.

I am, perhaps, most conscious of the sound of surf just after I have gone to bed. Even here I read myself to drowsiness, and, reading, I hear the cadenced trampling roar filling all the dark. So close is the Fo'castle to the ocean's edge that the rhythm of sound I hear oftenest in fair weather is not so much a general tumult as an endless arrival, overspill, and dissolution of separate great seas. Through the dark, mathematic square of the screened half window, I listen to the rushes and the bursts, the tramplings, and the long, intermingled thunderings, never wearying of the sonorous and universal sound.

Away from the beach, the various sounds of the surf melt into one great thundering symphonic roar. Autumnal nights in Eastham village are full of this ocean sound. The "summer people" have gone, the village rests and prepares for winter, lamps shine from kitchen windows, and from across the moors, the great levels of the marsh, and the bulwark of the dunes resounds the long wintry roaring of the sea. Listen to it a while, and it will seem but one remote and formidable sound; listen still longer and you will discern in it a symphony of breaker thunderings, an endless, distant, elemental cannonade. There is beauty in it, and ancient terror. I heard it last as I walked through the village on a starry October night; there was no wind, the leafless trees were still, all the village was abed, and the whole sombre world was awesome with the sound.

One reason for my love of this great beach is that, living here, I dwell in a world that has a good natural smell, that is full of keen, vivid, and interesting savours and fragrances. I have them at their best, perhaps, when hot days are dulled with a warm rain. So well do I know them, indeed, that were I blindfolded and led about the summer beach, I think I could tell on what part of it I was at any moment standing. At the ocean's very edge the air is almost always cool—cold even—and delicately moist with surf spray and the endless dissolution of the innumerable bubbles of the foam slides; the wet sand slope beneath exhales a cool savour of mingling beach and sea, and the innermost breakers push ahead of them puffs of this fragrant air. It is a singular experience to walk this brim of ocean when the wind is blowing almost directly down the beach, but now veering a point toward the dunes, now a point toward the sea. For 20 feet a humid and tropical exhalation of hot, wet sand encircles one, and from this one steps, as through a door, into as many yards of mid-September. In a point of time, one goes from Central America to Maine.

Atop the broad eight-foot back of the summer bar, inland 40 feet or so from the edge of low tide, other odors wait. Here have the tides strewn a moist tableland with lumpy tangles, wisps, and matted festoons of ocean vegetation—with common sea grass, with rockweed olive-green and rockweed olive-brown, with the crushed and wrinkled green leaves of sea lettuce, with edible, purple-red dulse and bleached sea moss, with slimy and gelatinous cords seven and eight feet long. In the hot noontide they lie, slowly, slowly withering—for their very substance is water—and sending an odor of ocean and vegetation into the burning air. I like this good natural savor. Sometimes a dead, surf-trapped fish, perhaps a dead skate curling up in the heat, adds to this odor of vegetation a faint fishy rankness, but the smell is not earth corruption, and the scavengers of the beach soon enough remove the cause.

Beyond the bar and the tidal runnel farther in, the flat region I call the upper beach runs back to the shadeless bastion of the dunes. In summer this beach is rarely covered by the tides. Here lies a hot and pleasant odor of sand. I find myself an angle of shade slanting off from a mass of wreckage still embedded in a dune, take up a handful of the dry, bright sand, sift it slowly through my fingers, and note how the heat brings out the fine, sharp, stony smell of it. There is weed here, too, well buried in the dry sand—flotsam of last month's high, full-moon tides. In the shadowless glare, the topmost fronds and heart-shaped air sacs have ripened to an odd iodine orange and a blackish iodine brown. Overwhelmed thus by sand and heat, the aroma of this foliage has dissolved; only a shower will summon it again from these crisping, strangely colored leaves.

Cool breath of eastern ocean, the aroma of beach vegetation in the sun, the hot, pungent exhalation of fine sand—these mingled are the midsummer savour of the beach.

3 Cape Cod

In the 1950s, a Patti Page song promised: "If you're fond of sand dunes and salt sea air, quaint little villages here and there, you're sure to fall in love with old Cape Cod." The tourism boom of the next few decades certainly proved her right. So popular did the Cape become, in fact, that today it risks losing much of the charm that brought everyone here in the first place. While the traditional associations—weathered-shingle cottages, long dune-backed beaches, fog-enshrouded lighthouses—are still valid, the serenity of the landscape has been eroded. More and more open land so restful to eyes wearied by concrete has been lost to housing developments, condominium complexes, and strip malls, built to service the expanding population. In summer, the large crowds mean having to seek out the tranquillity that once met one at every turn.

Yet, for those who do seek it out, it will be found, for much of the Cape remains compellingly beautiful and unspoiled. Even at the height of the season, there will be no crowds at the less-traveled nature preserves and beaches and in well-preserved old villages off the beaten path. In the off-season, still-beautiful beaches welcome solitary walkers, and life everywhere returns to a small-town hum.

In 1961, the Cape Cod National Seashore was established to preserve virtually the entire eastern shoreline in its natural state for all time, and in 1990 the Cape Cod Commission was created to put a stop to the unplanned development of years past. For the sake of its economy, which is based on the area's continued appeal to tourists, and for the sake of preserving a landscape just as dear to most of the people who live here, Cape Cod has seen the light and has taken its first steps toward it.

Separated from the Massachusetts mainland by the 17.4-mile Cape Cod Canal (and linked with it by three bridges), the Cape is always likened in shape to an outstretched arm bent at the elbow, with fist turned back toward the mainland at Provincetown. Within the arm's embrace is Cape Cod Bay; to the east is the open Atlantic; to the south, Nantucket Sound. Being surrounded by all this water has its cost: Tides regularly eat away at the land, sometimes at an alarming rate. In his book *Cape Cod*, Henry David Thoreau described the Atlantic-side beach—which he walked from end to end on several trips in the mid-19th century—as "the edge of a continent wasting before the assaults of the ocean." Through the years, many lighthouses—some built hundreds of feet from water's edge—have fallen into the sea, and others are now in danger of being lost. Billingsgate Island off Wellfleet, which once held a number of cottages and a lighthouse, today is a bare sandbar occupied only by resting birds. Sand eroded from one shore often ends up on another—Provincetown and Monomoy Island, for instance, continue to grow. Nevertheless, the U.S. Geological Survey estimates that "at some distant time—not for many generations, however—Cape Cod will be nothing more than a few low sandy islands surrounded by shoals."

The Cape's Atlantic coast is notorious for its shoals, which have accounted for more than 3,000 shipwrecks in 300 years of recorded history. Nicknamed "the graveyard of ships," the area once had 13 lifesaving stations from Monomoy to Provincetown. They were manned by a crew of surfmen who drilled in lifesaving techniques during the day and took turns walking the beach at night in all kinds of weather, watching for ships in distress.

The stories of shipwrecks in Thoreau's book and Henry Beston's *The Outermost House* are riveting in their revelation of the awesome power of the sea, the tragedy of lives lost in icy waters, and the bravery of the men of the U.S. Life Saving Service, whose motto was "You have to go out, but you don't have to come back." (In the service's 43-year history, hundreds of victims were rescued; only twice were surfmen's lives lost.) When the tide is low, you can sometimes see the skeletons of wrecked ships emerge briefly from the sand in which they lie buried.

The Cape consists of 15 towns, each broken up into villages (for example, the town of Dennis comprises the villages of Dennis and East Dennis on the north shore, Dennis Port and West Dennis on the south, and South Dennis midway between, much to the dismay of precisionists). The term *Upper Cape* (think "upper arm," relating to the Cape's shape) refers to the towns of Bourne, Falmouth, Mashpee, and Sandwich; *Mid-Cape,* to Barnstable, Yarmouth, and Dennis; and *Lower Cape* ("lower arm"), to Harwich, Chatham, Brewster, Orleans, Eastham, Wellfleet, Truro, and Provincetown. The term *Outer Cape* ("outer reaches") refers to Wellfleet, Truro, and Provincetown, and sometimes is used synonymously with *Lower Cape.*

The Upper Cape, like each of the areas embraced by these designations, contains enough diversity to make generalizations about its character rife with exceptions. The area just before and after the canal and bridges, it encompasses a vast military complex and air base, the Massachusetts Military Reservation; a major training school for seamen, the Massachusetts Maritime Academy; the Cape's second-largest town (in population), Falmouth, still green and historic yet active with shopping and culture; the Cape's oldest town, Sandwich, whose center is picture-postcard old New England; an international center of marine and biological scientific research, Woods Hole; and the Native American township of Mashpee. Along the west coast are wooded areas ending in secluded coves; along the south coast, long-established seaside resort communities.

The central section of the region, the Mid-Cape, includes the largest town, Barnstable; the main commercial hub, Hyannis, a village in Barnstable; Hyannis Port, a well-groomed enclave of wealth and site of the Kennedy Compound; lots of heavily touristed areas and a number of historic districts and well-preserved back roads.

From the elbow to the fist of the Cape arm is the Lower Cape, the least developed Cape segment, which encompasses Chatham, a traditional and very Capey yet sophisticated town with good shopping and strolling; the Monomoy National Wildlife Refuge, a two-island Audubon bird sanctuary; Nickerson State Park, offering plenty of recreation and the Cape's prime camping in a forest setting; the beaches, woods, swamps, walking trails, historic sites, and visitor centers of the Cape Cod National Seashore; the small fishing town of Wellfleet, with a number of art and crafts galleries; the high, sweeping dunes of Truro and the Province Lands; and, last but not least, Provincetown, in winter a quiet fishing village, in summer a wild and crazy place with important galleries, wonderful crafts shops,

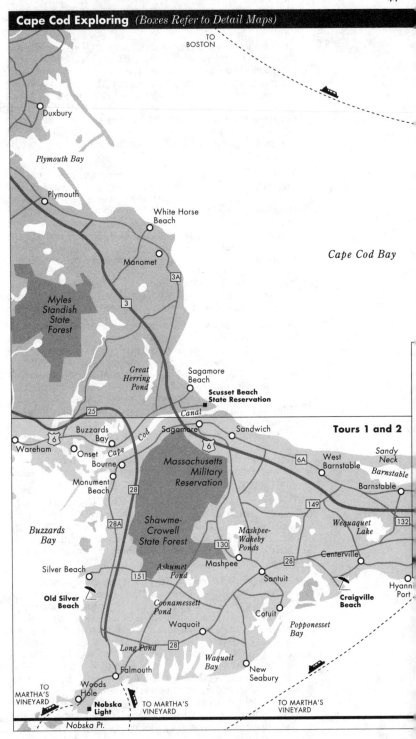

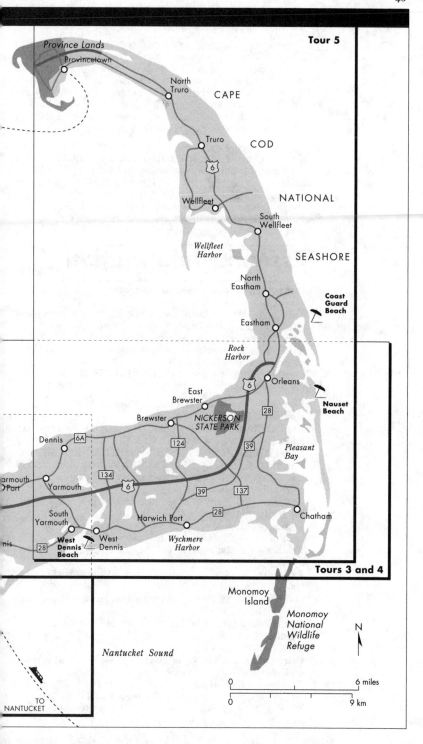

whale-watch excursion boats, good restaurants and people-watching, and lots of nightlife.

Crossing these boundaries on the north is Route 6A, the Old King's Highway, preserved for miles as a National Historic District, and true to its 17th- to 19th-century origins. On the south, Route 28 is a busy, mostly commercial highway that includes the most overdeveloped areas on the Cape. And everywhere there are bay and sound beaches, calm or wild, dune- or forest-backed, blanket-paved or secluded, which continue to offer just about every option for seekers of sun and sea.

Cape Cod is only about 70 miles from end to end, and you can make a cursory circuit of it in about two days. But it is really a place for relaxing—for swimming and sunning; for fishing, boating, and playing golf or tennis; for attending the theater, hunting for antiques, and making the rounds of the art galleries; for lobsters and fish fresh from the boat; or for leisurely walks, bike rides, or drives along pretty country roads that continue to hold out against modernity.

Essential Information

Important Addresses and Numbers

Tourist Information The **Cape Cod Chamber of Commerce** (junction of Rtes. 6 and 132, Hyannis, tel. 508/362–3225) is open year-round, weekdays 8:30–5; Memorial Day–Columbus Day, also weekends 9–4. It has information booths (open Memorial Day–Columbus Day) at the Sagamore Bridge rotary (tel. 508/888–2438) and just over the Bourne Bridge on Route 28 (tel. 508/759–3814) heading toward Falmouth.

Local chambers of commerce, many open only in season, put out literature on their area:
Brewster Board of Trade (Box 1241, 02631, tel. 508/896–8088; information center at old Town Hall, Rte. 6A).
Cape Cod Canal Region, for Sandwich and Bourne (70 Main St., Buzzards Bay 02532, tel. 508/759–3122; information centers at the Sagamore rotary, at the train depot in Buzzards Bay, and on Rte. 130 in Sandwich).
Chatham (533 Main St., Box 793, 02633–0793, tel. 508/945–5199; information center at 553 Main St.).
Dennis (junction of Rtes. 28 and 134, West Dennis; Box 275, South Dennis 02660, tel. 508/398–3568 or 800/243–9920).
Eastham (Rte. 6 at Fort Hill Rd., Box 1329, 02642, tel. 508/255–3444).
Falmouth (Academy La., off Main St., Box 582, 02541, tel. 508/548–8500 or 800/526–8532).
Harwich (Rte. 28, Box 34, Harwich Port 02646, tel. 508/432–1600 or 800/441–3199).
Hyannis Area (1481 Rte. 132, 02601, tel. 508/775–2201).
Mashpee (Mashpee rotary, Rte. 28, Box 1245, 02649, tel. 508/477–0792).
Orleans (Box 153, 02653, tel. 508/255–1386; information booth on Eldredge Pkwy., off Rte. 6A, tel. 508/240–2484).
Provincetown (MacMillan Wharf, Box 1017, 02657, tel. 508/487–3424); **Provincetown Business Guild** (115 Bradford St., Box 421–89, 02657, tel. 508/487–2313; gay tourism).

Truro (Rte. 6 at Head of the Meadow Rd., Box 26, North Truro 02652, tel. 508/487–1288).

Wellfleet (Box 571, 02667, tel. 508/349–2510; information center off Rte. 6 in South Wellfleet).

Yarmouth Area (657 Rte. 28, Box 479, West Yarmouth 02673, tel. 508/778–1008 or 800/732–1008; information center on Rte. 6 between Exits 6 and 7).

Emergencies For **police** emergencies, dial 911. For **fire and ambulance** emergencies anywhere on the Cape, call 800/352–7141.

For rescues at sea, call the **Coast Guard** (Woods Hole, tel. 508/548–5151; Sandwich, tel. 508/888–0020; Chatham, tel. 508/945–3830; Provincetown, tel. 508/487–0070).

Hospitals **Cape Cod Hospital** (27 Park St., Hyannis, tel. 508/771–1800). **Falmouth Hospital** (100 Ter Heun Dr., Falmouth, tel. 508/548–5300).

Walk-in Clinics The many Cape clinics include:
Dennis Health Stop (434 Rte. 134, South Dennis, tel. 508/394–7113).
Falmouth Walk-in Medical Center (309 Main St. [Rte. 28], Teaticket, tel. 508/540–6790).
Mashpee Family Medicine (Rte. 28, Mashpee, tel. 508/477–4282).
Medi-Center Five (525 Long Pond Dr., Harwich, tel. 508/432–4100).
Mid-Cape Medical Center (Rte. 28 at Bearse's Way, Hyannis, tel. 508/771–4092; Rte. 28, South Yarmouth, tel. 508/394–2151).
Outer Cape Health Services (Rte. 6, Wellfleet, tel. 508/349–3131; Harry Kemp Way, Provincetown, tel. 508/487–9395).

Dentists **Dental Associates of Cape Cod** (Cape Cod Mall, Hyannis, tel. 508/778–1200) accepts emergency walk-ins.

Late-night Pharmacies Most of the Cape's 20 **CVS** stores (in the Cape Cod Mall, Hyannis, tel. 508/771–1774) are open Monday–Saturday until 9 PM, Sunday until 6; most have extended hours in summer. Two are open 24 hours: in Dennis (Patriot Sq., Rte. 134, tel. 508/398–0133) and in Falmouth (64 Davis Straits, tel. 508/540–4307). They usually accept out-of-town prescription refills with the prescribing doctor's phone verification. Most pharmacies post emergency numbers on their doors.

Other Information **Army Corps of Engineers 24-hour hotline** (tel. 508/759–5991) for canal-area events, tide, and fishing information.

Tide, marine, and weather forecast (tel. 508/771–5522 or 508/255–8500).

WCOD hotline (tel. 508/790–1061) for time, temperature, weather, beach and marine reports, and concert updates.

Arriving and Departing by Plane

Airports **Barnstable Municipal Airport** (Rte. 28 rotary, Hyannis, tel. 508/775–2020) is the region's main air gateway. **Provincetown Municipal Airport** (Race Point Rd., tel. 508/487–0241) has year-round Boston service through Cape Air (*see* Airlines, *below*). Both airports are just a few minutes from the town center.

Airlines Airline service is extremely unpredictable because of the seasonal nature of Cape travel—carriers come and go, others juggle their routes. The Barnstable airport will always know which carriers fly in, should you encounter difficulty in making reservations. **Business Express/Delta Connection** (tel. 800/345–3400) flies into Hyannis nonstop from Boston year-round, direct from New York (LAG) in season. **Cape Air** (tel. 508/487–0240 or 800/352–0714) flies direct from Boston year-round; it also has joint fares with Continental, Delta, Midwest Express, and USAir and ticketing-and-baggage agreements with eight major U.S. airlines and KLM. **Northwest Airlink** (tel. 800/225–2525) and **USAir Express** (tel. 800/428–4322) fly nonstop from Boston year-round. Connections are made at Boston with the airlines' other routes. Charters serving Hyannis include **Hyannis Air Service** (tel. 508/775–8171) and **Thompson's** (tel. 508/771–0044). **Westchester Air** (tel. 800/759–2929) flies from White Plains, New York.

Arriving and Departing by Car

From Boston (60 miles), take Route 3, the Southeast Expressway, south to the Sagamore Bridge. From New York (220 miles), take I–95 north to Providence; change to I–195 and follow signs for the Cape to the Bourne Bridge. At the Sagamore Bridge, take Route 6 east to reach the Lower Cape and central towns quickly. At the Bourne Bridge, you can also get onto Route 6, or take Route 28 south to Falmouth and Woods Hole (about 15 miles). On summer weekends, when more than 100,000 cars a day cross each bridge, make every effort to avoid arriving in the late afternoon, especially on holidays. Routes 6, 6A, and 28 are heavily congested eastbound on Friday evening and westbound on Sunday afternoon.

Arriving and Departing by Train, Bus, and Boat

By Train **Amtrak** (tel. 800/USA–RAIL) offers limited, weekend train service to the Cape, with stops at Buzzards Bay, Sandwich, West Barnstable, and Hyannis; each year the company re-evaluates the routes, so don't be surprised if you find changes. The *Cape Codder,* on weekends from mid-June through Labor Day, travels between Hyannis and New York, with stops in Connecticut and Rhode Island; club and sleeper service is available. Connections with trains on other routes can of course be made at any point along the route. The rest of the year, you can travel to Boston by train and connect with buses there for Hyannis; Amtrak makes the arrangements, and connections are guaranteed. The tour desk (tel. 800/321–8684) offers packages including Hyannis hotels.

By Bus **Bonanza Bus Lines** (tel. 508/548–7588 or 800/556–3815) offers direct service to Bourne, Falmouth, and the Woods Hole steamship terminal from Boston, Providence, Fall River, and New Bedford, and connecting service from New York and Connecticut. Another route travels between Boston, Wareham, and Buzzards Bay. **Plymouth & Brockton Street Railway** (tel. 508/775–5524 or 508/746–0378) travels to Hyannis from Boston and Logan Airport, with stops en route.

By Boat **Bay State Cruise Company** makes the three-hour trip between Commonwealth Pier in Boston (tel. 617/723–7800) and MacMillan Wharf in Provincetown (tel. 508/487–9284) from Memorial Day to Columbus Day. *Cost, one way/same-day round-trip:*

$15/$28 adults, $13/$22 children under 13 and senior citizens, $5/$10 bicycles.

Capt. John Boats' passenger ferry makes the 1½- to two-hour trip between Plymouth's Town Wharf and Provincetown from Memorial Day through September. Schedules allow for day excursions. *Tel. 508/747–2400 or 800/242–2469 in MA. Cost, round-trip: $21 adults, $14 children 2–11, $18 senior citizens.*

Getting Around

Sample Distances From Sagamore Bridge to: Bourne Bridge, 5 miles; Falmouth, 20 miles; Hyannis, 18 miles; Chatham, 36 miles; Provincetown, 62 miles.

By Car Traffic on Cape Cod in summer can be maddening, especially on Route 28, which traces the populous south shore. Route 6 is the main artery, a limited-access (mostly divided) highway running the entire length of the Cape. On the north shore, the Old King's Highway, or Route 6A, parallels Route 6 and is a scenic country road lined with crafts and antiques shops. When you're in no hurry, use the back roads—they're less frustrating and much more rewarding. Good to know: Massachusetts permits a right turn on a red light (after a stop) unless a sign says otherwise. Also, when approaching one of the Cape's numerous rotaries (traffic circles), note that cars already on the rotary have the right of way.

Rental cars are available at the airport in Hyannis from **Avis** (tel. 508/775–2888), **Hertz** (tel. 508/775–5825), and **National** (tel. 508/771–4353), or through town branches of the other major chains (*see* Chapter 1, Essential Information).

By Bus The **Cape Cod Regional Transit Authority** (tel. 800/352–7155) operates the SeaLine bus service Monday–Saturday between Hyannis and Woods Hole. Its many stops include Cape Cod Community College, Cape Cod Mall, Mashpee Commons, Falmouth, and the Woods Hole steamship docks (fares 75¢–$4); the driver will stop when signaled along the route, and all buses have lifts for the disabled. **Plymouth & Brockton** (tel. 508/775–5524 or 508/746–0378) has service between Boston and Provincetown, with stops at many towns in between. **Bonanza** (tel. 508/548–7588 or 800/556–3815) plies between Bourne, Falmouth, Woods Hole, and Hyannis. All service is year-round.

By Bicycle Bicycling is a satisfying way of getting around the Cape. There are many flat back roads, as well as a number of well-developed and scenic bike trails (*see* Bicycling in Sports and the Outdoors, *below*). The following is a sampling of the many bike-rental shops available.

Upper Cape **Corner Cycle** (115 Palmer Ave., Falmouth, tel. 508/540–4195). **Holiday Cycles** (465 Grand Ave., Falmouth Heights, tel. 508/540–3549), with surrey, tandem, and other unusual bikes. **P&M Cycles** (29 Main St., Buzzards Bay, tel. 508/759–2830), across from the canal path.

Mid-Cape **All Right Bike & Mower** (627 Main St., West Yarmouth, tel. 508/790–3191). **Cape Cod Ski, Bike and Scuba** (323 Barnstable Rd., Hyannis, tel. 508/775–3301). **Cascade Motor Lodge** (201 Main St., Hyannis, tel. 508/775–9717), by bus and train station.

Outdoor Shop (50 Long Pond Dr., South Yarmouth, tel. 508/394–3819).

Lower Cape **Arnold's** (329 Commercial St., Provincetown, tel. 508/487–0844).

Bert & Carol's Lawnmower & Bicycle Shop (347 Orleans Rd., Rte. 28, North Chatham, tel. 508/945–0137).

Black Duck Sports Shop (Rte. 6, South Wellfleet, tel. 508/349–9801; off-season, tel. 508/349–2335).

Cape Cod Ski, Bike and Scuba (Rte. 6A, Orleans, tel. 508/255–7547; 815 Main St., Harwich, tel. 508/432–9035).

The Little Capistrano (Rte. 6, across from Salt Pond Visitor Center, Eastham, tel. 508/255–6515).

Rail Trail Bike Rentals (302 Underpass Rd., Brewster, tel. 508/896–8200), with parking for the Rail Trail.

By Moped **All Right Bike & Mower** and the **Outdoor Shop** (*see* By Bicycle, *above*) rent mopeds.

By Limousine **Aristocrat Limousine** (tel. 508/420–5466 or 800/992–6163), **Cape Escape Tours & East Coast Limousine Co.** (tel. 508/430–0666 or 800/540–0808 in MA), **Windsor Limousine Service** (tel. 508/420–1306 or 617/958–2489), and **John's Taxi & Limousine** (tel. 508/394–3209) provide 24-hour Cape-wide limo service.

By Taxi There are taxi stands at the Hyannis airport and bus station and at the Cape Cod Mall in Hyannis. You can arrange pickups by calling **All Village Taxi** (Falmouth, tel. 508/540–7200), **Eldredge Taxi** (Chatham, tel. 508/945–0068), **Hyannis Taxi** (tel. 508/775–0400), **Martin's Taxi** (Provincetown, tel. 508/487–0243), **Nauset Taxi** (Orleans, tel. 508/255–6965), and **Town Taxi** (Hyannis, tel. 508/775–5555).

Guided Tours

Cruises **Hy-Line** offers one-hour narrated tours of Hyannis harbor, including a view of the Kennedy compound; sunset and evening cocktail cruises are available. *Ocean St. dock, Pier 1, tel. 508/778–2600. Cost: $8 adults, $3.50 children 5–12.*

Cape Cod Canal Cruises (two or three hours, narrated) leave from Onset, just before the bridges onto the Cape. A Sunday jazz cruise, sunset cocktail cruises, and evening dance cruises are available. *Onset Bay Town Pier, tel. 508/295–3883. Cost: $6–$8 adults, $3–$4 children 6–12; $1 senior citizen discount Mon. and Fri.*

Patriot Party Boats offers two-hour day, sunset, and moonlight cruises between Falmouth and the Elizabeth Islands on a 68-foot schooner. Charters are available. *227 Clinton Ave., Falmouth, tel. 508/548–2626 or 800/734–0088 in MA. Cost: $15 adults, $10 children 6–12.*

Water Safaris offers 1½-hour tours of Bass River, past windmills, wilderness areas, and old captains' homes, on a 32-foot aluminum boat with an awning. *Rte. 28, West Dennis, just east of the Bass River Bridge, tel. 508/362–5555. Cost: $8.50 adults, $4.50 children under 13.*

The gaff-rigged schooner *Bay Lady II* makes two-hour sails, including a sunset cruise, across Provincetown Harbor into Cape Cod Bay. *MacMillan Wharf, Provincetown, tel. 508/487–9308. Cost: $10–$12 adults, $5 children under 12.*

Most of the above operate from April or May into October. For information on boats and ferries to the islands, *see* Chapter 4, Martha's Vineyard, and Chapter 5, Nantucket.

Train Tours   **Cape Cod Scenic Railroad** runs 1³/₄-hour excursions (round-trip) between Hyannis and Sagamore with stops at Sandwich and the canal. The train passes ponds, cranberry bogs, and marshes. A Dinner Train begins and ends in Hyannis (3 hours); the five-course gourmet meal is elegantly served as diners watch the passing scenery (floodlighted after sunset). New Ecology Discovery Tours (by reservation) are narrated by a naturalist and include a nature walk. *Main and Center Sts., Hyannis, tel. 508/771–3788. Excursions: several departures per day (no service Mon.) in each direction mid-June–Oct. (weekends starting in May). Cost: $10.50 adults, $6.50 children 3–12, $9.50 senior citizens. Dinner Train: Feb.–Dec., departs various evenings (reservations required at least 24 hrs in advance). Cost: $39.95. Ecology tour: call for times. Cost: same as Excursions (ask about family rates).*

Plane Tours   Sightseeing by air is offered by **Cape Cod Flying Service** (Cape Cod Airport, 1000 Race La., Marstons Mills, near Hyannis, tel. 508/428–8732), **Chatham Municipal Airport** (George Ryder Rd., West Chatham, tel. 508/945–9000), **Hyannis Air Service** (Barnstable airport, tel. 508/775–8171), **Cape Copters** (helicopters; Barnstable airport, tel. 508/790–1998), and **Cape Air** (Provincetown airport, tel. 508/487–0240). Among Cape Air's offerings are helicopter tours and tours in a 1930 Stinson. **Cape Cod Soaring Adventures** (tel. 508/540–8081 or 800/660–4563) offers glider flights and lessons out of Marstons Mills.

Dune Tours   **Art's Dune Tours** are hour-long narrated auto tours through the National Seashore and the dunes around Provincetown. *Tel. 508/487–1950 or 508/487–1050. Cost: $8 daytime, $9 sunset. Tours mid-Apr.–late Oct.*

Trolley Tours   The **Provincetown Trolley** leaves from the Town Hall, with pickups at other locations, on the hour from 10 to 8 and on the half-hour from 10:30 to 3:30. Points of interest on the 40-minute narrated tours include the downtown area and the Province Lands Visitor Center of the Cape Cod National Seashore. Riders can get on and off at four locations. *Tel. 508/487–9483. Cost: $7 adults, $5 children under 13, $6 senior citizens. Tours May–Oct.*

Nature Tours   The **Massachusetts Audubon Society** (contact Wellfleet Bay Wildlife Sanctuary, Box 236, South Wellfleet 02663, tel. 508/349–2615) sponsors naturalist-led wildlife tours year-round, including a tour of Nauset Marsh, with a walk on a barrier beach and a stop at a tern nesting colony; trips to the bird sanctuary of Monomoy Island; plus canoe trips, bay cruises, bird and insect walks, hikes, and more.

The Audubon Society's **Ashumet Holly and Wildlife Sanctuary** in East Falmouth (Ashumet Rd., tel. 508/563–6390) offers nature day trips and cruises to Cuttyhunk Island (including seal cruises in winter and spring), with guided birding walks in season. Phone reservations are required.

The **Cape Cod National Seashore** (Salt Pond, tel. 508/255–3421; South Wellfleet, tel. 508/349–3785; Province Lands, tel. 508/487–1256; *see also* Tour 5: Orleans to Provincetown, *below*) has guided walks, canoe trips, and more, daily from Memorial

Day to Columbus Day and on weekends in early spring and late fall; plus self-guided walking trails with accompanying leaflets.

Cape Cod Museum of Natural History (*see* Tour 3: Route 6A, Hyannis to Orleans, *below*) offers tours to Monomoy, some including overnights at the lighthouse, plus cruises exploring Nauset Marsh.

Whale-watching One of the joys of Cape Cod is the opportunity it affords for making trips to the whale feeding grounds at Stellwagen Bank, about 6 miles off the tip of Provincetown. On a sunny day especially, the boat ride out into open ocean is part of the pleasure, but the thrill, of course, is the sightings. You may spot minke, humpback, or finback whales, or the most endangered great-whale species, the right whale; just as welcome are dolphins, which in fact are toothed whales, and the seabirds that tag along for the ride.

Several operators offer whale-watch tours, with morning, afternoon, or sunset sailings lasting three to four hours. Provincetown is the main center. All boats have food service, but remember to bring sunscreen and a sweater or jacket—the breeze makes it chilly. Some boats stock seasickness pills, but if you're susceptible, come prepared!

Dolphin Fleet tours are accompanied by scientists who provide commentary while collecting data on the whale population they've been monitoring for years. They know the whales by name and tell you about their habits and histories. *Reservations are required. Ticket office in Chamber of Commerce building at MacMillan Wharf, tel. 508/349–1900 or 800/826–9300. Cost: $15.50–$16.50 adults (seasonal variation), $13.50–$14.50 children 7–12 and senior citizens. Tours Apr.–Oct.*

The ***Portuguese Princess*** sails with a naturalist on board to narrate. The snack bar offers Portuguese specialties. *Tickets available at 70 Shank Painter Rd. ticket office or at Whale Watchers General Store, 309 Commercial St., tel. 508/487–2651 or 800/442–3188 in MA. Cost: $15–$18 adults, $13–$16 children 7–12 and senior citizens. Tours Apr.–Oct.*

The ***Ranger V,*** the largest whale-watch boat, also has a naturalist on board. *Ticket office on Bradford St. at the corner of Standish St., tel. 508/487–3322 or 800/992–9333. Cost: $16–$19 adults, $12 children 7–11, $14–$17 senior citizens. Tours May–mid-Nov.*

Out of Barnstable Harbor, there's **Hyannis Whale Watcher Cruises.** A naturalist narrates and gives commentary on the sightings and Cape Cod Bay. *Millway, Barnstable, tel. 508/362–6088 or 800/287–0374 in MA. Cost: $18–$22 adults, $10 children 4–12, $17–$18 senior citizens. Tours Apr.–Nov.*

Exploring Cape Cod

The bridges over the canal are welcome sights to those approaching the Cape by land—signs every return vacationer eagerly awaits and never takes for granted. They're a bit magical, glistening silver arcs in the air, with boats small and large gliding smoothly below. The **Bourne Bridge** is the longest, at 2,384 feet; the **Sagamore Bridge** is 1,408 feet long. Each is supported by 44 steel cables suspended from the arch. They were completed in 1935, as was the **Railroad Bridge,** whose 500-foot-long movable span—the world's second-longest—lowers on the approach of a train (it takes about 2½ minutes).

Beyond the bridges, Cape Cod is traversed by three main highways. Route 6, the Mid-Cape Highway, passes through the relatively unpopulated center of the Cape, characterized by a landscape of scrub pine and oak. This is the fastest route east–west, and to Provincetown.

Paralleling Route 6 but following the north coast is Route 6A (also known as the Old King's Highway, the Cranberry Highway, and the Grand Army of the Republic Highway), in most sections a winding country road that passes through some of the Cape's best-preserved old New England towns. Here are main streets lined with stately sea captains' mansions and shaded by ancient, leafy trees. The bay side, as the north coast is called, tends to be marshy, and the water in the protected Cape Cod Bay is calmer than that of Nantucket Sound and the Atlantic.

The south shore of the Cape, traced by Route 28 and encompassing Falmouth, Hyannis, and Chatham, is heavily populated and is the major center for tourism. Its growth as a resort area has been abetted by its abundance of scenic harbors overlooking Nantucket Sound and its beaches with white sand and gentle surf. Route 28 itself is a busy highway, in summer densely packed with cars. Between about Hyannis and Harwich Port, it is flanked by strip malls, restaurants, motels, and kiddie attractions.

At Orleans, Routes 6A and 28 join with Route 6, which then continues alone through the sparsely populated Outer Cape (also called the back side) to the tip of Cape Cod.

More is included in each of the tours that follow than can be comfortably covered in one day, on the assumption that visitors will select the stops that are of most interest to them. Hyannis and Orleans are used as convenient beginning and end points; Hyannis itself is covered in Tour 1, Orleans in Tour 3.

Highlights for First-time Visitors

Cape Cod National Seashore (*see* Tour 5)
Chatham Light (*see* Tour 4)
Heritage Plantation, Sandwich (*see* Tour 1)
Julia Wood House, Falmouth (*see* Tour 2)
Kennedy Memorial and JFK Hyannis Museum, Hyannis (*see* Tour 1)
Pilgrim Monument, Provincetown (*see* Tour 6)
Route 6A, Sandwich to Orleans (*see* Tours 1 and 3)
Sandwich center (*see* Tour 1)
Sandy Neck, Sandwich (*see* Tour 1)
Whale watching (*see* Guided Tours, *above*)

Tour 1: Route 6A, Sagamore Bridge to Hyannis

This tour traverses a quiet section of the north shore, on a country road lined with small shops. All of Route 6A from Sandwich east—encompassing the oldest settlements on the Cape—is part of the Old King's Highway historic district and therefore protected from development. In fall, the foliage along the road is bright because of the many ponds and marshes, and along 6A in Sandwich you can stop to watch cranberries being harvested in flooded bogs. The whole tour covers about 25 miles.

Numbers in the margin correspond to points of interest on the Tours 1 and 2: The Canal to Hyannis map.

Take the first exit after crossing the Sagamore Bridge. Past the entrance (first right) to the Cape Cod Factory Outlet Mall, take a right at the light. On the left, across from the entrance to the Christmas Tree Shop (for both, *see* Shopping, *below*), is **Pairpont Crystal,** where you can watch richly colored lead crystal being hand-blown in the factory, as it has been for 150 years. The shop sells finished wares, including ornamental cup plates (used to hold the cup in the days when tea was poured into the saucer to drink) and reproductions of original Boston & Sandwich Glass pieces. *Rte. 6A, Sagamore, tel. 508/888–2344 or 800/899–0953. Open daily 9–6; demonstrations weekdays 8:30–4:30.*

❶ Continuing along Route 6A, you enter **Sandwich,** the oldest town on the Cape (founded in 1637). At the lights and sign directing you to Sandwich center, turn left instead, onto Jarves Street. Past the train depot, turn left (onto Factory Street) and then right (onto Harbor Street) to reach the **Sandwich Boardwalk,** leading across marsh, creek, and low dunes to Town Neck Beach, a rocky, cold beach with a sandy strip near the dunes. Destroyed by 1991's Hurricane Bob and October nor'easter, the boardwalk was rebuilt by volunteers using planks donated by individuals and businesses. Inscribed on the planks are donors' names, jokes (GET OFF OUR BOARD), thoughts (SIMPLIFY/THOREAU), and memorials to lovers, grandparents, and boats. From the viewing platform at the end, there's a very nice view (especially at sunset) of a long sweep of bay in both directions, the white cliffs beyond Sagamore, Sandy Neck, stone jetties, dunes and waving grasses, and the entrance to the canal.

Back at Route 6A, follow the sign into **Sandwich center,** a perfect old New England village and a good place for a leisurely stroll. At the end of Jarves Street, turn right onto Main Street, where the **Dan'l Webster Inn,** a reconstruction of a historic inn (*see* Dining and Lodging, *below*) with a restaurant and a gift shop worth a visit, sits amid little shops selling antiques, gifts, and art. On the right is **Yesteryears Doll Museum,** housed in the unfortunately rundown 1833 First Parish Meetinghouse. The enormous collection includes antique German, French, and Chinese dolls in bisque, china, wax, and many other media; Henry VIII and his wives, elegantly clothed in velvets and brocades; samurai warriors; and Balinese shadow puppets. The museum also has some wonderful miniature sets, such as a toy millinery shop with display cases, hatboxes, even ladies trying on hats; period German kitchens, complete with pewter, brass, copper, and tin implements; and an elaborately detailed four-story late Victorian dollhouse with wedding feast going on. A shop sells antique dolls. *143 Main St., tel. 508/888–1711. Admission: $3 adults, $2.50 senior citizens, $1.50 children under 12. Open mid-May–Oct., Mon.–Sat. 10–4. Closed Nov.–mid-May.*

Cross River Street and continue on Main Street, bearing right to find the **Sandwich Glass Museum.** Unlike other Cape towns, whose deep-water ports opened the doors to prosperity in the whaling days, Sandwich was an industrial town for much of the

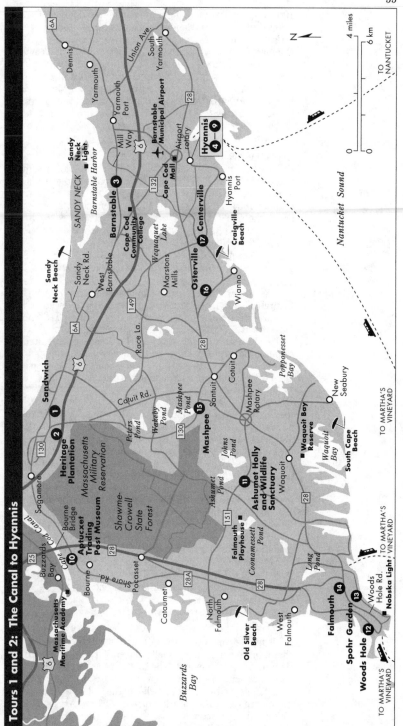

Tours 1 and 2: The Canal to Hyannis

19th century. The main industry was the production of vividly colored glass, called Sandwich glass, which is today a collector's item. The glass was made in the Boston & Sandwich Glass Company's factory here from 1825 until 1888, when competition with glassmakers in the Midwest—and finally a union strike—closed it. The museum contains relics of the town's early history, a diorama showing how the factory looked in its heyday, and an outstanding collection of blown and pressed glass. *129 Main St., tel. 508/888–0251. Admission: $3 adults, 50¢ children 6–12. Open Apr.–Oct., daily 9:30–4:30; Nov.–Dec. and Feb.–Mar., Wed.–Sun. 9:30–4; closed Jan.*

Cross the village green to the park around the lovely **Shawme Pond,** where children seem always to be fishing and the ducks and swans love to be fed. Here a little wooden bridge leads over a watercourse to the waterwheel-operated **Dexter Gristmill,** built in 1654. In season, the miller demonstrates and talks about the mill's operation and sells the ground corn. *Admission: $1.50 adults, 75¢ children 6–12; combination ticket with Hoxie House (below), $2.50 adults, $1 children. Open July–Labor Day, Mon.–Sat. 10–4:45, Sun. 1–4:45; Memorial Day–June and Labor Day–mid-Oct., weekends (call for hours).*

Time Out Across Water Street (and near the tall, white spired **First Church of Christ,** built in 1848 and inspired by a design of London architect Christopher Wren) is the **Dunbar Tea Shop** (1 Water St., tel. 508/833–2485). In a little room decorated in colonial style with paneled walls, dark beamed ceiling, and antiques, or at outdoor tables, an English cream tea and pub fare are served from 11 to 4:30 daily year-round. There's also a gift shop with antiques, books, and home decorator items.

Recrossing to the pond side of Water Street (Route 130), head left for the **Thornton W. Burgess Museum,** dedicated to this Sandwich native whose stories about Peter Rabbit, Reddy Fox, and a host of other creatures of the Old Briar Patch have been part of children's bedtimes for decades. Burgess, an avid conservationist, made his characters behave true to their species in order to educate children as he entertained them. A storytelling session, featuring the live animal that the Burgess story is about, is held regularly in July and August. The museum is best for small children or nostalgic adults; the many displays crowded into the small old house include some of Burgess's 170 books (and information about him), as well as changing exhibits on nature and children's hands-on exhibits. The small gift shop carries inexpensive items, including stuffed animals and Pairpont Crystal cup plates decorated with Burgess characters. Out back, benches overlook Shawme Pond and the ducks and swans bathing along its shore. *4 Water St., tel. 508/888–4668. Donations accepted. Open Mon.–Sat. 10–4, Sun. 1–4; Jan.–Mar., may close Sun.–Mon.*

A bit farther on is the **Hoxie House,** a saltbox remarkable in that it has been virtually unaltered since it was built in 1675—though it was lived in until the 1950s, it was never modernized with electricity or plumbing. Overlooking Shawme Pond, it has been furnished to reflect daily life in the Colonial period; some pieces are on loan from the Museum of Fine Arts in Boston. Highlights are diamond-shaped leaded-glass windows and a collection of small antique textile machines (spinning wheels, a 17th-century harness loom). *Rte. 130, tel. 508/888–1173. Admission: $1.50 adults, 75¢ children 12–16; combination ticket with Dexter Gristmill* (above) *$2.50 adults, $1 children. Open mid-June–mid-Sept., Mon.–Sat. 10–5, Sun. 1–5. Closed mid-Sept.–mid-June.*

School Street, across from the Hoxie House, leads back to Main Street. Leaving the village, take Grove Street to **Heritage Plantation,** an extraordinary complex of museum buildings, gardens, and a new café on 76 beautifully landscaped acres overlooking Shawme Pond. The grounds, crisscrossed by paths, include daylily, hosta, heather, herb, fruit-tree, and other gardens, as well as an extensive dell of rhododendrons begun by onetime estate owner Charles O. Dexter, an expert in hybridization. (In 1967, pharmaceuticals magnate Josiah K. Lilly III purchased the estate and turned it into a nonprofit museum.) The Shaker Round Barn showcases classic and historic cars, including a 1930 yellow-and-green Duesenberg built for Gary Cooper, a 1919 Pierce-Arrow, and a 1911 Stanley Steamer. The Military Museum houses antique firearms, a collection of 2,000 hand-painted miniature soldiers, military uniforms, and Native American arts. The Art Museum exhibits Colonial tools, an extensive Currier & Ives collection, Americana (including a mechanical-bank collection), antique toys such as a 1920 Hubley Royal Circus, and a working 1912 "Coney Island–style" carousel. In summer, evening concerts are held in the gardens. Peak bloom time for rhododendrons is mid-May–mid-June; for daylilies, July–early August. *Grove and Pine Sts., tel. 508/888–3300. Admission: $7 adults, $3.50 children 6–18, $6 senior citizens. Open mid-May–Oct., daily 10–5. Closed Nov.–mid-May.*

Return to Sandwich center and from there to Route 6A, then head east. Passing the **Sandwich Fish Hatchery** (*see* Off the Beaten Track, *below*) on the right, you'll come to the **Green Briar Nature Center and Jam Kitchen,** owned by the Thornton Burgess Society, which runs the Burgess museum as well. The nature center offers small changing exhibits on natural history, such as live frogs or turtles, aquariums, Indian artifacts, and seashells, as well as nature classes, walks, and lectures for adults and children. Great smells waft from the vintage stoves in the Jam Kitchen, and you can watch as jams, cranberry dishes, sun-cooked fruits, and pickles are made according to the recipes used here since 1903. Jam-making classes for adults and children are offered. *6 Discovery Hill Rd., off Rte. 6A, East Sandwich, tel. 508/888–6870. Donations accepted. Open Mon.–Sat. 10–4, Sun. 1–4; Jan.–Mar., may close Sun.–Mon.*

Sandy Neck Road (3.7 miles farther on 6A, on the left, opposite Michael's at Sandy Neck restaurant) leads to **Sandy Neck Beach.** On a peninsula, with the bay to the north and Barnstable Harbor and the 4,000-acre **Great Salt Marsh**—once harvested for salt hay, now a haven for birds—to the south, this is a good beach for walking; all you see is dunes and sand and sea in both directions. At the tip of the neck, the **Sandy Neck Light,** nonoperational since 1952 and now privately owned, stands just a few feet from the eroding shoreline. It was built in 1857 (to replace an 1827 light) of steel painted white, and it ran on acetylene gas.

As you continue east on 6A, past fine views of meadows and the bay, you enter the town of **Barnstable,** the Cape's largest, with

41,000 year-round residents, and the second oldest, having been founded in 1639, two years after Sandwich. You've just left the cozy Upper Cape for the busy Mid-Cape, but here in the historic district you won't notice the difference.

A mile and a half past the junction of Route 132 (which leads to the Cape Cod Community College, set on 120 wooded acres, and opposite it, the Cape Cod Conservatory of Music and Arts), a left at Scudder Lane will bring you to a town landing with a peaceful view of Sandy Neck across the water. At low tide the flats are exposed almost all the way out to the neck. A bit farther on 6A and you're in **Barnstable Village,** a lovely area of large old homes and the county seat. The **Olde Colonial Courthouse,** on the left, built in 1772 as the colony's second courthouse, is the home of the historical society Tales of Cape Cod (tel. 508/362–8927), which is restoring it to serve as a museum; a series of slide-illustrated lectures is held in summer. Across the street is **St. Mary's Episcopal Church,** with old-fashioned English gardens.

Just past the county courthouse, on the left, is the **Sturgis Library** (3090 Main St., tel. 508/362–6636), established in 1863 in a 1644 building on the National Register of Historic Places. Its holdings, which date back to the 17th century, include more than 1,500 maps and land charts, the definitive collection of Cape Cod genealogical material, and an extensive maritime-history collection.

Beyond the library is the little village center. Here the Barnstable Village Hall is home to the **Barnstable Comedy Club,** one of the oldest community theater groups in the country. A left onto Millway at the traffic light leads to **Barnstable Harbor,** with a fleet of fishing, charter, and whale-watch boats. Beyond the light, on the right, is the **Trayser Museum Complex.** Listed on the National Register of Historic Places, the red-painted brick main building houses a small collection of maritime exhibits (telescopes, captains' shaving boxes, items brought back from voyages, ship models and paintings), plus ivory, Sandwich glass, and Indian arrowheads. The downstairs re-creates the way the building looked in 1856, when it served as a customs house (don't miss the bronze acanthus-leaf capitals on the pillars). On the second floor is the restored customs-keeper's office with the original safe and a harbor view. Also on the grounds are a circa 1690 jail with two cells bearing former inmates' grafitti; and a carriage house with early tools, fishing implements, and a 19th-century horse-drawn hearse. *Rte. 6A, Barnstable, tel. 508/362–2092. Donations accepted. Open late June–mid-Oct., Tues.–Sat. 1:30–4:30. Closed mid-Oct.–late June.*

If you return to the traffic light, a left there will take you into Hyannis (about 2 miles) along a favorite local traffic-avoiding route. Beyond the intersection with Route 6, a left onto Route 132 leads past the **Cape Cod Mall** to what's called the Airport rotary, with the **Barnstable Municipal Airport** just beyond, on Route 28. Signs at the rotary will lead you to downtown **➍ Hyannis,** the Cape's year-round commercial hub, and a visibly different scene from what you've just left. Now you're well and truly in the Mid-Cape.

Numbers in the margin correspond to points of interest on the Hyannis map.

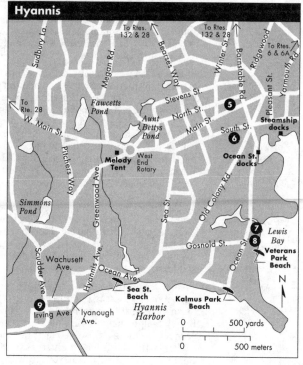

Hyannis

A right turn onto Main Street will take you through the downtown. Three parallel streets run through the heart of Hyannis. Busy, shop-filled Main Street is one-way, from east to west; South Street runs from west to east; and North Street is open to two-way traffic. At one end of Main Street is the West End rotary; just beyond it, on West Main Street, is the famous **Melody Tent,** opened in 1950 by the actress Gertrude Lawrence and her husband, producer/manager Richard Aldrich, to showcase Broadway musicals and concerts. Today the focus has shifted away from theater to music and stand-up comedy (*see* The Arts, *below*).

5 In Main Street's Old Town Hall, the **John F. Kennedy Hyannis Museum** explores JFK's Cape years (1934–63) through enlarged and annotated photographs culled from the archives of the JFK Library in Boston. Ongoing expansion plans, including adding a video (expected for 1994) and exhibits of memorabilia, await only money. *397 Main St., tel. 508/775–2201. Donations accepted. Open daily 10–4.*

6 On South Street is **St. Francis Xavier Church,** where Rose Kennedy and her family worshiped during their summers on the Cape (the pew that John F. Kennedy used regularly is marked by a plaque). At Ocean Street, turn right. Beyond the bustling docks—with boats for deep-sea fishing, harbor tours, and ferries to the islands, as well as waterfront seafood restau-
7 rants—is the **John F. Kennedy Memorial,** a quiet esplanade overlooking boat-filled Lewis Bay, with a plaque and fountain pool erected in 1966 by the people of Barnstable in memory of

the president who loved to sail these waters. Adjacent to the memorial is **Veterans Park,** with a beach, a tree-shaded picnic and barbecue area, and a playground. At the end of Ocean Street is **Kalmus Park Beach,** a long sandy beach with an area for windsurfers.

Hyannis Port was a mecca for Americans during the Kennedy presidency, when the **Kennedy compound** became the summer White House. The days of hordes of Secret Service men and swarms of tourists trampling down the bushes are gone, and the area is once again a community of quietly posh estates, though the Kennedy mystique is such that tourists still seek it out. To get a glimpse of the compound, less than 2 miles from the memorial, take a right onto Gosnold Street across from Veterans Park. At the stop sign, turn left at Sea Street; bear right onto Ocean Avenue, past Sea Street Beach; at the next stop sign, turn left onto Hyannis Avenue. If you stop a minute by the stone tower here, you'll get a good view of the long, narrow dock of the **Hyannis Port Yacht Club,** on Irving Avenue, stretching out into the harbor. Take the next left onto Iyanough Avenue, right onto Wachusett Avenue, then left onto Scudder Avenue. The compound is one block over, bounded by Scudder and Irving avenues.

Joseph P. and Rose Kennedy bought their house here—the largest one, closest to the water—in 1929, as a healthful place to summer with their soon-to-be-nine children. Sons Jack and Bobby bought neighboring homes in the 1950s. Jack's (now Jacqueline Onassis's) is the one at the corner of Scudder and Irving, with the 6-foot-high stockade fence on two sides. Bobby's (now Ethel's) is next to it, with the white fieldstone chimney. Ted bought a home on Squaw Island, a private island connected to the area by a causeway at the end of Scudder Avenue; it now belongs to his ex-wife, Joan. And Eunice (Kennedy) and Sargent Shriver have a house near Squaw Island, on Atlantic Avenue.

The compound is relatively self-sufficient in terms of entertainment: Rose Kennedy's home (with 14 rooms and nine baths) has a movie theater, and there's a private beach, a boat dock, a swimming pool, a tennis court, and a sports field that was the scene of the famous Kennedy touch-football matches. More recently, Maria Shriver, Caroline Kennedy, and other family members have had their wedding receptions here. The Hy-Line harbor cruise (*see* Guided Tours, *above*) passes in front of the compound, close enough for a good overview.

Scudder Avenue leads back to the West End rotary and from there to town.

Tour 2: Route 28, Bourne Bridge to Hyannis

Route 28 from the Bourne Bridge south to Falmouth is commercial in many areas; Route 28A, between Pocasset and West Falmouth, is more scenic, with side roads leading to attractive beaches and small harbors. The Falmouth–Hyannis segment of Route 28 traverses some little-developed south-coastal areas, a situation that quickly changes at Hyannis. The tour covers about 50 miles.

Numbers in the margin correspond to points of interest on the Tours 1 and 2: The Canal to Hyannis map.

Just over the Bourne Bridge, take a right at the rotary onto
⑩ Trowbridge Road and follow signs to the **Aptucxet Trading Post
Museum,** a monument to the birth of commerce in the New
World. Here, in 1627, Plimoth Plantation leaders established a
way station between the Indian encampment at Great Herring
Pond, 3 miles to the northeast; the Dutch colonists in New Am-
sterdam (New York) to the south, beyond Buzzards Bay; and
the English colonists on Cape Cod Bay. Before the canal was
built, the Manomet River connected the pond with Buzzards
Bay (no, scavengers don't frequent it—it was misnamed for the
migrating osprey that do), and a short portage connected the
pond to Scusset River, which met Cape Cod Bay. The Indians
traded furs; the Dutch, linen cloth, metal tools, glass beads, and
sugar and other staples; the Pilgrims, wool cloth, clay beads,
sassafras, and tobacco (which they imported from Virginia).
Wampum was the medium of exchange.

A replica of the post, including the original brick hearth, was
erected on the original's foundations; inside are 17th-century
cooking utensils, firearms, furniture, and other artifacts, plus
Indian arrowheads, tools, and tomahawks. Also on the grounds
are a gift shop in a Dutch-style windmill; a small Victorian railroad station built for the sole use of President Grover Cleveland, who had a summer home in Bourne; a saltworks; herb and
wildflower gardens; and a picnic area overlooking the canal.
*Aptucxet Rd., tel. 508/759–9487. Admission: $1.50 adults, 50¢
schoolchildren, $1.25 senior citizens. Open May–Columbus
Day, Tues.–Sat. 10–5, Sun. 2–5 (July–Aug. and Mon. holidays,
also Mon. 10–5). Closed Columbus Day–Apr.*

Return to Route 28 and head south. On your left sprawls the
21,000-acre **Massachusetts Military Reservation,** consisting of
the Camp Edwards Army National Guard and Reserve Training Site, the Coast Guard Air Station Cape Cod, and the Otis
Air National Guard Base (with the PAVE PAWS radar station,
a sophisticated system designed to track military satellites and
nuclear missiles). The main entrance is at the so-called Otis
rotary on Route 28; others are on Route 130 in Forestdale and
on Route 151 in Falmouth. Tours can be arranged (*see* Off the
Beaten Track, *below*).

The reservation, more often referred to as Otis Air Base, holds
a free two-day open house each summer with exhibitions that
may include precision flying by teams of the Air Force's Thun-
derbirds or the Navy's Blue Angels. Other highlights may be
performances by the Air Force Band, the Air Force honor
guard and drill team, the National Guard's Equestrian Unit,
or the Army's Golden Knights Parachute Team. Military
planes are on display, and concession stands serve the crowds.
For dates and information, call 508/968–4090 or 508/968–4003.

Leave Route 28 at the Otis rotary for Route 28A, which winds
past the little villages of Pocasset and Cataumet, with their old
houses, pretty streets, and ocean views. A left toward
Cataumet Village takes you on an even more scenic drive along
County Road, past cranberry bogs and an old graveyard, then
rejoins 28A. A left onto Route 151 leads you to the renowned
Falmouth Playhouse, one of the Cape's top theater venues.

Beyond the playhouse sign on Route 151, before the fair-
⑪ grounds, a left leads to the **Ashumet Holly and Wildlife Sanctuary,** a 45-acre tract of woods, shady groves, meadows, and

hiking trails (self-guided maps are available). Operated by the Massachusetts Audubon Society, the reservation features more than 1,000 holly trees, including 65 American, Oriental, and European varieties. Like the Heritage Plantation in Sandwich, it was purchased and donated by Josiah K. Lilly III for preservation purposes. Grassy Pond is home to many turtles and frogs, and in summer, 35 nesting pairs of barn swallows live in open rafters of the barn (they can be viewed Tues.–Sat. 9–4); downstairs is a small gift shop with handcrafted items. In spring, there's an open house when the dogwoods and rhododendrons are in bloom; in December, a three-day holly sale. Fall through spring, crafts and nature classes are given. *286 Ashumet Rd., East Falmouth, tel. 508/563–6390. Admission: $3 adults, $2 senior citizens and children. Trails open daily sunrise–sunset; office open Tues.–Sat. 9–4.*

Retrace your route 5 miles on 151 back to 28A and continue south, past a sign leading to **Old Silver Beach,** one of the Cape's prettiest. Passing antique Colonial homes ablaze in spring with flowering trees and bushes, Route 28A meanders under a canopy of leafy green through the center of **West Falmouth,** with a few antiques and other shops and a general store/post office. Just before 28A merges with 28, turn right at the blue camping sign for a scenic drive through the **Sippewissett** area.

Time Out **Peach Tree Circle Farm** (881 Old Palmer Ave., Falmouth, tel. 508/548–4006) includes a bakery, a farm stand, and a cheery tearoom where inexpensive lunches of soups, sandwiches, salads, and a few entrées like quiche or chicken pot pie are served year-round, amid the smells of baking bread and herbs hung to dry.

The road ends at the Cape's southwest tip, in the village of **⑫ Woods Hole,** a center for international marine research and home to several major scientific institutions. The National Marine Fisheries Service was here first, established in 1871 to study fish management and conservation. In 1888, the Marine Biological Laboratory (MBL), a center for research and education in marine biology, moved in across the street. In 1930, the Woods Hole Oceanographic Institution (WHOI) arrived, followed by the U.S. Geological Survey's Branch of Marine Geology in the 1960s.

WHOI is the largest of the institutions, with several buildings in the village and a 200-acre campus nearby. During World War II its research focused on underwater explosives, submarine detection, and the development of anti-fouling paint. Today it is the largest independent oceanography research laboratory in the country, with an $87 million annual operating budget. A graduate program is offered jointly with MIT, in addition to undergraduate and postdoctoral studies. WHOI's several research vessels range throughout the world's waters; its staff led the successful U.S.–French search for the *Titanic* (found about 400 miles off Newfoundland) in 1985.

Most of the year, Woods Hole is a peaceful community of intellectuals, who quietly go about their work. In summer, however, the basically one-street village teems with the 1,000 or more scientists and graduate students from all over the world who come either to participate in summer studies at MBL or WHOI or to work on independent research projects. A handful of waterside cafés and shops along Water Street compete for most bicycles stacked up at the door.

What accounts for this incredible concentration of scientific minds is, first, the variety and abundance of marine life in Woods Hole's unpolluted waters, and the natural deep-water port. Second is the opportunity for easy interchange of ideas and information and the stimulation of daily lectures and discussions (many open to the public) by important scientists. Third, the pooling of resources among the various institutions makes for economies that benefit each while allowing all access to highly sophisticated equipment.

A good example of this pooling of resources is the **MBL-WHOI Library**, possessor of one of the best collections of biological, ecological, and oceanographic literature in the world, including access to over 200 computer data bases and the Internet, and subscriptions to more than 5,000 scientific journals in 40 languages (with complete collections of most from their first issue). During World War II, the librarian arranged with a German subscription agency to have German periodicals sent to neutral Switzerland, to be stored until the end of the war; thus the library's German collections are uninterrupted whereas even many German institutions' are not. All journals are always accessible, because they cannot be checked out and because the library is open 24 hours a day. The Rare Books Room contains photographs, monographs, and prints, as well as journal collections dating back to 1665. However, unless you are a scientific researcher, the only way you'll get to see the library is by taking the **Marine Biological Laboratory tour** (tel. 508/548-3705, ext. 623; call for reservations, at least a week in advance if possible, and meeting instructions). The 1½-hour tours are led by retired scientists (mid-June–July, weekdays at 1 PM) and include an introductory slide show, as well as stops at the library, the marine resources center (where live sea creatures collected each day are kept), and one of the many research labs, where scientists will demonstrate the project they are working on.

The Oceanographic Institution is not open to the public, but you can learn about it at the small **WHOI Exhibit Center**, with videos and exhibits on the institution and its various projects, including research vessels. *15 School St., tel. 508/457-2000, ext. 2663. Admission free. Open mid-May–Oct., Mon.–Sat. 9:30–5, Sun. noon–5; call for spring and fall hours. Closed Jan.–Mar.*

The **National Marine Fisheries Service Aquarium** displays 16 tanks of regional fish and shellfish, plus microscopes for kids to examine marine life and several hands-on pools with banded lobsters, crabs, snails, starfish, and other creatures. The star attractions are two harbor seals, who can be seen in the outdoor pool near the entrance in summer (they winter in Connecticut). *Corner of Albatross and Water Sts., tel. 508/548-7684. Admission free. Open mid-June–mid-Sept., daily 10–4; mid-Sept.-mid-June, weekdays 9–4.*

Free guided walking tours of the village are available Tuesdays at 4 in July and August from the **Woods Hole Historical Museum,** across from the Martha's Vineyard ferry parking lot. In the archives you'll find old ships' logs, postcards, newspaper articles, maps, diaries, photographs; more than 200 tapes of oral history provided by local residents; and a 100-volume library on maritime history. The museum houses paintings, a restored Woods Hole Spritsail boat, boat models, and a model of the town as it looked in the 1890s. *573 Woods Hole Rd., tel. 508/548–7270. Donations accepted. Museum open July–Aug., Tues.–Sat. 10–4. Closed Sept.–June. Archives open year-round, Tues. and Thurs. 10–2.*

Beyond the museum, a right onto Church Street takes you past some fine estates. On the left is the 1888 **Episcopal Church of the Messiah,** a stone church with a conical steeple and a small medicinal herb garden in the shape of a Celtic cross. The garden is enclosed by an ilex hedge and provided with a bench for meditation. Inscriptions on either side of the carved gate read "Enter in hope" and "Depart in peace."

Turning into a shore road, Church Street leads to **Nobska Light,** from which the views of the nearby Elizabeth Islands and of Martha's Vineyard, across Vineyard Sound, are spectacular. The 42-foot cast-iron tower lined with brick was built in 1876 with a stationary light; depending on a ship's position, it shows red (indicating dangerous waters) or white. Since the light was automated in 1985, the adjacent keeper's quarters have been the headquarters of the Coast Guard group commander—a fitting passing of the torch from one safeguarder of ships to another.

Follow the road around, always bearing right, for the coast road back to Route 28 in Falmouth center. Alternatively, retrace your route to Woods Hole, and at the stoplight 1.7 miles to the north on Route 28, a left onto Oyster Pond Road and

13 another onto Fells Road takes you to the **Charles D. and Margaret K. Spohr Garden,** a private garden of 3 planted acres on Oyster Pond that the generous owner invites the public to enjoy. In spring, there are glorious displays of more than 700,000 daffodils, plus lilies, tulips, azaleas, magnolias, flowering crabs, rhododendrons, climbing hydrangeas, and more. A collection of old millstones, bronze church bells, and ship's anchors are woven into the landscaping.

14 Four miles north of Woods Hole via Route 28 is **Falmouth.** The Cape's second-largest town was settled in 1660 by Congregationalists from Barnstable who had been ostracized from their church and deprived of voting privileges and other civil rights for being sympathizers with the Quakers, then the objects of severe repression. The **Village Green**—a spare triangle of grass with a few trees, a flagpole ringed by flowers, and a low white fence—was used as a militia training field in the 18th century and a grazing ground for horses in the early 19th. Today it is flanked by attractive old homes, some built by sea captains, and the 1856 **Congregational Church** (built on the timbers of its 1796 predecessor), with a bell made by Paul Revere. The cheery inscription reads: "The living to the church I call, and to the grave I summon all."

Opposite the green, on Palmer Avenue, are the two museums maintained by the Falmouth Historical Society. The 1790 **Julia Wood House** retains wonderful architectural details (a widow's walk, wide-board floors, leaded-glass windows, a Colonial kitchen with wide hearth), plus antique embroideries, baby shoes and clothes, toys and dolls, portraits, furniture, and an authentically equipped doctor's office (from the house's onetime owner). Out back is a barn museum with antique farm implements, a 19th-century horse-drawn sleigh, and more. The smaller **Conant House** next door, a 1794 half-Cape, has military memorabilia, whaling items, scrimshaw, sailors' valentines, and a genealogical and historical research library. There's also a collection of books, portraits, and other memorabilia relating to Katharine Lee Bates, the native daughter who wrote "America the Beautiful." Docents lead you through the museums; free walking tours of the town are also available in season (call for meeting times). Adjacent to the museums is a pretty formal **garden** with a gazebo and flagstone paths. *Palmer Ave., tel. 508/548–4857. Admission: $2 adults, 50¢ children under 13. Open mid-June–mid-Sept., weekdays 2–5.*

On the other side of the green, a right onto Main Street will take you to the white Cape house (at No. 16) that is the **birthplace of Katharine Lee Bates.** Owned by the historical society, the 1812 house is no longer open to the public; a plaque on a rock out front commemorates Bates's birth, in 1859.

Time Out   **Peking Palace** (452 Main St., tel. 508/540–8204) offers good Mandarin, Szechwan, and Cantonese food in a quiet, attractively Oriental setting, and is open until 2 AM nightly in summer, weekends year-round.

Leaving town by Route 28 toward Hyannis, watch for a rotary with a sign for the **New Seabury Resort,** a 2,000-acre luxury complex with restaurants (including the Popponesset; *see* Dining, *below*) and the **Popponesset Marketplace,** a lively seasonal shopping center with entertainment and cafés (*see* Shopping, ⓑ *below*). Another sign on Route 28 leads to **Mashpee,** one of two Massachusetts towns (the other is Gay Head, on Martha's Vineyard) that have been governed continuously by Native Americans for more than 100 years. More than 600 residents are descended from the original Wampanoags who were given a 16-square-mile parcel in 1660 by a missionary, Rev. Richard Bourne. On the left is the **Wampanoag Indian Museum,** a small and somewhat disappointing museum on the history and culture of the tribe, set in a 1793 half-Cape. Exhibits include baskets, weapons, hunting and fishing tools, clothing, arrowheads, and a small diorama depicting a scene from an early settlement. At the end of the parking lot is a herring run. *Rte. 130, tel. 508/477–1536. Donations accepted. Open Tues.–Fri. 9–2, Sat. 10–2.*

Across the way, a town landing gives a view of the interconnecting **Mashpee and Wakeby ponds,** the Cape's largest freshwater expanse, popular for swimming, fishing, and boating.

Return to Route 28; just past the junction is the **Cahoon Museum of American Art,** in a 1775 Georgian Colonial farmhouse. Its several rooms display selections from the permanent collection of primitive paintings by Ralph and Martha Cahoon and other 19th- and early 20th-century art, including a number of pieces from the Hudson River School. Special exhibitions, classes, talks, and demonstrations are held throughout the summer. A gift shop offers books, cards, prints, and so forth. *4676 Rte. 28, Cotuit, tel. 508/428–7581. Donations accepted. Open Apr.–Jan., Wed.–Sat. 10–4, Sun. 1–4. Closed Feb.–Mar.*

⓰   Two miles farther you'll see signs for **Osterville,** a wealthy Barnstable enclave, with upscale shopping in its downtown. Off

Wianno Avenue is Seaview Avenue, lined with elegant water-front houses, including a few of the large "cottages" built beginning in the 19th century, when the area became popular with a monied set. A left off Wianno onto East Bay Road skirts the bay and has more lovely homes.

17 The next village along Route 28 is **Centerville.** Once a busy seafaring town, it still boasts 50 or so shipbuilders' and sea captains' homes along its quiet, tree-shaded streets. A right onto Main Street takes you to the **Centerville Historical Society Museum.** Set in a 19th-century house, the museum features furnished period rooms, Sandwich glass, miniature carvings of birds by Anthony Elmer Crowell, models of ships, marine artifacts, military uniforms and artifacts, perfume bottles (1760 to 1920), and 300 quilts and costumes (1650 to 1950). Guided tours are given (last tour at 3:30). *513 Main St., tel. 508/775–0331. Admission: $2.50 adults, 50¢ children 6–12. Open mid-June–mid-Sept., Wed.–Sun. 1:30–4:30. Closed mid-Sept.–mid-June.*

A few doors down is the **1856 Country Store** (555 Main St., tel. 508/775–1856)—what used to be called the penny-candy store, now stocked with nickel and dime candy. Today more of a country-gifts shop, it has crafts, jams, and all kinds of gadgets and toys, and in summer the pickles and slabs of cheddar cheese return.

Time Out Take your next left to sample the homemade offerings at **Four Seas Ice Cream** (360 S. Main St., tel. 508/775–1394), a tradition with generations of summer visitors.

Follow Main Street to **Craigville Beach,** a busy beach community of weathered-shingle cottages. Main Street continues to rejoin Route 28, which takes you to Hyannis, 3 miles away.

Tour 3: Route 6A, Hyannis to Orleans

For this tour, we return to the Old King's Highway and the north shore (beginning about 2½ miles east of where Tour 1 ended) for attractive old towns, fine beaches, and varied scenery, from marshland and kettle ponds to forest. Also along this stretch are antiques shops and excellent restaurants, several with views of the marsh. The tour covers about 25 miles.

Numbers in the margin correspond to points of interest on the Tours 3 and 4: Hyannis to Orleans map.

Heading east out of Hyannis on Route 28, turn left onto Willow Street. Three miles along you come to Route 6A. Cross 6A onto Mill Lane for a scenic loop (even better on foot); keep left at
18 the intersection of Water Street to go over **Keveney Bridge,** a one-lane wooden bridge over marshy Mill Pond that will make you want to grab a pole and join the others quietly fishing from it. The loop comes back out onto Route 6A, west of where you began. Across the street, on 6A, is **Cummaquid Fine Art** (*see* Shopping, *below*), an art gallery in a lovely old home.

19 Turn left onto 6A for **Yarmouth Port,** with some impressive captains' homes, many now B&Bs. On the right, watch for **Hallet's Store,** a country drugstore preserved as it was in 1889, when the current owner's grandfather, Thacher Hallet, opened it. Hallet served not only as druggist but as postmaster and justice of the peace as well. The oak cabinetry has ornate

Tours 3 and 4: Hyannis to Orleans

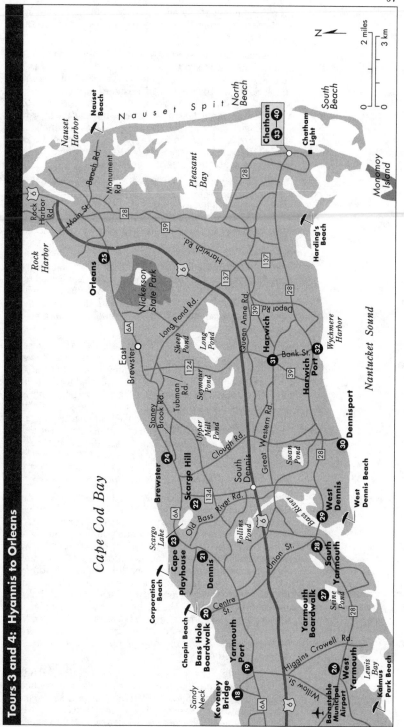

Cape Cod Bay

Nauset Spit

North Beach

South Beach

Chatham 33 40

Chatham Light

Monomoy Island

Nauset Harbor

Nauset Beach

Beach Rd.

Monument Rd.

Pleasant Bay

28

Harding's Beach

Rock Harbor

Rock Harbor Rd.

Main St.

6

6

28

39

25 Orleans

Nickerson State Park

137

137

Harwich Rd.

28

39

6A

East Brewster

Long Pond Rd.

Sheep Pond

Long Pond

Depot Rd.

Queen Anne Rd.

Harwich 31

Bank St. 32

Harwich Port

Wychmere Harbor

Nantucket Sound

124

Tubman Rd.

Seymour Pond

Upper Mill Pond

39

Staney Brook Rd.

24 Brewster

Scargo Hill

Clough Rd.

Great Western Rd.

Dennisport 30

Scargo Lake

6A

22

134

South Dennis

Swan Pond

28

Cape Playhouse 23

Old Bass River Rd.

Follins Pond

Bass River

29 West Dennis

West Dennis Beach

Corporation Beach

21 Dennis

Union St.

28 South Yarmouth

6

Chapin Beach

Bass Hole Boardwalk 20

Centre St.

Yarmouth Port

19

Seine Pond

27 Yarmouth Boardwalk

28

Sandy Neck

Keveney Bridge 18

6A

Higgins Crowell Rd.

West Yarmouth 26

Lewis Bay

Kalmus Park Beach

Willow St.

Barnstable Municipal Airport

6

N

2 miles

3 km

carved detailing; at the all-marble soda fountain with swivel stools, you can order the secret-recipe ice-cream soda, as well as an inexpensive lunch.

As the first real intersection—Summer Street, known as Cow Lane when it was the trail to the watering hole at Dennis Pond—approaches, try to pull over. The 1886 **Village Pump** is on the right, just before the **Old Yarmouth Inn,** the Cape's oldest inn (1696) and a onetime stagecoach stop. The black wrought-iron pump, long used for drawing household water, is surrounded by ironwork with cutouts of birds and animals and is topped by a lantern. In front is a stone trough for watering horses. In an old barn across the street is **Parnassus Bookshop** (*see* Shopping, *below*), great for browsing.

Behind the post office, a bit farther on the right, are the **Botanical Trails of the Historical Society of Old Yarmouth,** 50 acres of oak and pine woods and a pond, accented by blueberries, ladyslippers, Indian pipes, rhododendrons, holly, and more. Stone markers and arrows mark the trails, and benches are strategically placed for resting and appreciating the view. In the gatehouse's mailbox are trail maps. Just beyond, a right leads to the little **Kelley Chapel,** built in 1873 by a father for a daughter grieving over the death of a child, and moved to this site in 1960. The simple interior is dominated by an iron wood stove and a pump organ. *Off Rte. 6A. Admission: 50¢ adults, 25¢ children. Gatehouse open daily 1–4 in summer; trails open anytime.*

Across 6A, set back, is the 1780 **Winslow Crocker House,** an elegantly symmetrical two-story Georgian with 12-over-12 small-pane windows and rich paneling in every room. After Crocker's death, his two sons built a wall dividing the house in half. It was moved here from West Barnstable in 1936 by Mary Thacher, who donated it—along with her collection of 17th- to 19th-century furniture, pewter, hooked rugs, and ceramics—to the Society for the Preservation of New England Antiquities, which operates it as a museum. *250 Rte. 6A, tel. 508/362–4385. Admission: $4 adults, $2 children 5–12, $3.50 senior citizens. Open June–mid-Oct., Tues., Thurs., and weekends noon–5 for guided tours on the hour. Closed mid-Oct.–May.*

The next right, before the village green, leads to the **Captain Bangs Hallet House.** A white Greek Revival building with a hitching post out front and a weeping beech in back, it was built in 1840 (added onto a 1740 rear section) for a sea captain in the China trade, then bought by another, who swapped it with a third (this should give you an idea of the proliferation of sea captains hereabouts). In 1988, six 19th-century paintings and 200 pieces of scrimshaw were among the choice items stolen. Remaining are pewter, china, nautical equipment, antique toys and clothing, and more. The kitchen has the original 1740 brick beehive oven and butter churns. *11 Strawberry La., off Rte. 6A, tel. 508/362–3021. Admission: $1 adults, 25¢ children. Open June and Sept., Sun. 1–4; July–Aug., Thurs., Fri., and Sun. 1–4. Closed Oct.–May.*

For a virtually trafficless scenic loop, take a left off Route 6A past the green onto Church Street or Thacher Street, then left again onto Thacher Shore Road. In fall, this route is especially beautiful for its impressive stands of blazing red burning bush. Wooded segments alternate with open views of marsh. Keep bearing right; at the "Water St." sign, the dirt road on the right brings you to a wide-open view of marshland as it meets the bay. (Don't drive in too far, or you may get stuck.) Coming out, a right leads to Keveney Bridge, and back to Route 6A.

Turn left off 6A onto Centre Street (east of Church Street) and follow signs to Gray's Beach. At Homer's Dock Road, keep left; signs on the left point to a parking area for walking trails through a conservation area to the salt marsh. Adjacent to Gray's Beach, a little crescent of sand with still water good for **②** children, is the **Bass Hole Boardwalk,** which extends over a marshy creek; at the end are benches from which you can observe abundant marsh life and, across the creek, the beautiful, sandy shores of Dennis's Chapin Beach. At low tide you can walk out on the flats for almost a mile—a far cry from the 18th-century harbor that was the site of a schooner shipyard.

② Up ahead is **Dennis,** where the back streets, more so than the main route, have a beautifully preserved Colonial charm. The town has a number of conservation areas and nature trails (see the Dennis Chamber of Commerce guide), and many ponds for swimming.

About a mile east of the town line, you'll come to a collection of antiques shops. Just beyond, at an intersection of three roads, across from the Dennis Public Market, a left off Route 6A onto Nobscusset Road leads to the **Josiah Dennis Manse,** a saltbox with add-ons built in 1736 for Reverend Josiah Dennis, after whom the town was named. Inside, the rooms reflect Reverend Dennis's day. One room is set up as a child's room, with antique furniture and toys; the keeping room has an antique fireplace and cooking utensils; and the attic exhibits antique spinning and weaving equipment. Throughout are china, pewter, and portraits of sea captains. The Maritime Wing has ship models, paintings, nautical artifacts, and more. On the grounds is a 1770 one-room schoolhouse—furnished with wood-and-wrought-iron desks and chairs—moved in 1974 from a nearby site. *77 Nobscussett Rd., corner of Whig St., tel. 508/385–2232. Donations accepted. Open July–Aug., Tues. and Thurs. 2–4. Closed Sept.–June.*

Return to Route 6A; at Old Bass River Road, take a right and **②** follow signs for **Scargo Hill,** the highest spot in the area, at 160 feet. From here the view of wooded Scargo Lake and the village's scattered houses below and of Cape Cod Bay beyond is spectacular—on a clear day, you can see Provincetown. The panoramic view from atop the round tower (up a 38-step spiral staircase) makes sunsets and sunrises equally memorable.

Retrace your path to Route 6A and turn right. Just up on the **②** left is the complex built around the **Cape Playhouse,** one of the oldest summer theaters in the country. Californian Raymond Moore—having started a company in Provincetown but finding it too remote—bought an 1820s former Unitarian Meeting House here in 1927 and converted it into a theater. The opening performance featured Basil Rathbone in *The Guardsman;* other stars who performed here in the early days, many in their first professional appearances, include Bette Davis, Gregory Peck, and Henry Fonda. Also on the property are the **Cape Cinema,** with a huge ceiling mural designed by Massachusetts artist Rockwell Kent; the **Playhouse Restaurant** (*see* Dining, *below*); and an art museum.

The **Cape Museum of Fine Arts** showcases a permanent collection of more than 500 works by Cape-associated artists. Important works include a 1924 portrait of a Portuguese fisherman's daughter by William Paxton, one of the first artists to summer in Provincetown; a collection of wood-block prints by Varujan Boghosian, a member of Provincetown's Long Point Gallery cooperative; and an oil sketch by Karl Knaths, who painted in Provincetown from 1919 until his death in 1971. Offerings include classic films (*see* The Arts, *below*), lectures, art classes, and trips. *Tel. 508/385–4477. Admission: $2. Open Mar.–Nov., Tues.–Sat. 10–5, Sun. 1–5; Dec.–Feb., Tues.–Sat. 10–4, Sun. 1–4.*

A left onto Corporation Road, just after the Playhouse complex, leads to **Corporation Beach.** At one time a packet landing owned by a corporation formed of townsfolk, the beautiful crescent of white sand backed by low dunes now serves a decidedly noncorporate use, as a public beach.

Time Out Before leaving Dennis, you might want to stop for a bite at **Captain Frosty's** (219 Main St. [Rte. 6A], near the Yarmouth line, tel. 508/385–8548), a favorite local clam shack, with fried seafood, shellfish, and onion rings, as well as very good lobster rolls with more lobster than celery. For dessert, try homemade ice cream and frozen yogurt at the **Ice Cream Smuggler** (716 Main St., near the Dennis Public Market, tel. 508/385–5307).

㉔ The next town is **Brewster,** in the early 1800s the terminus of a packet cargo service from Boston and home to many seafaring families. In 1849, Thoreau wrote that "this town has more mates and masters of vessels than any other town in the country." A large number of mansions built for sea captains remain today, and quite a few have been turned into B&Bs. In the 18th and 19th centuries, the bay side of Brewster was the site of a major salt-making industry—in the 1830s almost 450 saltworks operated on the Cape, using a seawater-evaporation process developed by a Dennis sea captain. When the tide is low, you can walk out for about a mile on the **Brewster Flats** among tidal pools rich in sea life.

On a grassy rise on the left is the 1795 **Old Mill.** The octagonal, smock-type mill—shingled in weathered pine, with a roof like an upturned boat—was moved here in 1974 and has been restored. The millstones are original. At night the mill is often spotlit and makes quite a sight. Also on the grounds is a one-room house from 1795, the **Harris-Black House.** Once, amazingly enough, home to a family of 13, the restored 16-foot-square building is today partially furnished and dominated by a brick hearth and original woodwork. *Tel. 508/896–9521. Admission free. Open May–June and Sept.–Oct., weekends 1–4; July–Aug., Tues.–Fri. 1–4. Closed Nov.–Apr.*

Farther up on the left is the **Cape Cod Museum of Natural History,** which offers nature and marine exhibits (such as a working beehive and a pond- and sea-life room with live specimens), guided field walks, a natural history library, a museum shop, lectures, classes, and self-guided trails through 80 acres of forest, marshland, and ponds, all rich in birds and other wildlife. The exhibit hall upstairs has a wall display of aerial photographs documenting the process by which a barrier beach off Chatham's shore was split in two (*see* Tour 4, *below*). *Rte. 6A, Brewster, tel. 508/896–3867 or 800/479–3867 in MA. Admission:*

$3.50 adults, $1.50 children 6–14. Open Mon.–Sat. 9:30–4:30, Sun. 12:30–4:30.

Just beyond the bend in the road, turn right onto Paine's Creek Road, then left on Setucket Road, to reach the **Brewster Mill,** a restored 19th-century fulling mill—the area once had four— that is now a museum and gristmill. (Stoney Brook Road leads directly here from 28A.) The scene is wonderfully picturesque in true New England fashion: the old weathered-shingle mill, its waterwheel slowly turning, set on a little brook edged with leafy trees. Inside are exhibits, including old mill equipment and looms; during open hours you can watch cornmeal being stone-ground and get a lesson in weaving on a 100-year-old loom. Out back, across little wooden bridges, is a bench with a pleasant view of the pond and of the sluices leading into the mill area. *Stoney Brook Rd., no phone. Donations accepted. Open May–June, Thurs.–Sat. 2–5; July–Aug., Fri. 2–5. Closed Sept.– Apr.*

Early each spring, Stoney Brook's **Herring Run** is aboil with millions of alewives, which make their way from Cape Cod Bay by way of Paine's Creek to reach Stoney Brook and the ponds beyond to spawn. Walk across the street from the mill and down a path to the rushing stream spilling over rocks. Farther down the path is an ivy-covered stone wishing well and a wooden bridge with a bench.

Head back toward Paine's Creek Road, but instead of turning onto it, keep going straight; you will come out on Route 6A just before the **New England Fire & History Museum.** Set on a re-created 19th-century common with a picnic area, it features 35 antique vehicles (including the only surviving 1929 Mercedes-Benz fire engine), the late Boston Pops conductor Arthur Fiedler's private collection of fire-fighting memorabilia, a dozen mannequins in historical firefighter uniforms, a Victorian apothecary shop, an animated diorama of the Chicago Fire of 1871 (complete with smoke and fire), a historic working forge, and medicinal herb gardens. Guided tours are given. *1439 Main St. (Rte. 6A), Brewster, tel. 508/896–5711. Admission: $4.50 adults, $2.50 children 5–12, $4 senior citizens. Open mid-May–Labor Day, weekdays 10–4, weekends noon–4; Labor Day–Columbus Day, weekends 10–4. Closed Columbus Day– mid-May.*

At the junction of Route 124 is the **Brewster Store** (1935 Main St., tel. 508/896–3744), built in 1852. A local landmark, it is a typical New England general store, providing such essentials as the daily papers and penny candy. It's also a good stop for quick grocery-type refreshments, as the bicycles piled up out front in summer attest. Upstairs, the front of the store has been re-created, complete with benches, and memorabilia from antique toys to World War II bond posters are displayed. Downstairs is an antique nickelodeon you can play.

Nearby is the handsome **First Parish Church,** with Gothic windows and a capped bell tower. Known as the Church of the Sea Captains, it features pews marked with the names of famous Brewster seamen. Out back is an old graveyard, where militiamen, clergy, farmers, and captains rest side by side. Chowder suppers are held Wednesdays in July and August.

From here Breakwater Road leads to a former packet landing, and a right onto Route 124, then a left onto Tubman Road, takes you to the **Bassett Wild Animal Farm** (*see* What to See and Do with Children, *below*).

Back on 6A, you'll see the **Brewster Historical Society Museum** on the left. Inside the 1830s home are a sea captains' room, with paintings and artifacts; an 1890 barbershop; a child's room with antique toys and clothing; a room of women's period gowns and accessories; and other exhibits on local history and architecture. Out back is a ¼-mile labeled nature trail over dunes leading to the bay. *Tel. 508/896–7593. Admission free. Open May–June and Sept.–Oct., weekends 1–4; July–Aug., Tues.–Fri. 1–4. Closed Nov.–Apr.*

Farther up Route 6A on the right is **Nickerson State Park** (*see* Nature Areas, *below*). These 2,000-plus acres were part of a vast estate belonging to Roland C. Nickerson, son of Samuel Nickerson, a Chatham native who became a multimillionaire and founder of the First National Bank of Chicago. At their long private beach or their hunting lodge, Roland and his wife, Addie, lavishly entertained such visitors as President Grover Cleveland in English country house style, with coachmen dressed in tails and top hats and a bugler announcing carriages entering the front gates.

The estate was like a village unto itself. Its gardens provided much of the household's food, supplemented by game from its woods and fish from its ponds. It also had its own electric plant and a nine-hole golf course by the water. The enormous mansion Sam built for his son in 1886 burned to the ground in 1906, and Roland died two weeks later. The even grander stone mansion built in 1908 to replace it is now part of the Ocean Edge resort. In 1934, Addie donated the land for the state park in memory of her son, who died during the 1918 flu epidemic.

㉕ From the park it's about 2 miles to **Orleans.** Named for Louis-Philippe de Bourbon, duc d'Orléans, who reputedly visited the area during his exile from France in the 1790s, it is today the commercial center of the Lower Cape. Historically, it has the distinction of being the only spot in the continental United States to have received enemy fire during either world war. In July 1918, a German submarine fired on commercial barges off the coast; four were sunk, and one shell is reported to have fallen on American soil.

At the junction with Main Street, turn left; Main becomes Rock Harbor Road, a pleasant winding street lined with gray-shingled Cape houses, white picket fences, and neat gardens. At the end is **Rock Harbor,** a former packet landing and the site of a War of 1812 skirmish in which the Orleans militia kept a British warship from landing. In the 19th century Orleans had an active saltworks industry, and a flourishing packet service between Rock Harbor and Boston developed. Today the former packet landing is the base of charter-fishing and party boats in season, as well as of a small commercial fishing fleet whose catch can be sampled at the fish market and small restaurant here. Sunsets over the harbor are memorable.

A right at the junction of Route 6A and Main Street leads east (along what becomes Beach Road) to the town-owned **Nauset Beach,** a long, wide sweep of sand backed by high dunes.

At the intersection of 6A and Route 28, turn right; at Cove Road is the **French Cable Station Museum.** Built in 1890 to house a land extension of the transatlantic cable that originated in Brittany. In World War I, it was an essential link between Army headquarters in Washington and the American Expeditionary Force in France, and was guarded by Marines. In 1959, the station was closed as obsolete; the equipment is still in place. *41 S. Orleans Rd., tel. 508/240–1735. Donations accepted. Open July–Aug., Tues.–Sat. 2–4. Closed Sept.–June.*

Tour 4: Route 28, Hyannis to Chatham

There's no getting around it: The part of the Cape everyone loves to hate is Route 28 where it passes through Yarmouth—one motel, strip mall, nightclub, and miniature golf course after another. In 1989, as *Cape Cod Life* magazine put it, "the town [began] to plant 350 trees in hopes that eventually the trees' leaves, like the fig leaf of Biblical lore, will cover the shame of unkempt overdevelopment."

This tour takes you into the fray; it is a good way to go if you want to intersperse amusements with your sightseeing, because Route 28 is the main locus of such activities. A sensible option if you don't is to take speedy Route 6 to the exit nearest the first place you want to visit, then cut across the interior to 28. This route covers about 30 miles. The proliferation of motels, restaurants, and stores thins out somewhat as you near Chatham.

26 Heading east out of Hyannis, the first village is **West Yarmouth.** A little past the town line, on the left, is the **Baxter Grist Mill,** by the shore of Mill Pond (take the next left to park). Built in 1710, it is the only mill on Cape Cod that is powered by an inside water turbine; the others use either wind or paddle wheels. The mill was converted to the indoor metal turbine in 1860 because of the pond's low water level and the damage done to the wooden paddle wheel by winter freezes; the original metal turbine is displayed on the grounds, and a replica powers the restored mill. A videotape tells the mill's history. *Tel. 508/398–2231. Admission free. Days and hours of operation are completely unpredictable; call before you go. Closed Columbus Day–Memorial Day.*

27 After 1½ miles, turn left at the lights across from Cuffy's onto Winslow Gray Road; after a mile or so, turn right onto Meadowbrook Lane; at the end is the **Yarmouth Boardwalk.** A short walk through swamp and marsh takes you to the edge of Swan Pond, a pretty pond ringed with woods.

A bit farther on Route 28 is **Aqua Circus** (*see* What to See and Do with Children, *below*), with sea lion shows and more.

Time Out Next door is **Jerry's Dairy Freeze** (tel. 508/775–9752; open mid-Feb.–mid-Nov.), offering fried clams and onion rings—along with thick frappes, frozen yogurt, and soft ice cream—at good prices. It stays open until 11 PM in season.

28 **South Yarmouth** was once called Quaker Village, for its large Quaker population. A left off Route 28 onto North Main Street (at a major intersection) takes you to the 1809 **Quaker Meeting House,** still open for meetings; the partition down the center was to divide the sexes. The adjacent cemetery has simple markers with no epitaphs, an expression of the Friends' belief that all are equal in God's eyes. Behind the cemetery is an 1820–30 one-room Quaker schoolhouse.

Bass River forms the dividing line between the southern portions of the towns of Yarmouth and Dennis; the area of South Yarmouth just before the bridge is commonly referred to as **Bass River.** Here you'll find charter boats and boat rentals, as well as a river cruise, plus seafood restaurants and markets.

㉙ **West Dennis** is at the other side of the Bass River Bridge. A right onto School Street at the Texaco station leads to the **West Dennis Beach,** one of the best on the south shore. An aborted breakwater here was begun in 1837 in an effort to protect the mouth of Bass River but abandoned when a sandbar formed on the shore side.

Time Out The 1855 lighthouse that originally watched over the coast here has been converted into part of the **Lighthouse Inn** (tel. 508/398–2244), a summer resort with a moderately priced Continental and seafood restaurant serving three meals a day. Now *you* can watch over the coast, from behind windows or at tables outside.

Back on Route 28, a left onto Old Main Street leads to the **Jericho House Museum** (at the corner of Trotting Park Road), built in 1801 for a sea captain. (The name was given by a subsequent owner, who said the walls seemed to be tumbling down.) The classic Cape, with a bow roof and large central chimney, has been fully restored. Antique furnishings include 1850s portraits, and Chinese and other items brought home from overseas by sea captains. In the barn museum is antique cranberry-harvesting and woodworking equipment, a model saltworks, marine antiques, and 19th-century sleighs and wagons. Also here is a 150-piece driftwood zoo: A local man collected wood on a beach, then added eyes and beaks to bring out animal shapes. *Tel. 508/398–6736. Donations accepted. Open July–Aug., Wed. and Fri. 2–4. Closed Sept.–June (may open by appointment).*

Bear left at the intersection here for the 1835 **South Parish Congregational Church,** which has the oldest working organ in the United States. The cemetery beside the church has markers dating from 1795; many of them are for early sea captains and say simply "Lost at sea," while one says only "The Chinese Woman."

Returning to Route 28, the Mid-Cape's last southern village is **㉚** **Dennisport,** a prime summer resort area, with gray-shingled cottages, summer homes, and condominiums, and lots of white picket fences covered with rambling roses. The Union Wharf Packing Company was located here in the 1850s, and the shore was lined with sailmakers and ship chandlers. The beach where sea clams were once packed is now packed with sunbathers.

Time Out Farther up Route 28 on the right is **Kream 'N Kone** (527 Main St., tel. 508/394–0808), a great clam shack that also offers grilled chicken breast sandwich and teriyaki steak. A turn here onto Sea Street leads to the **Sundae School Ice Cream Parlor** (corner of Lower County Rd., tel. 508/394–9122; open mid-Apr.–mid-Oct.). Set in a rustic mid-19th-century barn decorated with such memorabilia as a working nickelodeon, it serves great homemade ice cream and frozen yogurt with lots of toppings, sugar-free and soft ice cream, real whipped cream, and even Moxie from an antique marble soda fountain.

31 Back on Route 28, a left onto Route 39 takes you into the heart of the quiet New England village of **Harwich.** Just before the junction of Main Street is **Brooks Academy,** an 1844 Greek Revival building with fluted pillars that was once a private school and is now the museum of the Harwich Historical Society. In addition to a large photo-history collection and exhibits on artist Charles Cahoon, cranberries, and shoemaking, the museum displays antique clothing and textiles, china and glass, fans, toys, and much more. On the grounds is a powder house that was used to store gunpowder during the Revolutionary War, as well as a restored 1872 outhouse. *80 Parallel St., tel. 508/432–8089. Admission free. Open June–mid-Oct., Thurs.–Sun. 1–4.*

Also on Main Street is **Brooks Park,** with a playground, picnic tables, a ballpark, tennis courts, and a bandstand where summer concerts are held. Returning to Route 28 via Bank Street, you pass some of the town's many cranberry bogs, tours of which are part of the grand Cranberry Harvest Festival in September (*see* Festivals and Seasonal Events in Chapter 1, Essential Information).

32 Back on Route 28 at the seaside community of **Harwich Port,** a right onto Harbor Road leads to scenic **Wychmere Harbor,** busy with pleasure boats.

Time Out   The **Augustus Snow House** (528 Main St. [Rte. 28], tel. 508/430–0528) offers an elegant afternoon tea of finger sandwiches, scones with cream, and dessert cakes. It is served in the inn's very Victorian, fireplaced parlors, or on the screened porch or brick patio, Monday–Saturday 1–4 (call to confirm or reserve). Lunch, Sunday brunch, and creative American dinners are served in the Garden Room restaurant downstairs (or on the porch or patio).

33 The next town up is **Chatham.** Situated at the bent elbow of the Cape, with water on three sides, it has all the charm of a quiet seaside resort but with relatively little of the commercialism. And it *is* charming: gray-shingled houses with tidy awnings and cheerful flower gardens, an attractive Main Street with crafts and antiques stores alongside homey coffee shops and a five-and-ten. It's a traditional town, with none of Provincetown's flash yet not overly quaint; wealthy yet not ostentatious; casual and fun but refined, and never tacky.

Numbers in the margin correspond to points of interest on the Chatham map.

When you cross the town line via Route 28, begin to watch for **Marion's Pie Shop, Fancy's Farm,** and **Chatham Jam and Jelly,** all worth stopping for (*see* Farm Stands and Food in Shopping, *below*), as well as the **Chatham Winery** (tel. 508/945–0300), open for tastings of fruit and flower wines produced here. Behind Pate's restaurant on 28 is the **Chatham Glass Company** (*see* Shopping, *below*), where you can watch glassblowing demonstrations daily. Just before you hit downtown, at the intersection with Queen Anne Road, turn left onto Depot Road for the **34** **Railroad Museum,** in a restored 1887 depot. Exhibits include

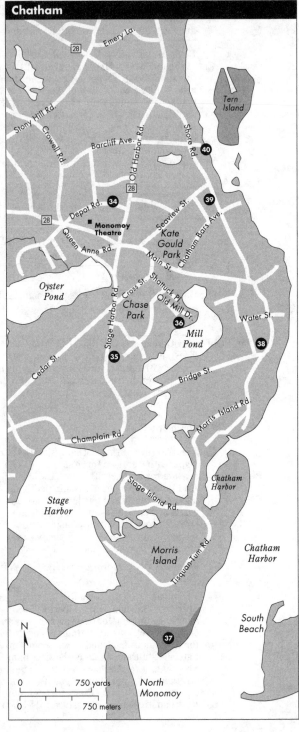

a walk-through 1910 New York Central caboose, old photographs, equipment, thousands of train models, and a new diorama of the 1915 Chatham railyards. *No phone. Donations accepted. Open mid-June–mid-Sept., Tues.–Sat. 10–4. Closed mid-Sept.–mid-June.*

Across from the museum (and behind the school) is the **Play-a-round,** a multilevel wood playground of turrets, twisting tubular slides, jungle gyms, and more, designed with the input of local children and built by volunteers. There's a section for the disabled and a fenced-in area for small children.

Return to the Queen Anne Road junction. For a scenic loop, turn down Queen Anne and skirt Oyster Pond, following bike-path signs. Half-Cape houses, open fields, and rolling pastures reveal the area's Colonial and agricultural history.

Winding around Stage Harbor—where Samuel de Champlain anchored in 1606 and was involved in a skirmish that marked the first blood shed in New England between Europeans and Native Americans—keep left at Bridge Street on Stage Harbor Road and you'll come to the **Old Atwood House and Museums** complex. Built by a sea captain in 1752 and occupied by his descendants until it was sold to the Chatham Historical Society in 1926, the Atwood House features a gambrel roof, variable-width floor planking, fireplaces, an old kitchen with a wide hearth and a beehive oven, and some antique dolls and toys. The New Gallery displays portraits of local sea captains. The Joseph C. Lincoln Room has the manuscripts, first editions, and mementos of the Chatham writer; in the basement is an antique tool room. The 1974 Durand Wing houses collections of seashells from around the world, threaded Sandwich glass, and Parian ware (unglazed porcelain vases, figurines, and busts). In a remodeled freight shed are a series of murals (1932–1945) by Alice Stallknecht Wight portraying religious scenes in Chatham settings; they have been exhibited at major galleries around the country. On the grounds are an herb garden, the old turret and lens from the Chatham Light, and a camp rescued from eroding North Beach. *347 Stage Harbor Rd., tel. 508/945–2493. Admission: $3 adults, $1 schoolchildren over age 12. Open mid-June–Sept., Wed.–Sat. 2–5. Closed Oct.–mid-June.*

A right onto Cross Street takes you past **Chase Park,** with a bowling green and picnic tables, to Shattuck Place; at the end is the **Old Grist Mill,** built in 1797, moved to the hill here from elsewhere in Chatham, and extensively renovated. Closed in 1992 for budgetary reasons, the mill may or may not be open in 1994.

Instead of completing the loop, backtrack and turn left onto Bridge Street, which crosses Mill Pond. There's fishing from the bridge, and "bullrakers" ply the pond's muddy bottom with 20-foot rakes in search of shellfish.

A right onto Morris Island Road and across the dike leads to the **Monomoy National Wildlife Refuge headquarters** (*see* Nature Areas, *below*), on the misleadingly named Morris Island. At the visitor center and bookstore (tel. 508/945–0594; open daily 8–5, with gaps) you can pick up pamphlets on **Monomoy Island,** a deserted barrier-beach area—once a fishing village—just south of Morris Island that is a paradise for bird-watchers. Actually two islands, North and South Monomoy, since a 1978 storm divided it, Monomoy was itself separated from the mainland in a 1958 storm. A ³/₄-mile interpretive walking trail (closed at high tide) around Morris Island gives a good view of the refuge and the surrounding waters. (For information on visiting the refuge, *see* Guided Tours, *above*.)

㊳ Returning to the junction of Bridge Street, follow the coast road (go straight) to **Chatham Light.** The view from here—of the harbor, the offshore sandbars, and the ocean beyond—justifies the crowds that gather to share it. When fog shrouds the area, pierced with darting beams from the beacon, there's a dreamlike quality about it.

Coin-operated telescopes allow a close look at the famous "Chatham Break," the result of a fierce 1987 storm that blasted a channel through a barrier beach (now known as North and South Beach) just off the coast. The Cape Cod Museum of Natural History in Brewster (*see* Tour 3: Route 6A, Hyannis to Orleans, *above*) has a display of photos documenting the process of erosion leading up to and following the break. If you're looking for a crowd-free sandy beach, boats at Chatham Harbor—such as the **Water Taxi** (tel. 508/430–2346)—will ferry you across to North Beach, a sandspit adjoining Orleans's Nauset Beach, or to South Beach or Monomoy. **Outermost Harbor Marine** (Morris Island Rd., tel. 508/945–2030) runs shuttles to South Beach.

Go straight on Shore Road, where elegant summer cottages share the view with stately houses of purebred Yankee architecture, including some of the finest bow-roof houses in the country. On the left past Main Street, set on a rise overlooking
㊴ the ocean, is the 1914 **Chatham Bars Inn** (*see* Lodging, *below*). The last of Chatham's grand old resort hotels, it has been thoroughly renovated and is as elegant and charming as it ever was.

Time Out Even if you're not staying at the inn, you can experience it in several ways. The main dining room (*see* Dining, *below*) offers dinner and elegant breakfast buffets year-round and Sunday Grand Buffets in summer. At the casual, elegant **Tavern at the Inner Bar**, choose from brick-oven pizzas, pastas, and wood-grilled selections year-round. In summer, the casual, oceanfront **Beach House Grill** offers clambakes and light lunches. And year-round there's dancing (*see* Nightlife, *below*). Call 508/945–0096 for information.

㊵ A bit farther along on the right is the entrance to the **Fish Pier.** The unloading of the boats after Chatham's fishing fleet returns, beginning sometime between noon and 2 PM, is a big local event, drawing crowds who watch it all from an observation deck. From their fishing grounds 10–100 miles offshore, the boats bring in haddock, cod, flounder, lobster, halibut, and pollock, which is packed in ice and shipped to New York and Boston or sold at the fish market here. Also here is *The Provider,* a monument to the town's fishing industry, featuring a hand pulling a fish-filled net from the sea.

Main Street, which you passed on Shore Road, takes you to the center of town. On Friday evenings in summer, the place to be is **Kate Gould Park** on Main Street for the Chatham band concert, the town's weekly party (*see* The Arts, *below*).

North of Chatham, Route 28 winds through wooded upland toward **Pleasant Bay,** to which a number of country roads to the right will take you for a good view of the Nauset spit and the little islands in between.

Tour 5: Orleans to Provincetown

Numbers in the margin correspond to points of interest on the Tour 5: Orleans to Provincetown map.

Starting at Orleans, this tour explores Eastham and the Outer Cape to the edge of Provincetown (which is covered in Tour 6: Provincetown, *below*), including the National Seashore. This part of the Cape is markedly different from the rest; much less populous and largely protected from development, it is an area of high dunes, endless beaches, and arty communities. The tour covers about 30 miles.

④ Traveling down-Cape (toward the tip) from Orleans, head east on Route 6. Once in **Eastham,** watch for a sign on the right (1½ miles from the town line) directing you to the Ft. Hill Area; on the approach road is the **Captain Edward Penniman House,** a large yellow, red, and white house in the French Second Empire style, built in 1868 by a whaling captain. The impressive exterior is noted for its mansard roof, its cupola (which once commanded a dramatic view of bay and sea), and the whale-jawbone entrance gate. To find out when the interior—which is slowly being renovated—is open for guided tours (only by reservation) or browsing through changing exhibits, call the Seashore at 508/255–3421.

④ Ahead, the road curves up over the Cape Cod National Seashore's **Ft. Hill Area,** dead-ending at a viewpoint overlooking a lovely pastoral scene: former farmland traced with stone fences, gently rolling down to Nauset Marsh, a red-maple swamp, and pastureland. Winding through the area are the 1-mile Red Maple Swamp Trail, which begins outside the Penniman house, and the Ft. Hill Trail, also 1 mile, beginning at the parking area; a map is available at the trailheads.

Return to Route 6; a half-mile up on the left, at Samoset Road, is the **Eastham Windmill,** a smock mill built in the early 1680s, moved to this site in 1808, and now the centerpiece of a park. The only Cape windmill still on a site on which it was in commercial use, it was recently restored by local shipwreck historian William Quinn and friends. *Rte. 6. Admission free. Open July–Labor Day, Mon.–Sat. 10–5, Sun. 1–5. Closed Labor Day–June.*

Opposite the park, next to the post office, is the 1741 **Swift-Daley House,** once the home of Gustavus Swift, founder of the Swift meat-packing company. Inside the full Cape with bow roof you'll find beautiful pumpkin pine woodwork and wide-board floors, a ship's-cabin staircase (which, like the bow roof, was built by ship's carpenters), and fireplaces in every downstairs room. The Colonial-era furnishings include an old cannonball rope bed, tools, a melodeon, a stereopticon, and a ceremonial quilt decorated with beads and coins. Antique clothing includes gloves, lacework, hankies, baby dresses, and a stunning 1850 wedding dress. Out back is a tool museum. *Rte. 6, tel. 508/240–1247. Admission free. Open July–Aug., weekdays 1–4. Closed Sept.–June.*

Tour 5: Orleans to Provincetown

ATLANTIC OCEAN

Race Point Beach

Province Lands Area 50

Pilgrim Heights Area 49

Pilgrim Lake

Race Point Light

Head of the Meadow Beach

Highland Light 48

Herring Cove Beach

Long Point Light

Provincetown Harbor

Provincetown 51–64

Wood End Light

North Truro

Ballston Beach

TO BOSTON

Corn Hill

Castle Rd.

Truro 47

CAPE

COD

NATIONAL

Chequesset Neck Rd.

Great Pond

Newcomb Hollow Beach

Griffin Island

Wellfleet 46

South Wellfleet

Cahoon Hollow Beach

SEASHORE

White Crest Beach

Great Island

Wellfleet Harbor

Marconi Station 45

Wellfleet Bay Wildlife Sanctuary 44

Marconi Beach

Nauset Light

Nauset Light Beach

Cape Cod Bay

North Eastham

Salt Pond Visitor Center

Coast Guard Beach

First Encounter Beach

Eastham 41 43

Samoset Rd.

Ft. Hill Area 42

Rock Harbor

Orleans

Nauset Harbor

East Brewster

Beach Rd.

Nauset Beach

Brewster

Nickerson State Park

28

39

Pleasant Bay

Dennis

6A

124

Yarmouth

134

6

39

137

Chatham Light

South Yarmouth

28

Harwich Port

Chatham

West Dennis

Wychmere Harbor

N

0   2 miles

0   3 km

Follow Samoset Road, past marshland, to **First Encounter Beach,** a great spot for watching sunsets. Near the parking lot is a bronze marker commemorating the first encounter between the local Indians and the passengers from the *Mayflower,* led by Captain Myles Standish, who explored the entire area for five weeks before moving on to Plymouth. Also here are the remains of a Navy target ship retired after 25 years of battering and now resting on a sandbar about a mile out.

Another half-mile up Route 6, on the right, is the entrance to the first visitor center of the **Cape Cod National Seashore.** Established in 1961 by a bill signed by President John F. Kennedy, the 27,700-acre seashore encompasses and protects 30 miles of superb ocean beaches; great rolling dunes; swamps, marshes, and wetlands; pitch pine and scrub oak forests; all kinds of wildlife; and a number of historic structures. Lacing through these landscapes are self-guided nature trails, as well as biking and horse trails. The two visitor centers, here in Eastham and in Provincetown, offer guided walks, tours, boat trips, demonstrations, and lectures from mid-April through Thanksgiving, as well as evening programs of beach walks, campfire talks, and more in summer (*see* The Arts and Nightlife, *below*).

❹❸ The **Salt Pond Visitor Center** has a museum with displays on the whaling and saltworks industries; exhibits of early Cape Cod artifacts, including scrimshaw; and the journal Mrs. Penniman kept while on a whaling voyage with her husband, as well as some of the Pennimans' possessions (such as their tea service and the captain's top hat). Also here are a bookstore and an air-conditioned auditorium for films on geology, sea rescues, whaling, Thoreau, and Marconi. Something's up every summer evening at the outdoor amphitheater, from slide-show talks to military-band concerts. *Tel. 508/255-3421. Admission free. Open Mar.–June and Sept.–Dec., daily 9–4:30; July–Aug., daily 9–6; Jan.–Feb., weekends 9–4:30.*

From here, hiking trails lead to a red-maple swamp, **Nauset Marsh,** and **Salt Pond,** in which breeding shellfish are suspended from floating "nurseries"; their offspring will later be used to seed the flats. Also here is the Buttonbush Trail, a nature path for the visually disabled. Roads and bicycle trails lead to **Coast Guard Beach** and **Nauset Light Beach,** which begin an unbroken 30-mile stretch of barrier beach extending to Provincetown—the "Cape Cod Beach" of Thoreau's 1865 classic *Cape Cod.* One can still walk its length, as Thoreau did, though the Atlantic continues to claim more of the Cape's eastern shore every year. To the south, near the end of Nauset spit, is the site of the famous beach cottage of Henry Beston's 1928 book *The Outermost House;* designated as a literary landmark in 1964, the cottage was completely destroyed in the Great Blizzard of February 1978.

From the center, signs direct you to Coast Guard Beach, where a turnout gives a good view over marsh and sea. A section of the cliff here was washed away in 1990, revealing remains of a prehistoric dwelling. Other signs lead from here to the much-photographed **Nauset Light,** the red and white lighthouse that tops the bluff where the "Three Sisters" lighthouses once stood. The Sisters themselves can be seen in a little landlocked park surrounded by trees, reached by paved walkways off Nauset Light Beach's parking lot.

How the lighthouses got there is a long story, but briefly it is this: In 1838, three brick lighthouses were built 150 feet apart on the bluffs in Eastham, overlooking a particularly dangerous shoals area; in 1892, after the eroding cliff dropped the towers into the ocean, they were replaced with three wood towers. In 1918, two were moved away, as was the third in 1923; eventually the National Park Service acquired the Three Sisters and brought them together here, where they would be safe, rather than returning them to the eroding coast. The Fresnel lens from the last working lighthouse is on display at the Salt Pond Visitor Center. Lectures on and guided walks to the lighthouses are conducted throughout the season.

44 A few miles farther on Route 6, on the left just over the Wellfleet line, is the **Wellfleet Bay Wildlife Sanctuary** (*see* Nature Areas, *below*), 1,000 acres of moors, marsh, and forest supervised by the Massachusetts Audubon Society.

45 A mile and a half farther, on the right, is the **Marconi Station,** the site of the first transatlantic wireless station erected on the U.S. mainland. From here, Italian radio and wireless-telegraphy pioneer Guglielmo Marconi sent the first American wireless message to Europe—"most cordial greetings and good wishes" from President Theodore Roosevelt to Edward VII of England—on January 18, 1903. The station broadcast news for 15 years. An outdoor shelter contains a model of the original station, of which only fragments remain as a result of cliff erosion (parts of the tower bases are sometimes visible on the beach below, where they fell). The Seashore's administrative headquarters is located here, and though it is not an official visitor center, it can provide information at times when the centers are closed; inside is a mock-up of the spark-gap transmitter used by Marconi. Off the parking lot a 1¼-mile (45-minute) trail and boardwalk lead through the Atlantic White Cedar Swamp, one of the most beautiful trails on the Seashore; free maps and guides are available at the trailhead. *South Wellfleet, tel. 508/349-3785. Open Jan.–Feb., daily 9–4:30; Mar.–Dec., weekdays 9–4:30.*

For a scenic loop through a classic Cape landscape, take a left onto LeCount Hollow Road (with scrub and pines on the left, heathland meeting cliffs with ocean below on the right) to **Cahoon Hollow Beach,** a town-managed beach with high dunes and a hot restaurant and dancing spot, the **Beachcomber** (*see* Nightlife, *below*). Turn left again onto Ocean View Drive, ending at **Newcomb Hollow,** a less-crowded town beach with a scalloped shoreline of golden sand; then backtrack to Cahoon Hollow and take the unmarked right just across from it to return to Route 6 via Great Pond. Head east (right) on 6 and turn off at the sign for Wellfleet Center.

46 **Wellfleet** was once the center of a large oyster industry and, with Truro, a Colonial whaling and codfishing port. Less than 2 miles wide, it is one of the more tastefully developed Cape resort towns, with a number of fine restaurants, historic homes, and more than 20 art galleries.

On the way into town, you pass the **First Congregational Church,** a handsome 1850 Greek Revival building said to have the only town clock in the world to strike on ship's time. The church's interior is lovely, with pale blue walls, a brass chandelier hanging from an enormous gilt ceiling rosette, subtly colored stained-glass windows, and pews curved to form an amphitheater facing the altar and the 1873, 738-pipe Hook and Hastings tracker-action organ. (Concerts are given in July and August on Sundays at 8 PM.) To the right is a Tiffany-style window depicting a clipper ship, with a dedication to the memory of a sea captain.

Farther on the right is a public lot where you can park if you want to wander the town. On Main Street, the **Wellfleet Historical Society Museum** exhibits furniture, paintings, shipwreck salvage, needlework, navigation equipment, early photographs, Indian artifacts, clothing, and more. The society's Samuel Rider House is no longer open to the public. *Tel. 508/349-9157. Admission: $1 adults and children 12 or older. Open late June–mid-Sept., Tues.–Sat. 2–5. Closed mid-Sept.–late June.*

From Main Street, Bank Street leads to Commercial Street, which has the flavor of the fishing town Wellfleet still is; galleries and shops occupy small weathered-shingle houses that look like fishing shacks. At the first intersection, turn left for a short walk across **Uncle Tim's Bridge**—with a much-photographed view over marshland and a tidal creek—leading to a small wooded island. Heading back, with the marsh on your left, follow Commercial Street to the **Wellfleet Pier,** busy with fishing boats, sailboats, yachts, charters, and party boats; at the twice-daily low tides you can shellfish on the tidal flats for oysters, clams, and quahogs (for a permit, call 508/349-9818).

Continue on the same road (which becomes Chequesset Neck Road) for a pretty 2½-mile drive along Cape Cod Bay past Sunset Hill—a great place to catch one. At the end, on the left, is a parking lot and wooded picnic area, from which nature trails lead off to **Great Island,** perfect for the beachcomber and solitude seeker. Actually a peninsula connected by a sand spit, Great Island offers more than 7 miles of trails (the most difficult on the Seashore, since they're mostly in soft sand) along the inner marshes and the water, and lots of windswept dunes—a beautiful place. The Seashore also offers occasional guided hikes and, from February through April, seal walks. To the right of the Great Island lot, a road leads to **Griffin Island,** with its own walking trail. Both Great and Griffin islands once actually were islands, but a tidal buildup of sand connected them with the mainland.

In the 17th century there were lookout towers for shore whaling, as well as a tavern, on Great Island; animals were pastured here, and oystering and cranberry harvesting were undertaken. By 1800, the hardwood forest that had covered it had been eradicated for use in ship and home building; the pitch pines and other growth you see today were introduced in the 1830s to keep the soil from washing into the sea.

❹⓻ Return to Route 6 and follow signs for the center of **Truro.** A town of high dunes, estuaries, and rivers fringed by grasses, rolling moors, and houses sheltered in tiny valleys, Truro is a popular retreat of artists and writers. Edward Hopper summered here from 1930 to 1967, finding the Cape light ideal for his austere brand of realism.

One of the largest towns in terms of area (almost 43 square miles), it is the smallest in population—only about 1,400 year-round. If you thought Wellfleet's downtown was small, wait until you see—or don't see—Truro's. It's a post office, a town hall, a shop or two; you'll know it by the sign that says "Downtown Truro," at a little plaza entrance. There's also a library, a firehouse, a police station, but that's about it.

From the center, Castle Road leads to Corn Hill Road, where a tablet commemorates the finding of a buried cache of corn by Standish and the *Mayflower* crew on **Corn Hill,** above; they took it to Plymouth and used it as seed, returning later to pay the Indians for the corn they'd taken.

Head east again on Route 6, and follow signs for the Cape Cod Light. As you near the lighthouse, you pass the **Truro Historical Museum,** built at the turn of the century as a summer hotel and now a repository of 17th-century firearms, mementos of shipwrecks, early fishing and whaling gear, ship models, a pirate's chest, scrimshaw, and more. One room exhibits wood carvings, paintings, blown glass, and ship models by Courtney Allen, artist and founder of Truro's historical society. An excellent self-guided historical tour of town is available at the gift shop. *Lighthouse Rd., North Truro, tel. 508/487–3397. Admission: $2 adults, $1.50 senior citizens, free for children under 12. Open mid-June–mid-Sept., daily 10–5. Closed mid-Sept.–mid-June.*

48 At the end of the road is **Highland Light,** also called Cape Cod Light, in which Thoreau boarded for a spell in his travels across the Cape's backside (as the Atlantic side of the Outer Cape is called). One of four active lighthouses on the Outer Cape, this one's a beauty, and you can drive right up to it. It is the Cape's oldest lighthouse, and the last to have become automated (in 1986). The first light on this site, powered by 24 whale-oil lamps, began warning ships off Truro's treacherous sandbars in 1798. The dreaded Peaked Hills Bars alone, to the north, have claimed hundreds of ships. The current light, a 66-foot tower built in 1857, is powered by two 1,000-watt bulbs, reflected by a huge Fresnel lens; its beacon can be seen for 20 miles. The lighthouse could fall into the sea within five to 30 years, depending on how quickly the 117-foot cliff on which it stands erodes, and on how successful a local committee is in finding the several million dollars necessary to move the lighthouse back from the cliff.

49 Back on Route 6 again, still going east, turn right for the **Pilgrim Heights Area** of the Cape Cod National Seashore. A short walking trail leads to the spring where a Pilgrim exploring party stopped to refill their casks, tasting their first New England water. Another path leads to a swamp, and a bike trail leads to Head of the Meadow Beach.

Walking through this still-wild area of oak, pitch pine, bayberry, blueberry, beach plum, and azalea gives you a taste of what it was like for these voyagers in search of a new home. "Being thus passed the vast ocean . . ." wrote William Bradford in *Of Plimoth Plantation,* "they had no friends to welcome them, no inns to entertain them or refresh their weatherbeaten bodies; no houses, or much less towns to repair to, to seek for succour."

From here you can take the coastal Route 6A—past countless ticky-tacky beach shacks and tidier rental cottages that line the bay—straight into **Provincetown,** or follow Route 6 to the
50 Seashore's **Province Lands Area.**

Tour 6: Provincetown

Numbers in the margin correspond to points of interest on the Tour 6: Provincetown map.

❺❶ This tour explores the 8-square-mile town of **Provincetown**— the Cape's smallest in area, second-smallest after Truro in year-round population—and its neighboring segment of the National Seashore. The town's main thoroughfare, Commercial Street, is 3 miles from end to end; street numbers are in the 300s around MacMillan Wharf, at the center, and get lower heading west and higher heading east.

Near the Provincetown border the massive dunes begin to appear on the right; in places they actually meet the road, turning Route 6 into a sand-swept highway. Scattered among the dunes are primitive cottages, called dune shacks, built from flotsam and other found materials, that have provided atmospheric as well as cheap lodgings to a number of famous artists and writers over the years—among them painter Harry Kemp, Eugene O'Neill, e.e. cummings, Jack Kerouac, and Norman Mailer. The few surviving shacks are privately leased from the National Seashore, which had planned to demolish them when their occupancy permits expire but was halted by their inclusion on the National Register of Historic Places in 1988. For dune tours, *see* Guided Tours, *above.*

❺❷ Turn right at the traffic light for the **Province Lands Visitor Center.** Inside you'll find literature and nature-related gifts, frequent short films (on local geology, the U.S. Life Saving Service, and more), and exhibits on the life of the dunes and the shore. You can also pick up information on guided walks, birding trips, lectures, bonfires, and other current programs throughout the Seashore, as well as on the Province Lands' own beaches (Race Point and Herring Cove) and walking, biking, and horse trails. Don't miss the wonderful 360° view of the dunes and the surrounding ocean from the observation deck. *Tel. 508/487–1256. Open Apr.–June and Sept.–Dec., daily 9–4:30; July–Aug., daily 9–6. Closed Jan.–Mar.*

Beyond the Visitor Center (and the Beech Forest picnic area and trails, across the way) is the small Provincetown airport, where sightseeing flights are available, and beyond that, the beautiful **Race Point Beach** (note that in summer the small parking lot fills up early in the day). Not far from the present Coast Guard Station is the **Old Harbor Station,** a U.S. Life Saving Service building towed here by barge from Chatham in 1977 to rescue it from an eroding beach. It is reached by a boardwalk across the sand; plaques along the way tell about the lifesaving service and the whales seen offshore. Inside are displays of such equipment as Lyle guns, which shot rescue lines out to ships in distress when the seas were too violent to launch a surfboat; and breeches buoys, in which passengers were hauled across those lines to safety. *No phone. Donations accepted. Open July–Aug., daily 10–4. Closed Sept.–June.*

Leaving Race Point Beach, a right onto Province Lands Road takes you through the heart of the dunes and woods, past **Herring Cove Beach** (the parking lot on the right is a great place to catch a sunset), and ultimately into the center of Provincetown. For this tour, instead return to Route 6 and turn right;

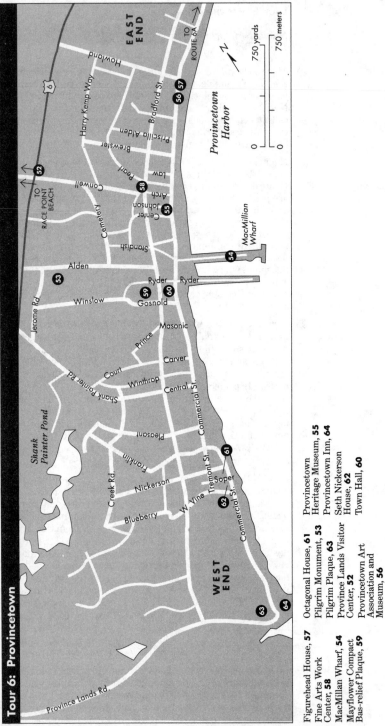

86

Tour 6: Provincetown

EAST END

TO ROUTE 6A

Howland

Harry Kemp Way

Brewster

Priscilla Alden

Bradford St.

Pearl

Conwell

Cemetery

C6

TO RACE POINT BEACH

Law

Arch

Johnson

Center

Standish

Alden

Winslow

Jerome Rd.

Ryder

Ryder

Gosnold

Masonic

Prince

Carver

Court

Winthrop

Central St.

Shank Painter Rd.

Pleasant

Franklin

Nickerson

Creek Rd.

Blueberry

W. Vine

Soper

Tremont St.

Commercial St.

Commercial St.

Shank Painter Pond

Province Lands Rd.

WEST END

Provincetown Harbor

MacMillan Wharf

750 yards

750 meters

0

N

Figurehead House, **57**
Fine Arts Work Center, **58**
MacMillan Wharf, **54**
Mayflower Compact Bas-relief Plaque, **59**

Octagonal House, **61**
Pilgrim Monument, **53**
Pilgrim Plaque, **63**
Province Lands Visitor Center, **52**
Provincetown Art Association and Museum, **56**

Provincetown Heritage Museum, **55**
Provincetown Inn, **64**
Seth Nickerson House, **62**
Town Hall, **60**

take the next two lefts, then a right onto Winslow Street. At the top of the hill, a sharp left leads to the parking lot of the

⑬ Pilgrim Monument, commemorating the first landing of the Pilgrims in the New World and their signing of the Mayflower Compact, America's first rules of self-governance, before setting off from Provincetown Harbor to explore the mainland. From atop the 252-foot-high tower (116 steps and 60 ramps) you get a panoramic view—the dunes on one side, the harbor on the other, and the entire bay side of Cape Cod beyond. At the base is a museum of Lower Cape and Provincetown history, with exhibits on whaling, shipwrecks, and scrimshaw, plus a diorama of the *Mayflower* and another of a glass factory. The exhibit on the pirate ship *Whydah*, sunk in a 1717 storm and discovered in 1984 off Wellfleet, includes a working laboratory doing conservation on artifacts from the ship (jewelry, weapons, coins), as well as audiovisual accounts of its discovery. The installation is elaborate, as befits a major find: The *Whydah* is the only pirate shipwreck ever recovered.

The tower was erected of granite shipped in from Maine, to a design modeled on a tower in Siena, Italy; President Theodore Roosevelt laid the cornerstone in 1907, and President Taft attended the 1910 dedication. On Thanksgiving Eve, in a ceremony including a museum tour and open house, 5,000 white and gold lights that drape the tower are lit, creating a display that can be seen as far away as the Cape Cod Canal. They are lit nightly into the New Year. *Tel. 508/487–1310. Admission: $5 adults, $3 children 4–12. Open July–Aug., daily 9–7; mid-Mar.– June and Sept.–Oct., daily 9–5; call for winter hours.*

Having looked down upon the town from this great height, it's time to come down and walk around in it. From the bottom of the hill, take a left, then a right, which brings you to MacMillan Wharf. The parking lot here is the most central one, which is why it fills up so fast, but there are other lots. In season especially, driving from one end of the main street to the other could take forever, so walking is definitely the way to go. In season, narrated trolley sightseeing tours make the downtown circuit throughout the day (*see* Guided Tours, *above*), or the romantically inclined can hire a horse-drawn carriage (tel. 508/487– 4246) from the stand in front of the Town Hall.

Provincetown is a place of creativity, sometimes startling originality, and infinite diversity. In the busy downtown, Portuguese-American fishermen mix with painters, poets, writers, and, in season, whale-watching families, cruise-ship passengers on brief stopovers, and gays and flamboyant cross-dressers who come to enjoy the freedom of a town with a large, visible gay population. In summer, Commercial Street is packed with sightseers and shoppers after the treasures of the many first-rate galleries and crafts shops. At night, raucous music and people spill out of bars, drag shows, and sing-along lounges galore. It's a fun, crazy place, with the extra dimension of the fishing fleet unloading their catch at MacMillan Wharf, in the center of the action.

During the early 1900s, Provincetown became known as Greenwich Village North. Artists from New York and Europe discovered the town's unspoiled beauty, special light, lively community, and colorful Portuguese flavor; by 1916, with five art schools flourishing here, painters' easels were as common as shells on the beach. This bohemian community, along with the availability of inexpensive summer lodgings close to the beach, attracted young rebels and writers as well, including John Reed (*Ten Days That Shook the World*) and Mary Heaton Vorse (*Footnote to Folly*), who in 1915 began the Cape's first significant theater group, the Provincetown Players. A young, unknown playwright named Eugene O'Neill joined them in 1916, when his *Bound East for Cardiff* premiered in a tiny wharfside fish house, minimally fitted out as a theater, in the East End. After 1916 the Players moved on to New York. Their theater (where 571 Commercial Street now is) is long since gone, but a model of it and of the old Lewis Wharf on which it stood is on display at the Pilgrim Monument museum.

The Historical Society puts out a series of walking-tour pamphlets, available for less than $1 each at many shops in town, with maps and information on the history of many buildings and the (more or less) famous folk who have occupied them.

The center of town is where the crowds and most of the touristy shops are. The quiet East End is mostly residential, with some top galleries, and the similarly quiet West End has a number of small inns with neat lawns and elaborate gardens. Practically the entire town has been designated part of the Provincetown Historic District—1,100 buildings spanning many architectural styles, from 18th-century Cape houses to Federals and Victorians.

54 **MacMillan Wharf,** with a large municipal parking facility, is a sensible place to start a tour. One of the remaining five of the 54 wharves that once jutted into the bay, it is the base for whalewatch boats, fishing charters, and party boats. Also here is the **Chamber of Commerce,** which has all kinds of information and schedules of events. Information columns at the wharf have rest room and parking lot locations, bus schedules, and other information for visitors.

55 Head east for two blocks to the **Provincetown Heritage Museum,** on the left. Exhibits include antique fire-fighting equipment, fishing artifacts, art (including donated works by Provincetown-related artists as well as antique prints and watercolors of schooners), wax figures, and a half-scale model (66 feet long, built by a master shipbuilder) of the fishing schooner *Rose Dorothea*, which won the Lipton Cup in 1907. *356 Commercial St., tel. 508/487–7098. Admission: $2 age 12 and over. Open mid-June–Columbus Day, daily 10–6. Closed Columbus Day–mid-June.*

Time Out **Juventino's Portuguese Bakery** (338 Commercial St., tel. 508/487–2303) puts out fresh Portuguese breads and pastries every day year-round, until 9 or 10 some nights in summer.

56 Ten more blocks up is the **Provincetown Art Association and Museum** (PAAM), founded in 1914 to collect and show the works of Provincetown-associated artists. Its 1,650-piece permanent collection is displayed in changing exhibits that combine up-and-comers with established artists of the 20th century. Some of the art hung in the four bright galleries is for sale. The museum store has books by or about local artists, authors, and topics, as well as posters, crafts, cards, and gift items. PAAM-sponsored year-round courses (one day and longer) offer the opportunity of studying under such talents as

Sal Del Deo and Tony Vevers. *460 Commercial St., tel. 508/487–1750. Admission: $2 adults; $1 children 3–12, senior citizens, and students. Open Nov.–Apr., weekends noon–4 and by appointment; Memorial Day–Labor Day, daily noon–5 and 7–10; May, Sept., and Oct., Mon.–Thurs. noon–5, Fri. and Sat. noon–5 and 7–10 (hours changeable).*

57 In the next block, at No. 476, is the **Figurehead House,** a yellow mansard-roofed house in the Second Empire style. The name comes from the figurehead of a woman—fished out of the sea during a whaling voyage in the early 19th century—that now adorns the front of this house. Turn up Cook Street and left onto Bradford Street, which runs parallel to Commercial Street and is known locally as Back Street. Several blocks up,

58 turn right onto Pearl Street for the **Fine Arts Work Center** (24 Pearl St., tel. 508/487–9960), a nonprofit organization begun in 1968 that sponsors 10 writers and 10 artists from October to May each year with a place to work, a stipend to live on, and access to artists and teachers. The center also has a gallery and sponsors off-season poetry readings and other events. The buildings in the complex around the center, which it owns, were formerly part of Day's Lumber Yard Studios, built above a lumberyard by a patron of the arts to provide poor artists with cheap accommodations. Among the studios' roster of residents over the years are Robert Motherwell, Hans Hoffmann, and Helen Frankenthaler.

Farther up are the former studios of two noted artists: Edwin W. Dickinson, at 46 Pearl Street, and Charles W. Hawthorne, at 48 Pearl. Hawthorne's Cape Cod School of Art, established here in 1899, put the town on its path to becoming a major art colony.

Farther along on Bradford Street, on your right, is the Duarte Motors parking lot, on the site of the former railroad depot. The train ran across Bradford and Commercial streets to the wharf, where it picked up passengers from the frequent Boston boats and crates of iced fish from the Commercial Street fish sheds. Train service ended in 1960.

Past Alden Street, in a little park on your right behind the Town

59 Hall, is the **Mayflower Compact bas-relief plaque** by sculptor Cyrus Dalin, depicting the historic signing.

60 The **Town Hall** was used by the Provincetown Art Association as its first exhibit space, and still exhibits paintings donated to the town over the years, including Provincetown scenes by Charles Hawthorne and WPA-era murals by Ross Moffett.

Time Out | **Provincetown Fudge Factory** (210 Commercial St., tel. 508/487–2850), across from the post office, makes silky peanut-butter cups, fudge, chocolates, saltwater taffy, caramel corn, yard-long licorice whips, and designer-flavor frozen yogurt—a must stop for those with a dental death wish, and they ship.

All the way at the west end of Commercial Street, at No. 74, between Soper and Nickerson streets, is an interesting piece

61 of Provincetown architecture: an **octagonal house** built in 1850.

Across Soper Street is the oldest building in town, dating to

62 1746. The small Cape-style **Seth Nickerson House**—a private home—was built by a ship's carpenter, with massive pegged, hand-hewn oak beams and wide-board floors.

63 At the bend in the road, the bronze **Pilgrim Plaque,** set into a boulder at the center of a green space, commemorates the first footfall of the Pilgrims onto Cape soil—Provincetown's humble **64** equivalent of the Plymouth Rock. Across the street is the **Provincetown Inn;** inside, a series of 19 murals (painted in the 1930s from old postcards) depicts life in the 19th-century town. For a day of fairly private beachcombing and great views, you can walk across the stone jetty at low tide onto the Long Point, a sandspit with two lighthouses. It's a 2-mile walk across soft sand, or hire a boat at Flyer's (*see* Sports and the Outdoors, *below*) to drop you off and pick you up.

What to See and Do with Children

The main component of children's summer vacations on the Cape is the same as their parents': the beach. Swimming, building sand castles, searching for shells and "neat rocks," and checking out the sea creatures and grasses that wash up have been the stuff of happy memories for generations of children.

Still, there are times when kids crave (and nag for) more modern diversions, and this family-oriented resort area offers enough activities to rival Myrtle Beach. Though miniature golf courses, go-cart racetracks, arcades, and the like are ubiquitous, much of the action centers on Route 28 between Yarmouth and Harwich Port. This strip is a monument to overdevelopment and a tangle of traffic in summer, but there's nothing like it when your kids (or you) are in the mood for some tacky fun.

Each town has a recreation program open to visitors. The morning activities, including sports, trips, and crafts, provide a good opportunity for your kids to meet others. Also, the **Cape Cod YMCA** (Box Y, Rte. 132, West Barnstable 02668, tel. 508/362–6500) offers summer one-week "fun clubs" (sports, crafts, nature), kids' evenings, summer day and resident camps, swimming classes, and more.

Amusements **Batter's Box** has softball and baseball batting cages and pitching machines, including one with fastballs up to 90 mph; a six-game video-arcade room; and video rentals. *322 Main St. (Rte. 28), Harwich Port, tel. 508/430–1155. Cost: $1.50 for 10 pitches, $5 for 40 pitches, or $10 for 40 pitches and a video of yourself. Open Apr.–May and Sept.–mid-Oct., Mon.–Sat. 11–7, Sun. 11–9; June–Aug., daily 9 AM–11 PM. Closed mid-Oct.–Mar.*

Bayberry Hollow Farm (W. Vine St. Ext., Provincetown, tel. 508/487–6584) offers pony rides year-round.

Bourne Kart Track has go-carts, minibikes, Hoops (a basketball game), a giant slide, a Ferris wheel, children's rides, minigolf, an arcade, bumper boats, and batting cages. *Rte. 28, Monument Beach, 2 mi south of Bourne Bridge, tel. 508/759–2636 or 800/535–2787. Cost: $1.50–$4 per ride. Open mid-Mar.–Nov., daily 9 AM–11 PM. Closed Dec.–mid-Mar.*

Bud's Go-Karts offers 20 top-of-the-line go-carts. *364 Sisson Rd., off Rte. 28, Harwich Port, tel. 508/432–4964. Cost: $5 for 6 min. Open June–Labor Day, Mon.–Sat. 9 AM–11 PM, Sun. 1–11 PM. Closed Labor Day–May.*

Cape Cod Storyland Golf is a 2-acre minigolf course set up as a mini-Cape Cod, with each of the 18 holes a Cape town. The course winds around small ponds and waterfalls, a full-size working gristmill, and reproductions of historic Cape buildings. There's an extra charge for the new bumper boats. *70 Center St. (by the railroad depot), Hyannis, tel. 508/778–4339. Admission: $5 adults, $4 children under 12. Open mid-Apr.–Oct., daily 8 AM–midnight. Closed Nov.–mid-Apr.*

Heritage Plantation (*see* Tour 1: Route 6A, Sagamore Bridge to Hyannis, *above*) has a working 1912 carousel for kids, with chariots and hand-carved horses.

Pirate's Cove is the most elaborate of the Cape's many minigolf emporiums, with a hill, a high waterfall, and a stream. In the works is a new 18-hole "Blackbeard's Challenge" course. *728 Main St. (Rte. 28), South Yarmouth, tel. 508/394–6200. Admission: $5 adults, $4 children under 13. Open July–Aug., daily 9 AM–11 PM; Apr.–June and Sept.–Oct., most days 10 AM–7 or 8 PM. Closed Nov.–Mar.*

Play-a-round is a megaplayground in Chatham (*see* Tour 4, *above*).

Rock Night at Orleans's Charles Moore Arena (*see* Sports and the Outdoors, *below*) is for kids 9–15 (no parents allowed). Every Friday from 8 to 10 PM year-round, kids rollerskate or ice-skate to DJ-spun rock and flashing lights.

Ryan Family Amusement Centers offer video-game rooms, minigolf, and bowling. *200 Main St., Buzzards Bay, tel. 508/759–9892; Town Hall Sq., Rte. 28, Falmouth, tel. 508/540–4877; Capetown Mall, Rte. 132, Hyannis, tel. 508/775–5566; 441 Main St., Hyannis, tel. 508/775–3411; 1067 Rte. 28, South Yarmouth, tel. 508/394–5644. Open daily; hours vary for each location.*

Trampoline Center has 12 trampolines at ground level over pits (so kids can't fall very far). *296 Rte. 28, West Harwich, tel. 508/432–8717. Cost: $3 for 10 min. Open mid-June–Labor Day, daily 9 AM–11 PM; Apr.–mid-June, weekends only (hours very changeable). Closed Labor Day–Mar.*

Water Wizz Water Park has a 50-foot-high water slide with tunnels and dips, a river ride, a kiddies' water park, a six-story tube ride, an arcade, volleyball courts and tournaments, minigolf, and food. *Rtes. 6 and 28, Wareham (2 mi west of the Bourne Bridge), tel. 508/295–3255. Admission: $15.75 adults ($12.75 on Sat.), $10 children under 48" and senior citizens. Open Memorial Day–mid-June, weekends 11–4; mid-June–Labor Day, daily 10–7. Closed Labor Day–Memorial Day.*

Arts **Academy of Performing Arts** (120 Main St., Orleans, tel. 508/255–5510) offers children 8 to 12 years old two-week sessions of theater, music, and dance classes, with a show at the end of each session; also, year-round classes for ages 4 to adult in dance, music, and drama.

Harwich Junior Theatre (Division St., Harwich [Box 168, West Harwich 02671], tel. 508/432–2002) gives theater classes for children year-round and presents four summer productions.

Mimsy Puppets (tel. 508/432–1279) give morning performances of fairy tales and folk tales for children late June through

August, Wednesdays at Community Hall in West Dennis and Thursdays at First Parish Church in Brewster.

Truro Center for the Arts at Castle Hill (Castle Rd., Box 756, Truro 02666, tel. 508/349–7511), housed in a converted 19th-century barn, offers summer arts and crafts workshops for children, as well as courses and single classes in art, crafts, photography, and writing for adults. Teachers have included notable New York– and Provincetown-based artists.

Children's programs are offered by the **Cape Cod Symphony Orchestra,** the **Cape Playhouse,** the **Falmouth Playhouse,** and the **Cape Cod Melody Tent** (*see* The Arts, *below*).

Camps The Massachusetts Audubon Society offers natural-history day camps for children in grades K–9 in July and August at its **Wellfleet Bay Wildlife Sanctuary** (Box 263, South Wellfleet 02663, tel. 508/349–2615). One-week sessions include classes and excursions. Reserve as early as possible—the camps are very popular. The **Cape Cod Museum of Natural History** (*see* Nature, *below*) and **Cape Cod Community College** (Rte. 132, West Barnstable 02668, tel. 508/362–2131, ext. 365) also offer summer day camps.

The Cape has a number of other day and residential summer camps; some teach sailing and water sports or horseback riding, such as **Cape Cod Sea Camps** (Box 1880, Brewster 02631, tel. 508/896–3451). **Cape Cod Baseball Camp** (Box S, Buzzards Bay 02532, tel. 508/295–6046) offers sessions of a week or more, either residential or day-camp, for children 8–19. For more information, write to the **Cape Cod Association of Children's Camps** (Box 38, Brewster 02631).

Museums **Cape Cod Children's Museum,** for children ages 1–10, has interactive play and science exhibits, playtime for toddlers and parents some mornings, and programs (about whales, cooking, germs) on Saturday mornings. *Falmouth Mall, Rte. 28, Falmouth, tel. 508/457–4667. Admission: 50¢. Open Mon.–Sat. 10:30–6, Sun. noon–5 (call to confirm hours).*

Also see **New England Fire & History Museum** (*see* Tour 3, *above*) in Brewster, **Plimoth Plantation** (*see* Off the Beaten Track, *below*) in Plymouth, and **Yesteryears Doll Museum** (*see* Tour 1, *above*) in Sandwich.

Nature **Army Corps of Engineers** (tel. 508/759–4431) has a summer junior-ranger program of outdoor activities for children 6–12 at Bourne Scenic Park on Route 6.

Aqua Circus of Cape Cod offers sea lion shows, a petting zoo, wandering peacocks, pony rides (in summer), shells, aquariums, educational programs, and the new Zoorific Theater, with presentations on small endangered animals. *674 Rte. 28, West Yarmouth, tel. 508/775–8883. Admission: $7.50 age 10 and up, $4.50 children 2–9. Open mid-Feb.–June and Sept.–late Nov., daily 9:30–5; July–Aug., daily 9:30–6:30. Closed late Nov.–mid-Feb.*

Bassett Wild Animal Farm has domestic and exotic birds and other animals (including lions), plus a petting zoo on 20 acres. Hayrides, pony rides, a snack bar, and a picnic area are available. *Tubman Rd., between Rtes. 124 and 137, Brewster, tel. 508/896–3224. Admission: $5.50 age 12 and up, $3.75* *children 2–11. Open mid-May–mid-Sept., daily 10–5. Closed mid-Sept.–mid-May.*

Cape Cod Museum of Natural History (*see* Tour 3, *above*) has a full program of children's and family activities in summer, including overnights and one- and two-week day camps of art and nature classes for preschoolers through grade 6.

Green Briar Nature Center in East Sandwich (*see* Tour 1, *above*) offers nature walks and other family activities all summer.

National Marine Fisheries Service Aquarium in Woods Hole (*see* Tour 2, *above*).

Whale watches (*see* Guided Tours in Essential Information, *above*).

Miscellaneous **Libraries** usually offer regular children's story hours or other programs—check them out on a rainy day. Hours are listed in the newspapers each week. **Hyannis Public Library** (401 Main St., Hyannis, tel. 508/775–2280) has a new children's multicultural center with books, tapes, and videos (some in foreign languages), programs, and a play area with puzzles and games.

Tot Drop (64 Enterprise Rd., Hyannis, tel. 508/778–6777) is a baby-sitting service by the Cape Cod Mall that lets you drop off your children for a few hours.

Baseball clinics (tel. 508/945–5199) for children 6–8 and 9–13 are offered in one-week sessions by the Chatham A's in summer.

Woodsong Farm Equestrian Center (121 Lund Farm Way, Brewster, tel. 508/896–5555) has a horsemanship program for children 7–18.

Off the Beaten Track

If you're not from an area like New England, traditional pastimes like barbecues, bazaars, and church suppers (chowder, lobster roll, perhaps ham and beans) are off the beaten track. If you're in the mood for a slice of regional Americana, give them a try—they're advertised in the papers.

Cape Cod Potato Chips (Independence Park, Rte. 132, Hyannis, tel. 508/775–7253) offers a free factory tour weekdays 10–4, including free samples of the all-natural chips hand-cooked in kettles in small batches.

In front of the **Dennis Police Department** (Rte. 134, South Dennis) is a display of Colonial-era punishment devices: stocks, pillories, and a whipping post.

At the Massachusetts Military Reservation (*see* Tour 2, *above*), a tour of **Air National Guard** grounds—including a slide briefing, a film, a look into F-15 fighter planes, and a tour of the museum, with old aircraft engines, missiles, models, and so forth—can be arranged by calling 508/968–4090. An attempt is made to schedule tours around flying activities, so you get to see the Guard in action.

Other of the reservation's tenants give tours as well: **Army National Guard** (tel. 508/968–5975), **Coast Guard** (tel. 508/968–6316), and **PAVE PAWS** (tel. 508/968–3206). It would be possible to see everything in a day, but you would have to reserve a couple of days in advance.

Massachusetts Maritime Academy, founded in 1891, is the oldest such academy in the country. At its 55-acre campus in Buzzards Bay, future members of the Merchant Marine receive their training. The library has scale models of ships from the 18th century to the present, as well as changing exhibits, and is open to the public at no charge (hours vary widely; call 508/759–5761, ext. 350). For a 20- to 30-minute tour of the academy weekdays at 10 and 2, call 48 hours in advance (ext. 314).

The **Nickerson Memorial Room** at the Cape Cod Community College (Rte. 132, West Barnstable, tel. 508/362–2131, ext. 445) has the largest collection of information on Cape Cod, including books, records, ships' logs, oral-history tapes, photographs, films, and more. It also has materials on the islands.

Plymouth, the settlement site the Pilgrims chose in December 1620 after scouting locations from their base at Provincetown, is just over 20 miles from the Sagamore Bridge via Route 3 or the coastal 3A. In addition to a number of historical museums, visitors can view **Plymouth Rock** (reputed first footfall) and tour a replica of the ship *Mayflower* as well as **Plimoth Plantation,** a reconstruction of the original settlement. At the last, actors in period costume and speaking Jacobean English carry on the daily life of the 17th century in character as early settlers in the furnished homes and walking the grounds. A crafts center features demonstrations of early techniques of making pottery, baskets, furniture, and woven goods. Self-guided tours start with a 12-minute film. *Warren Ave. (Rte. 3A), tel. 508/746–1622. Admission: $18.50 adults, $11 children 5–11, $17.50 senior citizens. Admission to* Mayflower II *only: $5.75 adults, $3.75 children 5–11. Plantation open Apr.–Nov., daily 9–5.* Mayflower II *open Apr.–June and Sept.–Nov., daily 9–5; July–Aug., daily 9–7.*

At the **Sandwich Fish Hatchery** (Rte. 6A, Sandwich, tel. 508/888–0008; open daily 9–3:30), rebuilt in 1993, you'll see over 200,000 brook, brown, and rainbow trout at various stages of development, being raised to stock the state's ponds. The mesh over the raceways is to keep kingfishers and herons from a free lunch. You can buy feed for a dime and watch the fish jump for it. An interpretive center may be added for 1994.

Area libraries with special collections include the **Centerville Library** (585 Main St., tel. 508/775–1787), with a 42-volume noncirculating set of transcripts of the Nuremberg Trials; **Cotuit Library** (871 Main St., tel. 508/428–8141), with a noncirculating set of luxurious leather-bound classics; **Hyannis Public Library** (401 Main St., tel. 508/775–2280), with a case full of books on JFK; and Barnstable's **Sturgis Library** (*see* Tour 1, *above*), with extensive Cape genealogical and maritime materials.

Shopping

Shopping is an important part of a Cape Cod vacation, especially on nonbeach days in summer (and in the rain, when the covered malls and factory outlets are mobbed). Favorite pastimes include antiquing and gallery hopping. Throughout the Cape you'll find weavers, candle makers, glassblowers, paper makers, and potters, as well as artists working in metal, enamel, and wood. You'll also find an inordinate number of shops specializing in country crafts, from straw dolls to handmade Christmas-tree ornaments.

Many shops close for the winter; in season, they tend to stay open late several nights a week, especially in Hyannis and Provincetown. For more on Cape specialties and shop hours, *see* Shopping in Chapter 1, Essential Information.

Shopping Districts

Provincetown has a long history as an art colony and remains an important art center, with many fine galleries and frequent exhibitions of Cape and non-Cape artists. Several artists represented in Provincetown are also shown in prominent New York galleries. **Wellfleet** has emerged as a vibrant center for art as well. Brochures on galleries in both towns are available by mail (*see* Shopping in Chapter 1, Essential Information).

Provincetown and Wellfleet also attract large numbers of craftsmen, who sell through a number of unique and sophisticated shops. **Route 6A,** the premier area for antiques and antiquarian bookshops, has its share of crafts shops as well, including many focusing on country crafts.

Hyannis's Main Street—the Cape's largest—is lined with bookshops, gift shops, jewelers, clothing stores, summer-wear and T-shirt shops, ice-cream and candy stores, plus minigolf places and fun or fancy eating places.

Main Street in **Chatham** is another busy shopping area, with more upscale and conservative merchandise than Hyannis. Here you'll find galleries, crafts, and clothing stores, plus a few good antiques shops.

Shopping Malls

Cape Cod Mall (between Rtes. 132 and 28, Hyannis, tel. 508/771–0200), the Cape's largest, has 90 shops, including Jordan Marsh, Filene's, Marshall's, Sears, F. W. Woolworth, restaurants, and a food court. It is open Monday–Saturday 9:30–9:30, Sunday noon–6, and is air-conditioned. Wheelchairs are available at no charge; strollers, for a small fee.

Falmouth Mall (Rte. 28, Falmouth, tel. 508/540–8329) has a theater, a children's museum, Bradlees, T. J. Maxx, and 30 other shops, generally open Monday–Saturday 9:30–9:30 and Sunday noon–5.

Mashpee Commons (junction of Rtes. 28 and 151, Mashpee, tel. 508/477–5400) has about 50 restaurants and shops, including The Gap and an art gallery, in an attractive village square setting. The shops are open Monday–Saturday 10–8 (Friday 'til 9), Sunday noon–5. There's also a movie theater, and free outdoor entertainment in summer.

Popponesset Marketplace (3 mi south of Rte. 28 from Mashpee rotary, New Seabury, tel. 508/477–9111), open late spring to early fall, offers 20 shops (boutique clothing, antiques), fun eating places (raw bar, pizza, ribs, Ben & Jerry's), minigolf, and weekend entertainment (bands, fashion or puppet shows, singalongs) by the sea.

Department Stores

These include **K mart** (Cape Town Mall, Rte. 132, Hyannis, tel. 508/771–0012); in the Cape Cod Mall, **F. W. Woolworth** (tel. 508/775–5212), **Jordan Marsh** (tel. 508/771–7111), **Filene's** (tel. 508/775–3800), and **Sears** (tel. 508/790–7300).

Factory Outlets

Cape Cod Factory Outlet Mall (Factory Outlet Rd., Exit 1 off Rte. 6, Sagamore, tel. 508/888–8417) has a food court and more than 20 outlets, including Corning/Revere, Carter's, Gitano, Bass Shoe, Bugle Boy, Van Heusen, and Toy Liquidators. Hours are Monday–Saturday 9:30–9, Sunday noon–6.

Factory Shoe Mart (Rte. 28, Dennisport, tel. 508/398–6000; Rte. 28 at Deer Crossing plaza, Mashpee, tel. 508/477–0017) has such brand names as Penaljo, Nickels, 9 West, Evan Picone, Unisa, Esprit, Nike, Reebok, and Rockport for men, women, and children.

Flea Market

The **Wellfleet Drive-In Theater** (Rte. 6, Eastham–Wellfleet line, tel. 508/349–2520) is the site of a giant flea market (mid-Apr.– June and Sept.–Oct., weekends and Mon. holidays 8–4; July and Aug., Mon. holidays, Wed., Thurs., and weekends 8–4). There's a snack bar and playground.

Farm Stands

Fancy's Farm Stands (199 Main St., East Orleans, tel. 508/255– 1949; The Cornfield, Rte. 28, West Chatham, tel. 508/945–1949) sell local and exotic produce, fresh-baked breads and pastries, dried flowers, baskets, hand-dipped candles, frozen prepared gourmet foods, spices and potpourri by the ounce, and more.

Tony Andrews Farm and Produce Stand (398 Old Meeting House Rd., East Falmouth, tel. 508/548–5257) lets you pick your own strawberries (mornings from mid-June), as well as peas, beans, and tomatoes (late June–late Aug.).

Auctions

You'll find an auction going on somewhere on the Cape all year long, from country-barn types to the internationally known Eldred's auctions. Though the high-end auctions deal in very fine antiques, they always include some lower-priced merchandise. (Write for schedules.) Church auctions often yield interesting Cape pieces, such as old sea chests, at good prices.

Eldred's (1483 Rte. 6A, Box 796, East Dennis 02641, tel. 508/385–3116) deals in mostly top-quality antiques, such as marine, Oriental, American, and European art; Americana; and estate jewelry. Its "general antiques and accessories" auctions feature less-expensive wares.

Merlyn Auctions (204 Main St., North Harwich, tel. 508/432– 5863) are homey affairs with moderate to inexpensive prices for old and new merchandise.

Sandwich Auction House (15 Tupper Rd., Sandwich, tel. 508/888–1926) has events weekly, usually estate sales.

Specialty Stores

"Cape Cod Antiques & Arts" (Box 2824, Orleans 02653–0039, tel. 508/255–2121 or 800/660–8999), a monthly supplement of *The Register* and *The Cape Codder* available at local news-stands, is chock-full of information on galleries, upcoming shows, Cape artists, antiques shops, auctions, and so forth.

Antiques **B.D. Hutchinson** (1274 Long Pond Rd., Brewster, tel. 508/896–6395), a watch- and clockmaker, sells antique and collectible watches, clocks, and music boxes.

Brown Jug (Main St. at Jarves St., Sandwich, tel. 508/833–1088) specializes in antique glass, such as Sandwich glass and Tiffany iridescent glassware, as well as Staffordshire china.

Ellipse Antiques (427 Main St. [Rte. 6A], Dennis, tel. 508/385–8626) specializes in mostly museum-quality early glass, such as rare Sandwich glass pieces, as well as Fiestaware, Staffordshire, Spatterware, and Americana.

Horsefeathers (454 Rte. 6A, East Sandwich, tel. 508/888–5298) sells antique linens, lace, bird cages, baby things, and Victoriana, such as valentines.

H. Richard Strand (Town Hall Sq., Sandwich, tel. 508/888–3230), in an 1800 home, displays very fine pre-1840 and Victorian antique furniture, paintings, American glass, and more.

Hyannis Antique Co-op (500 Main St., tel. 508/778–0512) offers a large selection of jewelry, glassware, porcelain, furniture, dolls, prints, collectibles, and more, at good prices.

Kingsland Manor (440 Main St. [Rte. 6A], West Brewster, tel. 508/385–9741) is like a fairyland, with ivy covering the facade, fountains in the courtyard, and everything "from tin to Tiffany"—including English hunting horns, full-size antique street lamps, garden and house furniture, weathervanes, jewelry, and chandeliers.

Remembrances of Things Past (376 Commercial St., Provincetown, tel. 508/487–9443) deals with articles from the 1920s to the 1960s, including Bakelite and other jewelry, telephones, neon items, ephemera, and autographed celebrity photographs.

Salt & Chestnut (651 Rte. 6A, West Barnstable, tel. 508/362–6085) has antique and custom-designed weathervanes displayed indoors and in the yard—a fun place to browse.

Shirley Walker Antiques at the Carriage House (3425 Rte. 6A, Brewster, tel. 508/896–6570) has American folk art, painted furniture, quilts, toys, and a roomful of garden accessories.

The Spyglass (618 Main St., Chatham, tel. 508/945–9686) carries telescopes, barometers, writing boxes, sea charts, and other nautical antiques.

Whitman House Gift Shop (Rte. 6, North Truro, tel. 508/487–3204) has Amish quilts and other country items.

Art **Animated Classics** (453 Commercial St., Provincetown, tel. 508/487–3668 or 800/795–CELS) deals in production, limited-edition, and serigraph cels from the major cartoon studios.

Berta Walker Gallery (208 Bradford St., Provincetown, tel. 508/487–6411) deals in Provincetown-affiliated artists, including Selina Trieff and Nancy Whorf, working in various media.

Blue Heron Gallery (Bank St., Wellfleet, tel. 508/349–6724) is one of the Cape's best galleries, with contemporary works—including Cape scenes, jewelry, and pottery—by regional and nationally recognized artists, including Sybil D'Orsi and Donald Voorhees.

Cummaquid Fine Arts (4275 Rte. 6A, Cummaquid, tel. 508/362–2593) has works by Cape Cod and New England artists, plus decorative antiques, beautifully displayed in an old home.

Ellen Harris Gallery (355 Commercial St., Provincetown, tel. 508/487–1414 or 508/487–0065), in its 25th year, deals in art and crafts, including jewelry, art glass, sculpture, and all media.

Hell's Kitchen Gallery (439 Commercial St., Provincetown, tel. 508/487–3570) features Provincetown-associated artists, including photographer Joel Meyerowitz and painter John Dowd.

Kendall Art Gallery (East Main St., Wellfleet, tel. 508/349–2482) carries contemporary art, including Harry Marinsky's bronzes in the sculpture garden and John Ffrench's brightly colored ceramic renderings of real and whimsical building facades.

Long Point Gallery (492 Commercial St., Provincetown, tel. 508/487–1795) is a cooperative of 17 well-established artists—including Varujan Boghosian, Robert Motherwell, Paul Resika, Judith Rothschild, and Tony Vevers—founded in 1977.

Tree's Place (Rte. 6A at 28, Orleans, tel. 508/255–1330) displays the work of New England artists, including Robert Vickery, Don Stone, and Elizabeth Mumford (whose popular folk art is bordered in mottos and poetic phrases). Champagne openings are held on Saturday nights in summer.

Books The Cape has a dozen bookshops that sell rare and out-of-print books (at any, ask for the brochure listing them), along with plenty of all-purpose bookstores.

Chart House Books (Liberty Sq., 1208 Rte. 132, Hyannis, tel. 508/771–4880) is a good new-book store with helpful staff.

Kings Way Books and Antiques (774 Rte. 6A, Brewster, tel. 508/896–3639) has out-of-print and rare books, including a large medieval section, plus small antiques, china, glass, silver, coins, and linens.

Parnassus Book Service (Rte. 6A, Yarmouth Port, tel. 508/362–6420), in an 1840 former general store, has a huge selection of old and new books—Cape Cod, maritime, Americana, antiquarian, and others—and is a great place to browse. They also carry Robert Bateman's nature prints.

Provincetown Art Association and Museum (460 Commercial St., Provincetown, tel. 508/487–1750) has a gift shop with many books on Provincetown and its artists.

Punkhorn Bookshop (672 Rte. 6A, Brewster, tel. 508/896–2114), an antiquarian- and rare-book seller, specializes in books on natural history, Cape and region, fine arts, and biography, plus antique prints and maps.

Titcomb's Bookshop (432 Rte. 6A, East Sandwich, tel. 508/888–2331) has used, rare, and new books, including a large collection of Cape and nautical titles and Americana and a new section with quality children's books.

Yellow Umbrella Books (501 Main St., Chatham, tel. 508/945–0144) has an excellent selection of new books, many on Cape Cod, plus used books.

Clothing **Cape Sailboards** (661 Main St., Falmouth, tel. 508/540–8800) has surf-type beachwear, Body Glove wet suits, and other beach gear, plus sail, boogie, and skim boards.

Hannah (47 Main St., Orleans, tel. 508/255–8234; Main St., Wellfleet, tel. 508/349–9884) has lovely upscale women's fashions—a blend of classic style with flair—by such labels as Hannah, No Saint, and Angel Heart.

Howlingbird (91 Palmer Ave., Falmouth, tel. 508/540–3787) carries detailed, hand-silkscreened, marine-theme T-shirts and sweatshirts, plus silver and shell jewelry, hand-painted cards, and silkscreened hats and handbags.

Karol Richardson (3 West Main St., Wellfleet, tel. 508/349–6378) creates classic women's designs in luxurious fabrics and sells interesting shoes, hats, and jewelry.

Kidstuff (381 Commercial St., Provincetown, tel. 508/487–0714) carries unusual, colorful children's wear.

Maxwell & Co. (200 Main St., Falmouth, tel. 508/540–8752) has traditional men's and women's clothing with flair, from European and American designers; handmade Italian shoes and boots; and leather goods and accessories.

Northern Lights Leather (361 Commercial St., Provincetown, tel. 508/487–9376) has high-fashion clothing, boots, shoes, and accessories of very fine, soft leather, plus silk clothing. Its shop around the corner sells all kinds of hammocks—rope, wood, Yucatan multicolor cotton—and has a waterfront deck where you can try them out.

Crafts **The Blacks Handweaving Shop** (597 Rte. 6A, West Barnstable, tel. 508/362–3955), in a barnlike shop with looms upstairs and down, makes beautiful hand-woven goods in traditional and jacquard weaves.

Cape Cod Cooperage (1150 Queen Anne Rd. at Rte. 137, Chatham, tel. 508/432–0788), set in an old barn, sells woodenware made in a century-old tradition by a barrelmaker on site, plus hand-decorated furniture, craft supplies, and more.

Chatham Glass Co. (17 Balfour La., West Chatham, tel. 508/945–5547) is a glassworks where you can watch glass being blown, and buy it, too—objects including marbles, Christmas ornaments, jewelry, and art glass.

Impulse (188 Commercial St., Provincetown, tel. 508/487–1154) has contemporary American crafts, including jewelry and an extraordinary kaleidoscope collection. The Autograph Gallery features framed photographs, letters, and documents signed by celebrities.

Kemp Pottery (Rte. 6A, Orleans, tel. 508/255–5853; 258 Rte. 6A, West Brewster, tel. 508/385–5782) has functional and decorative stoneware and porcelain, fountains, garden sculpture, pottery sinks, and stained glass.

Linda's Originals & the Yankee Craftsman (220 Rte. 6A, West Brewster, tel. 508/385–2285) brings together the work of 500 craftsmen in handcrafted country furnishings and gifts, plus many collectibles lines.

Oak & Ivory (1112 Main St., Osterville, tel. 508/428–9425) specializes in Nantucket lightship baskets made on the premises, as well as gold miniature baskets and scrimshaw.

Pewter Crafters of Cape Cod (927 Rte. 6A, Yarmouth Port, tel. 508/362–3407) handcrafts traditional and contemporary pewter objects from baby's cups to tea services.

Scargo Pottery (off Rte. 6A, Dennis, tel. 508/385–3894) is set in a pine forest, where potter Harry Holl's unusual wares—such as his signature castle birdhouses—sit on tree stumps and hang from branches. Inside are the workshop and kiln, plus work by Holl's four daughters .

The Spectrum (369 Rte. 6A, Brewster, tel. 508/385–3322; 342 Main St., Hyannis, tel. 508/771–4554) showcases imaginative American arts and crafts, including pottery, stained glass, art glass, and more.

Sydenstricker Galleries (Rte. 6A, Brewster, tel. 508/385–3272) features glassware handcrafted by a unique process, which you can watch in progress.

Tree's Place (Rte. 6A at Rte. 28, Orleans, tel. 508/255–1330), one of the Cape's best and most original shops, has a huge collection of handcrafted kaleidoscopes, plus art glass, hand-painted porcelain and pottery, hand-blown stemware, Russian lacquer boxes, jewelry, imported ceramic tiles, and much more. *See also* Art, *above.*

Whippletree (Rte. 6A, West Barnstable, tel. 508/362–3320) is a large barn, decorated for each season and filled with country gift items and a year-round Christmas section. Offerings include German nutcrackers, from Prussian soldiers to Casanova, plus characters from *The Nutcracker* ballet.

Food **Chatham Jam and Jelly Shop** (10 Vineyard Ave. at Rte. 28, West Chatham, tel. 508/945–3052) sells preserves (cranberry with strawberries and honey, Maine wild blueberry), nutty conserves, and ice-cream toppings, all made on site in small batches.

Chocolate House Fudge and Gift Shop (11 Cranberry Hwy., Sagamore, tel. 508/888–7065), just over the Sagamore Bridge on the Cape side, sells creamy fudge in 12 flavors, hand-dipped chocolates and truffles, and saltwater taffy and penny candy. The gift shop has cranberry glass and other Cape items.

Clambake Celebration (9 West Rd., Orleans, tel. 508/255–3289 or 800/423–4038) prepares full clambakes, including lobster, clams, mussels, corn, potatoes, onions, and sausage, for you to take away—or they'll deliver or air-ship year-round. The food is layered in seaweed in a pot and ready to steam.

Marion's Pie Shop (2022 Main St. [Rte. 28], West Chatham, tel. 508/432–9439) sells homemade and home-style fruit breads, pastries, prepared foods (lasagna, Boston baked beans, chowder base), and, of course, pies, both meat and fruit.

Gifts **Crystal Pineapple** (tel. 800/462–4009; 1540 Rte. 6A, West Barnstable, tel. 508/362–3128; 1582 Rte. 132, Hyannis, tel. 508/362–1330) has cranberry glass and many collectibles lines, including Dept. 56, Snowbabies, Swarovski crystal, and Disney Classics.

Home for the Holidays (154 Main St., Sandwich, tel. 508/888–4388), set in an old home, is a lovely place to browse for decorations, gifts, and handcrafted cards for nearly every holiday or special occasion—baby gifts, Christmas ornaments and papers, goblin lights for Halloween—as well as elegant glassware and china.

Odds and Ends **Baseball Shop** (26 Main St., Orleans, tel. 508/240–1063) sells everything relating to baseball and other sports—cards (new and collectible), hats, clothing, videos—plus comic books.

Bird Watcher's General Store (36 Rte. 6A, Orleans, tel. 508/255–6974 or 800/562–1512) has everything avian: feeders, paintings, houses, books, fountains, calls, ad infinitum.

Christmas Tree Shops (main shop at Exit 1 off Rte. 6, Sagamore, tel. 508/888–7010; others at Falmouth, Hyannis, Orleans, West Dennis, West Yarmouth, and Yarmouth Port) sell everything from thumbtacks to furniture to kitchen goods. This is not high-concept shopping, it's pure fun. The multicolor, Victorian-style Hyannis shop (Rte. 132, tel. 508/778–5521) is the largest.

Sports and the Outdoors

Many annual bike races, road races, marathons, triathlons, and golf and tennis tournaments are held on the Cape. Watch the local papers for upcoming events (*see also* Festivals and Seasonal Events in Chapter 1, Essential Information).

Bicycling

The Dennis Chamber of Commerce's guidebook includes bike tours and maps, and the Wellfleet chamber's pamphlet *Bicycling in Wellfleet* includes an annotated map (*see* Tourist Information in Essential Information, *above*). Also, a booklet on the marked and unmarked bike trails of Cape Cod, *The Cape Cod Bike Book*, is available in Cape bookstores and bike shops, or send $3.25 to Box 627, South Dennis 02660. For bike-rental shops, *see* Getting Around by Bicycle, *above*. **Cape Cod Cycle Tours** (Box 1356, North Eastham 02651, tel. 508/255–8281) offers guided tours with van support and motel accommodations.

For a brochure on the **Claire Saltonstall Bikeway** between Boston and Provincetown (135 miles) or Woods Hole (85 miles), using mostly bike paths and little-traveled roadways, send $2 and a business-size SASE to American Youth Hostels (1020 Commonwealth Ave., Boston 02215). It is also available in area bike shops and bookstores.

Bike Paths **Cape Cod Rail Trail,** the paved right-of-way of the old Penn Central Railroad, is the Cape's premier bike path. It is 20 miles long, from Dennis to Eastham, and passes salt marshes, cranberry bogs, ponds, and Nickerson State Park, which has its own path (*see below*). Along the way you can veer off to spend an hour or two on the beach, or stop for lunch. The terrain is easy to moderate. The trail begins in South Dennis (the start is at the parking lot off Rte. 134, south of Rte. 6, near Theophilus Smith Rd.) and ends at the entrance to the Salt Pond Visitor Center. There are parking lots along the route if you want to do only a segment: across from Pleasant Lake Store (on Pleasant Lake Ave.) in Harwich and at Nickerson State Park in Brewster. The Butterworth Company (38 Rte. 134, South Dennis 02660, tel. 508/760–2000 or 800/696–2762) sells a guide to the trail for $2.95.

On either side of the **Cape Cod Canal** is an easy straight trail (6½ miles on the south side, almost 8 miles on the north), offering a view of the bridges and canal traffic. They are accessed from many points along the trails.

The **Shining Sea Trail** is an easy 3½-mile route between Locust Street, Falmouth, and the Woods Hole ferry parking lot. It follows the coast, giving views of Vineyard Sound and dipping into oak and pine woods; a detour onto Church Street takes you to Nobska Light. A brochure is available at the trailheads.

The Cape Cod National Seashore maintains three bicycle trails (maps available at visitor centers). **Nauset Trail** is 1⅗ miles, from Salt Pond Visitor Center in Eastham through groves of apple and locust trees to Coast Guard Beach. **Head of the**

Meadow Trail is 2 miles of easy cycling between dunes and salt marshes from High Head Road, off Route 6A in North Truro, to the Head of the Meadow Beach parking lot. **Province Lands Trail** is a 5¼-mile loop off the Beech Forest parking lot on Race Point Road in Provincetown, with spurs to Herring Cove and Race Point beaches and to Bennett Pond. The paths wind up and down hills amid dunes, marshes, woods, and ponds, and offer spectacular views (on a really clear day, you can see the Boston skyline); there's a picnic grove at Pilgrim Spring.

Nickerson State Park (*see* Nature Areas, *below*) has 3 miles of trails through forest (trail map available).

Fishing

Fishing is one of the Cape's main pastimes, from surfcasting off beaches to angling in stocked ponds to deep-sea fishing trips. The Cape Cod Chamber's *Sportsman's Guide* gives fishing regulations, surf-fishing access locations, a map of boat-launching facilities, and more. The state Division of Fisheries and Wildlife (*see* Chapter 1, Essential Information) has a new book with 40 maps of Cape ponds. The "Fishing Around" column in the Friday *Cape Cod Times* tells the latest in fishing on the Cape—what's being caught and where.

The Cape Cod Canal is a good place to fish, from the service road on either side, for blues, cod, flounder, mackerel, and black and striped bass (Apr.–Nov.). The Army Corps of Engineers offers a **hotline on Canal fishing** (tel. 508/759–5991).

Hundreds of freshwater ponds offer good fishing for perch, pickerel, trout, and more; the required license (along with rental gear) is available at tackle shops, such as **Eastman's Sport & Tackle** (150 Main St., Falmouth, tel. 508/548–6900), **Goose Hummock Shop** (Rte. 6A, Orleans, tel. 508/255–0455; Rte. 28, Hyannis, tel. 508/778–0877), and **Truman's** (Rte. 28, West Yarmouth, tel. 508/771–3470). For rental boats, *see* Water Sports, *below*.

Fishing Trips Charter boats and party boats (per-head fees, rather than the charters' group rates) fish in season for bluefish, tuna, swordfish, marlin, and mako and blue sharks. Throughout the year there's bottom fishing for flounder, tautog, scup, fluke, cod, and pollock.

Fishing trips are operated on a walk-on basis from spring through fall by **Cap'n Bill & Cee Jay** (MacMillan Wharf, Provincetown, tel. 508/487–4330 or 800/675–6723), **Double Eagle Cruises** (Town Marina, Falmouth, tel. 508/548–2929), the *Golden Eagle* (Wychmere Harbor, Harwich Port, tel. 508/432–5611), **Hy-Line** (Ocean St. docks, Hyannis, tel. 508/790–0696; bottom fishing), the *Naviator* (Town Pier, Wellfleet, tel. 508/349–6003), and **Patriot Party Boats** (Falmouth Harbor, tel. 508/548–2626 or 800/734–0088 in MA; sport- or bottom fishing). Many of these offer charters as well, as do **Barnstable Harbor Charter Fleet** (186 Millway, tel. 508/362–3908) and **Rock Harbor Charter Boat Fleet** (Rock Harbor, Orleans, tel. 508/255–9757 or 800/287–1771 in MA).

Golf

The Cape Cod Chamber of Commerce has a "Golf Map of Cape Cod," locating dozens of courses on the Cape and islands. The Cape's mild climate makes golf possible almost year-round, and most of its 20 public courses stay open, though January and February do get nippy (temperatures average in the 30s). Summer greens fees range from $25 to $50.

Blue Rock Golf Course (off Highbank Rd., South Yarmouth, tel. 508/398–9295) is a highly regarded, easy-walking 18-hole, par-54 country club course crossed by a pond.

Captain's Golf Course (1000 Freeman's Way, Brewster, tel. 508/896–5100), with 18 holes, was voted among the top 25 public courses in the country by *Golf Digest* in 1990.

New Seabury Country Club (Shore Dr., New Seabury, tel. 508/477–9110) has one superior 18-hole, par-72 championship layout on water, and an 18-hole, par-70 course. Both are open to the public September–May (space-available basis, proper attire required).

Ocean Edge Golf Course (1 Villagers Rd., Rte. 6A, Brewster, tel. 508/896–5911), an 18-hole, par-72 course winding around five ponds, features Scottish-style pot bunkers, challenging terrain, and one hole over a cranberry bog. Weeklong residential or commuter golf schools are offered in spring and fall.

Tara Hyannis Hotel & Resort (West End Circle, Hyannis, tel. 508/775–7775) has a beautifully landscaped, challenging 18-hole, par-3 course.

Other courses: **Chatham Seaside Links** (Seaview St., tel. 508/945–4774), nine holes, a good beginner's course; **Cranberry Valley Golf Course** (Oak St., Harwich, tel. 508/430–7560), 18 well-groomed holes; and **Highland Golf Links** (Lighthouse Rd., North Truro, tel. 508/487–9201), a nine-hole, par-36 course on a cliff overlooking the Atlantic.

Health and Fitness Clubs

In addition to what's listed below, the following facilities may offer saunas and steam rooms; Nautilus, Biocycle, Airdyne, StairMaster, Gravitron, and other machines; treadmills; physical therapists or personal trainers; step and other aerobics; massage; and free weights.

Falmouth Sports Center (Highfield Dr., Falmouth, tel. 508/548–7433) is a huge facility with three all-weather tennis, six indoor tennis, one squash, and three racquetball/handball courts.

Fitness Club of Cape Cod (55 Attucks La., Independence Park, off Rte. 132, Hyannis, tel. 508/771–7734) has five racquetball/wallyball courts; basketball; day care; and a bar/restaurant with pool table and dart boards.

Mid-Cape Racquet Club (193 White's Path, South Yarmouth, tel. 508/394–3511) has one all-weather tennis, nine indoor tennis, two racquetball, and two squash courts; indoor and outdoor basketball; plus day care.

Norseman Athletic Club (Rte. 6, North Eastham, tel. 508/255–6370 or 508/255–6371) has four racquetball, two squash, six indoor tennis, and two indoor basketball courts; an indoor Olympic-size heated pool; swimming lessons; aerobics and children's self-defense classes; plus a pro shop and a restaurant.

The Tara Club (Tara Hyannis Hotel & Resort, West End Circle, tel. 508/775–7775) has two lighted outdoor tennis courts and indoor and outdoor pools.

Hiking/Walking

Many towns, such as Chatham, maintain walking trails in conservation or other scenic areas. Contact local chambers or information centers for details. The **Cape Cod Museum of Natural History** (*see* Tour 3, *above*), **Cape Cod National Seashore** (*see* Tour 5, *above*), and **Nickerson State Park** (*see* Nature Areas, *below*) offer guided walks and hikes in season.

The **Army Corps of Engineers** (tel. 508/759–4431) sponsors guided walks, bike trips, and hikes from its visitor center in Bournedale on Route 6; outside the center, on a bank of the canal with an excellent view, are a herring run, picnic tables, access to the canal bike path, and short self-guided walking trails through woodland.

The **Cape Cod National Seashore** has nine trails through varied terrain (brochures at visitor centers and trailheads). Among them are the moderately difficult 1½-mile Ft. Hill Trail in Eastham, exploring a red-maple swamp, and Wellfleet's 1¼-mile Atlantic White Cedar Swamp Trail. Easy trails in Truro include the ¾-mile Pilgrim Spring Trail through woodland in the Pilgrim Heights Area and the ½-mile Cranberry Bog Trail.

Horseback Riding

The **Province Lands Horse Trails** are three two-hour trails to the beaches through or past dunes, cranberry bogs, forests, and ponds—great at sunset; pick up a mount at **Nelson's Riding Stable** (43 Race Point Rd., Provincetown, tel. 508/487–1112). **Deer Meadow Riding Stables** (Rte. 137, East Harwich, tel. 508/432–6580) and **Haland Stables** (Rte. 28A, West Falmouth, tel. 508/540–2552) also offer trail rides, by reservation. **Woodsong Farm** (121 Lund Farm Way, Brewster, tel. 508/896–5555) offers instruction and day camps but no trail rides.

Ice-skating/Roller-skating

Fall through spring, ice-skating is available at several town rinks, including the **Charles Moore Arena** (O'Connor Way, Orleans, tel. 508/255–2971), **Falmouth Ice Arena** (Palmer Ave., Falmouth, tel. 508/548–9083), **John Gallo Ice Arena** (231 Sandwich Rd., Bourne, tel. 508/759–8904), **Kennedy Memorial Skating Rink** (Bearses Way, Hyannis, tel. 508/790–6346), and **Tony Kent Arena** (8 Gages Way, South Dennis, tel. 508/760–2400). Some offer roller-skating and rollerblading in summer. In winter, ponds and shallow flooded cranberry bogs sometimes freeze hard enough for skating; check conditions with the local fire department before venturing onto unfamiliar territory.

Jogging/Running

Aside from the state parks and forests, which have paved trails (*see* Nature Areas, *below*), the beaches are great places to run, as are the paths alongside the canal.

Lifecourse (Access and Old Bass River Rds., South Dennis) is a 1½-mile jogging trail through woods, with 20 exercise stations along the way. It is part of a recreation area that includes basketball and handball courts, a ball field, a playground, and a picnic area.

Many road races are held in season, including the world-class **Falmouth Road Race** (*see* Festivals and Seasonal Events in Chapter 1, Essential Information) in August and the **Cape Codder Triathlon** (Box 307, West Barnstable 02668) at Craigville Beach in July.

Shellfishing

For shellfishing licenses and information on sites, contact the local town hall.

Tennis and Racquetball

Public tennis courts abound: Falmouth, for example, has more than 20. To locate one near you, call the town chamber of commerce (*see also* Health and Fitness Clubs, *above*).

Ballymeade Country Club (Rte. 151, North Falmouth, tel. 508/457–7620) offers six Har-Tru and four hard courts, lessons, clinics, ball machines, a grass croquet court, and a pro shop.

Bissell's Tennis Courts (Bradford St. at Herring Cove Beach Rd., Provincetown, tel. 508/487–9512; open Memorial Day–Sept.) has five clay courts and offers lessons.

Chatham Bars Inn (Shore Rd., Chatham, tel. 508/945–0096, ext. 1155) offers four waterfront all-weather tennis courts, lessons, and a pro shop.

Chequessett Yacht & Country Club (Chequessett Neck Rd., Wellfleet, tel. 508/349–3704) is a semiprivate club (public use on space-available basis) with a nine-hole golf course and five hard-surface tennis courts across from the bay. Lessons are available.

Melrose Tennis and Sport Shop (606 Rte. 28, Harwich Port, tel. 508/430–2444) offers three Omni courts (synthetic grass and a sand layer, so it plays soft) and six Har-Tru courts, a pro shop, lessons, and daily round-robins and mixed doubles. You can also rent Rollerblades and buy sporting goods here.

Ocean Edge (Rte. 6A, Brewster, tel. 508/896–9000) has five clay and six Plexipave courts; offers lessons and round-robins; and hosts Tim Gullikson's World-Class Tennis School, including weekend packages and video analysis.

Oliver's (Rte. 6, Wellfleet, tel. 508/349–3330) offers one Truflex and seven clay courts and lessons and arranges matches.

Spectator Sports

The **Cape Cod Baseball League** (tel. 508/432–0340), begun in 1885, is an invitational league of college players that boasts Carlton Fisk, Ron Darling, and the late Thurman Munson as alumni. Considered the country's best summer league, it is scouted by all the major-league teams. Ten teams play a 44-game season from mid-June to mid-August; games are free.

Water Sports

Boating, Canoeing, and Kayaking

See also Sailing and Windsurfing, *below.*
Cape Cod Boats (Rte. 28 at Bass River Bridge, West Dennis, tel. 508/394–9268) rents powerboats, Sunfish, and canoes.
Cape Cod Waterways (16 Rte. 28, Dennisport, tel. 508/398–0080) rents canoes, kayaks, and manual and electric paddleboats for leisurely travel on the Swan River, as well as Windsurfers and sailboats delivered on the Mid-Cape.
Eastern Mountain Sports (Village Marketplace, 233 Stevens St., Hyannis, tel. 508/775–1072) rents kayaks and camping gear.
Wellfleet Bay Wildlife Sanctuary (*see* Nature Areas, *below*) and the **Cape Cod National Seashore** (*see* Tour 5, *above*) run canoe trips.

Sailing and Windsurfing

Aquaventures (tel. 800/300–3787; MacMillan Wharf, Provincetown; Sesuit Harbor, East Dennis) offers parasailing.
Arey's Pond Boat Yard (off Rte. 28, South Orleans, tel. 508/255–0994) has a sailing school with individual and group lessons.
Cape Water Sports (Rte. 28, Harwich Port, tel. 508/432–7079; other locations) rents Sunfish, Hobie Cats, Lasers, powerboats, sailboards, day sailers, paddleboats, and canoes, and gives instructions; sailboat charters are available.
Flyer's Boat Rental (131A Commercial St., Provincetown, tel. 508/487–0898 or 800/750–0898) rents Sunfish, sailboats, outboards, canoes, rowboats, and fishing poles and teaches sailing.
Jack's Boat Rentals (Rte. 6, Wellfleet, tel. 508/349–9808; locations on Flax Pond, Nickerson State Park, Brewster; Gull Pond, Wellfleet; Beach Point, Rte. 6A, North Truro) rents Sunfish, Hobie Cats, pedalboats, Aqua Bikes, canoes, kayaks, boogie boards, surfboards, and sailboards, and offers sailing and windsurfing lessons and guided "Canoe Eco-Tours"—sunset tours of connecting kettle ponds to observe wildlife.
Monomoy Sail & Cycle (275 Orleans Rd. [Rte. 28], North Chatham, tel. 508/945–0811) rents sailboards and Sunfish.
Nauset Sports (Rte. 6A, Orleans, tel. 508/255–4742; Rte. 6, North Eastham, tel. 508/255–2219) rents boards (surf, body, skim, sail) and wetsuits, plus in-line skates and tennis racquets.
Windsurfing Unlimited (277A Commercial St., Provincetown, tel. 508/487–9272) rents and provides instruction for sailboards, Sunfish, day sailers, and kayaks.

Scuba

Water temperatures vary from 50° to 70° in Nantucket Sound, and from 40° to 65° on the ocean side and in Cape Cod Bay. Check with a dive shop about local conditions and sites, as well as on dive boats. Wrecks in area waters include a steamship and schooners. Rentals, instruction, group dives, and information are available through **Aquarius Diving Center** (3239 Cranberry Hwy., Buzzards Bay, tel. 508/759–3483) and **Cape Cod Ski, Bike and Scuba** (tel. 800/348–4641 in MA; 323 Barnstable Rd., Hyannis, tel. 508/775–3301; 815 Main St. [Rte. 28], Harwich Port, tel. 508/432–9035; Rte. 6A, Orleans, tel. 508/255–7547).

Surfing

The Outer Cape beaches, including North Beach in Chatham, Nauset Beach in Orleans, Marconi Beach and White Crest Beach in Wellfleet, and Long Nook in Truro, are the best spots for surfing, which is best when there's a storm offshore. For a surf report (water temperature, weather, surf, tanning factor), call 508/255–9811. **Pump House Surf Co.** (9 Rte. 6A, Orleans, tel. 508/255–5832) rents wet suits and sells other surf gear. *Also see* Sailing and Windsurfing, *above.*

Swimming

Cape Cod Ski, Bike and Scuba in Harwich Port (*see* Scuba, *above*) offers an indoor, heated pool and swimming lessons year-round.

Beaches

Cape Cod has more than 150 ocean and freshwater beaches, with something for just about every taste. Bayside beaches generally have colder water, carried down from Maine and Canada, and gentle waves. Southside beaches, on Nantucket Sound, have rolling surf and are warmed by the Gulf Stream. Open-ocean beaches on the Cape Cod National Seashore are cold and have serious surf. Shell collecting is best on Nantucket Sound beaches, just after high tide or a storm; also check tidal pools and around jetties and wharf pilings.

To avoid the crowds, arrive either early in the morning or later in the afternoon (when the water is warmest, anyway). Parking lots fill up by 10 AM or so. Those beaches not restricted to residents charge (sometimes hefty) parking fees; for weekly or seasonal passes, contact the local town hall.

Cape Cod National Seashore

All of the Atlantic Ocean beaches on the National Seashore, though cold, are otherwise superior—wide, long, sandy, dune-backed, with great views. They're also contiguous: from Eastham to Provincetown, you can walk virtually without ever leaving sand. Seashore beaches also offer the luxury of length: You can always keep walking if you want privacy, whereas most everywhere else there's no escape from the crowds. Wellfleet beaches from late July through August are sometimes troubled with red algae in the water, which, while harmless, can be annoying; check with the Seashore on conditions.

All the Seashore beaches have lifeguards, showers (except Head of the Meadow Beach), and rest rooms; only Herring Cove has food. Beginning June 25, parking costs $5 per day, or $15 for a yearly pass good at all Cape beaches; walk-ins pay $2; senior citizens with Golden Eagle passports and disabled persons with Golden Age Passports (*see* Hints for Older Travelers and Hints for Disabled Travelers in Chapter 1, Essential Information) are admitted free.

Coast Guard Beach in Eastham is a long beach backed by low grass and heathland. (It doesn't have a parking lot; park at the Salt Pond Visitor Center and take the free shuttle to the beach.) The adjacent **Nauset Light Beach** is similar, with the lighthouse for a little extra Cape atmosphere. **Marconi Beach** in South Wellfleet is a narrow but long strand of golden sand backed by high dune cliffs. **Head of the Meadow Beach** in Truro is often less crowded; it has only temporary rest room facilities and no showers since the bathhouse burned down.

In Provincetown, **Race Point Beach** has a remote feeling, with a wide swath of sand stretching far off into the distance and around the point and Coast Guard Station. Behind the beach is pure duneland; bike trails lead off the parking lot. Because of its position, on a point facing north, the beach gets sun all day long, whereas the east-coast beaches tend to be sunniest early in the day. **Herring Cove Beach,** also in Provincetown, is calmer, a little warmer, and not as pretty, since the parking lot is not hidden behind dunes. There's a hot dog stand here, and sunsets from the parking lot to the right of the bathhouse are great.

Town and State Beaches

Cahoon Hollow Beach on Wellfleet's ocean side has a wide sandy beach, surf, lifeguards, rest rooms, and a restaurant and music club on the sand (*see* Nightlife, *below*).

Chapin Beach in Dennis is an attractive, dune-backed bay beach with long tidal flats at low tide that allow walking far out, but no lifeguards or services.

Corporation Beach in Dennis is an attractive crescent of white sand with lifeguards, showers, rest rooms, and a food stand.

Craigville Beach, near Hyannis, is a long, wide strand that is extremely popular, especially with the roving and volleyball-playing young (hence its nickname, "Muscle Beach"). It has lifeguards, showers, rest rooms, and food nearby.

Kalmus Beach, in Hyannis Port, is a fine, wide sandy beach with an area set aside for Windsurfers and a sheltered area good for children. It has a snack bar, rest rooms, showers, and lifeguards.

Nauset Beach in Orleans is 10 miles of wide, sandy ocean beach with low dunes and large waves good for bodysurfing or board surfing. There are lifeguards, rest rooms, showers, and a food concession. It's open to off-road vehicles.

Old Silver Beach in North Falmouth is a long, beautiful crescent of soft white sand, with the Sea Crest resort hotel at one end. It is especially good for small children because a sandbar keeps it shallow at one end and makes tidal pools with crabs and minnows. There are lifeguards, rest rooms, showers, and a snack bar.

Sandy Neck Beach in West Barnstable, a 6-mile barrier beach between the bay and marshland, is one of the Cape's most beautiful, a wide swath of pebbly sand backed by dunes extending to what looks like forever in both directions. There are lifeguards, a snack bar, rest rooms, and showers. Camping and four-wheel-drive vehicles are allowed on parts of the beach.

South Cape Beach in Mashpee is a mile-long state beach on warm Nantucket and Vineyard sounds, reachable via Great Neck Road south from the Mashpee rotary. Wide, sandy (pebbly in parts), with low dunes and marshland, it's a beach where you can walk a bit for privacy. Its only services are portable toilets. A 2-mile hiking trail loops through marsh areas and ponds.

Veterans Park in Hyannis has a small beach that is especially good for children since it is sheltered from waves and fairly shallow. It offers picnic tables, barbecue facilities, showers, rest rooms, and a playground.

West Dennis Beach is a popular, long and wide sandy beach on the warmer south shore. There's a very open feeling, since the beach goes on for 1½ miles, with marshland and Bass River across from it. Windsurfer rentals are available, as are bathhouses, lifeguards, a playground, food, and parking for 1,000 cars.

Freshwater Beaches

Flax Pond in Nickerson State Park (*see* Nature Areas, *below*) in Brewster, surrounded by pines, offers picnic areas, a bathhouse, and water sports rentals.

Flax Pond in South Yarmouth offers swimming, a lifeguard, and ducks but no beach, just pine-needle-covered ground. There's a piney picnic area with grills, as well as tennis and basketball courts.

Scargo Lake in Dennis has two beaches (access off Route 6A or Scargo Hill Road) that offer rest rooms and a picnic area. The sandy-bottomed lake is shallow along the shore (good for kids), surrounded by attractive woods, and stocked for fishing.

Nature Areas

Ashumet Holly and Wildlife Sanctuary (*see* Tour 2, *above*).

Cape Cod National Seashore (*see* Tours 5 and 6, *above*).

Monomoy National Wildlife Refuge is a 2,750-acre preserve on Monomoy Island, a fragile, 9-mile-long barrier-beach area (actually composed of two islands) south of Chatham (*also see* Tour 4, *above*). An important stop along the North Atlantic Flyway for migratory waterfowl and shore birds (peak migration times are May and late July), it provides nesting and resting grounds for 285 species, including large nesting colonies of great blackbacked, herring, and laughing gulls and several tern species. White-tailed deer also live on the islands, and harbor and gray seals frequent the shores in winter.

Monomoy is a very quiet, peaceful place of sand and beach grass; of tidal flats, dunes, marshes, freshwater ponds, thickets of bayberry and beach plum and a few pines. Because the refuge harbors several endangered species, visitors' activities are limited; certain areas are fenced off to protect nesting areas of terns and the endangered piping plover. The Audubon Society and others conduct tours of the island (*see* Guided Tours in Essential Information, *above*); the ***Rip Ryder*** (tel. 508/587–4540 or 508/945–5450) will taxi you over in season for some lone bird-watching. The only structure on Monomoy is the South Island Lighthouse. Built in 1849, the shiny red-orange structure, along with the keeper's house, was refurbished in 1988.

Roland C. Nickerson State Park (Rte. 6A, Brewster 02631, tel. 508/896–3491; map available on-site) is more than 2,000 acres of white pine, hemlock, and spruce forest dotted with seven freshwater kettle ponds (formed by glacial deposits). Some ponds are stocked with trout; other recreational opportunities are biking along 8 miles of paved trail (with access to the Rail Trail), canoeing, sailing, motorboating, picnicking, bird-watching (thrushes, wrens, warblers, woodpeckers, finches, larks, Canada geese, cormorants, great blue herons, hawks, owls, osprey), and ice-skating and cross-country skiing in winter. Wildlife includes red foxes and white-tailed deer. Tent and RV camping (418 sites; no hookups) is extremely popular here, and visitor programs are offered in season.

Scusset Beach Reservation (140 Scusset Beach Rd., off Rte. 3, Sandwich 02532, tel. 508/888–0859) is 450 acres near the canal, with a cold-water beach on the bay. Its pier is a popular fishing spot; other activities include biking, hiking, picnicking, and tent and RV camping on its 103 sites (some wooded).

Shawme-Crowell State Forest (Rte. 130, Sandwich 02563, tel. 508/888–0351) is 742 acres less than a mile from the canal. Activities include wooded tent and RV camping (280 sites; no hookups), biking, and hiking; campers get free day use of Scusset Beach. Open-air campfires are allowed.

Waquoit Bay National Estuarine Research Reserve (off Rte. 28, Falmouth; Box 3092, Waquoit 02536, tel. 508/457–0495) is 2,500 acres of estuary and barrier beach around the bay. It encompasses South Cape Beach (*see* Beaches, *above*), where interpretive walks are held; Washburn Island, reachable by private boat or by Saturday morning tours (call to reserve), offering 330 acres of pine barrens and trails, 11 primitive campsites (permit required), and swimming; and reserve headquarters, a 23-acre estate where, in summer, evening talks are held (*see* Nightlife, *below*) and guided field trips begin.

Wellfleet Bay Wildlife Sanctuary is a 1,000-acre haven for more than 250 species of birds, attracted by the varied habitats found here. Hiking trails lead through woods, past moors and salt marshes that rim Cape Cod Bay. The Massachusetts Audubon Society refuge sponsors walks, hikes, birding, nature classes, day camps for children (*see* What to See and Do with Children, *above*), and week-long field schools for adults, camping, seabird and marsh cruises, snorkeling, canoe and kayak trips, evening slide shows, and evening bat watches; a schedule is available on-site, or write for one. A new nature center has aquariums and other exhibits, plus a gift shop. *Off Rte. 6 (Box 236), South Wellfleet 02663, tel. 508/349–2615. Admission: $3 adults, $2 children 6–15. Open daily 8 AM–dusk.*

Dining

Based on reviews by Malcolm Wilson, the longtime restaurant reviewer for the Cape Cod Times.

New England cooking—hearty meat-and-potatoes fare—is the cuisine of choice on the Cape, plus, of course, the ubiquitous New England clam chowder and fresh fish and seafood. A number of extraordinary gourmet restaurants coexist with the bastions of tradition, however, along with the occasional purveyor of ethnic cuisines. Portuguese specialties such as kale soup or *linguiça* are found on many menus, thanks to the long history of seafaring Portuguese who have settled on the Cape. In Provincetown you'll find over 80 restaurants—some excellent—in season, and a few hearties year-round. At these little waterfront or back-street places, Italian and Portuguese cuisines and seafood predominate, but there's a wide variety.

In the off-season especially, many Cape restaurants offer "early-bird specials"—low-price dinners in early evening—and Sunday brunches and buffets, often with musical accompaniment. These are advertised in the newspapers.

Category	Cost*
Very Expensive	over $40
Expensive	$25–$40
Moderate	$15–$25
Inexpensive	under $15

*per person, excluding drinks, service, and sales tax (5%)

Upper Cape

Buzzards Bay
Inexpensive–Moderate

Stir Crazy. Southeast Asian dishes are served at this little box of a restaurant, given a bit of exotic flavor with baskets and posters from the owner's native Cambodia. There are no tame flavors here. The Thai *me-siam* is sautéed minced pork, tofu, soybean, coconut milk, and chili on a bed of bean sprouts and rice noodles topped with peanut sauce; the deep-fried finger egg roll appetizer is filled with chopped pork and vegetables and served with a very hot sauce. *100 Main St., tel. 508/759–1781. No reservations. Dress: casual. MC, V. BYOB. No lunch Sun. Closed Mon. and mid-Dec.–mid-Jan.*

East Sandwich
Moderate

Michael's at Sandy Neck. The twin-lobster special—in peak season, Michael's sells at least 3,000 lobsters a week—is the trademark of this relaxed restaurant, with a pubby dining room of exposed beams and white plaster walls, and a glassed-in porch with paper-covered tables you can color on. Fresh swordfish is another specialty, broiled, grilled, or blackened; Italian dishes include veal, chicken, and shrimp piccata and pasta primavera. Homemade loaves of bread accompany meals. *674 Rte. 6A, tel. 508/362–4303 or 800/362–4303. Reservations advised. Dress: casual. MC, V. No smoking.*

Falmouth
Expensive
★

Regatta of Falmouth-by-the-Sea. A spectacular view of the Inner Harbor and the Vineyard Sound from the window-wrapped front room is matched by creative Continental and ethnic cuisines. Classic sauces and reductions are applied to regional and local fish dishes (grilled swordfish, sautéed salmon) and to more exotic dishes such as Thai lobster and spicy lacquered duck with Oriental greens. New in 1993 were crabcakes and lobster, oyster, and corn fritters. The restaurant has a soft, elegant look, with contemporary decor in pinks, mauve, and white; tables set with Limoges porcelain and hand-blown oil lamps; a large Caribbean-color tropical fish tank inset into a room divider; and waterscape murals. *217 Clinton Ave., Falmouth harbor, tel. 508/548–5400. Reservations advised. Dress: smart casual. AE, MC, V. No lunch Sat.; closed Oct.–Memorial Day.*

Moderate–
Expensive
★

Coonamessett Inn. A classic New England hostelry, this elegant place built in 1796 retains all its old-fashioned charm. The main dining room features paintings by Ralph Cahoon; his signature hot-air balloons are re-created in copper and enamel to form hanging sculptures-cum-planters that add a touch of whimsy to an otherwise subdued and romantic room. The mostly white garden room has a window wall overlooking a leafy pond. The regional American menu focuses on fresh fish and seafood, such as lobster pie: crunchy chunks baked in a ramekin with a light breading and a filling of cream, butter, and sherry. A heart-healthy dish is offered each night. *Jones Rd., tel. 508/548–2300. Reservations advised. Dress: smart casual. AE, DC, MC, V. Closed Mon. Jan.–Mar.*

Moderate

The Flying Bridge. A huge infusion of cash from new owners has transformed this restaurant right on the Inner Harbor into a great waterfront dining spot. From spiffy, nautical-style decks you can watch yachts pass by or tie up at the dock as buoy bells clang and flags flap in the breeze. Behind glass walls are multiple dining rooms and three lounges (one with fireplace), which offer free hors d'oeuvres weekdays and weekend entertainment year-round. The menu emphasizes seafood and ranges from grazing fare (appetizers, salads, all-day sandwiches) to full meals, such as lobster pie, chicken Cordon Bleu, and seafood ravioli with salmon sauce. *220 Scranton Ave., tel. 508/548–2700. No reservations. Dress: casual. AE, DC, MC, V.*

Inexpensive–
Moderate

Amigo's. This busy strip-mall restaurant, its rough barn-board and plaster walls brightened with Mexican art and Tiffany lamps, serves good traditional Mexican fare—try the *sopa de elote*, a creamy soup of ground corn with nubbles of niblets, tomato, and crunchy onion—as well as "gringo food" and nightly specials such as blackened fish. A children's menu has several offerings for $3. *Tataket Sq., Rte. 28, tel. 508/548–8510. Reservations for 6 or more. Dress: casual. MC, V.*

Mashpee
Inexpensive–
Expensive
★

The Flume. For 20 years this clean, plain fish house, decorated only with a few Indian artifacts and crafts (the owner is a Wampanoag chief), has offered a small menu of New England–style food guaranteed to satisfy. The chowder is perhaps the Cape's best; other specialties are fried smelts and clams, broiled local scrod and bluefish, codfish cakes and beans, roast duck and turkey, pot roast, and Indian pudding. In spring, look for herring roe (from the local run) with bacon; in summer there's sautéed Maryland soft-shell crabs. *Lake Ave. (off Rte. 130), tel. 508/477–1456. Reservations limited. Dress: casual. MC, V. Closed some weekdays in the off-season.*

New Seabury
Expensive
★

Popponesset Inn. Combine a magnificent ocean view with comfortable dining in the ultimate Cape summer restaurant and you have this charming spot, which attracts a loyal clientele year after year. Gray-shingled buildings house a series of bright and airy white-and-blue dining rooms, some open to the sky, others enclosed by glass, but all witness to the varying moods of Nantucket Sound beyond the waving beach grass. Weather permitting, there's beachfront dining under a tent or at umbrellaed café tables. The cuisine is traditional New England with a strong emphasis on seafood, such as clam chowder; baked stuffed lobster with shrimp, scallops, and lobster; or herb-roast rack of lamb. The oceanview lounge, Poppy's, serves a lighter menu. There's dancing to a band weekends. *Shore Dr., tel. 508/477–1100 or 508/477–8258. Reservations advised. Jacket preferred. AE, MC, V. Closed Nov.–Mar.; closed Mon. and Tues. before May 1 and after Labor Day; no lunch before mid-June and after Labor Day.*

Sagamore
Inexpensive–Moderate
★ **The Bridge.** Known for good food and a warm welcome, The Bridge has several small dining rooms with recessed lighting. Helen Trout has been cooking Yankee pot roast for more than 30 years, and the menu doesn't lie when it says "nobody can cook a bottom round like Helen." The eclectic menu also offers two versions of *bijoux de la mer*—lobster, scallops, and shrimp with lemon-tarragon butter and a mushroom cream sauce or stir-fried with garlic butter and vegetables—and homemade tortellini *casagrande*, stuffed with chicken and topped with meat sauce. *Rte. 6A, tel. 508/888–8144. Reservations advised on weekends. Dress: casual. D, DC, MC, V.*

★ **Sagamore Inn.** Seek out this diamond in the rough for homestyle Italian and Yankee dishes and seafood served in a family atmosphere. Inside, the look is old Cape, with captain's chairs, wood tables and booths, stamped-tin ceilings, and bare varnished floors. The food is top-notch: large, sweet fried shrimp, rich and simple chicken cacciatore, flawless eggplant Parmesan. Also on the menu are lobsters, pot roast, and homemade bread pudding and grapenut custard. *Rte. 6A, tel. 508/888–9707. No reservations. Dress: casual. AE, MC, V. Closed Tues. and Dec.–Mar.*

Sandwich
Moderate–Expensive
★ **Dan'l Webster Inn.** The Colonial New England patina of this inn, conveyed in the decor and the costumed servers, belies its construction in 1971, on the ruins of the landmark original inn. The glassed-in conservatory has colonial-style chandeliers and lush greenery; another room has an open hearth. The changing regional American and Continental menu emphasizes seafood—such as lobster, shrimp, scallops, and scrod baked with white wine and breaded topping—and includes vegetarian offerings. Early-bird specials and Sunday brunch are offered year-round. The wine cellar has many times won the *Wine Spectator* Award of Excellence. *149 Main St., tel. 508/888–3622. Reservations advised. Dress: smart casual. AE, D, DC, MC, V.*

Mid-Cape

Barnstable
Moderate–Expensive
Mattakeese Wharf. Extending over the water on pilings, with a view of the warehouses and general helter-skelter of Barnstable Harbor, this relaxed restaurant has a popular waterside bar (entertainment on summer weekends), a nautical-look dining room, and a glassed-in deck (newly renovated and now heated) over the water. The varied menu features seafood (including bouillabaisse in a tomato-saffron broth) and several pasta dishes. Try the lightly breaded broiled scrod or roast prime rib. *271 Millway, Barnstable Harbor, tel. 508/362–4511.*

Reservations requested. Dress: casual. AE, DC, MC, V. Closed Nov.–Apr.

Cotuit   **Regatta of Cotuit.** This sister restaurant to the Regatta in Fal-
Moderate– mouth is set in an 18th-century landmark stagecoach inn with
Expensive original woodwork and wide-board floors (the restored original
★ taproom offers an inexpensive light menu and jazz piano).
Its intimate dining rooms are romantically lit with brass chandeliers and candle-bulb wall sconces. Oriental carpets and Limoges china add touches of luxury. The cuisine is elegant
American, with grilled foods a specialty (like the mixed grill of
three fish, each with its own sauce), as well as sautés and pâtés
of rabbit, veal, or venison. The signature dish, rack of lamb *en
chemise,* is outstanding: The lamb is carved from the bone, surrounded by *chèvre,* spinach, and pine nuts, wrapped in puff pastry, and served with a cabernet sauvignon sauce. *Rte. 28, tel.
508/428–5715. Reservations advised. Dress: smart casual. AE,
MC, V. Dinner only. Closed Jan.–Apr.*

Dennis   **Gina's by the Sea.** An intimate little bistro by the bay (perfectly
Moderate– situated for an after-dinner beach walk), Gina's serves some of
Expensive the tastiest food on the Cape. The interior has exposed beams,
knotty pine walls, a fireplace, and nicely set tables with white
cloths, flowers, and candles. The Northern Italian menu is supplemented with seafood specials. Chicken Gismonda is a moist
breast of chicken lightly breaded, sautéed in butter, and served
on a bed of spinach, garnished with mushrooms sautéed in Madeira sauce—a polished dish. *134 Taunton Ave., tel. 508/385–
3213. No reservations. Dress: casual. AE, MC, V. Closed
Dec.–Mar.; June–Aug., lunch and dinner daily; Apr.–May and
Sept.–Nov., dinner only, and closed Mon.–Wed.*

★ **Red Pheasant Inn.** The main dining room is pleasantly intimate
and rustic, with stripped pine floors, exposed beams, candle-
lighted tables, Victorian lighting, and two fireplaces; the Garden Room is hung with plants. The cuisine is American
regional, with a French twist in the sauces. The large menu
always features a roast lamb special—such as the rack with
garlic cream and a red-pepper coulis—as well as game and seafood. The grilled veal porterhouse chop comes with grilled endive and Stilton sauce. The long wine list is a *Wine Spectator*
award winner. *905 Main St. (Rte. 6A), tel. 508/385–2133. Reservations strongly advised. Dress: smart casual. D, MC, V. Dinner
only.*

Moderate   **Playhouse Restaurant.** This institution of pre- and post-theater
dining (where the chance of rubbing elbows with the perform-
ers adds an element of excitement) offers such simply prepared
dishes as broiled and baked fish, chicken pie, and lots of sautés,
such as shrimp with raisins, pine nuts, garlic, and basil. The
front room is bright and airy, surrounded on three sides by
small-pane windows and decorated in soft peach and powder
blue under a white cathedral ceiling. The back dining room, by
the bar, is a crowded, cozy spot prettily decorated with dark
navy flowered chintz. Charcoal etchings of stage stars add to
the theatrical ambience. *36 Hope La., off Rte. 6A, tel. 508/385–
8000. Reservations advised. Dress: casual. AE, D, MC, V. Usually dinner only (lunch on some matinee days). Closed
mid-Jan.–Mar.*

Rose's. Though Rose recently passed away, the restaurant she
and her husband, Angelo Stocchetti, opened in 1946 carries on
the tradition in her family's hands. There are several New Eng-

land–style dining rooms, as well as a glassed-in white room with a flagstone floor and a wishing well with (fake) birds on branches. Veal is the specialty, as in saltimbocca or veal scallops sautéed in lemon butter on fettuccine. The *calamaretti alla Ronaldo* (squid in a lobster-tomato sauce) and mussels in cream and wine, both served on linguini, are delicious. *Black Flats Rd., tel. 508/385–3003. Reservations advised on weekends. Dress: casual. MC, V. Dinner only. Closed Feb.–Mar.; also Mon. Apr.–May and mid-Oct.–Jan.*

Scargo Cafe. Across Route 6A from the Cape Playhouse stands this romantic old sea captain's house. One cozy room has a fireplace and exquisite, highly polished golden oak paneling, another has large windows that let in the sun at lunch, a third has nautical prints of whaling ships. New in 1993 were sauté dishes that allow you to pick your protein (beef, chicken, scallops, shrimp) and your sauces (peanut, Creole, garlic) for a meal served in the skillet. The rest of the menu mixes fish, Italian dishes and pastas, and such specials as chicken Wildcat (sautéed with apricot brandy, mushrooms, raisins, and sausage). Food is served until midnight in summer. *799 Rte. 6A, tel. 508/385–8200. Reservations accepted for 5 or more. Dress: casual. AE, D, MC, V.*

Dennisport
*Inexpensive–
Moderate*

Bob Briggs' Wee Packet. Famous for good food and good value since 1949, this little dinette/restaurant is done up in Cape kitsch—canary-yellow tables, Cape art, and driftwood and shells everywhere. From the kitchen—open to view and immaculate—comes fried or broiled fresh local seafood (fish-and-chips, charbroiled swordfish, Cape bay scallops), a light menu, and sandwiches. Desserts include homemade blueberry shortcake and bread pudding with lemon sauce. *Depot St., tel. 508/398–2181. No reservations. Dress: casual. MC, V. Closed Oct.–Apr.*

Hyannis
*Moderate–
Expensive*
★

The Paddock. Long the benchmark of consistent quality dining, this formal restaurant is decorated in Victorian style, from the dark, pubby bar to the airy summer-porch area filled with green rattan and large potted plants. The main dining room is a blend of dark beams, frosted-glass dividers, sporting art, upholstered banquettes, and Victorian armchairs. The wine list has won *Wine Spectator* awards for years. The traditional Continental-American menu emphasizes seafood (including 2-pound lobsters) and beef, such as steak *au poivre*—pounded with crushed peppercorns, sautéed in shallot butter, and flamed with cognac. Appetizers include escargots and chilled raspberry soup. *W. Main St. rotary (next to Melody Tent), tel. 508/775–7677. Reservations advised. Dress: smart casual. AE, DC, MC, V. Closed mid-Nov.–Mar.*

Penguin Sea Grill. The former Three Thirty One Main, or "Penguins Go Pasta," has undergone a sea change. In its new incarnation (under the same ownership and management) it is a classic seafood grill, serving pasta dishes such as pasta Fiore—shrimp, scallops, and lobster with mushrooms, scallions, sherry, and cream on angelhair—alongside Oriental, Caribbean, Spanish, Portuguese, and other choices. Chinatown seafood is shrimp, scallops, monkfish, and lobster Szechwan on angelhair with red chillies and black beans. Breads and desserts are homemade. The two-level dining room has been redone in earth tones; reflecting the new theme, wood carvings of crabs and a 9-foot-long fish adorn the brick walls (which alternate with mirrors and paneling). *331 Main St., tel. 508/775–*

2023. Reservations advised. Dress: casual. AE, DC, MC, V. No lunch weekends.

Roadhouse Cafe. This consistently fine downtown restaurant serves a mix of seafood (New England and Italian style, such as calamari marinara), pastas, and the very popular Italian cioppino, plus a light menu. The interior is cozy and attractive, with Oriental carpets on polished hardwood floors, exposed beams, lots of hanging plants, local art, and a fireplace. The Espresso Bar Lounge, in a new addition, is a clubby room with dark wood paneling and ceiling, Cape antiques, a fireplace, and a Chicago-style mahogany bar that offers 20 wines by the glass, 44 beers, and of course, espresso and cappuccino. Early-bird specials are offered year-round, and there's live jazz Thursday nights in the off season. *488 South St., tel. 508/775–2386. Reservations advised. Dress: casual. AE, D, DC, MC, V.*

Moderate **Fazio's Trattoria.** Chef/owners Tom and Eileen Fazio, formerly
★ of San Francisco's North Beach area, have brought their considerable talents to this small and warm trattoria, with candles on red-and-white-checkered tablecloths, photographs of Sicily, and robust Italian ballads adding the right atmospheric notes. From the new wood-burning ovens come breads and pizzas; everything from vegetables to chops to seafood are cooked on the new wood grill. Popular dishes include *pesce spada*, grilled swordfish with oil and lemon; and *penne salsiccia*, pasta with a sauce of sausages, roasted peppers, olives, onions, and fresh tomatoes. The sausages, along with desserts like cannoli and zabaglione, are strictly homemade. *586 Main St., tel. 508/771–7445. Reservations advised weekends. Dress: casual. MC, V. No lunch Sun.*

Harry's. Harry's is a great place for consistently good Continental and Cajun dishes that make use of local seafood. New Orleans and Toulouse-Lautrec posters decorate the walls, with plants and art-deco glass as accents. The hoppin' John (white rice and black-eyed peas), jambalaya, and blackened fish are all excellent, as are the substantial sandwiches. Sundays (three nights a week in summer) feature live jazz, blues, or rock. *700 Main St., tel. 508/778–4188. No reservations. Dress: casual. AE, MC, V.*

★ **Up the Creek.** House specialties at this comfortable, casual spot include the broiled seafood platter (half-lobster, scallops, scrod, baked stuffed shrimp) and seafood strudel—two hollandaise-sauced pastries filled with lobster, shrimp, crab, cheese, and more. The baked stuffed lobster is excellent. *36 Old Colony Rd., tel. 508/771–7866. Reservations advised. Dress: casual. AE, D, DC, MC, V. 10% senior discount at lunch. Closed some weekdays in off season.*

Inexpensive– **Barbyann's.** The success of this place is due to its casual, com-
Moderate fortable interior—exposed-beam ceilings, subdued lighting, and green, pink, and red color scheme—as well as its low-priced, tasty food. The menu mixes seafood, steak and prime rib, teriyaki, Mexican dishes, pizza, burgers, fun appetizers, and sandwiches. The Buffalo chicken wings, fried clams, and serious homemade chili are excellent. There's a patio with umbrella tables, and early birds are offered Monday–Thursday. *120 Airport Rd., tel. 508/775–9795. No reservations. Dress: casual. AE, D, DC, MC, V.*

★ **Baxter's Fish N' Chips.** Right on busy Lewis Bay, the ever-popular Baxter's gets a lot of swimsuit-clad boaters at its picnic tables for possibly the best fried clams on the Cape, as well as other fried, baked, and broiled fresh fish and seafood, lobsters, steamers, and mussels (plus burgers, chicken, and Cajun steak for landlubbers) and offerings from a raw bar on wheels in season. It's a fun place to watch boats at play while you dine. The indoor Baxter's Boat House Club—an airy, open room with sliding glass doors leading to deck tables, paintings of ships, copper lanterns, and a busy bar—has the same menu, plus specials. *Pleasant St., tel. 508/775-4490. No reservations. Dress: casual. MC, V. Closed Columbus Day–Apr.; weekdays Labor Day–Columbus Day.*

Sam Diego's. Traditional Mexican (and a few gringo) dishes are served until midnight amid a rather generic Mexican ambience—ornamental toucans, draped serapes, and sombreros. It's popular with families, but you'll find mostly young singles at the crowded good-time bar. An interesting dessert is the crusty deep-fried ice cream, served in a giant goblet. *950 Iyanough Rd. (Rte. 132), tel. 508/771-8816. No reservations. Dress: casual. AE, D, MC, V.*

Starbuck's. The decor is sort of Hard Rock Café but without a theme—from the rafters and on the walls of this "Good Time Eating and Drinking Place" hang flags, a sled, a mannequin, a miniature Fokker D-7, carved pigs, a tuba, and weather vanes. Everything is orchestrated in a glitzy, with-it way. The menu is huge and eclectic: Choose from burgers and sandwiches or Chinese, Japanese, Italian, Cajun, and Mexican dishes. If you're annoyed by the live band on off-season weekends, console yourself with the long menu of exotic and frozen drinks. *645 Rte. 132, tel. 508/778-6767. Reservations 1 hr in advance advised weekends. Dress: casual. AE, D, DC, MC, V.*

Osterville
Moderate–
Expensive
★

East Bay Lodge. The casually elegant main dining room, part glassed-in veranda, suggests the 1880s summer house the inn once was. The creative menu—presided over by a top-notch staff, including a full-time pastry chef—may feature such appetizers as wild mushroom tart, seafood sausage, and chilled poached salmon. Entrées, which include grilled fish, shellfish, and meat dishes, also feature such selections as crisp breast of duck with sour apples, almonds, and a bourbon sauce with vanilla, served with risotto cake; and lobster Royale for two (a sauté of scallops, the meat of a 3-pound lobster, and mushrooms in a velouté sauce served in the lobster shell). Sweetbreads and venison are featured in fall. Sundays there's a lavish brunch buffet, followed (in summer) by an evening shellfish buffet. The 425-item wine list boasts some extraordinary bottles. There's jazz and cabaret piano in the lounge many nights. *199 East Bay Rd., tel. 508/428-5200. Reservations advised. Jacket requested. AE, D, DC, MC, V. Dinner and Sun. brunch only.*

West Dennis
Inexpensive–
Moderate

Christine's. Lebanese specialties complement a mostly Italian menu offering homemade meatballs and sausages, excellent steaks, and baked and fried seafood. The dining room is large and pleasant, with etched glass, Tiffany lamps over booths and tables, lots of greenery, and watercolors and lithographs. There's a Sunday buffet brunch and a nightclub offering entertainment and dancing year-round (*see* Nightlife, *below*). *Rte. 28, tel. 508/394-7333. No reservations. Dress: casual. AE, D, MC, V.*

Yarmouth Port **Abbicci.** Inside an 18th-century cottage is a surprisingly mod-
Moderate– ern setting in Mondrianesque primary colors—white, black,
Expensive bright yellow and blue—with a black slate bar and steel-back
★ chairs. The contemporary Italian cuisine emphasizes a clean
taste, with light use of oils and fats in such dishes as calves'
liver with polenta and balsamic vinegar, grilled veal chop with
wild mushrooms, or roast duck with vinegar-apricot sauce.
Also on the menu are a dozen elegant pasta dishes and a few
Continental favorites, like rack of lamb. In summer, the emphasis is on fish. *43 Main St. (Rte. 6A), tel. 508/362–3501. Reservations advised. Dress: casual. AE, D, DC, MC, V.*

Anthony's Cummaquid Inn. The main dining room is a spacious, genteel place with window walls that reveal a water view
of great beauty. Complemented by an impressive wine list is a
traditional New England menu featuring bouillabaisse, baked
lobster-stuffed fillet of sole with Newburg sauce, rack of lamb
bouquettière (with vegetables and roast potatoes), and an ex-
ceptionally good, oversize roast beef *au jus. Rte. 6A, tel.
508/362–4501. Reservations advised. Jacket requested. AE, D,
MC, V. Dinner and Sun. lunch only.*

Inaho. A Georgian-style Cape house has been transformed into
an atmospheric setting for the Cape's only Japanese restaurant, adorned with shoji screens and light woods in the main
dining room and bamboo and mosses in the Japanese garden
outside. The traditional fare at this chef-owned and -operated
spot includes tempura, teriyaki, shabu-shabu, a wide range of
sushi, and of course sake. *157 Main St., tel. 508/362–5522. Reservations advised. Dress: casual. MC, V. Dinner only. Closed
Mon. in off-season.*

Inexpensive **Jack's Outback.** This quirky place where customers get their
★ own coffee while exchanging barbs with the staff offers basic
and satisfying American home cooking: pot roast with mashed
potatoes and gravy, prime rib, fresh fish and seafood, superb
soups, and simple but exceptional desserts. (Jack's is hidden
"out back," down the driveway by Inaho.) *161 Main St., tel.
508/362–6690. No reservations. Dress: casual. No credit cards.
No dinner Sun. and Mon. No liquor allowed.*

Lower Cape

Brewster **Chillingsworth.** This elegant jewel—lauded by many as the
Very Expensive Cape's best restaurant—is lit by candles and decorated in
★ Louis XV antique and reproduction furnishings. The award-
winning French cuisine is lightened by use of vegetable es-
sences and oils, and there's an outstanding wine cellar. The
frequently changing dinner menu is a seven-course (including
sorbet and "amusements") prix fixe ($40–$50), served at seatings in season, and features such entrées as roast lobster with
spinach, haricots verts, and lobster-basil sause; or caramelized
sea scallops with tomato-tarragon coulis, garnished with fresh
sea beans and leek hair. A new dinner bistro menu (no reservations) is served in the casual Garden Room. Lunch is à la
carte, with no seatings. Desserts, made in-house, are glorious
and are available to take out. *2449 Main St. (Rte. 6A), tel.
508/896–3640. Reservations recommended. Jacket preferred at
dinner. AE, DC, MC, V. Mid-June–mid-Oct., closed Mon., no
lunch Tues.; Memorial Day–mid-June and mid-Oct.–Thanksgiving, closed some weekdays. Closed Thanksgiving–Memorial
Day.*

Expensive **High Brewster.** The setting at High Brewster's is ideal: a restored farmhouse-cum-country inn, overlooking a pond, where low ceilings and dark exposed beams create a rich and intimate feel. Five-course prix-fixe menus ($33–$38) feature American regional cuisine and change seasonally; a fall menu might include pumpkin-and-sage bisque, tenderloin medallions with chives and cheese glaze, and apple crisp with maple syrup, walnuts, and apple rum ice cream. A six-course tasting dinner is offered once a week. Accommodations are available. *964 Satucket Rd., tel. 508/896–3636. Reservations required. Jacket suggested. AE, MC, V. Dinner only. Closed 1st 2 wks in Jan.; many weekdays in the off-season (call for days).*

Chatham **Chatham Bars Inn.** The high-ceilinged formal dining room of
Expensive– this grand hotel is a study in white, from walls and woodwork
Very Expensive to ceiling fans, crisp linens, and little bulbs in brass lantern wall sconces—set off admirably by the blue of the sea framed in the floor-to-ceiling windows. The creative American menu includes such temptations as pan-seared foie gras with figs, roasted shallots, and Armagnac sauce; and steamed salmon and cherrystone clams seasoned with bay leaves and lemon. Grand Sunday dinner buffets feature ice carvings, a raw bar (including caviar and half lobsters), and much more. Lavish buffet breakfasts are served daily year-round. A 17% service charge is added to all bills. *Shore Rd., tel. 508/945–0096 or 800/527–4884. Reservations required. Jacket and tie requested at night. AE, DC, MC, V. No lunch; no dinner Sun.–Thurs. (except holiday weekends) Nov.–Mar.*

Expensive **Christian's.** Billed as "an elegant Yankee restaurant," Chris-
★ tian's does have a certain panache. The look of the 1818 house's downstairs dining room is a mix of French country and old Cape Cod: exposed beams painted Colonial blue, wall sconces with parchment shades, and lace-covered tables. The cuisine is creative Continental and American, represented by such dishes as boneless roast duck with raspberry sauce, chicken with macadamia-nut breading and a grain-mustard cream sauce, or superior sautéed sole with lobster and a lemon-butter sauce. The mahogany-paneled piano bar/bistro upstairs serves a light, fish-based menu, and there's dining on an outdoor deck. *443 Main St., tel. 508/945–3362. Reservations advised. Dress: casual. AE, D, DC, MC, V. Closed some weekdays in off-season; downstairs closed Columbus Day–Apr. (except holidays).*

Moderate– **The Impudent Oyster.** A longtime favorite in this part of the
Expensive Cape, this restaurant just off Main Street is a big, comfortable room with a high ceiling, exposed beams, large hanging plants, and soft lighting from frosted-glass fixtures. The most popular menu items are grilled veal piccata—medallions with French mustard, rosemary, and lemon-butter sauce. In summer, bouillabaisse and seafoods *fra diavolo* are added to the menu. *15 Chatham Bars Ave., tel. 508/945–3545. Reservations requested in summer. Dress: casual. AE, MC, V.*

East Orleans **Kadee's Lobster & Clam Bar.** You can't help but feel happy sur-
Moderate– rounded by the bright colors of this souped-up summer clam
Expensive shack on the road to Nauset Beach. The choice seats are on the
★ deck, with flower boxes and flowered café-table umbrellas. From the immaculate and accomplished kitchen come oysters and littlenecks on the half shell, steamers and mussels with drawn butter or red pesto sauce, steamed peppered shrimp, seafood stews and a great Portuguese kale soup, chilled lob-

sters, clambakes, and broiled or fried seafood. Homemade
baked beans, corn on the cob, and steak fries are satisfying
accompaniments. There's takeout service, a gift shop with California-style summer items, and a minigolf course out back. *E.
Main St., tel. 508/255–6184. No reservations. Dress: casual. No
smoking indoors. MC, V. Closed Labor Day–Memorial Day.*

★ **Nauset Beach Club.** On the road to the beach, just past Kadee's,
is this casual restaurant that is packed inside and out (on the
deck) in summer. Set in an old duck-hunting cottage, it offers
superb, moderately priced Northern Italian dinners, including
homemade pastas (penne with pancetta in carbonara sauce,
lobster linguine with fresh tomato and sherry sauce), meat
dishes such as osso bucco, and specials based on local fish and
shellfish. The wine cellar is extensive. *222 E. Main St., tel.
508/255–8547. No reservations. Dress: casual. AE, D, DC, MC,
V. Dinner only. Thanksgiving–Mar., closed Sun.–Mon.*

Harwich Port **Thompson's Clam Bar.** A perennial favorite for fresh fish,
Moderate– Thompson's has been renovated extensively over the past few
Expensive years. The new look is swanky/clubby nautical, with a window
wall overlooking the scenic harbor, varnished wood tables, a
huge mahogany circular bar, and a cranberry-glass clerestory.
The harborfront patio is a popular spot for lunch or watching
sunsets over cocktails and selections from the raw bar or a light
menu. Regular menu highlights are lobster served several
ways, a fisherman's platter (an oversize assortment of fried fish
and shellfish, onion rings, and shoestring potatoes), and a true
shore dinner (chowder, steamers, boiled lobster, corn on the
cob, and watermelon, plus sausage); nonfish choices are available, as is a children's menu. There's acoustic entertainment
on summer weekends in the bar. The upstairs HarborWatch
Room offers a more expensive Continental menu in more formal, Victorian surroundings, with a harbor view (reservations
advised; dress: smart casual; closed mid-Sept.–May). *Snow
Inn Rd., off Rte. 28, tel. 508/432–3595. No reservations. Dress:
casual. AE, D, DC, MC, V. Closed mid-Sept.–mid-June.*

North Truro **Whitman House.** An inn since 1894, this elegant tavern has a
Moderate cozy Early American feel, with brick and dark barnboard walls,
handhewn posts, exposed ceiling beams, and hurricane lanterns on cloth-draped tables. Crackers and cheese, lavish salads, and loaves of homebaked bread accompany such finely
prepared traditional entrées as lobsters and prime rib, several
surf-and-turf combinations, teriyakis, or lightly blackened
swordfish or chicken. *Rte. 6, tel. 508/487–1740. Reservations advised on weekends, nightly in summer. Dress: casual. AE, DC,
MC, V. Dinner only. Closed Jan.–Mar.*

Orleans **Captain Linnell House.** Framed by huge trees, this neoclassic
Moderate– structure with dramatic Ionic columns looks like an antebellum
Expensive mansion transported to Cape Cod. Inside is a small dining room
★ with pecan-paneled fireplace, Aubusson rug, and crystal chandeliers beneath a ceiling rosette; in another room, rose chintz
drapes frame floor-to-ceiling windows overlooking a Victorian
folly garden. Among offerings on the classic American menu
are rack of lamb; sautéed Wellfleet oysters with Champagne-
ginger sauce and julienned vegetables; and scrod in parchment
with crabmeat, shrimp, and a lime-vermouth sauce. There's
dancing Friday nights in the off-season to big band or '50s
sounds in the lounge. *137 Skaket Beach Rd., tel. 508/255–3400.*

Reservations required in season. Dress: casual. MC, V. No lunch June–Oct. (except Sun. buffet brunch year-round).

Off the Bay Cafe. This is an easygoing storefront restaurant with pressed-tin ceiling, antique brass fixtures, lots of polished woodwork (including golden pine wainscoting) and a hunter-green-and-white color scheme softened with floral-print linens. The regional American cooking centers on fresh grilled seafood, aged beef, wild game, and pastas. Highlights may include paillard of veal with garlic, shallot, and lemon cream sauce; simple broiled scrod with lemon butter and capers; smoked fish and meats; and rotisseried game birds and duck. An inexpensive light menu is always available. There's a jazz brunch on Sunday. *28 Main St., tel. 508/255–5505. Reservations advised on Sat., nightly in season. Dress: casual. AE, D, DC, MC, V. Closed Mon. in off-season.*

Old Jailhouse Tavern. Tucked away on a rural side road is this 100-year-old house, renovated with a prize-winning architectural design and an all-glass conservatory addition. The contemporary interior—a stunning display of brass, etched glass, and the original grouted stone (the stone room was once used as a jail by the sheriff who lived in the house)—is softened with natural oak and greenery. The cuisine is eclectic, including everything from barbecued chicken and ribs to filet mignon and broiled seafood sampler. The taste bud–popping toast Nelson is crusty French bread smothered with bacon, crunchy onion, crabmeat, shrimp, scallops, hollandaise sauce, and Parmesan cheese. A late-night menu is offered until midnight. Sunday brunch is served in the off season. *28 West Rd., tel. 508/255–5245. No reservations. Dress: casual. D, MC, V.*

Moderate **Land Ho!** Walk in, grab a newspaper from the lending rack, take a seat, and relax—for 25 years Land Ho! has been making folks feel right at home. Decorated in a jumble of quarter boards and business signs, this casual spot serves kale soup that has made *Gourmet* magazine, plus burgers, hearty sandwiches, fresh native seafood, and very good chicken wings, chowder, and fish-and-chips. *Rte. 6A, tel. 508/255–5165. No reservations. Dress: casual. MC, V.*

Wellfleet **Aesop's Tables.** This restaurant in an 1800s house built from
Moderate– ships' timbers has served consistently fine meals since 1965.
Expensive The many dining areas include a summer porch, a brick patio overlooking the town, a romantic room with a fireplace, and a large art-deco-flavored room. The cuisine is new American, as in pan-roasted lamb chops with port-rosemary demiglaze and "uptown duck"—roast marinated duck with an orange-ginger reduction. Organic vegetables are featured, and Death by Chocolate, a heavy mousse cake, was voted best dessert on Cape Cod by *Boston* magazine. Late-afternoon "tea" offers scones, appetizers, and salads. There's acoustic and jazz entertainment in the tavern (a spacious parlor with sofas and marble-topped antique tables) Thursday nights in summer. *Main St., tel. 508/349–6450. Reservations advised. Dress: smart casual. AE, DC, MC, V. Dinner, afternoon tea, and Sun. brunch only. Closed Columbus Day–Mother's Day.*

Provincetown

Moderate– **Ciro's.** After three decades, Ciro's stage-set Italian restau-
Expensive rant—raffia-covered Chianti bottles hanging from the rafters,
★ plaster and brick walls, slate flooring, strains of Italian opera—

plays out its role with all the confidence of years on the boards. Hand-cut veal and pasta dishes are specialties; the extensive seafood selections include scampi *alla griglia*, grilled shrimp with lemon, parsley, garlic, butter, leeks, and shallots. *4 Kiley Ct., tel. 508/487–0049. Reservations strongly advised in summer and Sat. night year-round. Dress: casual. MC, V. Dinner only. Nov.–Memorial Day, closed Mon.–Thurs.*

Euro Island Grill & Café. An umbrella table on Euro's second-floor deck is a great vantage point for observing the Commercial Street parade while dining on Caribbean, Sicilian, or New England dishes, choosing from the raw bar, or sipping drinks from the outdoor Tiki bar. Other offerings, served outdoors or in the dramatic nightclub (*see* Nightlife, *below*), include Sicilian pizzas cooked on a stone hearth, clambakes, or grilled ribs, chicken, fish, and lobsters. *258 Commercial St., tel. 508/487–2505. No reservations. Dress: casual. AE, DC, MC, V. Closed Halloween–Memorial Day.*

Lobster Pot. A wide selection of seafood (including sashimi, 2-plus-pound lobsters, full clambakes), award-winning chowder, and homebaked breads are the specialties at this bustling family-run restaurant. The unfussy glass-walled dining room and the bar and outdoor deck upstairs overlook MacMillan Wharf and the harbor. There's a takeout lobster market and bakery on the premises. *321 Commercial St., tel. 508/487–0842. No reservations. Dress: casual. AE, D, DC, MC, V. Closed Jan.*

The Mews. A move in 1993 occasioned a stunning new look for this longtime local favorite. The downstairs main dining room (serving dinner and Sunday brunch) is bathed in light from a window wall with french doors that open onto the beach, offering views of boats in the harbor and moored at the breakwater. Pale-peachy plaster walls, adorned with art on loan from local galleries, match the color of the sand, spotlit at night. Furnishings and floor are in bleached woods; small Tiffany-style lamps light glass-topped tables. The seafood-centered menu offers an exciting mix of cuisines, which may include hummus, escargots *en croûte*, lobster dumplings (with ginger, scallions, and tomato and basil cream sauce), bouillabaisse, ratatouille with saffron couscous, glazed roast duck, and blackened scallops with tequila-lime butter. The upstairs piano bar (which serves lunch and dinner from a café menu) has the old Mermaid Bar's mahogany paneling and a water view. *429 Commercial St., tel. 508/487–1500. Reservations advised. Dress: casual. D, DC, MC, V. Closed mid-Nov.–mid-Feb.*

★ **Napi's.** A Provincetown institution, Napi's serves original and well-prepared food in a warm, casual art- and antiques-filled house of natural wood, exposed beams and brickwork, and stained-glass windows. The menu is large and eclectic: Middle Eastern, Moroccan, European, Oriental, vegetarian. Shrimp feta is shrimp flamed with ouzo and Metaxa, baked in tomato sauce, and topped with feta cheese. Chicken *chambeaux* is boneless chicken in white wine, tarragon, and a mushroom cream reduction. *7 Freeman St., tel. 508/487–1145. Reservations required in summer, advised off-season. Dress: casual. D, DC, MC, V. May–Oct., dinner only.*

Sal's Place. Homemade and imported Italian pastas and homemade desserts like *tiramisù* highlight the southern Italian menu at this waterfront trattoria. Specialties include shrimp Adriatica (shrimp and calamari with pesto sauce), saltimbocca, and spinach lasagna. The decor leans to wine basket-bottles and old photos and posters in the nonsmoking room out front; the back dining room and deck overlook the water. *99 Commercial St., tel. 508/487–1279. Reservations advised. Dress: casual. MC, V. Dinner only. Closed Nov.–Apr.; also Mon.–Thurs. before mid-June and after Oct. 1.*

Moderate **The Moors.** Built in 1956 by the townsfolk with flotsam and jetsam found on the beach after the original place burned down, this unique restaurant has authentic old-fishing-town flavor. Yellow light from two dozen lanterns and tabletop candle globes reveals walls and ceiling of driftwood planking hung with nautical items. The specialties are seafood and Portuguese cuisine, such as a delicious soup made from chourico and linguiça sausages; sea-clam pie and marinated swordfish steaks; and chicken with Madeira. Complete Portuguese dinners with a choice of three entrées are offered at $16–$18. There's entertainment in the lounge (*see* Nightlife, *below*). *5 Bradford St. Ext., tel. 508/487–0840. Reservations advised. Dress: casual. AE, D, DC, MC, V. Closed late Nov.–Mar.*

Lodging

With a tourism-based economy, the Cape naturally abounds in lodging places, including self-contained luxury resorts, grand old oceanfront hotels, chain hotels, mom-and-pop motels, antiques-filled bed-and-breakfasts, cottages, condominiums, and apartments. The Cape Cod Chamber of Commerce's "Resort Directory" lists hundreds of establishments, as well as many real-estate agencies dealing in rentals (*see also* Lodging in Chapter 1, Essential Information). Local chambers' guidebooks all carry information on realtors in their area, and the monthly full-color "Real Estate Book" (Box 10, West Hyannisport 02672, tel. 800/841–3401) includes rentals.

Choosing where to stay depends on the kind of vacation you have in mind. Beach lovers may choose on the basis of water temperature (bay and National Seashore waters are coldest, south-shore sound waters are warmest) or beach scenery and atmosphere (Seashore beaches are the dune-backed, windswept ones with no development allowed along the shore and miles of contiguous beaches for long walking and private sunning; Mid-Cape and Falmouth beaches are generally more circumscribed and crowded with families, though some are quite pretty, wide, and sandy).

Quiet, traditional villages with old-Cape flavor and several charming B&Bs with gardens and sometimes woodland settings are found in Sandwich and other towns along the north-shore Route 6A historic district. Access to the bay beaches and a number of shops and historical museums combine with the real country-road feeling of 6A to make for a leisurely getaway. Falmouth has village charm while providing all the amenities of the Cape's second-largest town, as well as proximity to the warmer south-shore beaches and to the ferry to Martha's Vineyard. Quiet, traditional Chatham, with upscale shops and superior accommodations, is well-positioned for day trips to Provincetown, Seashore beaches, and Hyannis.

Those who like more action should head for the Mid-Cape. The center of it all is Hyannis, with a busy Main Street and plenty of nightlife, along with some fine warm-water beaches; if you want to be near but not in it, consider one of the pretty surrounding villages, such as Centerville. Yarmouth encompasses the most developed stretch of Route 28 and is wall-to-wall tourist amenities, from motels with pools to seafood restaurants to minigolf and other activities—possibly a good choice for families with action-oriented children—as well as fishing and boating on Bass River.

For the austere Cape of dunes and sea, try the beach cottages of the sparsely developed Lower Cape between Wellfleet and Provincetown. Except in these two towns of artists and fishermen, there's not a lot of activity here, but especially in Truro there's escape and open vistas not possible elsewhere on the Cape, as well as spectacular long beaches. Provincetown is something completely different, a fun and (in summer) frantic wall-to-wall jumble of shops and houses bursting with colorful people, and a very active nighttime scene. Staying in town makes getting to everything by foot or bike possible; the edges of Commercial Street, away from the center, are relatively quiet. (The Provincetown Chamber of Commerce has a listing of inexpensive shared-bath guest houses that offer clean but very basic accommodations.) For a more secluded setting, you can stay in nearby Truro or Wellfleet and make day (or night) trips to town; the bayfront motels and cottages on Route 6A in North Truro, just outside Provincetown, are perhaps the best option for families, offering long sandy beaches, picnic areas, and often pools.

Finally, remember that the Cape is only 70 miles from end to end, so wherever you stay, you can always get there from here.

In summer, lodgings should be booked as far in advance as possible—several months for the most popular cottages and B&Bs. Assistance with last-minute reservations is available at the Cape Cod Chamber of Commerce information booths (*see* Essential Information, *above*). Off-season rates are much reduced, and service may be more personalized.

Reservations Services B&B services include **House Guests Cape Cod and the Islands** (Box 1881, Orleans 02653, tel. 508/896–7053 or 800/666–4678, fax 508/896–7054), with more than 100 B&Bs, cottages, and efficiencies; **Bed and Breakfast Cape Cod** (Box 341, West Hyannisport 02672–0341, tel. 508/775–2772, fax 508/775–2884), with about 90 on the Cape and islands; and **Orleans Bed & Breakfast Associates** (Box 1312, Orleans 02653, tel. 508/255–3824 or 800/541–6226, fax 508/255–2863), with 70 no-smoking B&Bs on the Lower Cape from Harwich to Truro. **Provincetown Reservations System** (293 Commercial St., Provincetown 02657, tel. 508/487–4620 or 800/648–0364) makes reservations year-round for accommodations, shows, restaurants, transportation, and more. **DestINNations** (tel. 800/333–4667) handles a limited number of hotels and B&Bs on the Cape and islands but will arrange any and all details of a visit.

Youth Hostels The homey **HyLand AYH-Hostel** (465 Falmouth Rd., Hyannis 02601, tel. 508/775–2970), on 3 acres of pine woods, offers 42 dorm beds and rental bikes March–November. **Mid-Cape AYH-Hostel** (75 Goody Hallet Dr., Eastham 02642, tel. 508/255–2785; open mid-May–mid-Sept.), on 3 wooded acres a 15-minute walk to the bay, has eight cabins sleeping six to eight each, plus volleyball and ping-pong. **Little America AYH-Hostel** (N. Pamet Rd., Box 402, Truro 02666, tel. 508/349–3889; open mid-June–

Labor Day), in a former Coast Guard station right on the dunes, has 42 beds.

Camping The Cape has many private campgrounds (ask the Cape Cod Chamber of Commerce for its listing), as well as camping at state parks and forests; tent and sleeping-bag rentals are available from **Eastern Mountain Sports** (Village Marketplace, 233 Stevens St., Hyannis, tel. 508/775–1072). Most popular with nature lovers is **Nickerson State Park** (*see* Nature Areas, *above*, for more on this and other state facilities). A surprise in this very traditional area is a family nudist campground, **Sandy Terraces** (Box 98, Marstons Mills 02648, tel. 508/428–9209). Although private campgrounds serve the area, the only camping permitted on the Cape Cod National Seashore itself is in nonrental, self-contained RVs at Race Point Beach.

Category	Cost*
Very Expensive	over $150
Expensive	$100–$150
Moderate	$75–$100
Inexpensive	under $75

all prices are for a standard double room in high season, excluding 5.7% state tax and 4% local tax

Upper Cape

East Sandwich **Earl of Sandwich Motor Manor.** Single-story Tudor-style buildings are ranged in a *U* around a duck pond and wooded lawn set with lawn chairs. Most rooms in the main building (1963) and the newer buildings (1981–83) have air-conditioning; all have phones and TVs. The decor is rather somber, with dark exposed beams on white ceilings, dark paneled walls, quarry-tile floors with Oriental throw rugs, and chenille bedspreads, but the rooms are a good size and have large Tudor-style windows and small tiled baths. *378 Rte. 6A, 02537, tel. 508/888–1415 or 800/442–3275. 24 rooms. Facilities: minifridges available. AE, D, DC, MC, V.*
Inexpensive

Falmouth **Coonamessett Inn.** Since 1953, this inn has been providing gracious accommodations and fine dining. One- or two-bedroom ★ suites are located in five buildings ranged around a broad, landscaped lawn that spills down to a scenic wooded pond—a tranquil country setting. Three suites directly overlook the pond. Rooms are casually decorated, with bleached wood or pine paneling, New England antiques or reproductions, upholstered chairs and couches, cable TV, and phones. A large collection of art by Ralph Cahoon is displayed throughout the inn. *Jones Rd. and Gifford St., Box 707, 02541, tel. 508/548–2300, fax 508/540–9831. 25 suites, 1 cottage. Facilities: 2 restaurants, lounge with entertainment, clothing shop. AE, DC, MC, V. Closed Mon. Jan.–Mar.*
Expensive

★ **Mostly Hall.** Set in a landscaped park far back from the street and separated from it by tall bushes, trees, and a wrought-iron fence, this inn looks very much like a private estate. The 1849 house itself is imposing, with a wraparound porch and a dramatic cupola (fitted out as a guest den with TV and travel library). Accommodations are in corner rooms, with leafy views through shuttered casement windows, reading areas, antique pieces and reproduction queen-size canopy beds, floral wallpapers, wall-to-wall carpeting, and Oriental accent rugs. First-floor rooms have 13-foot ceilings; most baths are small. *27 Main St., 02540, tel. 508/548–3786 or 800/682–0565. 6 rooms. Facilities: full breakfast, afternoon tea, central air-conditioning, bicycles, common TV/VCR, lending library, lawn games. MC, V. No smoking. Closed Jan.–mid-Feb.*

Moderate– Expensive **Quality Inn.** This inn, across from a pond a mile outside Falmouth center, has three buildings that were remodeled in 1989–90. Rooms are now large, with plush carpeting, contemporary pastel decor, wood-tone furniture, cable TV/HBO, and phones; suites have king-size beds, wet bars, and minifridges. The large pool area is bright and nicely arranged with patio furniture and greenery. Discount packages are available. *291 Jones Rd., 02540, tel. 508/540–2000 or 800/228–5151, fax 508/548–2712. 88 rooms, 5 suites. Facilities: heated indoor pool, room service, sauna, video game room, restaurant (in season), lounge with top-40s entertainment. Children under 18 stay free. AE, D, MC, V.*

Moderate **Admiralty Resort.** Rooms and suites at this large roadside motel outside Falmouth offer air-conditioning, phones, cable TV, wet bars, minifridges, and coffee-makers; the decor is contemporary, with mauve carpeting and pastel Formica and wood. Standard rooms (which could be better maintained) have two queen-size beds or one queen and one Murphy bed. King Jacuzzi rooms have king-size beds and mirror-backed whirlpool tubs in the bedroom, plus VCRs, microwaves, and hairdryers. Townhouse suites have cathedral ceilings with skylights; two baths (one with whirlpool); a loft with a king-size bed; a living room with a sofabed and a queen-size Murphy or king-size bed; and a second bath. Golf and other packages are available. *51 Teaticket Hwy. (Rte. 28), 02540, tel. 508/548–4240 or 800/341–5700, fax 508/457–0535. 98 rooms and suites. Facilities: outdoor pool with bar, heated indoor pool with spa, restaurant, lounge with live entertainment and dancing, playground, children's activities room (supervised in summer and school vacations), town/beach/ferry shuttle, no-smoking rooms, 4 disabled-accessible rooms; access to sister property's private beach, water sports. Children under 18 stay free. AE, D, DC, MC, V.*

Capt. Tom Lawrence House. Set back from the street, just steps from downtown, is this pretty white house with a cupola and green shutters, surrounded by flowers and bushes and a lawn shaded by old maple trees. Built in 1861 for a whaling captain, this intimate B&B offers fresh and romantic rooms with antique and painted furniture, French country wallpapers, soft colors, and thick carpeting. The beds, all queen-size canopy or king-size, have firm mattresses, Laura Ashley or Ralph Lauren linens, and down comforters in winter. The large common room has a piano and a fireplace. The full breakfast is lavish and delicious. *75 Locust St., 02540, tel. 508/540–1445. 6 rooms. MC, V. No smoking. Closed Jan.*

New Seabury Very Expensive ★ **New Seabury Resort and Conference Center.** On a 2,000-acre point surrounded by the waters of Nantucket Sound, this self-contained resort community offers rental apartments in some of its 13 "villages." Maushop Village is a Nantucket-look oceanfront complex of gray-shingled buildings set among narrow lanes of crushed seashells, with rugosa roses trailing over white picket fences and trellises; the interiors attractively mix Cape-style and modern furnishings. The Mews, overlooking a beautifully landscaped golf course, offers contemporary California-style condos with cathedral ceilings, lots of white and natural wood, and some private pools and hot tubs. Town house units in Sea Quarters have solariums with whirlpools and gas-log fireplaces. All units have full kitchens, washer/dryers, cable TV, and phones. Among the amenities (many of them seasonal) are fine oceanfront dining, a lounge and restaurant overlooking the fairways, a vast tennis facility, warm sea bathing and an oceanfront pool, miles of jogging trails through the woods, and Popponesset Marketplace (*see* Shopping, *above*). Golf and other packages are available. *Box 549, 02649, tel. 508/477–9111 or 800/999–9033. 167 1- and 2-bedroom units. Facilities: 5 restaurants, health club (Nautilus, stairclimbers, Airdyne, rowers, recumbent bikes, aerobics), 2 championship 18-hole golf courses (1 at water's edge), 16 all-weather tennis courts, pro shops and lessons, 3¹/2-mi private beach, Windsurfer and bike rentals, beach clubs, 2 outdoor pools (1 waterfront), kiddie pool, children's activities (including tennis and golf clinics; fee), soccer, baseball, jogging and bike trails, minigolf. AE, DC, MC, V.*

North Falmouth
Expensive

Sea Crest. Location and amenities are strong drawing cards at this conference center and resort, whose six buildings sprawl along one end of beautiful Old Silver Beach. All rooms have TVs, phones, and minifridges; many have ocean views, and some have gas-log fireplaces. Newer rooms are modern, done in pastels with a flashy painting of flowers above each bed; others date from the 1940s and are traditional Cape Cod. Many packages are available. *350 Quaker Rd., 02556–2903, tel. 508/540–9400 or 800/225–3110, fax 508/548–0556. 256 rooms (8 disabled accessible), 10 suites. Facilities: restaurant, lounge, piano bar, deli, health club (StairMaster, Nautilus, rowing machines, indoor pool, whirlpool, dry and steam saunas), 4 tennis courts, outdoor pool and cabana bar, shuffleboard, putting green, video arcade, children's day camp, room service, movie room, 8 conference and meeting rooms, 2 ballrooms, rental bikes and water-sports equipment; special arrangements with local golf course. AE, D, DC, MC, V.*

Sandwich
Expensive–
Very Expensive

Bay Beach. Sliding glass doors lead from bedrooms' private decks directly onto a bay beach edged in waving sea grass. Inside, the spacious rooms—with contemporary light woods, skylights, rattan, and pastel fabrics—have air-conditioning, minifridges, cable TV with remote, phones, and bright new baths with hair dryers and heat lamps; all but one room have CD/cassette players and radios. The honeymoon suite has a two-person Jacuzzi, an extralarge shower, and a mirrored wall behind the king-size bed. The common area, wrapped with windows to take advantage of the wide-open sea view, has a fireplace, a dining table, and sliders out to the shared deck. Nearby, a boardwalk leads across marshland to Sandwich center, a mile away. *1–3 Bay Beach La., Box 151, 02563, tel. 508/888–8813. 4 rooms. Facilities: Continental breakfast, wine and cheese on arrival, Lifestep and Lifecycle machines, newspaper, private beach, beach chairs, bikes. MC, V. No smoking. Closed Veteran's Day–Apr.*

Moderate–
Expensive
★

Dan'l Webster Inn. A re-creation of an 18th-century inn that stood on the site, this is a classy, quiet, traditional New England inn with an excellent restaurant. Guest rooms (which are mostly in the main inn and wings; two nearby historic homes have four suites each) have floral fabrics and fine reproduction mahogany and cherry furnishings, including some canopy beds, for a generally colonial look. All rooms have phones, cable TV, and air-conditioning; some suites have fireplaces or whirlpools, and one has a baby grand piano. A common room was added in 1993. *149 Main St., 02563, tel. 508/888–3622 or 800/444–3566, fax 508/888–5156. 37 rooms, 9 suites. Facilities: outdoor pool, membership in local health club, access to private golf club, room service, turndown service, no-smoking rooms, gift shop, restaurant, piano lounge. AE, D, DC, MC, V. 2-night minimum year-round.*

West Falmouth
Very Expensive

Inn at West Falmouth. In a secluded area of this exclusive village is a luxurious inn set in a renovated 1898 estate house. A mood of casual elegance is created through a mixture of contemporary and antique furnishings, mostly queen-size beds (including canopies), Italian marble bathrooms with whirlpool tubs, and polished hardwood floors. All rooms have phones, hair dryers, and wall safes; some have wood-burning fireplaces and private decks. Beyond the french doors off the breakfast room—a sunroom washed dreamily in pale pink and mint green—is a patio spilling over with lush potted plants and trees, overlooking woods, gardens, and the tennis court and leading to the small pool and deck. The distant view of the ocean is brought closer by the telescope in the tower sitting area. *Box 1208, 02574, tel. 508/540–7696 or 508/540–6503. 9 rooms. Facilities: Continental breakfast, afternoon tea in winter, heated outdoor pool, clay tennis court. Smoking restricted. AE, MC, V.*

Mid-Cape

Barnstable
Expensive–
Very Expensive

Ashley Manor. Set back from the Old King's Highway by high boxwood hedges and a wide lawn is this fine B&B, just a walk from the village and the bay beach. Begun in 1699, with later additions, the inn preserves the antique wide-board floors (some spatter-painted) and the two living rooms' big open-hearth fireplaces with beehive ovens. Antique and country furnishings, Oriental rugs, and brass and crystal accents create an elegant atmosphere. All but one room has a working fireplace or wood stove, and all provide such amenities as crystal glasses and coffee-makers; a country-Colonial one-room cottage has a kitchenette for light cooking. Breakfast is served on the backyard terrace, looking onto fruit trees, a gazebo, and the tennis court, or in the formal dining room with candlelight, china, and crystal. *3660 Rte. 6A, Box 856, 02630, tel. 508/362–8044. 4 rooms, 2 suites. Facilities: full breakfast, afternoon snacks, complimentary wine (or sherry or port), all-weather tennis court, bikes, croquet, access to yacht club, beach chairs, common grand piano. Smoking restricted. AE, MC, V.*

Expensive
★

Beechwood. This yellow and pale green 1853 Queen Anne Victorian is trimmed with a touch of gingerbread, wrapped by a wide porch with wicker and tinkling wind chimes, and shaded by big old beech trees. While the parlor is pure mahogany-and-red-velvet Victorian, guest rooms are beautifully decorated with antiques in unheavy earlier Victorian styles (including Eastlake); all have minifridges, and two have fireplaces. Breakfast is served by candlelight in the dining room, with pressed-tin ceiling, fireplace, and tables set with lace, flowers, and crystal. *2839 Main St. (Rte. 6A), 02630, tel. 508/362–6618. 6* *rooms. Facilities: full breakfast, afternoon tea on request. No smoking in common areas. AE, MC, V.*

Centerville
Expensive

Inn at Fernbrook. Part of a parcel originally landscaped by Frederick Law Olmsted, designer of New York's Central Park, the inn features duck ponds, a heart-shaped sweetheart rose garden, exotic trees, and a windmill; a right-of-way grants access to the eponymous fern-rimmed brook. The house itself, an 1881 Queen Anne Victorian mansion on the National Register of Historic Places, is a beauty, from the turreted exterior to the fine woodwork and furnishings within. Most rooms have garden views; some have bay-windowed sitting areas, canopy beds (all beds are queen- or king-size), and working fireplaces. The gourmet breakfast is friendly and delicious. *481 Main St., 02632, tel. 508/775–4334, fax 508/778–4455. 4 rooms, 1 2-bedroom suite, 1 cottage (no kitchen). Facilities: full breakfast, afternoon tea, massage (fee). AE, D, MC, V.*

Dennis
Moderate
★

Isaiah Hall B&B Inn. Lilacs and pink roses trail the white picket fence outside this 1857 Greek Revival farmhouse on a rural back road on the bay side. Inside, guest rooms feature country antiques, some canopy beds and Oriental carpets, floral-print wallpapers, and such homey touches as quilts and priscilla curtains. In the attached carriage house, rooms have a Cape Cod look, with three stenciled white walls, one knotty pine; some have small balconies overlooking a wooded lawn with gardens, grape arbors, and berry bushes. Make-it-yourself popcorn, tea, coffee, and soft drinks are always available. *152 Whig St., 02638, tel. 508/385–9928 or 800/736–0160, fax 508/385–5879. 11 rooms. Facilities: Continental breakfast, common TV and fridge, no-smoking rooms, croquet, badminton, picnic tables, grills. AE, MC, V. Closed mid-Oct.–Mar.*

Hyannis
Expensive–
Very Expensive
★

Tara Hyannis Hotel & Resort. For its beautifully landscaped setting, extensive services and pampering, and superior resort facilities (including a well-equipped health club, an 18-hole golf course, a large indoor pool with a window wall overlooking the golf course, and a popular night spot), it's hard to beat the Tara. The lobby area is elegant but the rooms—each with a private balcony—are a bit dull, done in pale colors and standard contemporary hotel style; a gradual upgrade is under way. Rooms overlooking the golf greens or the courtyard garden have the best views. *West End Circle, 02601, tel. 508/775–7775 or 800/843–8272, fax 508/778–6423. 224 rooms, 8 suites. Facilities: golf course (fee), 2 putting greens, 2 lighted tennis courts, indoor pool with Roman bath, outdoor pool with grill, health club (fee; see Sports and the Outdoors, above), restaurant, lounge (see Nightlife, below), pub, hair salon, gift shop, full children's program (school vacations and summer), business services, room service, minifridges (fee). AE, D, DC, MC, V.*

Moderate–
Expensive

Capt. Gosnold Village. An easy walk to the beach and town, this colony of motel rooms and cottages is ideal for families. Children can ride their bikes around the quiet street and compound; the pool is fenced in and is manned by a lifeguard. In some rooms, walls are attractively paneled in knotty pine; floors are carpeted; furnishings are colonial or modern, simple, and pleasant. All units have cable TV and heat; motel rooms have minifridges and coffee-makers, and cottages have phones and decks. *230 Gosnold St., 02601, tel. and fax 508/775–9111. 18 cottages (divisible into rooms, efficiencies, and 1- to 3-bedroom cottages). Facilities: outdoor pool, basketball area, game nets,* *picnic areas, gas grills, maid service. MC, V. Closed Nov.–mid-Apr.*

Hampton Inn Cape Cod. All the rooms at this business- and family-oriented cinderblock motel just off the highway have new white-oak-veneer furnishings, including one king-size or two double beds, a table and chairs or a desk and chair, and a wardrobe. All have air-conditioning, a phone, and cable TV with HBO, ESPN, and remote; some have microwaves and minifridges, and some king rooms have sofabeds. The quietest rooms are those on the top floor that face the pond and woods. *1470 Rte. 132, 02601, tel. 508/771–4804 or 800/999–4804, fax 508/790–2336. 104 rooms (no-smoking rooms available). Facilities: Continental breakfast, indoor pool, whirlpool, saunas, sun deck, free use of nearby health club, children under 18 stay free, senior discounts available. AE, D, DC, MC, V.*

Moderate **Inn on Sea Street.** This charming, relaxed B&B just a walk from
★ the beach and downtown Hyannis consists of two 19th-century homes furnished with country antiques and lacy fabrics by Lois, one of the personable innkeepers. (Car buffs will enjoy the antique cars J.B. keeps around.) Delicious breakfasts are served on china, silver, and crystal in the antiques-and-lace dining room of the 1849 main house or in the glassed-in sun porch. The house across the street offers a common living room, a shared kitchen, large guest rooms with queen-size canopy beds and cable TV, and one room with a private porch. Out back is a small cottage all in white, with a kitchen. *358 Sea St., 02601, tel. 508/775–8030. 9 rooms, 2 with shared bath; 1 cottage. Facilities: full breakfast, common TV, games. AE, D, MC, V. Smoking discouraged. Closed mid-Nov.–Mar.*

South Yarmouth **Seaside.** Right on a warm, sandy Nantucket Sound beach, with
Inexpensive– a view of scalloped beaches in both directions, is a compound
Expensive of Cape-style cottages (efficiencies and one- or two-bedroom units) built in the 1930s. The decor varies, as each unit is individually owned. All have kitchens or kitchenettes and cable TV; many have wood-burning fireplaces. The oceanfront cottages, right off a strip of green grass set with lounge chairs and adirondacks, have the best view and decor. Cottages in the adjacent pine grove are generally very pleasant, though the least expensive units at the back, with knotty pine walls and ceilings, have an outdated '50s look. Shoulder-season rates are very attractive. *135 S. Shore Dr., Box 172, 02664, tel. 508/398–2533. 50 cottages. Facilities: private beach, barbecue facilities, picnic tables. MC, V. Closed mid-Oct.–Apr.*

West Dennis **Lighthouse Inn.** On a small private beach adjacent to West
Expensive Dennis Beach is this old-style Cape resort, in family hands since 1938. The main inn, built around a still-operational 1855 lighthouse, has five guest rooms; scattered along a landscaped lawn are 23 individual weathered-shingle Cape cottages (one-room to three-bedroom; no kitchens) and five multiroom buildings. Cottages have decks, knotty pine and some painted walls, and generally nice, cabiny bedrooms. (A five-year room-refurbishment program started in 1993.) The oceanfront Guest House has a common room with a fireplace. In the main inn is a living room, a glassed-in waterfront porch with a TV, a library, and the restaurant—three glass-wrapped waterfront rooms serving New England cuisine and seafood, plus weekly shore dinners. Daily in summer, supervised day and evening activities and dinners for children give parents some private time.

MAP rates and inexpensive single rooms are available. *Lighthouse Rd., Box 128, 02670, tel. 508/398–2244, fax 508/398–5658. 63 rooms. Facilities: full breakfast, restaurant, cocktail lounge (sometimes piano, dancing), room service, private beach and after-hours fishing, heated outdoor pool, poolside snack bar (July–Aug.), 2 Har-Tru tennis courts, minigolf, putting green, shuffleboard, playground, children's program (July–Aug.), game room (ping-pong, pool, video games), comedy and music club (Sand Bar). Closed Columbus Day–Memorial Day.*

Yarmouth Port
Expensive
★
Wedgewood Inn. This handsome Greek Revival building, white with black shutters and fan ornament, is on the National Register of Historic Places and dates from 1812. Inside, the decor is sophisticated country, a mix of fine Colonial antiques, upholstered wing chairs, Oriental rugs, large Stobart and English sporting prints and maritime paintings, brass accents, handcrafted cherry pencil-post beds, antique quilts, period wallpapers, and Claire Murray hooked rugs on wide-board floors. All rooms are air-conditioned. Two spacious suites have canopy beds, fireplaces, and porches; one has a separate den. *83 Main St., 02675, tel. 508/362–5157 or 508/362–9178. 4 rooms with bath, 2 suites. Facilities: full breakfast, afternoon tea, common TV, bicycles. No smoking in common areas. AE, DC, MC, V.*

Moderate–
Expensive
★
Liberty Hill. The 1825 Greek Revival mansion stands on a rise set back from Route 6A, in an attractive setting of trees and flower-edged lawns. The large rooms, with tall windows and high ceilings, are romantically but unfussily decorated with fine antiques, upholstered chairs, and thick carpets. The third-floor Waterford Room has a king-size bed, an oversize bath, and bay and garden views. *77 Main St. (Rte. 6A), 02675, tel. 508/362–3976 or 800/821–3977. 5 rooms. Facilities: full breakfast, afternoon tea, dinner on request (fee), common TV, guest fridge with mixers. AE, MC, V.*

Lower Cape

Brewster
Very Expensive
Ocean Edge. This huge, self-contained resort is more like a town, with 17 "villages" of residential and rental condominiums, as well as a major conference center. The sports facilities are superior, including a world-class golf course; activities such as concerts, tournaments, and clambakes are scheduled throughout the summer. Accommodations range from oversize hotel rooms with sitting areas in the conference center, with direct access to the health club and tennis courts, to luxurious one- to three-bedroom condos in the woods. All are tastefully decorated in modern style, are air-conditioned, and have cable TV and phones; condos have washer/dryers and some fireplaces; some units have ocean views. The resort is very spread out; you may need your car to get from your condo to the pool. Weekend B&B packages are available. *Rte. 6A, 02631, tel. 508/896–9000 or 800/343–6074, fax 508/896–9123. 125 condominium units, 90 hotel rooms. Facilities: 1,000-foot private beach, championship golf course, golf and tennis schools, driving range and putting greens, 2 heated indoor pools (1 lap pool, 1 with whirlpool), heated Olympic-size outdoor pool, ponds, 6 all-weather tennis courts, well-equipped fitness room, saunas, jogging and bike trails, 3 restaurants, pub entertainment, room service (hotel), concierge, basketball court, bicycle rentals, children's program, playground. AE, D, DC, MC, V.*

Moderate– **Brewster Farmhouse.** Inside a restored 1845 farmhouse on his-
Expensive toric Route 6A are sophisticated guest rooms offering modern
baths, Lane reproduction furnishings, goose-down pillows,
thick white towels, cable TV, air-conditioning, hair dryers, and
turndown service with bedside sherry and chocolates. One
room has a fireplace; another has a king-size rice bed and sliders out to a private patio. In good weather, breakfast is served
on the patio looking onto the 2-acre backyard, rimmed with
apple trees and centered by a pool. *716 Main St., 02631, tel.
508/896–3910 or 800/892–3910, fax 508/896–4232. 5 rooms, 3 with
private bath. Facilities: full breakfast, afternoon tea, heated outdoor pool and spa, beach towels and blankets. No smoking in
rooms. AE, D, DC, MC, V. Closed Jan.*

★ **Captain Freeman Inn.** A splendid 1866 Victorian built for a
packet schooner fleet owner has been renovated to show off its
original opulence, including the ground floor's ornate Italian
plaster ceiling medallions, marble fireplace, herringbone-inlay
flooring, and 12-foot ceilings and windows. Guest rooms have
hardwood floors, antiques and Victorian reproductions, eyelet
spreads, and some fishnet or lace canopies. In a 1989 addition
are three "Luxury Suites"—spacious bedrooms with queen
canopy beds, sofas, fireplaces, cable TV and VCR, minifridges,
private phone lines, air-conditioning, and French doors leading
to small enclosed porches with private whirlpool spas. Winter
weekend cooking schools share the innkeeper's skills, as do
dinners (on request; fee) in the off season. An exercise room is
planned for 1994. *15 Breakwater Rd., 02631, tel. 508/896–7481 or
800/843–4664. 12 rooms, 9 with private bath. Facilities: full
breakfast, afternoon tea, outdoor heated pool, croquet, badminton, bikes, movie library, common minifridge, ice machine. No
smoking. AE, MC, V.*

Moderate **Old Sea Pines Inn.** The inn, fronted by a white-columned por-
★ tico and wraparound veranda overlooking a broad lawn,
strongly evokes the feel of a summer estate of an earlier day.
The living room is spacious, with an appealing seating area before the fireplace. A sweeping staircase leads to guest rooms
decorated with antique-look wallpaper, framed old photographs, and nicely matching antique furnishings. Many rooms
are very large; fireplaces are available, including one in the
inn's best room, which has a sitting area in an enclosed sun
porch. Rooms in a newer building are well but sparely decorated, with bright white modern baths, and have cast-iron
queen-size beds and cable TV. The shared-bath rooms are *very*
small but sweetly done, and a steal at $40 in summer. *2553 Main
St. (Rte. 6A), Box 1026, 02631, tel. 508/896–6114, fax 508/896–
8322. 19 rooms (5 share 2 1/2 baths), 2 suites. Facilities: full breakfast, afternoon tea Jan.–Mar., restaurant (dinners) in season.
No smoking in bedrooms. AE, DC, MC, V.*

Chatham **Chatham Bars Inn.** The ultimate oceanfront resort in the old
Very Expensive style, this Chatham landmark comprises the main building,
★ with its grand-hotel lobby and formal restaurant (*see* Dining,
above), and 26 one- to eight-bedroom cottages on 20 landscaped
acres. The inn has been renovated to create a casual Cape Cod
elegance, though you'll feel free to dress in your best. Some
rooms have ocean-view porches or oceanfront decks by the
Fish Pier; all have phones, cable TV (complimentary VCRs and
movies available), and traditional Cape-style furnishings.
Service is attentive and extensive. Theme weekends and B&B
packages (including a sumptuous breakfast buffet) are offered

in the off-season. MAP rates are available. *Shore Rd., 02633, tel. 508/945–0096 or 800/527–4884, fax 508/945–5491. 130 rooms, 20 suites. Facilities: private beach, 4 tennis courts, fitness room, putting green, heated outdoor pool, shuffleboard, volleyball, harbor cruises, launch service to North Beach, baby-sitting, children's program (July–Aug.), 3 restaurants, clambakes, lounge with entertainment, bar; 9-hole golf course adjacent. AE, DC, MC, V.*

Wequassett Inn. This tranquil, traditional resort offers first-rate accommodations in 19 Cape-style cottages along a little bay and on 22 acres of woods, plus luxurious dining, attentive service, evening entertainment, and plenty of sunning and sporting opportunities. Guest rooms have received design awards; the decor is Early American, with country pine furniture and such homey touches as handmade quilts and duck decoys. Each room has air-conditioning, a minifridge, cable TV/HBO, and a phone; some have fireplaces or wet bars. *Pleasant Bay, 02633, tel. 508/432–5400 or 800/225–7125, fax 508/432–5032. 102 rooms, 2 suites. Facilities: 5 all-weather tennis courts, heated outdoor pool, fitness equipment, boat tours, beach drop-off, transport to town, restaurant, poolside grill, piano lounge, room service, walking path; for extra fee, sailboats, Windsurfers, sailing lessons. AE, DC, MC, V. Closed Nov.–Apr.*

Expensive **Captain's House Inn.** Finely preserved architectural details,
★ superb taste in decorating, opulent home-baked goods, and an overall feeling of warmth and quiet comfort are just part of what makes this one of the Cape's finest small inns. Each room in the three inn buildings has its own personality. Some are quite large, some have fireplaces; some are lacy and feminine, some refined and elegant. The general style of the inn is Colonial Williamsburg. The Hiram Harding Room in the Captain's Cottage has 200-year-old handhewn ceiling beams, a wall of raised walnut paneling centered by a large working fireplace, and a rich red Oriental carpet. Teatime provides a good chance to meet fellow guests. *371 Old Harbor Rd., 02633, tel. 508/945–0127, fax 508/945–9406. 14 rooms, 2 suites. Facilities: Continental breakfast, afternoon tea. No smoking. AE, MC, V. Closed mid-Nov.–mid-Feb.*

★ **Moses Nickerson House.** Warm, thoughtful service and a love of fine antiques and decorating characterize this B&B. Queen-bedded guest rooms in the 1839 house feature wide-board pine floors; some have gas-log fireplaces. Each room has an individual look: one with dark woods, leathers, Ralph Lauren fabrics, and English hunting antiques; another with a high canopy bed, puffy feather mattress, and Nantucket hand-hooked rug. Breakfast is served on china and crystal in a pretty glassed-in sun room with views of the garden and fish pond. *364 Old Harbor Rd., 02633, tel. 508/945–5859 or 800/628–6972. 7 rooms. Facilities: full breakfast, afternoon wine or tea, complimentary fruit and sherry, turndown service. AE, MC, V. No smoking. Closed Jan.*

Eastham **Sheraton Ocean Park Inn.** Located at the entrance to the Na-
Expensive tional Seashore, with a nicely landscaped atrium pool area at its center, this Sheraton offers standard modern-decor rooms with TV, phone, two double beds or one king-size bed, and tiled baths. Rooms have views of the pool or the woods; the outside rooms are a little bigger and brighter and have minifridges. *Rte. 6, 02642, tel. 508/255–5000 or 800/533–3986, fax 508/240–*

1870. 105 rooms, 2 suites. Facilities: fitness room with Universal and other equipment, whirlpool, 2 outdoor tennis courts (lighted in summer), saunas, outdoor pool with poolside bar, heated indoor atrium pool, restaurant, lounge with dancing, game arcade, no-smoking rooms, room service, children under 18 stay free. AE, D, DC, MC, V.

East Orleans
Moderate–Expensive
★

Kadee's Gray Elephant. A mile from Nauset Beach, next to shops, a grocery store, a farm stand, a post office, and Kadee's Lobster & Clam Bar (*see* Dining, *above*), is this 200-year-old house offering small vacation studio and one-bedroom apartments. Unique on the Cape, they are a cheerful yet tasteful riot of color, from wicker painted lavender or green to bright pink bows and flowers painted on furniture to beds layered in quilts and comforters mixing plaids and florals to colorfully framed art. Each room has cable TV with remote, a phone, and individual heat and air-conditioning. Kitchens are fully equipped with microwaves, attractive glassware, irons and boards, even lobster crackers. Everything looks fresh and new, since renovations began in 1992; eventually eight apartments will be available. *Main St., Box 86, 02643, tel. 508/255–7608, fax 508/240–2976. 3–6 apts. Facilities: outdoor patio and grill; restaurant and minigolf course (fee) in season. MC, V.*

Harwich Port
Expensive

Augustus Snow House. While rooms at this inn, a Princess Anne Victorian with gabled dormers and wraparound veranda, are done up in Victorian style, down to reproduction furnishings and (dark) wallpapers and authentic period brass bathroom fixtures, they also offer a host of 20th-century comforts. All rooms have king- or queen-size beds, TVs, and phones; some have whirlpool tubs, and one has a working fireplace. An afternoon English tea open to the public is served in the lovely fireplaced Victorian drawing rooms or on the patio. *528 Main St., 02646, tel. 508/430–0528 or 800/339–0528 in MA. 5 rooms. Facilities: full breakfast, restaurant, turndown service. No smoking in common areas. AE, MC, V.*

★

Beach House Inn. Truly right on the beach, and a private, warm, sandy Nantucket Sound beach at that, this inn is the beach house you've always dreamed of—the one where you spill out of bed and walk barefoot a few feet along a sand path lined with rosa rugosa to hit the water. From umbrella tables on the deck you can watch the sweep of coast and surrounding grasslands while enjoying breakfast; in the off-season, there's a fireplace in the common room. Guest rooms, off a central hallway, are beautifully maintained and simply decorated. All have knotty pine walls, cable TV, minifridge, and air-conditioning; two baths have whirlpool tubs. Planned for construction by 1994 is a new room with bay windows on three sides for a panoramic view. *4 Braddock La., 02646, tel. 508/432–4444 or 800/870–4405. 12 rooms. Facilities: Continental breakfast, outdoor shower. MC, V.*

North Truro
Expensive

Kalmar Village. A good choice on the bayfront strip just outside Provincetown is this cheerful, family-owned (since 1968) complex of cottages grouped around a large pool and lawns edged in lilacs, pines, and rosa rugosa. Nicest and closest to the wide sandy beach are the six new two-bedroom cottages, all white and bright with lots of windows and blond wood and new kitchens. Old Cape-style two-bedrooms have fireplaces but less living area and rougher edges than the nicer one-bedrooms (knotty-pine walls, large living room with two sofabeds). All cottages have cable TV, individual heat, picnic tables, and hibachis. *Rte. 6A, Box 745, 02652, tel. 508/487–0585; in winter, 246 Newbury St., Boston 02116, tel. 617/247–0211. 50 cottages, 6 efficiencies, 4 motel rooms. Facilities: heated outdoor pool, laundry, daily maid service. AE, D, MC, V. Closed Columbus Day–Memorial Day.*

Moderate **East Harbour.** This meticulously maintained complex outside Provincetown offers simple accommodations ranged around a manicured lawn separated from the bay beach by low grasses. The two-bedroom cottages have paneled walls, colonial-style furnishings, and full kitchens. Motel rooms have large picture windows, minifridges and coffee-makers, light paneling, and '60s motel-style furnishings. A new apartment is all white and bright, with skylights, Shaker-reproduction furnishings, a modern kitchen, and second-floor views of the harbor from a private deck. All units have individual heat and cable TV. *Rte. 6A, Box 183, 02652, tel. 508/487–0505, fax 508/487–6693. 7 cottages, 8 rooms, 1 apartment. Facilities: beach, laundry, gas grills, picnic tables, umbrellas. AE, D, MC, V. In season, 1-wk min for cottages, 2-night min for rooms. Closed Nov.–Mar.*

South Harwich **Handkerchief Shoals Motel.** Located about 2 miles from Har-
Inexpensive wich Port and 3 miles from downtown Chatham, the single-story property is set back from the highway and surrounded by well-maintained lawn and trees. Rooms are sparse but large and sparkling clean, with sitting and desk areas, tiled baths, cable TV with remote, fridge, and microwave—a very good value for the money. *Rte. 28, Box 306, 02661, tel. 508/432–2200. 26 units. Facilities: morning coffee, outdoor pool, lawn games, ping-pong. AE, D, MC, V. Closed mid-Oct.–mid-Apr.*

South Wellfleet **Surf Side Colony.** There's very little in the way of accommoda-
Expensive tions on the Atlantic shore of the Outer Cape, so these one- to
★ three-bedroom cottages are an especially lucky find. Scattered on either side of Ocean View Drive, they range from units in a piney grove to deluxe ocean-side cottages (the two closest to the water have the best views) a one-minute walk from Maguire's Landing town beach, a beautiful, wide strand of sand, dunes, and surf. Though the exteriors are retro Florida, with pastel shingling and flat roofs, inside the cottages are tastefully decorated in Cape style, including knotty pine paneling. All units have wood-burning fireplaces, screened porches, kitchens, (mostly) tiled baths, rattan furniture, and carpeting; some have roof decks, outdoor showers, and grills. The two-bedroom ocean-side deluxes have dishwashers and VCRs (no TV reception). *Box 272, 02663, tel. 508/349–2017, fax 508/349–1345. 18 cottages. Facilities: laundromat; for a fee, daily maid service, baby-sitting. MC, V. 1-wk min late June–Labor Day. Limited availability Nov.–Feb.*

Moderate **Wellfleet Motel & Lodge.** A mile from Marconi Beach and opposite an Audubon sanctuary is this well-maintained and tasteful highway-side complex. Rooms in the single-story motel, built in 1964, have attractive knotty-pine paneling. Those in the two-story lodge, built in 1986, are bright and spacious, with white walls, oak furniture, king- or queen-size beds, and patios. All rooms have cable TV/HBO, radios, phones, air-conditioning, minifridges, microwave ovens, and coffee-makers. *Rte. 6, Box 606, 02663, tel. 508/349–3535 or 800/852–2900. 57 rooms, 8 suites. Facilities: heated indoor pool and whirlpool in cedar-lined room, small heated outdoor pool, coffee shop (breakfast* *only), bar, basketball hoop, disabled-accessible rooms. AE, DC, MC, V. Lodge and facilities closed Dec.–Mar.*

Wellfleet

Inexpensive–Moderate

Inn at Duck Creek. A walk from town is this old-time inn with a sweet country feel. Set on 5 wooded acres by a pond, creek, and salt marsh, it consists of the 1800s main inn and two other old houses. Rooms in the main inn (except rustic third-floor rooms) and in Saltworks have a simple charm, with a few rough edges; typical furnishings include clawfoot tubs, country antiques, light floral wallpapers, lace curtains, chenille spreads, and rag rugs on hardwood floors. The two-room Carriage House is cabiny, with rough barnboard and plaster walls. The inn's parlors, screened porches, and marsh-view deck invite relaxation. There's elegant dining at Sweet Seasons or pub dining with entertainment at The Tavern Room (*see* Nightlife, *below*). *Main St., Box 364, 02667, tel. 508/349–9333. 25 rooms, 17 with private bath. Facilities: Continental breakfast, 2 restaurants, guest fridge. AE, MC, V. Closed mid-Oct.–mid-May; 2-night min weekends in season.*

Inexpensive

Holden Inn. If you're watching your budget and can deal with a few fashion don'ts, like the occasional shag carpet or milk-glass lamp, try this old-fashioned place in a country setting just out of the town center. Rooms are very clean and simply decorated with grandma's-house wallpapers, country antiques (brass-and-white-iron or spindle beds, wicker, a marble-top table), hardwood floors, and ruffled sheers or country-style curtains. Private baths with old porcelain sinks are available in adjacent 1840 and 1890 buildings. The lodge has shared baths, an outdoor shower, and a big screened porch—a soothing place filled with birdsong from the surrounding trees and open land—with a lovely view of the ocean and Great Island far below. The main house has a common room and a screened front porch with rockers and a bay view through trees; there are picnic tables and gardens in the back yard. *Commercial St., Box 816, 02667, tel. 508/349–3450. 26 rooms (14 with shared baths). No credit cards. Closed mid-Oct.–mid-Apr.*

Provincetown

Expensive–Very Expensive

★

Hargood House. This apartment complex on the water, a half-mile from the town center, is a great option for longer stays and families. Many of the individually decorated units have decks and large water-view windows; all have full kitchens and modern baths. No. 8 is like a light, bright beach house: on the water, with three glass walls, cathedral ceilings, private deck, dining table and chairs. No. 20 has a fireplace and a home-style kitchen. Rental is mostly by the week in season; two-night minimum off-season. *493 Commercial St., 02657–2413, tel. or fax 508/487–9133. 20 apartments. Facilities: private beach, daily maid service in season, barbecue grills, parking. AE, MC, V.*

Expensive

Best Western Chateau Motor Inn. The personal attention of the owners, whose family has run the place since it was built in 1958 (additions completed in 1972; total remodeling in 1986), shows in the beautifully landscaped lawn and garden that surround the pool, as well as in the well-maintained modern hotel rooms, with wall-to-wall carpeting and tiled baths. All rooms have color cable TV with HBO, satellite, and remote; two phones; shower-massage heads; card-key locks; and individual heat and air-conditioning. Atop a hill with expansive views from pic-

ture windows of marsh, dunes, and sea, t[...]
ish walk to the center of town, yet a[...]
Bradford St., Box 558, 02657, tel. 5[...]
fax 508/487–3557. 55 rooms. Facil[...]
heated outdoor pool, fax service; [...]
available. Children under 18 stay f[...]
AE, D, DC, MC, V. Closed Nov.–Ap[...]

Moderate–Expensive **Anchor Inn.** A short walk from to[...]
guest house with turret and porch [...]
ing doors that open out to a deck overlooking or on the water
(corner rooms are brightest). The decor is very simple but
pleasant, with light-painted wood furnishings; all rooms have
TVs and ceiling fans. *175 Commercial St., 02657, tel. 508/487–
0432 or 800/858–2657 outside MA, fax 508/487–6280. 24 rooms.
Facilities: morning coffee in season, beach. AE, MC, V.*

Dinghy Dock. In the quiet West End, this waterfront apartment house is a vestige of old Provincetown, as is the funny and
wise proprietress. The decor is minimal and baths are small,
but the apartments are cheerful and comfortable and have full
kitchens (some TVs). The nicest have picture windows and
decks overlooking the water and the lighthouse on the sand spit
just across the harbor; one has sliding doors that open out to a
small deck and garden. For summer, book by April 1 (one-week
minimum). *71 Commercial St., 02657, tel. 508/487–0075. 8 apartments. Facilities: laundry, grills, beach (no parking, but can be
arranged). No credit cards.*

Inexpensive– **The Masthead.** Families in particular are welcome at these un-
Expensive pretentious but homey seaside cottages and apartments—
some with room for seven—within walking distance of town,
but far enough away to escape the frenetic summer pace. This
is classic Provincetown—friendly, down-to-earth, with cooking
facilities, plants, phones, color cable TV, air-conditioning, and
private decks. The best and most expensive units overlook the
water. Cottage #35 is like a ship's cabin, with wainscoting on
the walls and ceiling. *31–41 Commercial St., Box 577, 02657, tel.
508/487–0523 or 800/395–5095, fax 508/487–9251. 6 apartments,
4 cottages, 3 efficiencies, 8 rooms. Facilities: beach, free moorings and launch service, daily New York Times. Children under
12 stay free. AE, D, DC, MC, V.*

Moderate **Fairbanks Inn.** On the next street over from Commercial
Street is this comfortable and nicely decorated inn that includes the 1776 main house and auxiliary buildings. Guest
rooms have four-poster or canopy beds, Oriental rugs on wide-
board floors, antique furnishings, and cable TV; some have fireplaces or kitchens. The wicker-filled sun porch and the garden
are good places for afternoon cocktails. *90 Bradford St., 02657,
tel. 508/487–0386. 15 rooms (4 with semiprivate baths), 1 suite.
Facilities: Continental breakfast; common TV, VCR, stereo,
phone, and rooftop sun deck; BYOB bar and fridge. AE, D, MC,
V.*

The Arts and Nightlife

Arts and entertainment events are listed in the *Cape Cod
Times*'s "CapeWeek" section on Friday or in its daily editions.
Also check out the Tuesday "What's On Cape" section or Fri-

day "Weekend" page of *The Register* and *The Cape Codder.* In Provincetown, look for *The Advocate,* a weekly.

The Arts

Since before the turn of the century, creative people have been drawn to Cape Cod summers, and their legacy and ongoing contribution is a thriving arts scene. Vital art galleries exist in Provincetown and elsewhere (*see* Shopping, *above*). In addition to the professional theaters, which offer top-name talent in season, almost every town has a community theater that provides quality entertainment—often mixing local players with visiting pros—throughout the year. The Cape also gets its share of music stars, from pop to classical, along with local groups ranging from barbershop quartets to Bach chorales to early music or chamber ensembles, often playing at school auditoriums or town halls.

Theater The top summer-stock venues, often featuring name performers, are the Equity **Cape Playhouse** (off Rte. 6A, Dennis, tel. 508/385–3911 or 508/385–3838) and the **Falmouth Playhouse** (off Rte. 151, North Falmouth, tel. 508/563–5922). Both offer Broadway-style shows and morning children's plays and have restaurants.

The **Barnstable Comedy Club** (Village Hall, Rte. 6A, Barnstable, tel. 508/362–6333), the Cape's oldest amateur theater group, gives much-praised performances of musicals and dramas throughout the year.

Monomoy Theatre (776 Main St., Chatham, tel. 508/945–1589) presents summer productions—thrillers, musicals, classics, modern drama—by the Ohio University Players.

The **College Light Opera Company** (Highfield Theatre, off Depot Ave., Falmouth, tel. 508/548–0668), founded in 1969, presents Oberlin and other college music majors in summer operettas and musical comedies. The company includes more than 30 singers and an 18-piece orchestra.

The **Wellfleet Harbor Actors Theater (W.H.A.T.;** box office on Main St., tel. 508/349–6835) presents new American plays, satires, farces, and black comedies in its mid-May–mid-October season.

The **Academy Playhouse** (120 Main St., Orleans, tel. 508/255–1963), one of the oldest community theaters on the Cape, presents 10–12 productions year-round, including original works.

The **Provincetown Theatre Company** (tel. 508/487–3466 or 508/487–4715) presents classics, modern dramas, and new works by local authors year-round, as well as staged readings and playwriting workshops.

The **Cape Cod Melody Tent** (*see* Music, *below*) hosts a Wednesday-morning children's theater series in July and August.

Music **Heritage Plantation** (*see* Tour 1, *above*) sponsors summer jazz and other concerts in its gardens from June to mid-September; bring chairs or blankets. Most concerts are free with admission to the complex.

The **Provincetown Playhouse Mews Series** (Town Hall, 260 Commercial St., tel. 508/487–0955) presents classical chamber, folk, ethnic, and jazz concerts in summer.

Popular The Cape's top venue for popular music concerts and comedy
is the **Cape Cod Melody Tent** (21 W. Main St., Hyannis 02601,
tel. 508/775–9100), an institution since 1950. Performances
are held late June–early September in a 2,300-seat theater-in-
the-round under a tent. Performers have recently included the
Preservation Hall Jazz Band, Willie Nelson, Tony Bennett,
the Doobie Brothers, and George Carlin.

The **Summer Songs** series, presented by the Cape Cod Museum of Natural History (*see* Tour 3, *above*), features folk and
Native American music Wednesday nights in July and August
in the auditorium.

The **Beach Plum Music Festival,** held in August at the Provincetown Town Hall (260 Commercial St., tel. 508/349–6874), is
a series of popular folk and jazz concerts by such performers
as Wynton Marsalis, Arlo Guthrie, Queen Ida, and Holly Near.

Club Euro (258 Commercial St., Provincetown, tel. 508/487–
2505 or 487–2511; *see* Nightlife, *below*) offers weekend concerts
by big names in world music, including African music, Jamai-
can reggae, Chicago blues, and Cajun zydeco.

Classical The 100-member **Cape Cod Symphony Orchestra** (Mattacheese Middle School, Higgins Crowell Rd., West Yarmouth,
tel. 508/362–1111), under former D'Oyly Carte Opera conductor Royston Nash, gives regular and children's concerts, with
guest artists, October–May; in summer, two outdoor pops concerts are given, in Mashpee and Orleans.

The **Cape & Islands Chamber Music Festival** (Box 2721, Orleans 02653, tel. 508/255–9509) is three weeks of top-caliber
performances and master classes at various locations in
August.

Band Concerts Traditional New England town band concerts are held weekly
each summer in many Cape towns; bring along chairs, blankets, sweaters, and a picnic supper if you like, and go early to
get a good spot. **Chatham**'s (Kate Gould Park, Main St., tel.
508/945–5199), beginning at 8 PM on Friday, draws up to 6,000
people; as many as 500 fox-trot on the roped-off dance floor,
and there are special dances for children and sing-alongs for
all.

Other locations: **Buzzards Bay** (Buzzards Bay Park, off Main
St., tel. 508/759–3122), Thursdays at 7. **Falmouth** (Marina
Park, Scranton Ave., tel. 508/548–2416), Thursdays at 8. **Harwich** (Brooks Park, tel. 508/432–1600), Tuesdays at 7:30. **Hyannis** (Bismore Park, Ocean St. docks, tel. 508/775–2201),
Wednesdays at 7:30. **Sandwich** (bandstand, Henry T. Wing Ele-
mentary School, Rte. 130, tel. 508/888–5281), Thursdays at
7:30. **West Yarmouth** (Mattacheese Middle School, off Higgins
Crowell Rd., tel. 508/778–1008), Mondays at 7:30.

Opera Two performances a year, in spring and fall, are given at Sandwich High School (Quaker Meetinghouse Rd., East Sandwich)
by the touring group from New York City's Opera Northeast
under Donald Westwood. For dates, contact **Opera New England of Cape Cod** (tel. 508/775–3974). (*See also* College Light
Opera Company under Theater, *above*.)

Film Besides the first-run theaters, the **Cape Museum of Fine Arts
Cinema Club** (Cape Playhouse complex, Rte. 6A, Dennis, tel.

508/385–4477) presents classic and avant-garde movies in an intimate setting year-round.

That fast-disappearing American tradition, the drive-in movie, is living still on Cape Cod: At the **Wellfleet Drive-In Theater** (Rte. 6, tel. 508/349–7176 or 508/255–9619), films start at dusk nightly in season, and there's a minigolf course.

Dance The **Cape Ballet** (Canterbury Plaza, Cotuit Rd., Sandwich, tel. 508/833–0699 or 508/477–8052), a semiprofessional company, performs classical and contemporary ballet year-round and offers lessons.

Nightlife

Nighttime on Cape Cod can be very special, in many ways. In the less developed areas, the stars are amazingly bright and make beach walks in blackness and silence even more wondrous—more of an experience in the elemental. Also, the power of the lighthouse beacons as they cut through the night sky has a fascination impossible to resist. If you're up *really* late, you might head for Chatham Light to catch a terrific sunrise.

Many daytime activities, such as fishing, take on a completely different aspect at night. Scuba enthusiasts might consider night diving; colors are more vivid by flashlight, a lot of sea life is phosphorescent or bioluminescent, and nocturnal species come out to play. It's important to know the tides and safe locations—check with a dive shop.

A number of organizations sponsor outdoor activities at night, including the **Cape Cod Museum of Natural History**'s stargazing sessions (*see* Tour 3, *above*) and **Wellfleet Bay Sanctuary**'s bat walks, night hikes, and lecture series (*see* Nature Areas, *above*). The **Army Corps of Engineers** (tel. 508/759–4431), which maintains the Cape Cod Canal, offers free evening programs in summer, including slide shows about the canal, sing-alongs, night walks, and storytelling around campfires at the Bourne Scenic Park and Scusset Beach State Park. The **Cape Cod National Seashore** offers summer evening programs, such as slide shows, sunset beach walks, concerts (local groups, military bands), and sing-alongs, at its Salt Pond Amphitheater (Eastham, tel. 508/255–3421) and Province Lands Visitor Center (Provincetown, tel. 508/487–1256) and sunset campfire talks at the beaches at Provincetown. **Waquoit Bay reserve** (*see* Nature Areas, *above*) holds summer "Evenings on the Bluff," talks for families (who are invited to bring picnics) on environmental, historical, and artistic subjects; activities for children are often provided.

In summer, just walking Main Street in Hyannis or Commercial Street in Provincetown is nightlife in itself. The streets are filled with a fascinating array of people who are from everywhere and into everything, all on vacation and having a great time. All you require to be a part of "the stroll" is an appreciation of life's infinite variety—and maybe an ice-cream cone.

Of course, the Cape certainly has plenty of what is more traditionally defined as nightlife. Hyannis and Yarmouth have a lot of rowdy dance clubs, bars, and restaurant lounges packed with college students on summer vacation. Most of the Upper and Lower Cape is quiet, except for Provincetown (with the added spice of drag shows) and a few places in Chatham. And scattered throughout the Cape are places to dine and dance in elegant style. In season, many restaurant and hotel lounges have entertainment nightly; in the off-season, those that remain open cut back to weekends.

Mixed Menu **Christine's** (Rte. 28, West Dennis, tel. 508/394–7333; *see* Dining, *above*) has entertainment nightly in season in its new 300-seat showroom. Concerts (sometimes with dancing) feature name bands from the 1950s to 1970s, Top-40 bands, or jazz; there are also standup comedy nights and Sunday-night cabaret with cruise-ship-style buffet. Off-season, there's live entertainment and dancing to a DJ on weekends, plus special events.

Crown & Anchor Complex (247 Commercial St., Provincetown, tel. 508/487–1430) consists of a number of bars under one roof, including a leather bar, a disco (with new light shows), a cabaret of gay and straight comics and drag shows, a pool bar, and a game room with pool tables and video games.

The Flying Bridge (220 Scranton Ave., tel. 508/548–2700; *see* Dining, *above*) on Falmouth Harbor has acoustic entertainment in its lounges weekends year-round (more often in season), plus steel bands and acoustic music on the outdoor deck on summer afternoons.

Sea Crest resort (350 Quaker Rd., North Falmouth, tel. 508/540–9400; *see* Lodging, *above*) offers a summer and holiday-weekend schedule of nightly entertainment on the outdoor terrace, including dancing to country, Top 40, reggae, and jazz bands and big-band DJ, plus karaoke and comedy.

Bars and Lounges **Bobby Byrne's Pubs** (Rte. 28, Harwich Port, tel. 508/430–1100; Rte. 28, Hyannis, tel. 508/775–1425; Mashpee Commons, Rtes. 28 and 151, tel. 508/477–0600; Rte. 6A, Sandwich, tel. 508/888–6088) offer a comfortable pub atmosphere, a jukebox, and good light and full menus. **Chatham Squire** (487 Main St., Chatham, tel. 508/945–0945), with four separate bars (including a raw bar), is a rollicking year-round local hangout, drawing a young crowd to the bar side and a mixed crowd of locals to the quieter restaurant side. Aside from occasional live acoustic music, a jukebox and the crowd itself are the only entertainment. **Oliver's** restaurant (Rte. 6A, Yarmouth Port, tel. 508/362–6062) has live acoustic music in its tavern weekends year-round (nightly in summer). **Sheraton Ocean Park Inn** in Eastham (Rte. 6, tel. 508/255–5000; *see* Lodging, *above*) features a folk guitarist/comedian/singalong leader in its lounge weekends year-round; in summer there's some kind of entertainment most nights.

The Tavern Room (Main St., Wellfleet, tel. 508/349–7369), set in an 1800s building, with beamed ceiling, fireplace, and a bar covered in nautical charts, features live entertainment from jazz to pop to country to Latin ensembles. Munchies are served alongside the menu of traditional and Latin/Caribbean-inspired dishes. **The Woodshed** (Rte. 6A, Brewster, tel. 508/896–7771), the rustic bar at the Brewster Inn, is a good place to soak up local color and dance to pop duos or bands that perform most nights. **The Yacht Club,** the sophisticated lounge of the Tara Hyannis Hotel (West End Rotary, tel. 508/775–7775), has live pop entertainment nightly in season, mostly DJs in the off-season. The bar has a wide-screen TV for sports events and a window wall overlooking the pool and golf course.

The Moors restaurant (Bradford St. Ext., Provincetown, tel. 508/487–0840; *see* Dining, *above*) has presented Lenny Grand-champ in its lounge for more than 15 years; he plays the piano, sings, does jokes, and leads sing-alongs up to six nights a week in season. **Napi's** (7 Freeman St., Provincetown, tel. 508/487–1145; *see* Dining, *above*) offers easy-listening piano in its up-stairs lounge on weekends, nightly in season.

Dance Clubs **Asa Bearse House** (415 Main St., Hyannis, tel. 508/771–4444) has dancing nightly year-round on a small dance floor to live acoustic, blues, rock, and progressive rock (headliners and local), as well as DJ music. Frozen drinks and happy hours with appetizers attract a largely college crowd in summer.

Beachcomber (Cahoon Hollow Beach, off Rte. 6, Wellfleet, tel. 508/349–6055)—right on the beach, with live Boston rock bands most nights, weekend happy hours with live reggae, and dancing nightly in summer—is hot with the college crowd at night and on breaks from the sun. Indoors or at tables by the beach-front bar, order from a menu featuring fun appetizers, salads, burgers, seafood, barbecue, frozen drinks, and raw bar.

Casino-By-The-Sea (Grand Ave. S, Falmouth Heights, tel. 508/548–0777) is the Upper Cape's hot beachfront club, with dancing in the nightclub and outdoor deck to high-energy rock and Top-40 bands in season. Saturday-afternoon beach parties with entertainment and activities (volleyball tournaments, raft races), pool tables and tournaments, college nights, and happy hours contribute to the fun. Selections from the upstairs Wharf restaurant's full or light menu or from the deli keep up the energy.

Club Euro (*see* The Arts, *above*) in Provincetown has world-music concerts weekends in season, plus vintage and urban dance videos five nights a week (and at concert intermissions) in a great room—1843 Congregational church, later movie theater—done in an eerie ocean dreamscape: oceanic-green-sea walls with half-submerged three-dimensional mermaid and sprouting fish, black ceiling high above. Pool tables and a late-night menu (*see* Euro Island Grill in Dining, *above*) are available.

Jammer's (Rte. 28, Hyannis, tel. 508/775–2922) is a huge, 1,500-seat club across from the airport, with three dance floors and two stages, as well as a volleyball court and a pool. Entertainment includes a guitarist and sing-along at happy hour and dancing to Top-40 and dance bands nightly, plus weekly male and female body contests and Pro-Beach Volleyball Tour games.

Mill Hill Club (164 Rte. 28, West Yarmouth, tel. 508/775–2580) has dancing to a DJ nightly and Top-40 and alternative dance bands Thursday–Saturday year-round, plus videos and satel-lite sports on large-screen TVs, a regular hypnotist act, bikini contests, and a singer/guitarist at happy hour in season.

Starbuck's in Hyannis (Rte. 132, tel. 508/778–6767; *see* Dining, *above*) has live acoustic entertainment in its bar many nights year-round.

Sundancer's (116 Rte. 28, West Dennis, tel. 508/394–1600) has dancing to a DJ and live bands year-round and Sunday-after-noon reggae bands in season.

Ballroom Dancing   **Betsy's Ballroom** (Yarmouth Senior Center, 528 Forest Rd., South Yarmouth, tel. 508/362–9538) has Saturday-night dancing to bands on the Cape's largest dance floor year-round.

Captain Linnell House (137 Skaket Beach Rd., Orleans, tel. 508/255–3400; *see* Dining, *above*) has dancing to big band and '50s music in its fireplaced lounge Fridays in the off-season.

Chatham Bars Inn (Shore Rd., tel. 508/945–0096; *see* Lodging, *above*) has dancing in its South Lounge in July and August and to a pianist or other soft music year-round in its dark and clubby Tavern at the Inner Bar restaurant. Proper dress is required in season.

Coonamessett Inn (Jones Rd. and Gifford St., Falmouth, tel. 508/548–2300; *see* Dining, *above*) has dancing to soft piano, jazz trios, or other music in its lounge on weekends year-round, as well as ballroom dancing a few Sunday nights in winter.

East Bay Lodge (East Bay Rd., Osterville, tel. 508/428–5200; *see* Dining, *above*) has dancing to jazz or cabaret-style piano (sometimes with major jazz pianists) and occasional vocals in its lounge several nights a week year-round.

Popponesset Inn (Shore Dr., New Seabury, tel. 508/477–1100 or 508/477–8258; *see* Dining, *above*) has dancing to bands in its water-view lounge, on a large dance floor, weekends in season.

Rof-Mar Diplomat Club (Popple Bottom Rd., Sandwich, tel. 508/428–8111; reservations required), a function room, has ballroom dinner dances and dancing to country bands year-round. There's a large dance floor and seating on outdoor porches.

Country and Western   **Bud's Country Lounge** (Bearses Way and Rte. 132, Hyannis, tel. 508/771–2505) has pool tables and features live country music, lessons, and dancing year-round. (*See also* Rof-Mar, *above*.)

Folk   Three well-established coffeehouses present a mixture of professional and local folk and blues in a no-smoking, no-alcohol environment, with refreshments available during intermission: **Benefit Coffeehouse** of the Liberty Folk Society (Liberty Hall, Main St., Marstons Mills, tel. 508/428–1053), with benefit concerts the first Saturday of each month featuring mostly local musicians; **First Encounter Coffee House** (Chapel in the Pines, Samoset Rd., Eastham, tel. 508/255–5438), booking national acts the first and third Saturday of each month (closed May and September); and **Woods Hole Folk Music Society** (Community Hall, Water St., Woods Hole, tel. 508/540–0320), with concerts of nationally known performers the first and third Sundays of the month from October into May.

Irish Music   **Cape Cod Irish Village** (512 Main St., West Yarmouth, tel. 508/771–0100) has dancing to two- or three-piece bands performing traditional and popular Irish music year-round. The crowd is mostly couples and over-35s.

Clancy's (8 Upper County Rd., Dennisport, tel. 508/394–6661; 175 Rte. 28, West Yarmouth, tel. 508/775–3332) has singer/guitarists year-round.

Irish Pub (126 Main St. [Rte. 28], West Harwich, tel. 508/432–8808) has dancing to bands—a mix of Irish, American, and dance music and sing-alongs—plus pool, darts, sports TV, and pub food in the bar.

Shamrock Lounge (Mitchells Steak and Rib House, 451 Iyanough Rd. [Rte. 28], Hyannis, tel. 508/775–6700) has duos performing Irish and American songs, sing-alongs, and comedy year-round.

Jazz The Cape Cod Jazz Society operates a 24-hour hotline (tel. 508/394–5277) on jazz events throughout the Cape.

Bishop's Terrace restaurant (Rte. 28, West Harwich, tel. 508/432–0253) has dancing to jazz trios most Saturday nights in its small lounge, set in a converted barn with tools hanging from barnboard walls. Several nights in season, a pop/classical pianist performs.

Dome Restaurant (Woods Hole Rd., Woods Hole, tel. 508/548–0800) has dancing to a Dixieland jazz band in its lounge, under a geodesic dome, Sundays in July and August; there is easy-listening piano on Friday and Saturday in season.

Wequassett Inn (Pleasant Bay, Chatham, tel. 508/432–5400; *see* Lodging, *above*) has a jazz duo nightly in its lounge (jacket requested).

Yarmouth Inn (Rte. 6A, Yarmouth Port, tel. 508/362–3191) has jazz duos in its country French restaurant's lounge several nights year-round.

Cruises **Hy-Line** in Hyannis and **Cape Cod Canal Cruises** in Onset (*see* Guided Tours in Essential Information, *above*), as well as **Patriot Party Boats** (*see* Guided Tours, *above*) and the *Island Queen* (tel. 508/548–4800) in Falmouth, run sunset or moonlight cruises in season. Some include dancing under the stars to live music.

Miscellaneous **Boatslip** (161 Commercial St., Provincetown, tel. 508/487–1669) has a tea dance on its huge beachfront deck and indoor dance music to DJ dance music from 3:30 to 6:30 on summer afternoons. The crowd is mostly gay, and the place is always packed.

The many venues for drag shows in Provincetown include the **Town House** (291 Commercial St., Provincetown, tel. 508/487–0292), which has these and other entertainment for a mixed crowd in its "Backroom Cabaret" most nights in season.

Cape Cod Ocean Waves (Yarmouth Senior Center, 528 Forest Rd., South Yarmouth, tel. 508/945–3196 or 508/398–0416), the **Nau-Sets** (Willy's Gym, Rte. 6A, Orleans, tel. 508/255–1680 or 508/255–5079), and the **Village Squares** (Kennedy Skating Rink, Bearses Way, Hyannis, tel. 508/771–3341) hold square dances weekly most of the year.

Coconuts Comedy Club (Holiday Inn, Rte. 132, Hyannis, tel. 508/775–6600) offers standup with cable veterans Thursday-Saturday nights in season.

On Saturday evenings in July and August during the **Wellfleet Gallery Crawl,** Wellfleet's art galleries are open for cocktail receptions to celebrate show openings. Walk from gallery to gallery meeting the featured artists and checking out their works.

4 Martha's Vineyard

Much less developed—by stringently enforced design—than Cape Cod, yet more diverse and cosmopolitan than neighboring Nantucket Island, Martha's Vineyard is an island with a split personality. From Memorial Day through Labor Day it is a vibrant, star-studded place. Edgartown is flooded with seekers of chic who've come to wander the tidy streets lined with boutiques and stately whaling captains' homes. The busy main port, Vineyard Haven, welcomes day-trippers fresh off a ferry or private yacht to browse in its own array of swank shops. Oak Bluffs, where pizza and ice-cream emporiums reign supreme, has a boardwalk-town air, and several night spots that cater to the high-spirited, tanned young.

Those too long in city pent find escape on the island's many bike paths, in nature preserves, and on miles of spectacular white-sand beaches paved with multicolor beach towels. Summer regulars return, including a host of celebrities such as William Styron, Art Buchwald, Walter Cronkite, Katherine Graham, Jacqueline Onassis, Patricia Neal, Beverly Sills, and Carly Simon (joined more recently by new homeowners Spike Lee and Billy Joel). Concerts, theater and dance performances, and lecture series draw top talent to the island, while a county agricultural fair, weekly farmer's markets, and fireworks displays viewed from Oak Bluffs' village green offer earthier pleasures.

This summer persona is the one most people know, but in many ways the Vineyard's other self is even more appealing, for in the off-season the island becomes a place of peace and simple beauty. On drives along country lanes through the agricultural center of the island, there's time to linger over pastoral and ocean vistas without deference to a throng of other cars, bicycles, and mopeds. In the many conservation areas, the voices of the summer crowds are gone, leaving only the sounds of birdsong and the crackle of leaves underfoot. The beaches, always lovely, now can be appreciated in solitude, and the water seems to sparkle more under the crisp blue skies.

The locals, too, are at their convivial best in the off-season. After struggling to make the most of the short money-making season, they reestablish contact with friends and take up pastimes previously crowded out by work. The result for visitors—besides the extra dose of friendliness they are likely to encounter—is that cultural, educational, and recreational events continue to be offered year-round.

Bartholomew Gosnold charted Martha's Vineyard for the British Crown in 1602 and is credited with naming it, supposedly after his infant daughter and the wild grapes he found growing in profusion. Later, a Massachusetts Bay Colony businessman, Thomas Mayhew, was given a grant to the island, along with Nantucket and the Elizabeth Islands, from King Charles of England. Mayhew's son, Thomas Mayhew, Jr., founded the first European settlement here in 1642, at Edgartown, finding the resident Wampanoag Indians good neighbors. Among other survival skills, they taught the settlers to kill whales on shore; when moved out to sea, this skill would bring the island great prosperity, at least for a while. (Historians estimate a Wampanoag population of 3,000 upon the arrival of Mayhew; today there are fewer than 300. The tribe is now working hard to reclaim and perpetuate its cultural identity, and it has reclaimed ancestral lands in the town of Gay Head.)

Martha's Vineyard

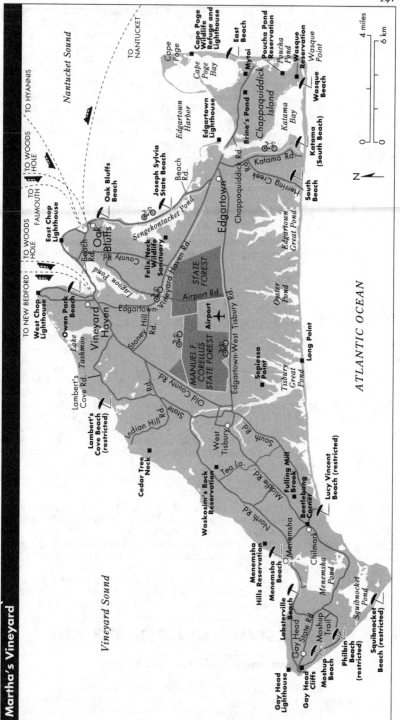

Vineyard Sound

Nantucket Sound

ATLANTIC OCEAN

TO NEW BEDFORD

TO WOODS HOLE

TO WOODS HOLE FALMOUTH

TO WOODS HOLE

TO HYANNIS

TO NANTUCKET

West Chop Lighthouse

East Chop Lighthouse

Owen Park Beach

Lambert's Cove Beach (restricted)

Lake Tashmoo

Vineyard Haven

Lambert's Cove Rd.

Cedar Tree Neck

Indian Hill Rd.

State Rd.

Stoney Hill Rd.

Lagoon Pond

Oak Bluffs

Oak Bluffs Beach

Beach Rd.

County Rd.

Felix Neck Wildlife Sanctuary

Sengekontacket Pond

Joseph Sylvia State Beach

Beach Rd.

STATE FOREST

Airport Rd.

Edgartown-Vineyard Haven Rd.

Edgartown

Edgartown Lighthouse

Edgartown Harbor

Cape Poge

Cape Poge Bay

Cape Poge Wildlife Refuge and Lighthouse

East Beach

Myroi

Poucha Pond Reservation

Poucha Pond

Wasque Reservation

Wasque Point

Chappaquiddick Island

Katama Bay

Wasque Beach

Katama (South Beach)

Chappaquiddick Rd.

Brine's Pond

Katama Rd.

Herring Creek

South Beach

Edgartown Great Pond

Oyster Pond

Edgartown-West Tisbury Rd.

Long Point

Tisbury Great Pond

Sepiessa Point

MANUEL F. CORELLUS STATE FOREST

Airport

Old County Rd.

West Tisbury

South Rd.

Fulling Mill Brook

Tea La.

Middle Rd.

North Rd.

Waskosim's Rock Reservation

Menemsha Hills Reservation

Menemsha Beach

Menemsha

Lobsterville Beach

Gay Head Lighthouse

Gay Head Cliffs

Moshup Trail

Philbin Beach (restricted)

Squibnocket Beach (restricted)

Squibnocket Pond

Menemsha Pond

Chilmark

Beetlebung Corner

Lucy Vincent Beach (restricted)

Gay Head

State Rd.

N

0   4 miles

0   6 km

Settled as a community of farmers and fishermen (both of which occupations continue to flourish here today), the island made a decided shift in the early 1800s to whaling as the basis of its economy. Never as influential as Nantucket or New Bedford, Martha's Vineyard still held its own, and many Vineyard whaling masters returned home wealthy men. Especially during the golden age of whaling—around 1830 to 1845—the captains built impressive homes with the profits, and these, along with many graceful houses from earlier centuries, still line the streets of the onetime whaling towns of Vineyard Haven and Edgartown. After the Civil War the industry went into decline, but by that time a new industry was on the rise, and it has continued to hold sway to this day: tourism.

The story of this development begins in 1835, when the first Methodist Camp Meeting—a two-week gathering of far-flung parishes for group worship and a healthy dose of fun—was held in the then-undeveloped Oak Bluffs area. From the original meeting's nine tents, the number grew to 250 by 1857.

Little by little, permanent platforms ranged around the large central tent of the preachers were built by returning campers; then the odd cottage popped up, fit into the same space a tent would occupy. By 1880, Wesleyan Grove, as it was called (after Methodism founder John Wesley), was a community of about 500 tiny cottages. Lacy filigree insets began to appear along the facades, becoming more and more ornate as neighbors tried to outdo one another. The style, emerging from Gothic Revival styles imported from Europe, was known as Carpenter Gothic, for the filigree work produced with jigsaws.

Meanwhile, burgeoning numbers of cottagers coming to the island each summer helped convince speculators of its desirability as a resort destination, and in 1867 a separate secular community was laid out alongside the Camp Ground. Steamers from New Bedford, Boston, New York, and elsewhere began bringing in fashionable folk for the bathing and the sea air, for picking berries or playing croquet. Grand hotels sprung up around Oak Bluffs Harbor; a railroad followed, connecting the town with the beach at Katama. The Victorian seaside resort became known as Cottage City; later, the name was changed to Oak Bluffs.

Today, more than 300 of the Camp Ground cottages remain, and just as Edgartown and Vineyard Haven attest to their origins as whaling ports, so Oak Bluffs—with its grassy, open parks, its porch-wrapped beach houses, and its village green and gazebo, where families still gather to hear the town band play—evokes the days of Victorian summer ease. If you close your eyes, the Day-Glo orange bikinis and cones of frozen yogurt seem to fade away, replaced for just a moment by flowing white dresses and parasols held languidly against the sun.

Essential Information

Important Addresses and Numbers

Tourist Information **Martha's Vineyard Chamber of Commerce** is two blocks from the Vineyard Haven ferry. (Look for town information booths by the Vineyard Haven Steamship terminal, across from Oak Bluffs' Flying Horses carousel, and on Church Street in Edgartown.) *Beach Rd., tel. 508/693–0085. Open weekdays 9–5; also Memorial Day–Labor Day, Sat. 10–2.*

Emergencies Dialing 911 will connect you with a **communications center,** where messages are quickly relayed to the hospital, physicians, ambulance services, police, fire departments, or Coast Guard. There's a 24-hour emergency room at **Martha's Vineyard Hospital** (Linton La., Oak Bluffs, tel. 508/693–0410). **Vineyard Medical Services** (State Rd., Vineyard Haven, tel. 508/693–6399) provides walk-in care; call for days and hours.

Late-night **Triangle Pharmacy** (245 Vineyard Haven Rd., Edgartown, tel.
Pharmacies 508/627–5107; night number 508/627–3175) and **Leslie's Drug Store** (Main St., Vineyard Haven, tel. 508/693–1010) are open daily year-round and have pharmacists on 24-hour call for emergencies.

Cash Machines ATMs are operated by the **Edgartown National Bank** (2 S. Water St. and 251 Upper Main St. [next to the A&P] in Edgartown; 129–131 Circuit Ave., near post office, in Oak Bluffs; tel. 508/627–3343) and by the **Martha's Vineyard National Bank** (opposite steamship offices in Vineyard Haven and Oak Bluffs; 19 Lower Main St., Edgartown; Up-Island Cronigs Market, State Rd., West Tisbury; tel. 508/693–9400).

Arriving and Departing by Plane

Airport **Martha's Vineyard Airport** (tel. 508/693–7022) is in West Tisbury, about 5 miles west of Edgartown.

Airlines **Cape Air** (tel. 508/771–6944 or 800/352–0714) connects the Vineyard year-round with Boston (including a summer hourly shuttle), Hyannis, Nantucket, and New Bedford; it also offers joint fares and ticketing-and-baggage agreements with several major carriers. In season, **Continental Express** (tel. 800/525–0280) has nonstop flights from Newark and **Northwest Airlink** (tel. 800/225–2525) flies from Boston. In 1993, **USAir Express** (tel. 800/428–4322) began offering service out of Boston and (via Allegheny) seasonal weekend service out of LaGuardia. **Air New England** (tel. 508/693–8899) and **Direct Flight** (tel. 508/693–6688) are year-round charter services with island bases. **Westchester Air** (tel. 800/759–2929) flies charters out of White Plains, New York.

Arriving and Departing by Ferry

Car-and-passenger ferries travel to Vineyard Haven from Woods Hole on Cape Cod year-round. In season, passenger ferries from Falmouth and Hyannis on Cape Cod, and from New Bedford, serve Vineyard Haven and Oak Bluffs. All provide parking lots for leaving cars overnight (cost: $6–$10 a night).

From Woods Hole The **Steamship Authority** operates the only car ferries, which make the 45-minute trip to Vineyard Haven year-round, and to Oak Bluffs from late May through September. *Tel. 508/540–2022 for auto reservations; on the Vineyard, 508/693–0367 or 508/693–0125 for information, 508/693–9130 for auto reservations; TDD 508/540–1394. Cost, one-way: mid-May–mid-Oct.: $4.50 adults, $2.25 children 5–12, $36 cars; mid-Mar.–mid-May and mid-Oct.–Nov., $4 adults, $2 children, $23 cars; Dec.–mid-Mar., $4 adults, $2 children, $17 cars. Bicycles: $2.75 one-way year-round.*

If you plan to take a car to the island (or to Nantucket) in summer or weekends in fall, you *must* reserve space on the ferry as far ahead as possible (in season, call weekdays from 7 to 9 PM for faster service). Those with reservations must be at the terminal 30 minutes (45 minutes in season) before sailing time. If you're without a reservation, get there very early and be prepared to wait, possibly for hours, for a space to open up. On the upside, a summer standby policy guarantees same-day passage from Woods Hole or Vineyard Haven to vehicles in the standby line by 2 PM.

A number of parking lots in Falmouth hold the overflow of cars when the Woods Hole lot is filled; free shuttle buses take passengers to the ferry, about 15 minutes away. Signs along Route 28 heading south from the Bourne Bridge direct you to open parking lots, as does AM radio station 1610, which can be picked up within 5 miles of Falmouth.

Available at the ticket office in Woods Hole is a free reservations phone connecting you with many lodgings and car- and moped-rental firms on the island.

From Hyannis Hy-Line makes the 1³/₄-hour run to Oak Bluffs May–October. From June to mid-September, the "Around the Sound" cruise makes a one-day round-trip from Hyannis with stops at Nantucket and Martha's Vineyard ($31 adults, $15.50 children 5–12, bicycles $13.50). If you intend to leave your car at the Hy-Line lot in Hyannis, reservations are a good idea during the high season. *Ocean St. dock, tel. 508/778–2600, 508/778–2602 for reservations; in Oak Bluffs, tel. 508/693–0112. Cost, one-way: $10.75 adults, $5.25 children 5–12, $4.50 bicycles.*

From Falmouth The *Island Queen* makes the 40-minute trip to Oak Bluffs from late May through Columbus Day. *Falmouth Harbor, tel. 508/548–4800. Cost: round-trip, $9 adults, $4.50 children under 13, $6 bicycles; one way, $5 adults, $2.50 children under 13, $3 bicycles. Children under 5 sail free Fri.–Mon.*

Patriot Party Boats (tel. 508/548–2626) allows passengers on its daily Falmouth Harbor–Oak Bluffs mail run in the off-season ($4 adults, $2 children) and operates a year-round 24-hour water taxi (you pay about $100 to charter the whole boat).

From New Bedford The *Schamonchi* travels between Billy Woods Wharf and Vineyard Haven from mid-May to mid-October. The 450-passenger ferry makes the 1¹/₂-hour trip at least once a day, several times in high season, avoiding Cape traffic. *Tel. 508/997–1688; Beach Rd., Vineyard Haven, tel. 508/693–2088. Cost, one-way/round-trip same day: $8.50/$15 adults, $4.50/$7.50 children under 12, $2.50/$5 bicycles. Senior citizens get a 10% discount.*

From Nantucket Hy-Line makes 2¹/₄-hour runs to and from Oak Bluffs from mid-June to mid-September—the only interisland passenger service. (To get a car from Nantucket to the Vineyard, you must return to the mainland and drive from Hyannis to Woods Hole.) *Tel. 508/778–2600 in Hyannis, 508/693–0112 in Oak Bluffs, 508/228–3949 on Nantucket. Cost, one-way: $10.75 adults, $5.25 children 5–12, $4.50 bicycles.*

Arriving and Departing by Private Boat

Town harbor facilities are available at **Vineyard Haven** (tel. 508/696–4200), **Oak Bluffs** (tel. 508/693–4355), **Edgartown** (tel. 508/627–4746), and **Menemsha** (tel. 508/645–2846). Private companies include **Vineyard Haven Marina** (tel. 508/693–0720), **Dockside Marina** (tel. 508/693–3392) in Oak Bluffs, and **Edgartown Marine** (tel. 508/627–4388).

Arriving and Departing by Bus and Train

From the Woods Hole ferryport, you can travel onwards with **Amtrak** (tel. 800/USA–RAIL) in summer, or, year-round, with **Bonanza Bus Lines** (tel. 800/556–3815) to Rhode Island, Connecticut, and New York.

Getting Around

By Car In season, the Vineyard gets overrun with cars and many innkeepers will advise you to leave your car home, saying you won't need it. This is true if you are coming over for just a few days and plan to spend most of your time in the three main towns, Oak Bluffs, Vineyard Haven, and Edgartown, which are connected in summer by a shuttle bus. Otherwise, you'll probably want a car. Driving on the island is fairly simple; there are few main roads, and these are all well marked. Sample distances from Vineyard Haven: to Oak Bluffs, 3 miles; to Edgartown, 8 miles; to Gay Head, 18 miles.

Rentals can be booked through the Woods Hole ferry terminal free phone; at the airport desks of **Budget** (tel. 508/693–1911), **Hertz** (tel. 508/693–2402), **All Island** (tel. 508/693–6868), and others; or from companies in the towns, including **Atlantic** (tel. 508/693–0480). **Adventure Rentals** (Beach Rd., Vineyard Haven, tel. 508/693–1959) rents cars as well as mopeds, Jeeps, and buggies, and offers half-day rates. Cost: $25–$65 per day for a basic model car. **Vineyard Classic and Specialty Cars** (tel. 508/693–5551) rents classic Corvettes, a '57 Chevy, and other cars, as well as mopeds and mountain bikes (*see* By Bicycle and Moped, *below*).

By Four-wheel-drive Four-wheel-drive vehicles are allowed on parts of South Beach with $50 annual permits sold on the beach in summer, or anytime at the Dukes County Courthouse (Treasurer's Office, Main St., Edgartown, tel. 508/627–4250). Wasque Reservation (*see* Tour 3: Edgartown, *below*) has a separate mandatory permit and requires that vehicles carry certain equipment, such as a shovel; call the rangers before setting out for the dunes. Jeeps are a good idea for exploring areas approachable only by dirt roads, but for over-sand travel, even in a Jeep the going can be difficult. Also, most rental companies (*see* By Car, *above*; By Bicycle and Moped, *below*) don't allow their Jeeps to be driven over sand, for insurance reasons. Renting a four-wheel-drive vehicle costs $40–$140 per day (prices fluctuate widely with the season).

By Bus From mid-May to mid-October, shuttles operate daily from 8 AM to midnight or so between Vineyard Haven (pickup on Union Street in front of the steamship wharf), Oak Bluffs (by the Civil War statue), and Edgartown (on Church Street). The rest of the year buses operate 8 AM to 7 PM, sometimes on weekends only; for the current bus schedule, call the shuttle hotline (tel. 508/693–1589) or flip through a Steamship Authority schedule. Shuttle tickets cost $1.50–$3 each way year-round. A three-town combination ticket costs an economical $4.

Buses from the Down-Island towns to Gay Head—which stop at the airport, West Tisbury, Chilmark, and on demand wherever it's safe to do so—run between 9 AM and 5 PM in July and August; at other times, call to confirm. Cost: $1–$5 one-way.

By Trolley The Martha's Vineyard Transit Authority (tel. 508/627–7448) offers two trolley routes in Edgartown.

Downtown From mid-May to mid-September, trolleys make a continuous circuit of downtown, beginning at free parking lots on the outskirts—at the Triangle off Upper Main Street, at the Edgartown School on Robinson Road (a right off the West Tisbury Road before Upper Main), and on Mayhew Lane. It's really worth doing to avoid parking headaches in town, and it's cheap (25¢) and convenient. Trolleys run every 10 minutes from 7:30 AM to 11:30 PM daily (mid-May–June, 7:30–7) and can be flagged along the route.

South Beach Trolley service to South Beach via Herring Creek and Katama roads is available mid-June–mid-September for $1.50 one-way (10-trip pass, $10). Pickup is at the corner of Main and Church streets. In good weather there are frequent pickups daily between 9 and 5:30, hourly in inclement weather, or you can flag a trolley whenever you see one. For information on weekly, monthly, or seasonal passes, call 508/627–9663.

By Taxi Taxis meet all scheduled ferries and flights, and there are taxi stands by the Flying Horses Carousel in Oak Bluffs, at the foot of Main Street in Edgartown, and by the Steamship office in Vineyard Haven. Companies serving the island include **All Island** (tel. 508/693–3705), **Marlene's** (tel. 508/693–0037), **Martha's Vineyard Taxi** (tel. 508/693–8660), and **Up Island** (tel. 508/693–5454). Fares range from $4 within a town to $35–$40 one way from Vineyard Haven to Gay Head; rates double after midnight.

By Limousine **Muzik's Limousine Service** (tel. 508/693–2212) and **Holmes Hole Car Rental & Limo Service** (tel. 508/693–8838) provide limo service on-island and sometimes travel off-island.

By Bicycle and Moped Martha's Vineyard is a great place for bicycling, though Up-Island roads are hilly, and during summer and fall the roads can be very crowded. There are several paved, scenic bike paths (*see* Sports and the Outdoors, *below*). To rent a moped, a driver's license is required; remember that many Vineyard roads are narrow, and watch out for loose gravel and sand. There are many accidents each year.

Rent bikes and mopeds in Oak Bluffs at **Anderson's** (tel. 508/693–9346), on the harbor, or at **De Bettencourt's** (tel. 508/693–0011; also Jeeps), **King's Bike & Moped** (tel. 508/693–1887), and **Ride-On Mopeds** (tel. 508/693–2076), all of which are located on Circuit Avenue Extension near the ferry docks. You can also try **Sun 'n' Fun** (Lake Ave., tel. 508/693–5457), which rents bikes, cars, Jeeps, and Jet Skis. In Edgartown try **R.W. Cutler Bike** (1 Main St., tel. 508/627–4052; Triangle, Upper Main St., tel. 508/627–7099) or **Wheelhappy** (8 S. Water St., tel. 508/627–5928), which delivers. In Vineyard Haven look for **Martha's Vineyard Scooter and Bike** (tel. 508/693–0782), just up from the ferry. No matter where you rent, expect to pay $7–$18 per day for bikes, $25–$50 per day for mopeds.

By Ferry The three-car **On Time** ferry—so named because it has no printed schedules and therefore can never be late—makes the five-minute run to Chappaquiddick Island (*see* Tour 3, *below*) June–mid-October, daily 7:30 AM–midnight; less frequently off-season. *Dock St., Edgartown, tel. 508/627–9427. Cost, round-trip: $1 individual, $4 car and driver, $2.50 bicycle and rider, $3.50 moped or motorcycle and rider.*

By Horse-drawn Carriage **Lysander Drives** (tel. 508/693–3789) offers rides in an antique surrey with Victorian-costumed driver.

Guided Tours

Orientation Buses meet all ferries for two-hour narrated tours of the island spring through fall, with a stop at the Gay Head Cliffs. See the island another way if possible.

Walking Tours **Liz Villard** (tel. 508/627–8619) leads walking tours on Edgartown's "history, architecture, ghosts, and gossip" that include visits to the historic Dr. Daniel Fisher House, the Vincent House, and the Old Whaling Church. Times for the tours, given April–December, are posted on the kiosk outside the church. Combination tickets with the Vineyard Museum are available.

Special-Interest Air Tours See the Vineyard by silent sailplane with **Soaring Adventures of America** (Katama Airfield, Herring Creek Rd., Edgartown, tel. 508/627–3833 or 800/762–7464). Tours are given daily in summer. It's just you and the pilot; you can even take a turn at the controls. **Katama Flights** (tel. 508/627–9018 or 508/627–4163) offers regular air tours.

Cruises The 50-foot sailing catamaran ***Arabella*** (tel. 508/645–3511) makes day sails out of Menemsha to Cuttyhunk and the Elizabeth islands with Captain Hugh Taylor. The teakwood sailing yacht ***Ayuthia*** (tel. 508/693–7245) offers half-day, full-day, and overnight sails to Nantucket or the Elizabeth Islands out of Coastwise Wharf in Vineyard Haven. Day sails, sunset cruises, and overnights to Nantucket or Cuttyhunk on the 54-foot Alden ketch ***Laissez Faire*** (tel. 508/693–1646) leave out of Vineyard Haven. ***Mad Max*** (tel. 508/627–7500), a 60-foot high-tech catamaran, offers day sails and charters out of Edgartown.

The ***Shenandoah*** (tel. 508/693–1699), a square topsail schooner, offers six-day cruises including meals; passengers are ferried to ports, which may include Nantucket, Cuttyhunk, New Bedford, Newport, Block Island, or others. One or two weeks each summer, day sails with lunch are offered (call for schedule). Cruises depart from Coastwise Wharf in Vineyard Haven.

Exploring Martha's Vineyard

The island is roughly triangular, with maximum distances of about 20 miles east to west and 10 miles north to south. The west end of the Vineyard, known as Up-Island (from the nautical expression of going "up" in degrees of longitude as you sail west), is more rural and wild than the east end, known as

Down-Island (comprising Vineyard Haven, Oak Bluffs, and Edgartown). Almost a fifth of the island (over 11,400 acres) is conservation land, and more is being acquired all the time by organizations—including the Land Bank, funded by a 2% tax on real estate transactions—that exist in order to preserve as much of the island in its natural state as is possible and practical.

Highlights for First-time Visitors

Edgartown (*see* Tour 3: Edgartown)
Felix Neck or **Cedar Tree Neck** (*see* Nature Areas)
Gay Head Cliffs (*see* Tour 4: Up-Island)
Lambert's Cove Beach (*see* Beaches)
Menemsha (*see* Tour 4: Up-Island)
Oak Bluffs Camp Ground (*see* Tour 2: Oak Bluffs)
The Vineyard Museum (*see* Tour 3: Edgartown)
Wasque Reservation on Chappaquiddick (*see* Tour 3: Edgartown)

Tour 1: Vineyard Haven

Numbers in the margin correspond to points of interest on the Vineyard Haven map.

Because most visitors to the island come by the Vineyard Haven ferry (the town is officially named Tisbury, but commonly referred to as Vineyard Haven, the name of the port), we begin here. There's an information booth by the steamship terminal, or a short walk from the steamship terminal along Water Street and a right onto Beach Road will take you to the
❶ **Martha's Vineyard Chamber of Commerce** for maps and information.

Time Out On Water Street, across from the A&P, the **Black Dog Bakery** (tel. 508/693–7550) offers fresh breads and baked goods, quick-lunch items, and Black Dog gift items (*see* Shopping, *below*). A new shop out back sells a wider range of Black Dog mementoes.

The next right after the chamber building is Main Street, with shops and places to eat. From here, a left onto Spring Street
❷ brings you to the **Association Hall.** The 1844 neoclassical structure houses the town hall as well as the Katharine Cornell Memorial Theatre, created in part with funds the actress—a long-time summer resident—donated in her will. The walls of the theater, on the second floor, are painted with murals depicting such island scenes as whaling and an Indian gathering; overhead is a blue sky with seagulls. Island artist Stan Murphy painted the murals on the occasion of the town's tercentenary, in 1971. In addition to theatrical performances, concerts and dances are held here.

❸ A path to the left of the hall leads to the **Centre Street Cemetery**, where tall pine trees shade grave markers dating as far back as 1817. Some stones are simple gray slate slabs; others are engraved with such motifs as the death's-head, or skull, common on early tombstones. A more recent grave is that of Katharine Cornell, who died in 1974.

Leave the cemetery via Center Street, turning right; past the town tennis courts is **William Street,** a quiet stretch of white

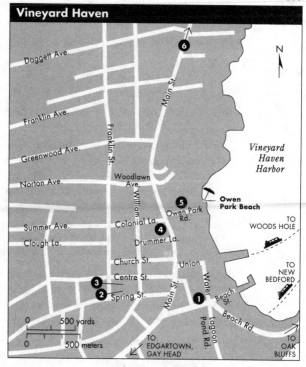

Vineyard Haven

picket fences and Greek Revival houses, many of them built for prosperous sea captains. Now a part of a National Historic District, the street was spared when the Great Fire of 1883 claimed much of the old whaling and fishing town.

At **108 William Street,** set back on a wide lawn behind a wrought-iron fence just before Colonial Lane, is an imposing monument to a later source of the town's prosperity: tourism. The elegantly detailed three-story house was built in 1873 by Benjamin C. Cromwell—captain not of a whaling ship but rather a steamer that brought New Bedford folk to the island.

4 Turn down the unmarked Colonial Lane. At the intersection of Main Street is the **Old Schoolhouse Museum,** built in 1829 as the first town school. Exhibits include items brought back from voyages during whaling days, including Polynesian and Inuit tools, as well as antique musical instruments, clothing, and records of 19th-century schoolchildren. Out front is the **Liberty Pole,** erected by the Daughters of the American Revolution in commemoration of three patriotic girls who blew up the town's liberty pole in 1776 to prevent it from being taken for use on a British warship. *110 Main St., tel. 508/693–3860. Admission: $2 adults, $1 children under 13. Open mid-June–mid-Sept., Tues.–Fri. and Sun. noon–4. Closed Sat. and Mon.; mid-Sept.–mid-June.*

5 Across the street and a block up Main is **Owen Park,** with swings, a bandstand where summer band concerts are held (*see* The Arts, *below*), and tree-shaded benches that give fine views of the harbor. At the end of the lawn is a public beach with a swing set and a close-up view of the boats coming in and out of the harbor.

In the 19th century, this harbor was one of the busiest ports in the world, welcoming thousands of coastwise vessels each year. The headlands on either side—West Chop in Vineyard Haven and East Chop in Oak Bluffs—each came to have a lighthouse at its tip to help bring ships safely into port. Both areas were largely settled in the late 19th to early 20th centuries, when the very rich from Boston and Newport built expansive bluff-top "summer cottages." These houses—built in what is called the Shingle Style, characterized by broad gable ends, dormers, and, of course, natural shingle siding that weathers to gray— were meant to eschew pretense, though they were sometimes gussied up a bit with a turret or two.

6 Today beautiful, green **West Chop** retains its exclusive air and boasts some of the island's most distinguished residents. A 2-mile drive or bike ride along Main Street, which becomes increasingly residential, will take you there. The 52-foot white-and-black **West Chop Lighthouse,** on the right, was built in 1881 of brick, to replace an 1817 wood light. It has been moved back twice from the edge of the eroding bluff. Just beyond the lighthouse, on the point, is a scenic overlook with a landscaped area and benches.

If you return to town via Franklin Street you pass the **West Chop Woods,** an 85-acre conservation area with marked walking trails through pitch pine and oak; there's parking off Franklin Street and a bike rack on Main Street.

Tour 2: Oak Bluffs

Numbers in the margin correspond to points of interest on the Oak Bluffs map.

Beach Road leads east out of Vineyard Haven across a narrow strip of land between the harbor on the left and Lagoon Pond: a haven for boats passing in storms, a good scalloping and water-sports area, and the site of the **State Lobster Hatchery** (*see* Off the Beaten Track, *below*). A left onto Highland Drive, after the drawbridge, takes you past **Crystal Lake** and the wild-
7 life preserve that surrounds it. Beyond the lake is **East Chop** and the **East Chop Lighthouse.** Built of cast iron in 1876 to replace an 1828 tower—used as part of a semaphore system between the island and Boston—that burned down, the 40-foot tower stands high atop a bluff from which the views of Nantucket Sound are spectacular. Keeping to the coast road, you'll come eventually to **Oak Bluffs Harbor.** Once the setting for a number of grand hotels—the 1879 **Wesley Hotel** on Lake Avenue is the last of them—the still colorful harbor now specializes in gingerbread-trimmed guest houses and minimalls hawking fast food and souvenirs.

8 A new attraction on the harbor in 1993 was **Butterflies in Flight,** a walk-through butterfly garden in an 1,800-square-foot greenhouse. Inside are a fish pond with waterfall, birds, 1,000 tropical and wildflower plants, and 500–600 North American butterflies. A taped narrative and exhibits on developmental stages inform you about the creatures flying around you, and there's a theme gift shop. *Circuit Ave. Ext., tel. 508/693–*

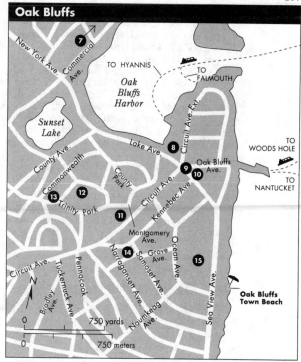

Oak Bluffs

*4006. Admission: $4 adults, $3 children 3–12. Open May–Sept.,
daily 9–sundown (gift shop open 9–9).*

This walking tour of town begins where Lake Avenue runs into
Oak Bluffs Avenue (which ends at the steamship dock). A good
first stop in season is the gingerbread-trimmed **information
booth.** Across the way is the building that houses the **Flying
Horses,** the nation's oldest continuously operating carousel,
and a National Historic Landmark. Handcrafted in 1876 and
extensively renovated in 1990–91, it offers small children entertainment from a Nintendo-less time. While waiting in line,
you can munch on popcorn, slushes, or cotton candy. In the
waiting area are a number of 20th-century diversions: ping-ing
arcade games. *Oak Bluffs Ave., tel. 508/693–9481. Rides cost $1;
$8 for a book of 10. Open mid-June–Labor Day, daily 10–10;
spring and fall, weekends only; closed in winter.*

Time Out   **Standby Diner** (Oak Bluffs Ave., tel. 508/693–5525), across the
street, is light and bright, with lots of small-paned windows and
a marble countertop salvaged from an old diner by the owner
and cook, Jack. Eggs and omelets are served all day, along with
lunches and dinners of homemade soups (like pork-and-green-
chili stew), burgers and clubs, fresh seafood, and blue-plate
specials (shepherd's pie, grilled pork chops, steak, fried
chicken) at $6–$8 off-season, $8–$12 in season. Seafood and
pasta dishes highlight in-season dinner menus. Senior citizens
get a 10% discount on request.

Just beyond the Flying Horses is Circuit Avenue, the center of the Oak Bluffs action, with most of the town's shops, bars, and ⑪ restaurants. Here, on the right, is the entrance to the **Oak Bluffs Camp Ground,** a 34-acre warren of streets tightly packed with more than 300 Carpenter Gothic Victorian cottages, gaily painted in pastels with wedding-cake trim. As you wander through this fairy-tale setting, imagine it at night, lit by the warm glow from hundreds of Japanese paper lanterns hung from every cottage porch. This is what happens each summer on Illumination Night, when the end of the Camp Meeting season—attended these days by some fourth- and fifth-generation cottagers—is marked as it has been for more than a century, with lights, singing, and open houses for families and friends. (Because of overwhelming crowds of onlookers in seasons past, the date is not announced until the week before.)

⑫ As you enter the grounds, before you is the **Tabernacle,** an impressive open-air structure of iron at the center of Trinity Park. On Wednesdays at 8 PM in season, visitors are invited to join in on an old-time community sing. If you know tunes like "The Erie Canal" or just want to listen in (music books are available for a donation), drop by the Tabernacle and take a seat. Also in the park is the 1878 **Trinity Methodist Church.**

The Cottage Museum, in an 1867 cream-and-orange cottage near the Tabernacle, exhibits cottage furnishings from the early days, including photographs, hooked rugs, quilts, and old Bibles. The gift shop offers Victorian and nautical items. *1 Trinity Park, tel. 508/693–0525. Donation: $1. Open mid-June– Sept., Mon.–Sat. 10–4. Closed Oct.–mid-June.*

Exit the Camp Ground as you entered, but don't leave until you've spotted what's called the **Wooden Valentine** (25 Washington Ave.); just think purple. At Circuit Avenue, cross the street and turn right. At the junction of the next street, again cross the street and head left. The octagonal building you see ⑭ is the nonsectarian **Union Chapel,** built in 1870 for the Cottage City resort folk who lived outside the Camp Ground's seven-foot-high fence. In summer, concerts are held here. Follow Grove Avenue to Ocean Avenue, a crescent of large Shingle-style cottages, with lots of turrets, breezy porches, and pastel ⑮ facades, circling **Ocean Park.** Band concerts take place at the gazebo here on summer nights, and in August the park hosts hordes of island families and visitors for a grand fireworks display over the ocean, across Sea View Avenue.

Tour 3: Edgartown

Numbers in the margin correspond to points of interest on the Edgartown map.

Edgartown is approached from Oak Bluffs via a scenic 6-mile section of Beach Road. On your left is Nantucket Sound and one of the island's best beach areas; soon the road narrows to an ever-eroding strip separating the Sound from Sengekontacket Pond, on your right. A protected bike path also runs the distance.

Edgartown, a world away from the honky-tonk of Oak Bluffs, is a tidy, polished town of upscale boutiques and elegant 17th- and 18th-century sea captains' houses ensconced in well-manicured gardens and lawns. To orient yourself historically a bit

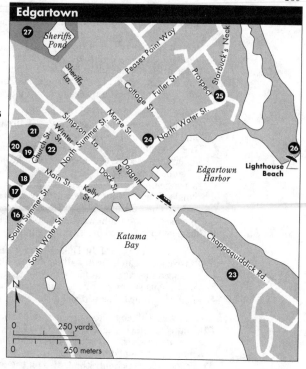

before touring the town, you might want to stop off at a complex of buildings and lawn exhibits that constitute the **Vineyard Museum**. The following opening hours apply to all the exhibits, which are detailed below. *Cooke St., corner of School St., tel. 508/627–4441. Admission: mid-June–mid-Sept., $4 adults, $2 senior citizens and children 12–17; mid-Sept.–mid-June, $2 adults, $1 senior citizens and children. Open July 4–Labor Day, daily 10–4:30; rest of year, call for hours.*

The one property open in summer only is the **Thomas Cooke House**, set in the 1765 home of a customs collector. The house itself is part of the display, including the low doorways, the wide-board floors, the original raised-panel woodwork with fluted pilasters, and the hearths in the summer and winter kitchens. Docents conduct tours of the 12 rooms, whose exhibits explore the island's history through furniture, tools, costumes, portraits, toys, crafts, and various household objects. One room is set up as a 19th-century parlor, illustrating the opulence of the golden age of whaling through such period pieces as a 2-foot-long inlaid Swiss-movement music box and a pianoforte. Upstairs are ship models, whaling paraphernalia, and old customs documents, as well as a room tracing the evolution of the Camp Meeting through photographs and objects.

The **Francis Foster Museum** houses a small collection of whaling implements, scrimshaw, navigational instruments, and lots of old photographs. One interesting exhibit is a collection of 19th-century miniature photographs of 110 Edgartown whaling masters, grouped by family. In the same building is the **Gale**

Huntington Reference Library, with genealogical records, rare island books, and ships' logs from the whaling days, plus some publications for sale. The **Capt. Francis Pease House,** an 1850s Greek Revival adjacent to the library, houses a permanent exhibit of Native American, prehistoric, pre-Columbian, and later artifacts, including arrowheads and pottery, plus changing exhibits from the collection. The Children's Gallery displays changing exhibits created by children.

The **Carriage Shed** displays a number of vessels and vehicles, including a whaleboat, a snazzy 1855 fire engine with stars inlaid in wood, and an 1830 hearse, considerably less ornate than the fire engine, and rightly so. The shed also houses some peculiar gravestones that once marked the eternal resting places of some strangely beloved chickens. In the yard outside it are a replica of a 19th-century **brick tryworks,** used to process whale oil from blubber aboard ship; and the 1,008-prism **Fresnel lens** installed in the Gay Head Lighthouse in 1854 and removed when the light was automated in 1952. Each evening the lens lamp is lighted briefly after sundown.

The museum, part of the Dukes County Historical Society, sells an excellent Edgartown walking-tour booklet ($4.95) that is full of anecdotes, as well as history, about the people who have lived in the houses along the route over the past three centuries. The following tour takes you along the most interesting streets.

Leaving the complex, proceed down School Street toward Main Street. On the left, at **60 Davis Lane,** is a handsome white clapboard Greek Revival with black shutters and fan ornament, surrounded by gardens. It was built in 1825 as a private school. At **20 School Street,** also on the left, is a white monumental Greek Revival fronted with four big Doric columns; built as a Baptist church in 1839, it is now a private residence.

At the end of School Street, turn left onto Main Street. On the right (at No. 89) is the **Old Whaling Church,** begun in 1843 as a Methodist church and now a performing-arts center. The massive Greek Revival building has a six-column monumental portico, unusual three-sash windows, and a 92-foot clock tower that can be seen for miles. The simple yet graceful interior is bright with 27-foot-tall windows and retains the original box pews and lectern. Aside from during performances, you can get inside only as part of the historical walking tours offered by Liz Villard (*see* Guided Tours, *above*), which also offer the only access to the Fisher and Vincent properties discussed below.

Next door is the graceful **Dr. Daniel Fisher House,** with wraparound roofwalk, small front portico with fluted columns topped by acanthus capitals, and a simple but elegant side portico with thin fluted columns. It was built in 1840 for one of the island's richest men, who was not only a doctor but also the owner of a whale-oil refinery, a spermaceti candle factory, and a gristmill, among other things. The house is now used for functions and office space.

In back of the Fisher House is the island's oldest dwelling: the 1672 **Vincent House,** a weathered-shingle farmhouse moved to this site in 1977, restored, and now maintained as an architectural museum. Most of the original wide-board floors, glass, brick, and hardware remain; parts of walls have been exposed to reveal the early wattle-and-daub construction methods.

㉒ Across Church Street (or around the corner from the Whaling Church) is the **Edgartown Visitors Center** (no phone), with information, rest rooms, and snacks.

Heading back down Main Street toward the harbor, you enter the commercial district of Edgartown. A left onto North Water Street brings you past Daggett Street, at the end of which is **㉓** the ferry to **Chappaquiddick Island** (*see* Getting Around by Ferry, *above*). A sparsely populated area with a surprising number of nature preserves, the island makes a great day trip or bike ride on a sunny day. Chappaquiddick Island is actually connected to the Vineyard by a long sand spit from South Beach—a spectacular 2³/₄-mile walk if you have the energy.

From the Chappy side of the ferry landing, past the striped cabanas of the Chappy Beach Club, the paved road leads to **Brine's Pond,** a 41-acre Land Bank area. The mown grasses around the serpentine pond with an island in the center and woodland behind make this a popular, scenic picnicking spot.

Continue on the paved road to a sharp bend, where a sign steers you onto the dirt Dyke Road for the Trustees of Reservations' 14-acre **Mytoi** preserve. On the left side of Dyke Road is a tranquil Japanese park, created in 1958 by a private citizen. The park was seriously lashed by 1991's Hurricane Bob, but you can still admire the creek-fed pool spanned by a bridge and rimmed with Japanese maples, azaleas, and irises. Walking trails across the street, which lead to a salt marsh with views to a barrier beach, have not yet been restored. *Tel. 508/693–7662. Admission free. Open daily sunrise–sunset.*

At the end of Dyke Road (.2 mile farther) is the **Dyke Bridge,** infamous as the scene of the 1969 accident in which a young woman was killed in a car driven by Ted Kennedy. Across the inlet here is the 509-acre **Cape Poge Wildlife Refuge,** with the spectacular **East Beach** and the **Cape Poge Light.** Until the rickety bridge is replaced (it was dismantled in 1991), the only access is by boat, as part of a naturalist-led Jeep tour (tel. 508/693–7662), or by four-wheel-drive from the Wasque Reservation (*see below*).

Back on the paved road, just before the pavement ends, a Land Bank marker on the left leads to the 99-acre **Poucha Pond Reservation.** Trails shaded by pines and oaks lead around the marshy pond; at the end of the trail is a great view of the pond, the Dyke Bridge, and the East Beach dunes in the distance. Bring binoculars for the birds and repellent for the mosquitoes. *3.8 mi from ferry landing, tel. 508/627–7141. Admission free. Open daily sunrise–sunset.*

After the paved road becomes dirt, continue on for ³/₄ mile to the gatehouse for the 200-acre **Wasque Reservation.** With the adjacent Cape Poge Wildlife Refuge, with which it is cooperatively managed by the Trustees of Reservations, Wasque (pronounced "WAYCE-qwee") is a wilderness of dunes, woods, moors, salt marshes, ponds, tidal flats, and barrier beach—as well as an important migration stopover or nesting area for many sea and shore birds. You'll need an over-sand four-wheel-drive vehicle to access much of the acreage; a Trustees annual permit ($60–$100) is required, available on site or for through Coop's Bait & Tackle (*see* Fishing, *below*).

Leading off from the gatehouse are the four-wheel-drive route and roads to two parking lots. Beyond the fishermen's lot, atop a bluff, is a pine-shaded picnic grove with a spectacular, practically 180° panorama. Below is Swan Pond, rich in bird life (including swans, of course) and surrounded by marsh and beach grasses. Beyond it is beach, sky, and boat-dotted sea. From the grove, a long boardwalk leads down amid the grasses to **Wasque Point,** a prime surfcasting spot. There's plenty of wide sandy beach here to sun on, but swimming is dangerous because of strong currents.

The other parking lot leads to **Wasque Beach**—just as wide and sandy as Wasque Point but better for swimming—via a flat boardwalk with benches overlooking the west end of Swan Pond. A walking path joins this parking lot with the picnic grove; it is a pretty walk, skirting the pond with lots of benches and ocean-view overlooks on one side, osprey poles on the other. *Tel. 508/627–7260. Admission: $3 cars, plus $3 adults over 15 Memorial Day–mid-Sept.; free rest of year. Property open 24 hrs; gatehouse open mid-June–Columbus Day, daily 9–5.*

Back on the "mainland," the upper part of North Water Street, the most photographed strip of architecture in town, is lined by many fine captains' houses. There's always some interesting detail you never noticed before—like a widow's walk with a mannequin poised, spyglass in hand, watching for her seafaring husband to return. The 1832 house where this piece of
㉔ whimsy can be seen is at **86 North Water Street,** which the Society for the Preservation of New England Antiquities maintains as a rental property.

㉕ At the bend in the road is the gray-shingled Victorian **Harbor View Hotel,** on the left. Built in the 1890s and a major player in the Vineyard's early resort days, the very upscale property was totally renovated in 1990; additions include period details such as the gazebo off the wraparound veranda and new turrets. A path off to the right just before the hotel leads down to
㉖ the **Edgartown Lighthouse,** surrounded by a public beach with a good view but seaweedy bathing. The original light guarding the harbor was built in 1828 on an island made from granite blocks. The island was later connected to the mainland by a bridge. By the time the 1938 hurricane made a new light necessary, sand had filled in the gap between the island and the mainland. The current white-painted cast-iron tower was floated over from Ipswich, Massachusetts, on a barge in 1939.

This area, called Starbuck's Neck, is a good place to wander about in, with views of ocean, harbor, a little bay, and moorland. Return to town by continuing past the hotel and turning left onto Fuller Street. Or take a right off Fuller to Peases Point Way; behind the tennis courts is a trail circling an old ice pond
㉗ that is at the center of **Sheriffs Meadow Sanctuary,** 17 acres of marsh, woodland, and field.

Tour 4: Up-Island

Numbers in the margin correspond to points of interest on the Up-Island map.

Much of what makes the Vineyard special is found here, in the agricultural heart of the island and the largely undeveloped lands along the perimeter, from West Chop in the north to Ed-

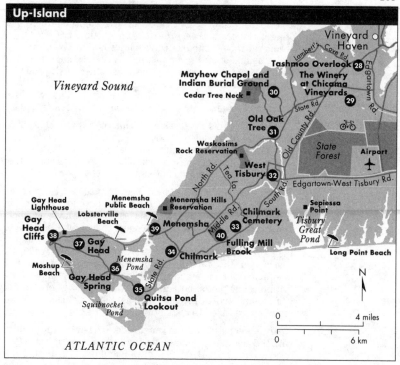

gartown in the southeast. Country roads meander through woods and tranquil farmland; dirt side roads lead past crystalline ponds, abandoned cranberry bogs, and conservation lands. In Chilmark, West Tisbury, and Gay Head, nature lovers, writers, artists, and others have established close ongoing summer communities. In winter, the isolation and bitter winds send even many year-round Vineyarders from their Up-Island homes to places in the Down-Island towns.

This tour starts from State Road in Vineyard Haven. Just outside the center of town, on the right, is a turnout. Called the

28 **Tashmoo Overlook,** it is a scenic viewpoint overlooking a meadow leading down to Lake Tashmoo and Vineyard Sound beyond. The meadow is public space; across the lane from it is the **amphitheater** where summer Vineyard Playhouse productions are held.

Time Out Before the overlook, turn in at John's Fish Market for **Sandy's Fish & Chips** (tel. 508/693-1220), a seasonal clam shack, with takeout fried fish and seafood, burgers, and soft ice cream.

29 After a mile or so, a green sign on the left directs you to **The Winery at Chicama Vineyards** (Stoney Hill Rd., tel. 508/693-0309). (From Edgartown, take the Edgartown–Vineyard Haven Road and turn off at the sign for Thimble Farm.) From 35 acres of trees and rocks, the Mathiesen family—George, a broadcaster from San Francisco; his wife, Cathy; and their six children—have created a vineyard, starting in 1971 with 75 vinifera vines. Today the winery produces nearly 100,000 bottles a year, from chardonnay, cabernet, Riesling, Pinot noir, and other European grapes. Free tours and tastings are given daily Memorial Day–Columbus Day; call for details about the limited schedule of off-season tastings. A shop selling wines and herbed vinegars, mustards, jellies, and other foods prepared on the premises is open year-round (closed July 4 and Labor Day). A Christmas shop with glassware, gift baskets, wreaths, and more is open mid-November through New Year's Eve.

Farther down this woodsy lane is **Thimble Farm** (tel. 508/693–6396), with pick-your-own strawberries and raspberries (and preboxed fruits in case you're not feeling so rural). Also available are cut flowers, melons, pumpkins, hydroponic tomatoes, and other produce grown here.

Return to State Road and bear right toward Gay Head at the next fork, remaining on State Road. Just beyond is Indian Hill Road; turning into a dirt road, this leads to the **Mayhew Chapel and Indian Burial Ground.** The small chapel, built in 1829 to replace an earlier one, and a memorial plaque are dedicated to the pastor Thomas Mayhew, Jr., leader of the original colonists who landed at Edgartown in 1642. Mayhew was an enlightened man, noted for his fair dealings with the local Wampanoags. Within a few years, he had converted a number of them to Christianity; called Praying Indians, they established a community here called Christiantown.

Near the chapel is a wildflower garden, and beyond the boulder with the plaque are stones marking Indian grave mounds (the dead are not named, for fear of calling down evil spirits). Behind the chapel is the beginning of a loop trail through the woods (there's a map at the first trail fork), which leads to a lookout tower.

A sign just before you rejoin State Road leads to the **Cedar Tree Neck** nature preserve (*see* Nature Areas, *below*). Back on State Road, turn right. Soon thereafter you'll pass **Takemmy Farm** (*see* What to See and Do with Children, *below*)—keep an eye out for llamas by the fence on the right. Farther on, on the right, is **Glassworks of Martha's Vineyard** (tel. 508/645–3367), where you can watch glass being blown (and buy some, too) by glassmakers who have works in the Boston Museum of Fine Arts. Just before the intersection of North Road (the sign points to Menemsha), in a field on the right, is what's fondly known as the **Old Oak Tree,** a massive, ancient oak that is an island landmark.

Soon State Road brings you into the center of **West Tisbury.** For centuries a sheep-farming region, the town continues its agricultural tradition with several active horse and produce farms; it also encompasses half of the 4,000-acre **State Forest.** West Tisbury's center looks very much the small New England village, complete with a white, steepled church. **Alley's General Store** (State Rd., tel. 508/693–0088), the heart of the town center since 1858, sells everything from hammers to dill pickles; the Martha's Vineyard Preservation Trust purchased the building in 1993 and plans a thorough restoration to preserve its rural character.

Time Out   Behind Alley's is **Back Alley's** (tel. 508/693–7367), serving tasty sandwiches, grocery items, and pastries to go year-round.

Past the mansard-roofed town hall is the 1859 **Agricultural Hall,** where a county fair, including livestock and produce judging, is held in August (*see* Festivals and Seasonal Events in Chapter 1, Essential Information) and weekly farmer's markets are held in summer (*see* Shopping, *below*). The Agricultural Society purchased a nearby parcel of land in 1992; when construction on a new, larger Ag Hall is finished, the fair and market will be moved there. Across from the present site is the **Field Gallery** (tel. 508/693–5595), where Tom Maley's large white sculptures, like a colonial horse and rider or a whimsical piper, are displayed on a wide lawn. Inside are changing summer exhibitions of island artists. Just after the First Congregational Church, on the right, is **Music Street,** a street of old sea captains' homes once noted for a preponderance of pianos bought with whaling profits.

33 About 3 miles out of West Tisbury center, on the right, is **Chilmark Cemetery,** where John Belushi is buried. His tree-shaded grave, near the entrance, is marked by a boulder in which his name is deeply engraved. Visitors often leave odd tokens of remembrance. Lillian Hellman, a longtime summer resident of the island, is also buried here. A mile farther, don't miss the view on your left of Chilmark's **Allen Farm**—an impressive vista across pastureland protected by the Land Bank. A shop here (tel. 508/645–9064) sells handwoven blankets and knitted items made from the farm's wool. Another half-mile up on the left, look for a big telephone pole at the center of a paved street entrance (if you see a grass road divider, you've gone too far); this dirt road leads to **Lucy Vincent Beach,** perhaps the island's most beautiful.

The crossroads you soon come to is called **Beetlebung Corner,** named for the stand of beetlebung, or black gum, trees on your
34 right. This is the center of **Chilmark,** whose scenic ocean-view roads, rustic woodlands, and lack of crowds have drawn chic summer visitors and, hard on their heels, stratospheric real estate prices. At Beetlebung are the town's public buildings, including the firehouse and the post office, as well as the **Chilmark Community Center,** where everything from town meetings to auctions to chamber music concerts are held. In summer, a general store, a clothing boutique, a restaurant and breakfast café, a gallery, and a bank turn the little crossroads into a minimetropolis.

Continue on State Road. After about 1½ miles, a paved road on the left leads to **Squibnocket Beach,** a rocky beauty with a tranquil, covelike look. Beyond the next bend on State Road is
35 the **Quitsa Pond Lookout,** with a good view of the adjoining Menemsha and Nashaquitsa ponds, the woods, and the ocean beyond. Just past the Gay Head town line, on the left, is
36 **Gay Head spring;** from an iron pipe gushes water cold enough to slake a cyclist's thirst on the hottest day. Feel free to fill a canteen; locals come from all over the island to fill jugs.

37 **Gay Head** is an official Native American township: In 1987, after more than a decade of struggle in the courts, the Wampanoag tribe won guardianship of 420 acres of land, which are being held in trust by the federal government in perpetuity and constitute the Gay Head Native American Reservation. Also in Gay Head is the 380-acre estate of Jacqueline Onassis.

At the fork beyond the spring, take a left onto Moshup Trail, the coastal route, with views of dunes and sea. Continue to the **38** western tip of the island and the **Gay Head Cliffs,** a National Historic Landmark and part of the reservation land. These dramatically striated walls of red clay are the island's major tourist attraction, as evidenced by the tour bus–filled parking lot. Native American crafts and food shops line the approach to the overlook, from which you can see the Elizabeth Islands, north across Vineyard Sound, and Noman's Land Island (part wildlife preserve, part military bombing-practice site—with fake bombs), 3 miles off the Vineyard's southern coast.

Time Out   The **Aquinnah** (tel. 508/645–9654), at the end of the row of shops, is a Wampanoag-owned restaurant with a great view from the deck: of the moor-covered cliffs over which it is perched, of the long white stretch of beach 135 feet below, of the sea and islands, and of spectacular sunsets over the water. Highlights of the simple menu are fresh fish, homemade chowder and pies, and delicious breakfasts, like pancakes with fresh raspberries or pecans.

Adjacent to the overlook is the **Gay Head Lighthouse** (the largest of the Vineyard's five), precariously stationed atop the rapidly eroding cliffs. In 1798, a wood lighthouse was built here—the island's first—to warn ships away from Devil's Bridge, an area of shoals a quarter-mile offshore. The current incarnation, built in 1856 of red brick, carries on with its alternating pattern of red and white flashes. Despite the light, the Vineyard's worst wreck occurred here in January 1884, when the *City of Columbus* sank, taking with it into the icy waters more than 100 passengers and crew. The original Fresnel lens was removed when the lighthouse was automated in 1952, but it is preserved at the Vineyard Museum in Edgartown (*see* Tour 3: Edgartown, *above*). The lighthouse is open to the public summer weekends for sunsets, weather permitting; private tours can also be arranged (tel. 508/693–4922 or 508/645–9954).

Head out from the cliffs area via State Road, which will take you past the "center" of Gay Head. This consists of a combination fire and police station, the town hall, a Tribal Council office, and a public library, formerly the little red schoolhouse (because the town's year-round population is only about 650, Gay Head children attend schools in other towns). A left onto Lobsterville Road and a right onto West Basin Road (off which another right leads to a parking lot for Menemsha Pond) take you along the shore of Menemsha Bight and through the **Cranberry Lands,** an area of cranberry bog gone wild that is a popular nesting site for birds. No humans can nest here, but you can drive by and look. At the end of the road, with marshland on the right and low dunes and grasses and the long blue arc of the bight on the left, you get a terrific view of the quiet fishing village of Menemsha, across the water. **Lobsterville Road Beach** here is public, but there's no parking.

Return to State Road via Lobsterville Road, and at Beetlebung **39** Corner, follow signs to **Menemsha.** If you think you've seen it before, you probably have: It was used for location shots in the film *Jaws*. The jumble of weathered fishing shacks, fishing and pleasure boats, drying nets and lobster pots, and dads and kids pole-fishing from the jetty is a picturesque scene not lost on myriad photographers and artists, but this is very much a working village. The catch of the day loaded off the boats coming in and out of the channel can be bought from markets along Dutcher's Dock, or from the restaurant Home Port (*see* Dining, *below*). Romantics bring picnic suppers to the public **Menemsha Beach** for catching perfect sunsets over the water. In season, **Creek Charters** (tel. 508/645–9097) offers a water taxi across the channel to the Gay Head side—a saving of a dozen or so strenuous miles by bike—as well as overnight charters to the Elizabeth Islands and Nantucket.

Back at Beetlebung, turn left onto **Middle Road** to enjoy pastoral Chilmark at its best, with gently rolling farmland and woodland marked off by low stone fences, as well as ocean views here and there from elevated points. On the right, a small **40** brown sign marks the parking lot for **Fulling Mill Brook**, a 50-acre town-owned conservation area; a walking trail slopes gently down along the brook (with big boulders to sit and sun on) to the property's edge at South Road, where there's a bike rack and another sign. A right at the end of Middle Road brings you back to West Tisbury center, from which roads lead anywhere you want to go on the island.

What to See and Do with Children

The **Chilmark Community Center** (Beetlebung Corner, tel. 508/645–9484) has activities for children of all ages in summer, including dances, concerts, and movies. It's a great place for kids to meet other kids. Other towns have recreation programs as well: Edgartown (tel. 508/627–6145), Oak Bluffs (tel. 508/693–2303), Vineyard Haven (tel. 508/693–6220), and West Tisbury (tel. 508/693–2723).

The Children's Theatre in Oak Bluffs (at the high school, Edgartown–Vineyard Haven Rd., tel. 508/693–4060) has weekday classes for children in summer. **Vineyard Playhouse** (*see* The Arts, *below*) has theater-related activities for children and teens in summer.

Island Cove Mini Golf (State Rd., Vineyard Haven, tel. 508/693–2611), across from Cronig's, is a nine-hole, disabled-accessible course featuring bridges, a cave, fake rocks, sand traps, and a stream that powers a watermill.

Storytelling hours for children are offered by all the island's libraries. Call about days and times: **Chilmark** (Beetlebung Corner, tel. 508/645–3360), **Edgartown** (N. Water St., tel. 508/627–4221), **Oak Bluffs** (Circuit Ave., tel. 508/693–9433), **Vineyard Haven** (Upper Main St., tel. 508/696–4210), and **West Tisbury** (Music St., tel. 508/693–3366).

In summer, **Oak Bluffs** has all kinds of attractions to keep kids entertained. In a big white building across the street from the **Flying Horses Carousel** (*see* Tour 2: Oak Bluffs, *above*) is **The Game Room** (Oak Bluffs Ave., tel. 508/693–5163), with 85 arcade games, as well as pool tables, air hockey, and skeeball; planned for '94 is an addition for water bumper boats. At **Dockside Minigolf** (upstairs at Dockside Marketplace, Oak Bluffs Harbor, tel. 508/696–7646) each of the 18 holes—half indoors, half in the open—has an island motif, such as a ferryboat, a lighthouse, or a gingerbread house.

Nip 'n' Tuck Farm (State Rd., West Tisbury, tel. 508/693–1449) offers pony-cart rides in summer from 3 to 5 PM (and by arrangement), as well as hayrides for groups. Children can visit with the farm's baby lambs, ducks, and pigs on free tours (parents pay $1). The farm stand sells vegetables, raw milk, and soft-serve ice cream.

Arrowhead Farm (*see* Horseback Riding, *below*).

Takemmy Farm (State Rd., North Tisbury, tel. 508/693–2486) invites children to visit with the llamas (raised as pets and breeding stock) and miniature donkeys on Wednesday and Saturday afternoons year-round. Every day year-round, the farm stand sells eggs and yarn; in season, there are vegetables, flowers, and honey as well.

Gymnastics and movement day camps for children from age 3½ through high school are available in one-week summer programs through the U.S. Academy of Gymnastics (Sept.–mid-June, 11 Allen Rd., Norwalk, CT 06851, tel. 203/847–4994; mid-June–Aug., Box 2271, Vineyard Haven 02568, tel. 508/693–5225).

Felix Neck Wildlife Sanctuary (*see* Nature Areas, *below*) runs the **Fern & Feather Day Camp,** with one- or two-week summer sessions (including campouts) in which children learn about wildlife, plants, and the stars. Early registration is advised and begins in February.

Spinnaker Lanes (State Rd., Vineyard Haven, tel. 508/693–9691) offers 12 lanes of candlepin bowling and six tournament pool tables. Lanes are disabled-accessible.

Off the Beaten Track

The **Nathan Mayhew Seminars** (167 N. William St., Box 1125, Vineyard Haven 02568, tel. 508/693–6603) offer college-level two-day to seven-week courses in humanities, social science, business, and visual and performing arts year-round, as well as lectures, music and arts events, and workshops. In spring and fall, week-long, live-in Elderhostel academic programs are offered. The **Henry Beetle Hough Memorial Library,** in the same building (open by appointment only), is a research library on island studies. The basis of the collection is the personal library of the Pulitzer Prize-winning journalist who was editor of the *Vineyard Gazette* from 1920 to 1985.

A memorial to Thomas Mayhew, Jr.—called **Place on the Wayside**—was erected on the Edgartown–West Tisbury Road, just east of the airport entrance, on the opposite side. A plaque identifies the spot where Mayhew had his "last worship and interview with them before embarking for England" in 1657, never to return. (The ship was lost at sea.) Wampanoags passing this spot would leave a stone in Mayhew's memory; the stones were later cemented together to form the memorial.

June through August, the **State Lobster Hatchery** (end of Shirley Ave. on Lagoon Pond, Oak Bluffs, tel. 508/693–0060), which stocks all of coastal Massachusetts and does marine research, offers weekday tours of its visitor room, with rearing tanks and wall displays.

Martha's Vineyard Shellfish Group (tel. 508/693–0391) grows seed clams, scallops, and oysters to stock lagoons and beds throughout the county. From spring through fall, tours of the solar shellfish hatchery on Lagoon Pond in Vineyard Haven can be arranged with advance notice.

Shopping

A specialty of the island is wampum—black, white, or purple beads made from shells that are fashioned into jewelry and sold at the cliffs and elsewhere. Antique and new scrimshaw jewelry and the ultra-expensive, sometimes scrimshaw-topped pocket-books called Nantucket lightship baskets can be found at many island shops. Many Vineyard shops close for the winter, though quite a few in Vineyard Haven and a few elsewhere remain open; call to make sure a shop is open before making a special trip.

Shopping Districts The three main towns have the largest concentrations of shops. Most of Vineyard Haven's line Main Street. Edgartown's, the toniest, are clustered together within a few blocks of the dock, on Main, Summer, and Water streets. Primarily fun, casual clothing and gift shops line Circuit Avenue in Oak Bluffs. At Gay Head Cliffs, you'll find touristy Native American crafts and souvenirs in season.

Shopping Complexes **Tisbury Marketplace,** on Beach Road between Oak Bluffs and Vineyard Haven across from the Mobil station, has crafts and gift shops, a toy store, a music store, a sporting-goods shop, and a pizza parlor. In Edgartown, the **Colonial Inn Shops** (38 N. Water St.) sell art, crafts, and sports gear; the adjacent **Nevin Square** (Winter St.) has leather, clothing, art, antiques, and crafts. **Crispin's Landing** in Vineyard Haven (Main St.) has shops selling leather, pottery, jewelry, and crafts.

Department Store **The Fligors** (27 N. Water St., Edgartown, tel. 508/627–8811) is the closest thing to a department store on the island, with varied offerings, including preppy clothing and a Christmas shop.

Food and Flea Markets A **flea market** is held on the grounds of the Chilmark Community Church (Menemsha Cross Rd., tel. 508/645–3177) Wednesday and Saturday in season from about 7 AM until 2:30 or 3 PM.

A **farmers market**—offering fresh flowers, plants, fruits and vegetables, homemade baked goods and jams, honey, and fun— is held at the Agricultural Hall (tel. 508/693–9549) on South Road in West Tisbury mid-June–mid-October on Saturday from 9 to noon.

Specialty Stores **All Things Oriental** (Beach Rd., Vineyard Haven, tel. 508/693–
Antiques 8375) has jewelry, porcelains, paintings, furniture, and more.
Bramhall & Dunn (Main St., Vineyard Haven, tel. 508/693–6437; Red Barn Emporium, Old County Rd., West Tisbury, tel. 508/693–5221) carries stripped 19th-century English country pine furniture, as well as fine crafts, linens, and housewares.
C. W. Morgan Marine Antiques (Beach Rd., Vineyard Haven, next to MV Shipyard, tel. 508/693–3622) offers a wide range of museum-quality nautical items (instruments, sea chests, ship models, paintings, prints, and so forth).
Soulagnet Collection (Colonial Inn Shops, Edgartown, tel. 508/627–7759; Basin Rd., Menemsha, tel. 508/645–3735) has Americana, including furniture, folk art, and crafts, as well as local photographs and prints.

Art **Edgartown Art Gallery** (20 S. Summer St., Edgartown, tel. 508/627–8508), across from the Charlotte Inn, has 19th- and 20th-century oils and watercolors, including English sporting prints, marine art, and works by major local artists, plus small English antiques.

Goff's Gallery & Book Store (State Rd., North Tisbury, tel. 508/693–4484) sells books by Vineyard writers, Clark Goff's New England-themed prints and notepapers, Heather Goff's painted pottery (including her signature plates with farmscapes, cows, and other Vineyard scenes), Ingrid Goff's jewelry, and yarn from Vineyard sheep.

Granary Gallery (Red Barn Emporium, Old County Rd., West Tisbury, tel. 508/693–0455 or 800/472–6279) showcases sculptures and mostly representational paintings by island and international artists, including the photographs of Alfred Eisenstaedt. Biweekly shows spotlighting a local artist are preceded by Sunday-evening receptions.

Hermine Merel Smith Fine Art (Edgartown Rd., West Tisbury, tel. 508/693–7719) specializes in paintings and drawings by contemporary American impressionists.

Willoughby's (Old Post Office Sq., Edgartown, tel. 508/627–3369) features mostly island landscapes and scenes by Vineyard and Cape artists, including limited-edition prints and drawings.

Books The **Bunch of Grapes Bookstore** (Main St., Vineyard Haven, tel. 508/693–2291) and the newly enlarged **Bickerton & Ripley Books** (Main St., Edgartown, tel. 508/627–8463) carry a wide selection of new books, including many island-related titles, and sponsor book signings—watch the papers for announcements.

Book Den East (New York Ave., Oak Bluffs, tel. 508/693–3946) has 20,000 out-of-print, antiquarian, and paperback books housed in an old barn.

Clothing **Bramhall & Dunn** (*see* Antiques, *above*) in Vineyard Haven carries fine hand-knit sweaters and original women's accessories and shoes.

Island Children–Althea and Emily Designs (94 Main St., Vineyard Haven, tel. 508/693–6130) has children's and women's clothing in 100% cotton, hand-block-printed with unique African- and Caribbean-inspired and classic designs.

Lakota (by appointment, tel. 508/693–9044) has sophisticated, upscale women's dresses (some with a summery island feel), suits, and blouses in natural fibers, all designed by Lorraine Parrish (designer of Carly Simon's wedding dress). Some clothing uses fabrics designed by island artists.

Laughing Bear (138 Circuit Ave., Oak Bluffs, tel. 508/693–9342) has fun children's and women's wear made of Balinese or Indian batiks and other unusual materials, plus jewelry and accessories from around the world.

Murray's of the Vineyard (Main St., Vineyard Haven, tel. 508/693–2640), sister shop of Nantucket's Murray's Toggery, has classic men's and women's fashions, shoes, and accessories, from such names as Ralph Lauren and Liz Claiborne.

Nature Knits (Tisbury Marketplace, Beach Rd., Vineyard Haven, tel. 508/693–7776) sells natural-fiber clothing for children, as well as adult and maternity items.

Pandora's Box (Menemsha, tel. 508/645–9696) has unique and funky women's clothing and accessories.

Crafts **Chilmark Pottery** (off State Rd., West Tisbury, tel. 508/693–7874; Crispin's Landing, Main St., Vineyard Haven, tel. 508/693–2013) is a workshop and gallery showcasing hand-formed stoneware, porcelain, and Raku by island potters.

Edgartown Scrimshaw (Main St., tel. 508/627–9439) carries a large collection of scrimshaw, including some antique pieces, as well as Nantucket lightship baskets and 14-karat lightship-basket jewelry.

Michaela Ltd. Gallery of American Crafts (Towanticut Ave., Oak Bluffs, tel. 508/693–8408) has pottery, blown glass, jewelry, soaps, candles, baskets, woven goods, and more.

Gifts **Black Dog Bakery** (*see* Tour 1: Vineyard Haven, *above*) sells T-shirts, sweatshirts, beach towels, and many other gift items, all emblazoned with the signature Black Dog logo.

Chilmark Chocolates (State Rd., near Beetlebung Corner, tel. 508/645–3013) sells superior chocolates and buttercrunch that you can sometimes watch being made in the back room.

The Secret Garden (148 Circuit Ave., Oak Bluffs, tel. 508/693–4759), set in a yellow gingerbread cottage, has linens, lace, baby gifts, wicker furniture, prints, and more.

Tashtego (29 Main St., Edgartown, tel. 508/627–4300) is one of the island's most interesting shops, with small antiques, island crafts, and home furnishings.

At **Vineyard Photo Emporium** (115 Circuit Ave., Oak Bluffs, tel. 508/693–7733), you can have a sepia-style picture taken in costume before exotic backdrops.

Jewelry **Optional Art** (35 Winter St., Edgartown, tel. 508/627–5373) sells fine jewelry mostly in 18-karat gold, handcrafted by 30 award-winning American artisans.

Sioux Eagle Designs (Crispin's Landing, Main St., Vineyard Haven, tel. 508/693–6537) offers unusual handmade pieces.

Vivian Wolfe & Co. (42 Main St., Edgartown, tel. 508/627–5822) has antique and estate jewelry, as well as antique silver tea services, and so forth.

Sporting Goods **Brickman's** (Main St., Vineyard Haven, tel. 508/693–0047; Main St., Edgartown, tel. 508/627–4700) sells beach and sports gear, such as camping, fishing, snorkeling equipment and boogie boards; also sportswear, surfer-type clothing, and major-label footwear for the family.

Wind's Up! (Tisbury Market Place, Beach Rd., Vineyard Haven, tel. 508/693–4340) sells swimwear, windsurfing and sailing equipment, boogie boards, and other outdoor gear.

Sports and the Outdoors

Edgartown Recreation Area (Robinson Rd., tel. 508/627–9726) has four tennis courts, a basketball court, a softball field, a roller hockey court, a picnic area, and playground equipment. All areas are lighted some nights in summer. Activities (published in the papers) include tennis round-robins; softball and basketball games; arts and crafts; and rainy-day events. Also see the "Island Recreation" section of *The Vineyard Gazette*'s calendar for open Frisbee, rugby, and other games.

Bicycling There are well-maintained, flat paved paths along the coast road from Oak Bluffs to Edgartown—very scenic—and inland from Vineyard Haven to Edgartown to South Beach. These connect with paths—potholed in some places—that weave through the State Forest. Middle Road in Chilmark is a lovely winding country road with less traffic than the main roads. For information on unofficial group rides, call Cycleworks (tel. 508/693–6966). For bike rentals, *see* Getting Around by Bicycle and Moped, *above.*

The biggest race of the year is the **Tour of Martha's Vineyard** (tel. 508/693–1656), held on Tivoli Day in September, and beginning and ending in Oak Bluffs. The 60-mile race attracts contestants from all over the world.

Fishing Huge trawlers unload their catch daily at the docks in Vineyard Haven and Menemsha, attesting to the richness of the waters surrounding the island. One of the most popular spots for sport fishermen is **Wasque Point** (*see* Tour 3, *above*) on Chappaquiddick. Another is **South Beach** (*see* Beaches, *below*) and the jetty at the mouth of the **Menemsha Basin.** Striped bass and bluefish are island stars. Both island newspapers carry fishing columns as well as plentiful ads for fishing charters.

The annual **Martha's Vineyard Striped Bass & Bluefish Derby** (Box 2101, Edgartown 02539, tel. 508/627–8342), from mid-September to mid-October, offers daily, weekly, and derby prizes for striped bass (reintroduced in the '93 derby), bluefish, bonito, and false albacore catches, from boat or shore.

Pick up the current listing of fishing regulations at **Larry's Tackle Shop** (141 Main St., Edgartown, tel. 508/627–5088), **Coop's Bait and Tackle** (147 West Tisbury Rd., Edgartown, tel. 508/627–3909), and **Dick's Bait and Tackle** (New York Ave., Oak Bluffs, tel. 508/693–7669). All rent gear and sell accessories and bait.

The party boat *Skipper* (tel. 508/693–1238) leaves out of Oak Bluffs Harbor in season. Several outfits offer fishing charters, including **North Shore Charters** (Menemsha, tel. 508/645–2993), **Big Eye Charters** (Edgartown, tel. 508/627–3649), and the *Slapshot II* (Edgartown, tel. 508/627–8087).

Golf **Farm Neck Golf Club** (Farm Neck Rd., Oak Bluffs, tel. 508/693–3057), a semiprivate club on marsh-rimmed Sengekontacket Pond, has 18 holes in a championship layout, plus a driving range. The public **Mink Meadows Golf Course** (Golf Club Rd., off Franklin St., Vineyard Haven, tel. 508/693–0600), on West Chop, has nine holes and ocean views.

Health and Fitness Clubs Both the **Health Club at the Tisbury Inn** (Main St., Vineyard Haven, tel. 508/693–7400) and the **Vineyard Racquet & Fitness Center** (12 Mariner's Way, off Vineyard Haven Rd., Edgartown, tel. 508/627–7760) feature Lifecycle, Nautilus, Universal, and Stair Master machines, plus bikes, free-weight rooms, sauna and tanning facilities, aerobics classes, personal trainers, and day care. The latter also has two racquetball courts and a steam room.

Hiking The nature preserves and conservation areas (*see* Nature Areas, *below*) are laced with well-marked, scenic trails through varied terrains and ecological habitats. The miles of uninterrupted beaches are perfect for long walks.

Horseback Riding **Arrowhead Farm** (Indian Hill Rd., West Tisbury, tel. 508/693–8831) offers lessons for adults and children year-round, as well as children's summer horsemanship programs. The farm has an indoor ring and leases horses out but does not offer trail rides. **Martha's Vineyard Riding Center** (across from the airport, off the Edgartown Rd., West Tisbury, tel. 508/693–3770) offers English riding lessons, clinics, and horse shows; it also has indoor and outdoor rings, a hunt course, and scenic trails. Dawn, sunset, and moonlight rides are available. **Misty Meadows Horse Farm** (Old County Rd., West Tisbury, tel. 508/693–1870) offers trail rides and lessons. At any stable, be sure to call ahead to reserve. The **State Forest** (*see* Nature Areas, *below*) has horse trails through it.

Ice-skating   **Martha's Vineyard Ice Arena** (Edgartown–Vineyard Haven Rd., Oak Bluffs, tel. 508/693–5329) is open August–March.

Sailing and Boating   The **Harborside Inn** in Edgartown (S. Water St., tel. 508/627–4321 or 800/627–4009) rents O'Day 17s, Hobie Cats, and Boston Whalers and offers sailing lessons. **Sun 'n' Fun** (Lake Ave., tel. 508/693–5457) rents sailboats, as well as Jetboats and Jet Skis. **Vineyard Boat Rentals** (Dockside Marketplace, Oak Bluffs Harbor, tel. 508/693–8476) rents Boston Whalers, Bayliners, and Jet Skis. **Wind's Up!** (Beach Rd., Vineyard Haven, by Lagoon Pond, tel. 508/693–4252) rents day sailers, catamarans, and Sunfish, as well as Windsurfers and boogie boards, and offers lessons. For chartered cruises, *see* Guided Tours, *above*.

Scuba-diving   Vineyard waters hold a number of sunken ships, including several schooners and freighters off East Chop and Gay Head. **Vineyard Scuba** (S. Circuit Ave., Oak Bluffs, tel. 508/693–0288) has diving information and equipment rental.

Shellfishing   Each town issues shellfish licenses for the waters under its jurisdiction. Contact the town hall of the town in which you wish to fish for a permit, as well as information on good spots and a listing of areas closed because of seeding projects or contamination: **Chilmark** (tel. 508/645–2651), **Edgartown** (tel. 508/627–6180), **Gay Head** (tel. 508/645–9915), **Oak Bluffs** (tel. 508/693–5511), **Vineyard Haven** (tel. 508/696–4200), and **West Tisbury** (tel. 508/693–9659).

Tennis   Tennis is very popular on the island, and at all times reservations are strongly recommended. Public clay courts (reserve court with the attendant the previous day) are on Church Street in Vineyard Haven; they're open in season only, and small fees are charged. Hard-surface courts are in Niantic Park in Oak Bluffs, on Robinson Road in Edgartown, and at the grammar school on Old County Road in West Tisbury; all cost a small fee and are open year-round.

Farm Neck Tennis Club (County Rd., Oak Bluffs, tel. 508/693–9728; open mid-Apr.–mid-Nov.) is a semiprivate club with three clay courts, lessons, and a pro shop. **Island Country Club** (Beach Rd., Oak Bluffs, tel. 508/693–6574; open May–Columbus Day) has three Har-Tru courts and a pro shop.

Water Sports   Martha's Vineyard is an ideal place for windsurfing. With the many bays and inlets there is always a patch of protected water for the neophyte; the oceanside surf provides plenty of action for the expert. **Wind's Up!** (*see* Sailing and Boating, *above*) provides windsurfing lessons and rentals, plus an invaluable brochure including best locations and safety tips.

Dogfish Sea Kayaks (tel. 508/645–9281) rents (closed-top) sea kayaks and offers instruction and guided trips. **M.V. Kayak** (tel. 508/627–0151) rents (open-top) ocean kayaks.

MV Ski Waterskiing and **MV Parasail** (tel. 508/693–2838) offer
waterskiing lessons and rides (including pair, slalom, and trick
riding), plus kneeboarding, innertubing, and parasailing.

Beaches

The beaches on the south shore, on the Atlantic Ocean, offer
strong surf. Those on the Nantucket or Vineyard sound tend
to be protected and calmer. Inns sometimes make available to
guests a parking sticker for town beaches that are otherwise
limited to residents; these restricted beaches are often much
less crowded than the popular public beaches, and some, such
as Lucy Vincent and Lambert's Cove, are the most beautiful.
There are, however, miles of superb public beaches on which a
couple minutes' walk will get you a private patch of sand. Surprisingly, beach rest rooms are in short supply.

Public **Bend-in-the-Road Beach,** Edgartown's town beach, is a protected area marked by floats adjacent to the state beach.
Backed by low, grassy dunes and wild roses, Bend-in-the-Road
offers calm, shallow waters, some parking, and lifeguards. It
can be reached by bike path or shuttle bus.

East Beach, on Chappaquiddick Island, one of the area's best
beaches, is accessible only by boat or Jeep from the Wasque
Reservation (*see* Tour 3: Edgartown, *above*). It offers heavy
surf, good bird-watching, and relative isolation in a lovely setting, but there are no facilities.

Joseph A. Sylvia State Beach, between Oak Bluffs and Edgartown, is a mile-long sandy beach with a view of Cape Cod across
Nantucket Sound. The calm, warm water and food vendors
make it popular with families. There's parking along the roadside, and the beach is accessible by bike path or shuttle bus.

Lake Tashmoo Town Beach, at the end of Herring Creek Road
in Vineyard Haven, offers swimming in the warm, relatively
shallow brackish lake or in the cooler, gentle Vineyard Sound.
There is a lifeguarded area and some parking.

Lobsterville Road Beach comprises 2 miles of beautiful sand
and dune beach on the Vineyard Sound in Gay Head. It is a
seagull nesting area and a favorite fishing spot. Though the
water tends to be cold, the beach is protected and suitable for
children. There is no public parking.

Long Point (*see* Nature Areas, *below*) has a beautiful beach on
the Atlantic, as well as freshwater and saltwater ponds for
swimming, including the brackish Tisbury Great Pond. There
are rest rooms.

Menemsha Public Beach, adjacent to Dutcher's Dock, is a pebbly beach with gentle surf on Vineyard Sound. Located on the
western side of the island, it is a great place to catch the sunset.
The fishing boats and people angling from the jetty add atmosphere. There are rest rooms and lifeguards. Snack stands and
restaurants are a short walk from the parking lot.

Moshup Beach, in Gay Head, off Moshup Trail, is a Land Bank
property offering surf and sand backed by low grasses. At the
cliffs are food shops and rest rooms. From the parking lot, a
boardwalk path leads to the beach, a five-minute walk away;
there's a dropoff point at the edge of the beach. Heading to the

right along the shore, you can walk below the cliffs, but climbing them is against the law—they're eroding much too quickly even without the added human factor.

Oak Bluffs Town Beach, between the steamship dock and the state beach, is a crowded, narrow stretch of calm water on Nantucket Sound, with snack joints, lifeguards, parking, and rest rooms at the steamship office.

Owen Park Beach, a small, sandy harbor beach off Main Street in Vineyard Haven, is a convenient spot, with a children's play area, lifeguards, and a harbor view.

South Beach (also called Katama Beach), the island's largest and most popular, is a 3-mile ribbon of sand on the Atlantic, with strong surf and ocassional riptides (check with the lifeguards before swimming). From Edgartown, take the bike path to Katama or catch the trolley. There is limited parking.

Uncle Seth's Pond is a warm freshwater pond on Lambert's Cove Road in West Tisbury, with a small lifeguarded beach right off the road.

Wasque Beach, at the Wasque Reservation on Chappaquiddick (*see* Tour 3: Edgartown, *above*), is an uncrowded half-mile sandy beach with sometimes strong surf and currents, a parking lot, and rest rooms.

Restricted **Lambert's Cove Beach** (West Tisbury), one of the island's prettiest, has fine sand and very clear water. On the Vineyard Sound side, it has calm waters good for children and views of the Elizabeth Islands.

Lobsterville Beach, off Lobsterville Road in Gay Head, is a shallow, calm, sandy beach on Menemsha Pond with resident-only parking and an attractive setting.

Lucy Vincent Beach (Chilmark), on the south shore, is a very beautiful, wide strand of fine sand and surf backed by high clay bluffs. Keep walking to the left for the unofficial nude beach.

Squibnocket Beach (Chilmark), on the south shore, offers an appealing boulder-strewn coastline; a narrow beach that is part smooth rocks and pebbles, part fine sand; and gentle waves.

Nature Areas

Several of the island's nature areas offer bird walks, special kids' programs, and a schedule of events that are listed in the newspapers year-round and in the *Best Read Guide,* available free in shops and hotels. All have nature trails. A free map to the islands' conservation lands, including detailed directions, parking information, and usages permitted, is available from the Martha's Vineyard Land Bank (167 Main St., Edgartown 02539, tel. 508/627–7141) or from any town hall or library.

Cape Poge Wildlife Refuge and Wasque Reservation, on Chappaquiddick (*see* Tour 3: Edgartown, *above*).

Cedar Tree Neck, 300 hilly acres of unspoiled West Tisbury woods managed by the Sheriff's Meadow Foundation, offers varied environments, rich wildlife, freshwater ponds, brooks, low stone walls, and wooded trails ending at a stony but secluded North Shore beach (swimming, picnicking, and fishing prohibited). A trail starting at the parking lot leads to the summit of the headland with views of Gay Head and the Elizabeth Islands. Other trails lead to a bird refuge. *Indian Hill Rd. (off State Rd.) for 2 mi, then right 1 mi down steep, rocky dirt road to parking lot. Tel. 508/693–5207. Admission free. Open daily 8:30–5:30.*

Felix Neck Wildlife Sanctuary, a Massachusetts Audubon Society preserve 3 miles out of Edgartown, has 350 acres, including 6 miles of hiking trails traversing marshland, fields, oak woods, seashore, and wildfowl and reptile ponds. A full schedule of events is offered throughout the year, including sunset hikes along the beach, exploration of salt marsh, stargazing, snake or bird walks, snorkeling, and more, all led by trained naturalists. An exhibit center has aquariums, snake cages, and a gift shop. *Off Edgartown–Vineyard Haven Rd., tel. 508/627–4850. Admission: $3 adults, $2 children under 13, $1 senior citizens. Center open mid-June–mid-Sept., daily 8–4; mid-Sept.–mid-June, Tues.–Sun. 9–4. Trails open sunrise–sunset.*

Long Point, a 633-acre Trustees of Reservations preserve, is an open area of grassland and heath bounded on the east by the freshwater Homer's Pond, on the west by the saltwater West Tisbury Great Pond, and on the south by a mile of South Beach on the Atlantic Ocean. Tisbury Great Pond and Long Cove Pond (a sandy freshwater swimming pond) are ideal spots for duck- and bird-watchers. *Mid-June–mid-Sept., turn left onto the unmarked dirt road (Waldron's Bottom Rd., look for mailboxes) 3/10 mi west of airport on Edgartown–West Tisbury Rd.; at end, follow signs to Long Point parking lot. Mid-Sept.– mid-June, follow unpaved Deep Bottom Rd. (1 mi west of airport) 2 mi to lot. Tel. 508/693–7392. Admission: mid-June– mid-Sept., $6 per vehicle, $3 adults over 15; free rest of year. Open daily 10–6.*

Manuel F. Correllus State Forest. At the center of the island is a 4,000-acre forest of pine and scrub oak laced with hiking trails and circled with a paved but rough bike trail (mopeds are prohibited). There's also a 2-mile nature trail, a 2-mile parcourse, and horse trails. *Headquarters on Barnes Rd., between Edgartown–Vineyard Haven Rd. and Edgartown–West Tisbury Rd., tel. 508/693–2540. Admission free. Open daily sunrise–sunset.*

Menemsha Hills Reservation, a 210-acre Trustees of Reservations property, includes a mile of rocky shoreline and high sand bluffs along Vineyard Sound; excellent views of the Elizabeth Islands and beyond; hilly walking trails through scrub oak and heathland, with interpretive signs at viewpoints; and Prospect Hill, the island's highest at 309 feet. *Off North Rd., Chilmark, 1 mi east of Menemsha Cross Rd., tel. 508/693–7662. Call ahead about naturalist-led tours. Admission free. Open daily sunrise– sunset.*

Mytoi, on Chappaquiddick (*see* Tour 3: Edgartown, *above*).

Sepiessa Point. This Land Bank property, 164 acres on Tisbury Great Pond, offers expansive pond and ocean views, walking trails and bird-watching around coves and saltwater marshes, horse trails, and swimming and boating. *1.2 mi on right down New La./Tiah's Cove Rd., off West Tisbury Rd., West Tisbury, tel. 508/627–7141. Admission free. Open daily sunrise–sunset.*

Waskosim's Rock Reservation. After years of fighting for it, the Land Bank bought this unique 145-acre property in 1990 from a developer who'd planned to build 40 houses on it. The preserve comprises diverse habitats—rolling green hills, wetlands, oak and beetlebung woods, and 1,500 feet of frontage on Mill Brook—as well as the ruins of an 18th-century homestead. The rock itself—deposited by the retreating glacier and said to resemble the head of a breaching whale—is on a high ridge above the valley, from which there is a panoramic overview of more than 1,000 acres of protected land. At the trailhead off North Road there's a map outlining a 3-mile hike. *Parking areas are in Chilmark: on North Rd. or 1 mi off Tea La., a rough dirt road. Tel. 508/627–7141. Admission free. Open daily sunrise–sunset.*

Dining

The focus of island cuisine is seafood fresh from the surrounding waters, though you will find Mexican, Chinese, and other more exotic cuisines. Dining out here is not the highly developed, gourmet experience it is on Nantucket, but a few establishments do offer sophisticated cooking in equally sophisticated settings.

Note: Only Edgartown and Oak Bluffs allow the sale of liquor. In the "dry" towns, restaurants are glad to provide setups for patrons' bottles.

Box or picnic lunches are available at **Vineyard Gourmet** (Main St., Vineyard Haven, tel. 508/693–5181). **Bill Smith** (tel. 508/627–8809 or 800/828–6936) and **New England Clambake Co.** (tel. 508/627–7462) prepare clambakes to go.

Category	Cost*
Very Expensive	over $40
Expensive	$25–$40
Moderate	$15–$25
Inexpensive	under $15

*per person, excluding drinks, service, and 5% tax

Edgartown

Very Expensive **L'étoile.** The Charlotte Inn's restaurant is set in a glass-
★ wrapped summerhouse, with a flagstone floor and a skylight-punctuated peaked roof. An open, airy room with lots of white and lots of greenery—hanging ferns, citrus trees in big clay pots—it has the civilizing influence of liberally placed English antiques (brass lighting fixtures, spotlighted oil paintings in gilt frames, a collection of shining wood mailboxes) and elegant dinner service of bone china, crystal, and silver. The contemporary French menu highlights imaginative native seafood and shellfish as well as game. The four-course dinner menu ($48–$54) includes such entrées as assiette of steamed lobster, littlenecks, and scallops with a sauce of lobster, sweet pepper, and basil, or grilled swordfish with ginger, lime, and cilantro butter. The outdoor patio, a little secret garden with fountain and cas-

cading wisteria, is a good choice on a sunny day for the prix-fixe brunch ($22). The wine list is extensive and includes half-bottles. *27 S. Summer St., tel. 508/627–5187. Reservations required. Jacket suggested. AE, MC, V. Dinner and Sun. brunch only. Closed Jan.–mid-Feb.; also weekdays mid-Feb.–mid-May and mid-Nov.–Dec.*

Expensive **The Navigator.** Here, the setting's the thing: right on Edgartown Harbor, with umbrella-topped café tables outside taking full advantage of the terrific view. It's a great place for lunch, and a nice escape from the shopping streets when you need it, though the food—"hearty New England fare," spotlighting fresh seafood and lobster—is fairly pedestrian. It's also a good place for afternoon cocktails on the patio or later in the nautical Boathouse Bar. *2 Main St., tel. 508/627–4320. Dress: casual. Reservations advised for 7 or more. AE, D, DC, MC, V. Closed mid-Oct.–Apr.*

Moderate– **Daggett House.** The inn's intimate cellar dining room, lit by
Expensive candle sconces on rustic wood tables, retains the flavor of the Colonial tavern it once was (*see* Lodging, *below*), with raised paneling, a large open-hearth fireplace, and wide-board floors. From the little open kitchen come such entrées as grilled veal chop with caramelized-onion sauce, grilled swordfish with salsa of smoked tomato and yellow pepper, and seafood pie, all prettily presented. Prix-fixe dinners at $16–$22 are usually available. *59 N. Water St., tel. 508/627–4600. Reservations required. Dress: casual. MC, V. No smoking. Breakfast and dinner only. Closed Mon.–Tues.; Sun. and Wed. dinner.*

Sandcastles. The spot where Martha's used to be is now occupied by this place dedicated to "grazing." In addition to regular entrées, there's a long list of appetizers ranging from raw bar selections to "pizzettas" (tortilla shells topped with gourmet ingredients like sun-dried tomatoes and goat cheese) to half-lobsters. You can mix and match like tapas, or lunch on just one and a frozen drink from the upstairs bar, backed by a curtain of cascading water. Sit downstairs, done in soft salmon with banquettes, tables, and local art; in the bright upstairs dining room; or on the outdoor balcony that looks down over flower boxes to the leafy street below. *71 Main St., tel. 508/627–8446. Reservations advised. Dress: casual. AE, D, DC, MC, V. Closed mid-Oct.–mid-Apr. (or mid-May).*

Menemsha

Expensive **Beach Plum Inn and Restaurant.** Amid a wooded setting high
★ above Menemsha harbor is this romantic restaurant with window walls that catch the colors of the sunset, and a small menu of beautifully prepared Continental dishes, served on colorful, hand-painted Italian plates by candlelight. Three- to five-course prix fixe dinners ($35–$45) include such choices as roast boneless duck with honey-curry sauce, bouillabaisse, and salmon in puff pastry; appetizers may include Brie *en croûte* or house pâté. *North Rd., tel. 508/645–9454. Reservations required. Dress: casual. AE, D, MC, V. BYOB. Breakfast and dinner only. Closed Nov.–Apr.*

Moderate **Home Port.** Here you'll find very fresh fish and seafood (the specialties are lobsters and swordfish) simply baked, broiled, or fried, served in four-course prix fixe menus ($16–$26) that include steaming loaves of bread. The decor, too, is no-nonsense, with plain wood tables and a family atmosphere; window walls overlooking the harbor provide more than enough visual pleasure at sunset. The wait for a table is often very long; take a seat outside and order from the raw bar or the takeout menu, or use the time to wander around the fishing village. *North Rd., tel. 508/645–2679. Reservations required (a week in advance July–Aug.). Dress: casual. AE, MC, V. BYOB. Dinner only. Closed Nov.–Apr.*

Oak Bluffs

Expensive– **Oyster Bar.** Caterer of President Clinton's 1993 birthday din-
Very Expensive ner, the Oyster Bar (named for its 35-foot mahogany-and-mar-
★ ble bar with raw bar) has an art-deco look in white and pink, with a high embossed-tin ceiling, faux-marble columns, tropical greenery on Ionic-column pedestals, and a line of pink neon along the walls. Though the extensive menu includes pastas, pizzas, hearty soups, and specials such as gumbo filé with duck and shrimp or grilled muscovy duck breast with spaetzle, the stars are the many varieties of fish available each night—local catch as well as exotics like mahimahi—cooked any way you like: broiled, sautéed, grilled, steamed, *wasabi*-glazed, blackened, au poivre. Wine dinners with famous winemakers are featured throughout the season. *162 Circuit Ave., tel. 508/693–3300. Reservations strongly advised. Dress: casual. MC, V. Dinner only. Closed Dec.–mid-May; Tues. and Wed. in May and Oct.– Nov.*

Moderate– **Jimmy Seas Pan Pasta Restaurant.** Pasta to die for comes out
Expensive of this funky little place—a converted cellar with cinderblock
★ walls painted on one side with a giant shark and lobster, a few hanging buoys and nets, and Caribbean-color hunks of cloth on tables. While opera or Frank Sinatra rolls out of the sound system and happy customers chat from table to table, friendly waitresses deliver crisp family-style salads and individual pans heaped with pasta classics—primavera, mussels marinara, lobster fra diavolo, fettuccine Alfredo—plus daily specials like big fresh shrimp in garlic cream over linguine or pumpkin tortelloni with sage cream sauce. *14 Kennebec Ave., tel. 508/693–2948. No reservations. Dress: casual. No credit cards. Closed Columbus Day–May.*

Moderate **Zapotec.** Warm tortilla chips and terrific coriander-scented salsa accompany authentic and creative regional Mexican dishes such as lobster quesadilla or the grilled catch of the day, served perhaps with a fiery fruit salsa and pumpkin-seed tomatillas. Tag sales supplied the vaguely Mexican decor (like the used piñata). The glassed-in porch, lighted by red and green Christmas lights in the shape of chili peppers, feels comfortably intimate, even romantic. A selection of wine, Mexican beer, and recorded music (jazz, R&B, big bands, rock, zydeco) add to the informal, good-time atmosphere. *10 Kennebec Ave., tel. 508/693–6800. No reservations. Dress: casual. AE, MC, V. Dinner only. Closed mid-Oct.–mid-May.; Mon.–Tues. in shoulder seasons.*

Inexpensive– **Giordano's.** Bountiful portions of simply prepared Italian food
Moderate (pizzas, pastas, cacciatores, cutlets) and fried fish and seafood
★ at excellent prices keep Giordano's—run by the Giordano family since 1930—a family favorite. Several different children's meals are available for about $5 (including milk and Jell-O).

The ambience suits the clientele: hearty, noisy, and cheerful, with sturdy booths, bright green-topped wood tables, and hanging greenery. Lines often wrap around the corner. *107 Circuit Ave., tel. 508/693–0184. No reservations. Dress: casual. No credit cards. Closed late Sept.–early June.*

Ray's Bar-B-Q. Chickens turning on a spit over the window-front wood-fired roaster lure you into this hole-in-the-wall place, but it's the hickory-smoked St. Louis pork ribs, Texas beef ribs or brisket, and North Carolina pulled pork that most folks come for. Also on the menu are marinated prime rib (roasted) and colossal shrimp (grilled), plus sandwiches on French sourdough rolls. Accompaniments are down-home South, like sweet-potato fries, grits, and collard greens, but desserts get fancier, including whipped-cream-topped warm chocolate soufflé cake and pecan-bourbon-caramel squares. Opened in 1993 by Ray Schilcher, co-owner and chef at the Oyster Bar, Ray's has a very small, simple upstairs dining room; if you can't wait, order takeout and have a picnic. *Circuit Ave., tel. 508/693–7444. No reservations. Dress: casual. No credit cards. Closed Oct.–May.*

Vineyard Haven

Expensive **Le Grenier.** At this classic French restaurant, owner and chef Jean Dupon of Lyons offers a menu of more than 20 entrées, including delicacies such as quail flamed with cognac and grapes, maigret of duck in crème cassis, and poached salmon with cream of leeks. The *feuilleté d'escargot* appetizer is a puff pastry filled with a sauté of escargots, shallots, lemon juice, tarragon, and more, flamed with cognac and combined with garlic butter and heavy cream. Delectable desserts include dark-chocolate mousse cake and crème caramel. The look of this second-floor restaurant, entered through a green lattice, is a mix of garret (*grenier* means "loft" or "granary") and garden room. The exposed slats and beams of the slanted ceiling are painted light green, as are the walls; tables are romantically set with green and pink linens, candles in hurricane globes, and flowers in cut-glass vases. In the popular screened porch, painted vine tendrils climb posts to the roof. The owners also operate the Patisserie Française downstairs, offering breakfast, lunch, and fresh pastries. *Upper Main St., tel. 508/693–4906. Reservations strongly advised. Dress: casual. AE, MC, V. BYOB. Dinner only.*

Moderate– **Black Dog Tavern.** An island landmark, the harborside Black
Expensive Dog serves basic chowders, pastas, fish, and steak, along with such dishes as grilled bluefish with avocado salsa, sirloin tips with aïoli, or shrimp with Thai green curry sauce (you may have more success with the basics). The glassed-in porch, lighted by ship's lanterns, overlooks the harbor; the nautical theme is continued in rustic ship's-planking floors, photographs of sailing ships, and quarterboards. The wait for a table is often long; put your name on the list and walk around the harbor area to pass the time. The Black Dog Bakery on Water Street provides the little loaves served with dinner and a large selection of desserts. *Beach Rd. Ext., tel. 508/693–9223. No reservations. Dress: casual. BYOB. No smoking. AE, D, MC, V.*

West Tisbury

Expensive **Lambert's Cove Country Inn.** The country-inn setting (*see*
★ Lodging, *below*), soft lighting and music, and fine Continental
cuisine make this the coziest, most romantic dining spot on the
island. The daily selection of entrées may include poached
salmon with varied sauces, roast duck breast with cranberry-
honey glaze, or herb-crusted veal scaloppine with sun-dried
tomato and roast garlic butter. In summer, a Sunday brunch is
served on the deck overlooking the orchard. *Off Lambert's Cove
Rd., tel. 508/693–2298. Reservations required. Dress: smart casual. AE, MC, V. BYOB. Dinner and Sun. brunch only. Closed
weekdays in the off-season.*

Lodging

You can reserve a room year-round at many island establishments via the toll-free phone inside the waiting room at the
Woods Hole ferry terminal. The Chamber of Commerce maintains a listing of availability in the peak tourist season, from
mid-June to mid-September. During these months, rates are
at their highest and reservations are essential. In the winter,
rates go down by as much as 50%.

The following organizations book cottages, apartments, inns,
hotels, and B&Bs: **Martha's Vineyard and Nantucket Reservations** (Box 1322, Lagoon Pond Rd., Vineyard Haven 02568, tel.
508/693–7200 or 800/649–5671 in MA), **Accommodations Plus**
(RFD 273, Edgartown 02539, tel. 508/627–7374), and **House
Guests Cape Cod and the Islands** (Box 1881, Orleans 02653, tel.
800/666–4678, fax 508/896–7054). **DestINNations** (tel. 800/333–
4667) handles a limited number of Vineyard hotels and B&Bs,
but the staff will arrange any and all details of a visit.

The **Manter-Memoral AYH-Hostel** (Edgartown Rd., Box 158,
West Tisbury 02575, tel. 508/693–2665), near a bike path but 7
miles from the nearest beach, is open April–November. Accommodations are dorm style (78 beds).

Martha's Vineyard Family Campground (Box 1557, Edgartown
Rd., Vineyard Haven 02568, tel. 508/693–3772), open mid-May–
mid-October, has wooded sites, tent-trailer rentals, a rec room,
and cable TV hookups. **Webb's Camping Area** (Barnes Rd., Oak
Bluffs [RFD 3, Box 100, Vineyard Haven 02568], tel. 508/693–
0233), on 90 acres, is more woodsy and private, with some
water-view sites and a store. It is open mid-May–Labor Day.
Both campgrounds take tents and RVs but no pets, and offer
bathrooms, showers, laundry facilities, and playgrounds.

For information about rentals and long-term stays, contact one
of the realtors listed in the chamber of commerce's guidebook,
such as **Sandcastle Realty** (Box 2488, 256 Edgartown Rd., Edgartown 02539, tel. 508/627–5665 or 800/537–3721) or **Martha's
Vineyard Vacation Rentals** (51 Beach Rd., Box 1207, Vineyard
Haven 02568, tel. 508/693–7711).

Category	Cost*
Very Expensive	over $200
Expensive	$150–$200
Moderate	$100–$150
Inexpensive	under $100

all prices are for a standard double room in high season, excluding 5.7% state tax and (Down-Island only) 4% local tax

Chilmark

Moderate **Breakfast at Tiasquam.** Set amid acres of peaceful farmland and forest of oak and beech is this B&B, built in 1987 in a contemporary design with 20 skylights, sliding glass doors, and private decks that connect the interior with the natural setting. This is a location for people who want to get away from it all, to bike on country roads, walk in the woods, or just lie in the hammocks and read. Lots of common areas invite mixing. The decor is spare and soothing, emphasizing fine craftsmanship, as in the woodwork and the baths' hand-thrown ceramic sinks. The "master bedroom" has a two-person Jacuzzi and a wood stove. Breakfast is hearty and varied, served at a handcrafted dining room table. *Off Middle Rd., RR1, Box 296, 02535, tel. 508/645–3685. 8 rooms, 2 with private bath (6 share 3¹/2 baths). Facilities: full breakfast, bikes and car for rent, beach passes, 2 disabled-accessible rooms, outdoor showers, common TV and stereo. No credit cards. No smoking.*

Edgartown

Very Expensive ★ **Charlotte Inn.** From its original structure, the 1865 home of a whaling company owner, the Charlotte (now a Relais & Châteaux member) has grown into a five-building complex of meticulously maintained accommodations and an excellent restaurant, L'étoile (*see* Dining, *above*). Gery Conover, owner for more than 20 years, and his wife, Paula, supervise every detail of the inn, which they have furnished through annual antiquing trips to England. Hallways are hung with original oil paintings and prints; in one, Gery's large collection of antique brass flashlights is displayed in a glass case. Two superb rooms in the 18th-century Garden House, with a fireplaced common room open to all inn guests, have porches overlooking a flower-filled English garden. The Summer House has a veranda with wicker chairs and a very large room, No. 14, with a fireplace and a baby grand piano. All guest rooms have down pillows and comforters, rich fabrics, and comfy stuffed armchairs; some have working fireplaces, TVs, or phones. *27 S. Summer St., 02539, tel. 508/627–4751. 21 rooms, 3 suites. Facilities: Continental breakfast, afternoon tea, restaurant, art gallery, common TV. AE, MC, V.*

Harbor View Hotel. This historic hotel, centered on the 1891 gray-shingled main building with wraparound veranda and gazebo, was completely renovated in 1991 and is now a beautiful property with luxurious accommodations, full services, and a great location. Many rooms are spacious and have private decks that look out across landscaped lawns to the harbor, the lighthouse, and the ocean beyond. Town houses have cathedral ceilings, decks, kitchens, and large living areas with sofa beds; most rooms have phones, air-conditioning, cable TV with remote control, minifridges, and a wall safe. Room VCRs, fax machines, and rooms with kitchenettes are also available. The location is in a residential neighborhood just minutes from town. A beach good for walking stretches ³/₄ mile from the jetty, from which there's good fishing for blues; children enjoy swimming in the sheltered bay. Packages and theme weekends are available. *131 N. Water St., 02539, tel. 508/627–7000 or 800/225–6005, fax 508/627–7845. 124 units. Facilities: 2 all-weather tennis courts, heated outdoor pool, privileges at Farm Neck Golf Club, volleyball, boat slips, poolside food service, piano lounge, seafood restaurant, gift shop, concierge, room service, no-smoking rooms, daily newspaper, laundry service, baby-sitting. Children under 12 stay free. AE, DC, MC, V.*

Mattakesett. This community of individually owned three- or four-bedroom homes and condominiums is within walking distance of South Beach. All units have been recently renovated, are spacious, sleep eight, and have phone, full kitchen with dishwasher, washer/dryer (cable TV available), freestanding fireplaces, and decks with or without bay and ocean views. The staff provides plenty of service, and the children's program, pool, and barbecue grills add to the definite family atmosphere. Usually there's a one-week minimum stay, and it's best to book by January 15. *Katama Rd., tel. 508/627–4432; reservations c/o Stanmar Corp., 130 Boston Post Rd., Sudbury, MA 01776, tel. 508/443–1733. 92 units. Facilities: private tennis club with 6 Har-Tru and 2 all-weather courts, heated outdoor pool, swimming lessons, bicycles, aerobics classes, children's program, ferry auto reservations (July–Aug.). No credit cards. Closed Columbus Day–Memorial Day.*

Expensive   **Harborside Inn.** Right on the harbor, with boat docks at the end of a nicely landscaped lawn, the inn offers a central town location, harborview decks, and lots of amenities. Seven two- or three-story buildings are ranged around a wide lawn with formal rose beds, brick walkways, a brick patio with gas grills and café tables, and a pool. The rooms have colonial-style furnishings (which could use some updating), brass beds and lamps, and light floral wallpapers; each has cable TV/HBO, phone, minifridge, and individual heat and air-conditioning. *3 S. Water St., Box 67, 02539, tel. 508/627–4321 or 800/627–4009. 86 rooms, 3 suites. Facilities: heated outdoor pool, sauna and whirlpool room, recreation room (ping-pong, pool, large cable TV/VCR), gas grills, boat rentals, in-room VCR rentals, fax. AE, MC, V.*

Kelley House. At the center of town, this sister property of the Harbor View aims at combining services and amenities with a country-inn feel, through complimentary Continental breakfasts, afternoon wine and cheese receptions, and evening cookies and milk. Totally renovated in 1991, the 1742 white-clapboard main house and the adjacent Garden House are surrounded by pink roses; inside, the decor is an odd mix of country French and Shaker. Large suites in the Chappaquiddick House and the two spacious town houses with full kitchens in the Wheel House have porches (most with harbor views) and living rooms. All guest rooms have cable TVs, phones, and air-conditioning. The 1742 pub, with original handhewn timbers and ballast-brick walls, serves light fare, ribs from its own smoker, and 10 interesting beers on tap until 11 PM. *23 Kelly*

St., 02539, tel. 508/627–7900 or 800/225–6005, fax 508/627–8142. 52 rooms, 7 suites. Facilities: heated outdoor pool, use of Harbor View's tennis courts, daily newspaper, concierge, no-smoking rooms, laundry service, baby-sitting. Children under 12 stay free. AE, DC, MC, V. Closed Nov.–Apr.

★ **Shiverick Inn.** New innkeepers have added warmth to the elegance of this inn, in a striking 1840 house with mansard roof and cupola. Rooms are airy and bright, with high ceilings, lots of windows, American and English antiques, rich fabrics and wallpapers, and antique art. Beds are mostly queen-size canopies or carved four-posters. Several rooms have fireplaces or open-face wood stoves. Breakfast is served in a lovely summerhouse-style room with a wood-burning fireplace. There's a library with cable TV and stereo, and a flagstone garden patio. *Corner of Peases Point Way and Pent La., Box 640, 02539, tel. 508/627–3797 or 800/723–4292, fax 508/627–8441. 10 rooms. Facilities: Continental breakfast, air-conditioning in most rooms; bike rentals. No smoking. AE, D, MC, V.*

Moderate– **Colonial Inn.** Part of a busy downtown complex of shops, the
Expensive inn is hardly a tranquil escape, but if you like your modern conveniences and being at the center of the action, this may be for you. Rooms are pleasantly decorated in pale shades of either mauve and gray-blue or teal and peach, with new white pine furniture, wall-to-wall carpeting, and brass beds and lamps. Each has a good-size bath, cable TV in an armoire, a phone with computer modem port, and air-conditioning; suites have a sofa bed, two TVs, and a minifridge. One common fourth-floor deck (like some rooms) has a superb view of the harbor. *N. Water St., Box 68, 02539, tel. 508/627–4711 or 800/627–4701, fax 508/627–5904. 39 rooms, 2 suites, 1 efficiency. Facilities: Continental breakfast, restaurant, fax, beach towels, shops. Children under 16 stay free. AE, MC, V. Closed Jan.–mid-Apr.*

★ **Daggett House.** The flower-bordered lawn that separates the main house from the harbor makes a great retreat after a day of exploring town, a minute away. Breakfast and dinner are served in the 1750 tavern (*see* Dining, *above*), where raised-wood paneling hides a secret staircase (now a private entrance to an upstairs guest room, but the innkeeper may let you peek in if the room is unoccupied). This and two other buildings are decorated with fine wallpapers, antiques, and reproductions. The Widow's Walk Suite has a private roofwalk with a superb water view and a hot tub. *59 N. Water St., Box 1333, 02539, tel. 508/627–4600 or 800/468–3514, fax 508/627–4600. 20 rooms, 3 housekeeping suites. Facilities: Continental breakfast, common TV. AE, MC, V.*

Moderate **Edgartown Commons.** Just a block or two from town is this condominium complex of seven buildings, from an old house to motel units around a busy pool. The studios and one- or two-bedroom units all have full kitchens and cable TV/HBO, and some are very spacious. Each has been decorated by its owner, so the decor varies—some have an older look, some are new and bright (like pool units 29 and 30). Definitely family-oriented, the place has lots of kids to keep other kids company; units away from the pool are quieter. *20 Peases Point Way, 02539, tel. 508/627–4671, fax 508/627–4271. 35 units. Facilities: outdoor pool, playground, shuffleboard, picnic areas with barbecue grills, laundry. AE, D, DC, MC, V. Closed Nov.–Apr.*

Gay Head

Very Expensive **Outermost Inn.** In 1990, Hugh and Jeanne Taylor converted
★ the home they built 20 years ago by the Gay Head Cliffs into a
bed-and-breakfast. Their design takes full advantage of the superb location: Standing alone on acres of moorland, the house
is wrapped with windows revealing breathtaking views of sea
and sky in three directions. The Oak Room has a separate entrance and French doors leading onto a private deck with a
great view of the Gay Head Lighthouse, adjacent to the property; other guests enjoy the same view from the porch that
wraps the house on two sides. The decor is simple, with white
walls, local art, and polished light-wood floors; each room has
a phone, and one has a whirlpool tub. Dinners are served two
to four nights a week spring through fall and are open to the
public. The beach is a 10-minute walk away. Hugh has sailed
area waters since childhood and charters out his 50-foot catamaran for excursions to Cuttyhunk Island. *Lighthouse Rd., RR
1, Box 171, 02535, tel. 508/645–3511, fax 508/645–3514. 7 rooms.
Facilities: full breakfast, afternoon setups and hors d'oeuvres on
request, restaurant, beach passes, TVs, box lunches available in
season. AE, MC, V.*

Menemsha

Expensive– **Beach Plum Inn and Cottages.** The main draws of this 10-acre
Very Expensive retreat are the woodland setting, the panoramic view of the
ocean and Menemsha harbor, and the romantic gourmet res-
taurant offering spectacular sunsets. Cottages (one with whirlpool bath) are decorated in casual beach style. Inn
rooms—some with private decks offering great views—have
modern furnishings and small new baths; some are air-conditioned. Optional MAP rates include breakfast and dinner as
well as afternoon cocktails and hors d'oeuvres served on the
terrace. *North Rd., 02552, tel. 508/645–9454. 5 inn rooms, 4 cottages. Facilities: full breakfast, restaurant, tennis court, passes
to Chilmark beaches. AE, D, MC, V. Closed mid-Oct.–mid-May.*

Moderate **Menemsha Inn and Cottages.** For 40 years *Life* photographer
Alfred Eisenstaedt has returned to his cottage on the hill for
the panoramic view of Vineyard Sound and Cuttyhunk beyond
the trees below. Menemsha also comprises older cottages with
'50s motel furnishings and plaster and wood-paneled walls, as
well as several cottages newly remodeled with fireplaces and
full kitchens. All are nicely spaced on 10 acres and vary in privacy and water views; all have screened porches. You can also
stay in the 1989 inn building, or in the pleasant Carriage House,
both of which have white walls, plush blue or sea green carpeting, and Appalachian light pine reproduction furniture. All
rooms and suites have private decks, most with fine sunset
views; suites have sitting areas, desks, minifridges, and big
tiled baths. *North Rd., Box 38, 02552, tel. 508/645–2521. 9 rooms,
6 suites, 12 cottages. Facilities: Continental breakfast (inn only),
all-weather tennis court, passes to Chilmark beaches, shower
room. No credit cards. Closed Thanksgiving–Apr.*

Oak Bluffs

Moderate **Oak House.** The wraparound veranda of this pastel-front, 1872
★ Victorian looks across a busy street to the beach. Several rooms

have private terraces, and some have air-conditioners or TVs; if you're bothered by noise, ask for a room at the back. The decor centers on well-preserved woods—some rooms have oak wainscoting from top to bottom—choice antique furniture, and nautical-theme accessories. Afternoon tea with fancy cakes baked by the innkeeper, Betsi, a former pastry chef, is served in a glassed-in sun porch, with lots of white wicker and plants. *Sea View Ave., Box 299, 02557, tel. 508/693–4187. 8 rooms, 2 suites. Facilities: Continental breakfast, afternoon tea, pay phone. D, MC, V. Closed mid-Oct.–mid-May.*

Inexpensive– Moderate
Admiral Benbow Inn. On a busy road between Vineyard Haven and Oak Bluffs harbor, the Benbow is a small, homey B&B. The house, built for a minister at the turn of the century, features elaborate woodwork, a comfortable hodgepodge of antique furnishings, and a Victorian parlor with a stunning carved-wood-and-tile fireplace. *520 New York Ave., Box 2488, 02557, tel. 508/693–6825. 7 rooms. Facilities: full breakfast, afternoon tea, common TV, courtesy phone. No smoking. AE, MC, V.*

Martha's Vineyard Surfside Motel. Right in the thick of things (it gets noisy in summer) are these two buildings, the newest built in 1989. Rooms are spacious, bright (corner rooms more so), and well maintained, each with typical motel furnishings, carpeting, table and chairs, individual air-conditioning and heat, cable TV, and phone; deluxe rooms have minifridges, remote control, and water views, and two rooms are disabled-accessible. *Oak Bluffs Ave., Box 2507, 02557, tel. 508/693–2500 or 800/537–3007, fax 508/693–7343. 35 rooms. AE, D, MC, V.*

★ **Sea Spray Inn.** This porch-wrapped summer house is set in a quiet spot, on a drive circling an open park that borders an ocean beach. The decor is simple and restful, highlighted by cheerful splashes of color. In the Honeymoon Suite (one room), an iron-and-brass bed is positioned for viewing the sunrise through bay windows draped in lacy curtains; the cedar-lined bath includes an extra-large shower. The Garden Room has a king-size bed with gauze canopy and a private enclosed porch. The common living room is large and airy. *2 Nashawena Park, Box 2125, 02557, tel. 508/693–9388. 7 rooms (2 with shared bath). Facilities: Continental breakfast, common TV, barbecue grill. MC, V. No smoking. Closed mid-Nov.–mid-Apr.*

Inexpensive
Attleboro House. This guest house across from bustling Oak Bluffs harbor is a big 1874 gingerbread Victorian with wrap-around verandas on two floors. It offers small, simple rooms, some with sinks, powder-blue walls, lacy white curtains, and a few antiques; singles have three-quarter beds. Linen exchange but no chambermaid service is provided during a stay. The shared baths are rustic and old but clean. *11 Lake Ave., Box 1564, 02557, tel. 508/693–4346. 9 rooms share 4 baths. Facilities: Continental breakfast, common TV. MC, V. Closed Oct.–mid-May.*

Vineyard Haven

Expensive
★ **Thorncroft Inn.** Set on 3½ acres of woods about a mile from the ferry, the main inn, a 1918 Craftsman bungalow, has been renovated from top to bottom. Fine Colonial and richly carved Renaissance Revival antiques are combined with tasteful reproductions to create an environment that is somewhat formal but not fussy. All rooms have air-conditioning, phones, and wir-

ing for computers; nine have working fireplaces (used only in the off-season). Deluxe rooms have cable TV and minifridge, and some have whirlpools or canopy beds; two rooms have private hot tub rooms. Gourmet breakfasts are served in shifts and are conducive to meeting and chatting with other guests. *278 Main St., Box 1022, 02568, tel. 508/693–3333 or 800/332–1236, fax 508/693–5419. 12 rooms, 1 suite. Facilities: full breakfast, afternoon tea, restaurant, turndown service, newspaper. No smoking. AE, D, MC, V.*

Moderate **Aldworth Manor.** A 10-minute walk from Main Street, this secluded inn offers graciously appointed bedrooms and lots of space. Common areas in the sprawling 1902 house (with 1920s addition) include a living room with fireplace, game table, and grand piano; a patio with umbrella tables overlooking 2 acres of gardens and trees; and a sun room with TV. Guest rooms feature thick carpeting in soft pastels, floral wallpapers and borders, lace curtains, and carved antique and reproduction beds piled with pillows and quilts or crocheted coverlets. Two rooms have fireplaces. *26 Mt. Aldworth Rd., Box 4058, 02568, tel. 508/693–3203, fax 508/693–6813. 6 rooms, 1 suite. Facilities: Continental breakfast, afternoon tea, turndown service; beach chairs, towels, and coolers. No smoking. No credit cards.*

Captain Dexter House. Set in an 1843 sea captain's house at the edge of the shopping district, this B&B has an intimate, historic feeling about it. The small guest rooms are beautifully appointed, with period-style wallpapers, velvet wing chairs, and 18th-century antiques and reproductions, including several four-poster canopy beds with lace or fishnet canopies and hand-sewn quilts. The Captain Harding Room is larger, with original wood floor, fireplace, bay windows, canopy bed, desk, and bright bath with claw-foot tub. *100 Main St., Box 2457, 02568, tel. 508/693–6564. 7 rooms, 1 suite. Facilities: Continental breakfast, afternoon tea, common refrigerator and TV. No smoking in common areas. AE, MC, V. Closed Jan.–Mar.*

Tisbury Inn. At the center of the shopping district is this hotel offering tiled bathrooms with tub showers, firm beds, and amenities, including a well-equipped health club, cable TV/HBO, room phones, and air-conditioning. Rooms are simply done in soft pastels, floral fabrics, a few ruffles, rocking chairs, and pleasant art. In summer, stay three nights and the fourth is free. *Main St., Box 428, 02568, tel. 508/693–2200 or 800/332–4112, fax 508/693–4095. 27 rooms, 2 suites. Facilities: Continental breakfast, restaurant, health club (see Sports and the Outdoors, above), indoor pool. AE, D, DC, MC, V.*

West Tisbury

Moderate **Lambert's Cove Country Inn.** This secluded and peaceful coun-
★ try inn, approached by a road that snakes through tall pine woods, is set amid an apple orchard and a lovely English garden. Rooms in the 1790 farmhouse have light floral wallpapers and a sweet country feel. Rooms in outbuildings have screened porches or decks and a more rustic look. Among the common areas is a lovely gentleman's library with fireplace. The restaurant (*see Dining, above*) is intimate and romantic. *Lambert's Cove Rd., West Tisbury (RR1, Box 422, Vineyard Haven 02568), tel. 508/693–2298, fax 508/693–7890. 15 rooms. Facilities: Continental breakfast, restaurant, room service, tennis court in woods, passes to Lambert's Cove Beach. AE, MC, V.*

The Arts and Nightlife

Both island newspapers, the *Martha's Vineyard Times* and the *Vineyard Gazette*, publish weekly calendars of events. Also scan the *Best Read Guide*, free at many shops and hotels.

The Arts

Throughout the year, lectures, classic films, concerts, plays, and other events are held at the **Old Whaling Church** in Edgartown; watch the papers, or check the kiosk out front.

Theater Plays can be seen year-round, thanks to the island's numerous theater groups. The **Vineyard Playhouse** (10 Church St., Vineyard Haven, tel. 508/693–6450) offers a mid-June–early September season of drama, classics, and comedies, performed by a mostly Equity troupe on the air-conditioned main stage; summer Shakespeare and other productions at the natural amphitheater at Tashmoo Overlook on State Road in Vineyard Haven (bring insect repellent and a pillow); children's programs (*see* What to See and Do with Children, *above*) and late-night cabaret (*see* Nightlife, *below*), also in season; and a full winter schedule of community-theater and Equity productions. Local art exhibitions are held throughout the year. One performance of each summer main-stage show is interpreted in American sign language. **Island Theater Workshop** (tel. 508/693–5290), the island's oldest year-round company, performs at various venues.

Music The **Tabernacle** in Oak Bluffs is the scene of a popular Wednesday-night community sing (*see* Exploring, *above*), as well as other family-oriented entertainment. For a schedule, contact the Camp Meeting Association (Box 1176, Oak Bluffs 02557, tel. 508/693–0525).

Martha's Vineyard Chamber Music Society (tel. 508/645–9771 or 508/645–9606), formerly called the Chilmark Chamber Players, performs eight summer concerts and three in winter at various venues.

A free **organ recital** by David Hewlett is given on a rebuilt 1840 organ at Federated Church (S. Summer St., Edgartown, tel. 508/627–4421) every Friday at 12:10.

The Sunday night (8 PM) **Vineyard Haven Town Band concerts** take place on alternate weeks in summer at Owen Park in Vineyard Haven, and at the gazebo in Ocean Park on Beach Road in Oak Bluffs.

Dance The **Yard**—a colony of dancers and choreographers, formed in 1973—gives several performances throughout the summer at its 100-seat Barn Theater in a wooded setting (off Middle Rd., Chilmark, tel. 508/645–9662). Artists are selected each year from auditions that are held in New York. Dance classes are available to visitors.

Film Dial 508/696–7469 to reach a 24-hour hotline with schedules for all movie theaters on the Vineyard. The island has three first-run movie theaters: **Capawock** (Main St., Vineyard Haven) and Oak Bluffs' **Island Theater** (Circuit Ave.) and **The Strand** (Oak Bluffs Ave. Ext.). At least one stays open year-round. A new Edgartown movie house seemed imminent at press time. Films are shown at other locations from time to time; check the local newspapers.

Writing Workshop **Nancy Slonim Aronie,** a visiting writer at Trinity College and NPR host, leads week-long summer workshops in Chilmark (tel. 508/645–9085 or 203/233–0030).

Nightlife

Dances and other events for different age groups are held throughout the summer at the **Chilmark Community Center;** watch for announcements in the papers.

Coffeehouse **Wintertide Coffeehouse** (Five Corners, Vineyard Haven, tel. 508/693–8830) offers live folk, blues, and other music featuring local and national talent, including open-mike nights, in a homey alcohol- and smoke-free environment. Light meals, desserts, and freshly ground coffees and cappuccino are served at candlelit tables year-round.

Cabaret The **Vineyard Playhouse** (*see* The Arts, *above*) has musical or comedy cabaret after the Friday and Saturday performances, from 10:45 to midnight, in season (BYOB; seating limited).

Bars and Lounges At **David's Island House** (118–120 Circuit Ave., Oak Bluffs, tel. 508/693–4516), renowned pianist David Crohan entertains with popular and classical music throughout dinner in season. Other musical guests perform nightly in the lounge, where a light menu is served.

The **Ritz Café** (Circuit Ave., Oak Bluffs, tel. 508/693–9851), a popular bar with a pool table (off-season) and a jukebox, has live blues and jazz every weekend, more often in season.

Dance Clubs Two major clubs offer a mix of live rock, R&B, and reggae and DJ-spun dance music. **Hot Tin Roof** (at the airport, tel. 508/693–1137 or 508/693–9320), open in summer, is larger and airier, has more live music, and features comedy nights.

Atlantic Connection (124 Circuit Ave., Oak Bluffs, tel. 508/693–7129), open year-round, offers fancy light and sound systems (including a strobe-lit dance floor topped by a glitter ball) and live reggae, R&B, funk, and blues. There's also karaoke, comedy, DJ music, and an adjoining restaurant.

5 Nantucket

At the height of its prosperity, in the early to mid-19th century, the little island of Nantucket was the foremost whaling port in the world. In the bustling harbor, ships set off for or returned from the whaling grounds of the Pacific while coastal merchant vessels put in for trade or outfitting. Along the wharves, a profusion of sail lofts, ropewalks, ship's chandleries, cooperages, and other such shops stood cheek by jowl. Barrels of whale oil were off-loaded from the ships onto wagons, then wheeled along the cobblestone streets to refineries and candle factories. On the strong sea breezes the smoke and smells of booming industry were carried through the town as its inhabitants eagerly took care of business.

The boom years didn't last long, but before they ended, some of the hard-won profits had gone into the building of grand homes that remain as eloquent testimony to Nantucket's glory days. The wharves still teem with shops of merchants and craftsmen who tend to the needs of incoming ships, though today those vessels are filled with tourists whose needs tend more toward T-shirts and chic handbags than to ropes and barrels.

Thanks in no small part to the island's isolation, 30 miles out in the open Atlantic (the name Nantucket is a corruption of the Indian word *Nanticut,* meaning "faraway land"), and to its frequently depressed economy, Nantucket has managed to retain much of its 17th- to 19th-century character. Indeed, the town—with its streets lit by old-fashioned street lamps and its hundreds of beautifully preserved houses—hardly seems changed since whaling days. But this remarkable preservation also owes much to the foresight and diligence of people working to ensure that what makes Nantucket special can be enjoyed by generations to come. In 1955, legislation to designate the island an official National Historic District was begun. Now any outwardly visible alterations to a structure—even the installation of air conditioners or a change in the color of paint—must conform to a rigid code.

The code's success is obvious in the restful harmony of the buildings, most covered in weathered-gray shingles, sometimes with a facade of clapboard painted white or gray (in early Nantucket a clapboard facade was a sign of wealth, because it would need painting; these practical people saw no need for more than one showy side). In town, which is more strictly regulated than the outskirts, virtually nothing jars. You'll find no neon, stoplights, billboards, or fast-food franchises. In spring and summer, when the many neat gardens are in bloom and the gray shingles are blanketed with cascading pink roses, it all seems perfect.

The desire to protect Nantucket from change extends to the land as well. When the 1960s tourism boom began, it was clear that something had to be done to preserve the breezy, wide-openness of the island—its miles of clean, white-sand beaches, the heath-covered moors—that is as much a part of its charm as the historic town. A third of the 14- by 3-mile island's 30,000 acres are now protected from development, thanks to the ongoing efforts of several public and private organizations and the generosity of Nantucketers, who have donated thousands of acres to the cause. The Nantucket Conservation Foundation, established in 1963, has acquired through purchase or gift more than 8,200 acres, including working cranberry bogs and

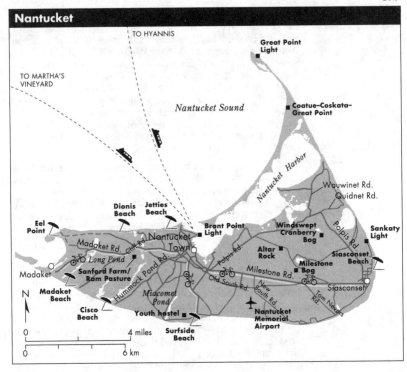

Nantucket

TO HYANNIS

TO MARTHA'S VINEYARD

Nantucket Sound

Great Point Light

Coatue–Coskata– Great Point

Nantucket Harbor

Wauwinet Rd.
Quidnet Rd.

Dionis Beach

Jetties Beach

Eel Point

Madaket Rd.

Cliff Rd.

Nantucket Town

Brant Point Light

Windswept Cranberry Bog

Polpis Rd.

Sankaty Light

Long Pond

Sanford Farm/ Ram Pasture

Hummock Pond Rd.

Altar Rock

Polpis Rd.

Siasconset Beach

Madaket

Milestone Bog

Milestone Rd.

Old South Rd.

New South Rd.

Tom Nevers Rd.

Siasconset

Madaket Beach

Miacomet Pond

N

Cisco Beach

Youth hostel

Surfside Beach

Nantucket Memorial Airport

0 ———— 4 miles

0 ———— 6 km

vast tracts of moorland. A land bank, funded by a 2% tax on real-estate transactions, was instituted in 1984 and has since acquired more than 1,000 acres. Most of these areas are open to the public and marked with signs on the roadside.

The first settlers came to the island to get away from repressive religious authorities on the mainland—having themselves fled to the New World to escape persecution in England, the Puritans of the Massachusetts Bay Colony proceeded to persecute Quakers and those who were friendly with them. In 1659, Thomas Mayhew, who had obtained Nantucket through royal grant and a deal with the resident Wampanoag tribe, sold most of the island to nine shareholders for £30 and two beaverskin hats. These shareholders then sold half shares to people whose skills the new settlement would need. The names of these families—Macy, Coffin, Starbuck, Coleman, Swain, Gardner, Folger, and others—are inescapable in Nantucket, where three centuries later many descendants still live.

The first year, Thomas Macy and his family, along with Edward Starbuck and the 12-year-old Isaac Coleman, spent fall and winter at Madaket, managing with the assistance of the local natives. The following year, 1660, Tristram Coffin and others arrived, establishing a community—later named Sherburne—at Capaum Harbor, on the north shore. When storms closed the harbor early in the 18th century, the center of activity was moved to the present Nantucket Town. Relations with the Wampanoags seem to have been cordial, and many of the tribe would become expert whalemen. Numbering about 3,000 when the settlers arrived, the native population was greatly reduced by a 1763 plague; the last full-blooded Wampanoag on the island died in 1855.

The settlers first tried their hand at farming, though their crops never thrived in the sandy soil. In 1690 they sent for a Yarmouth whaleman to teach them to catch right whales from small boats just offshore. In 1712 a boat was blown farther out to sea and managed to capture a sperm whale, whose oil was much more highly prized; thus began the whaling era on Nantucket.

In the 18th century, whaling voyages never lasted much longer than a year; by the 19th century the usual whaling grounds had been so depleted that ships had to travel to the Pacific to find their quarry and could be gone for five years. (Some Nantucket captains have South Sea islands named for them—Swain's Reef, Gardner Pinnacles, and so forth.) The life of a whaler was hard, and many never returned home. An account by Owen Chase, first mate of the Nantucket whaling ship *Essex*, of "the mysterious and mortal attack" of a sperm whale, which in 1820 ended in the loss of the ship and most of the crew, fascinated a young sailor named Herman Melville and formed the basis of his 1851 novel, *Moby-Dick*.

The fortunes of Nantucket's whaling industry rose and fell with the tides of three wars and ceased altogether in the 1860s—a result of diminished whale populations, the replacement of whale oil by cheaper kerosene, and the emergence of a sandbar that prevented the large whaling ships from entering Nantucket harbor. By the next decade tourism was being pursued, and hotels began springing up at Surfside, on the south shore. Developments at Siasconset, to the east, followed, and in the 1920s the fishing village became a fashionable resort for theater folk. The tourist trade waxed and waned until the 1960s; since then it has been the island's main industry.

Like the original settlers, most people who visit Nantucket today come to escape—from cities, from stress and hurry, and in some ways from the 20th century. Nantucket has a bit of nightlife, including two raucous year-round dance clubs, but that's not at all what the island is about. It's about small gray-shingled cottages covered with pink roses in summer, about daffodil-lined roads in spring. It's about moors swept with brisk salt breezes and scented with bayberry, wild roses, and cranberries. Perhaps most of all, it's about rediscovering a quiet place within yourself and within the world, getting back in touch with the elemental and taking it home with you when you go.

Essential Information

Important Addresses and Numbers

Tourist Information   The **Chamber of Commerce** (Pacific Club Bldg., 14 Main St., tel. 508/228–1700) is open Labor Day–Memorial Day, weekdays 9–5; Memorial Day–Labor Day, weekdays 9–5, Saturday 11–5. The **Nantucket Information Bureau** (25 Federal St., tel. 508/228–0925) is open July–Labor Day, daily 9 AM–11 PM; Labor Day–June, Monday–Saturday 9–5:30. Also look for information kiosks at Steamboat and Straight wharves and at the airport. The **Helpline** (tel. 508/228–7227) has information on island health services, activities, and transportation.

Emergencies   Dial 911 to reach the **police** or **fire department.** The **Nantucket Cottage Hospital** (S. Prospect St., tel. 508/228–1200) has a 24-hour emergency room.

Late-night   **Island Pharmacy** (Finast Plaza, Sparks Ave., tel. 508/228–6400)
Pharmacies   is open daily until 8 or 9 year-round. Aside from normal business hours off-season, **Congdon's** (47 Main St., tel. 508/228–0020) is open nightly until 10 from mid-June to mid-September; **Nantucket Pharmacy** (45 Main St., tel. 508/228–0180), until 10 nightly from Memorial Day to Labor Day.

Cash Machines   ATMs are at the **airport, Steamboat Wharf, Nantucket Bank** (2 Orange St. or 104 Pleasant St., tel. 508/228–0580), **Pacific National Bank** (61 Main St., tel. 508/228–1917), **A&P** (Straight Wharf, tel. 508/228–9756), and **Finast** (Lower Pleasant St., tel. 508/228–2178).

Arriving and Departing by Plane

Airport and   **Nantucket Memorial Airport** (tel. 508/325–5300) is about 3½
Airlines   miles southeast of town via Old South Road. A taxi from the airport to town costs about $6.

Business Express/Delta Connection (tel. 800/345–3400) flies from Boston year-round and from New York (LAG) in season. **Cape Air** (tel. 508/771–6944 or 800/352–0714) connects the island with Boston, Martha's Vineyard, and New Bedford year-round; it also has joint fares with Continental, Delta, Midwest Espress, and USAir and ticketing-and-baggage agreements with eight major U.S. carriers and KLM. **Colgan Air** (tel. 800/272–5488) flies from Newark and Hyannis year-round. **Continental** (tel. 800/525–0280) has nonstops from Newark in season. **Island Airlines** (tel. 508/775–6606, 508/228–7575, or 800/248–7779) and **Nantucket Airlines** (tel. 508/790–0300, 508/228–6234, or 800/635–8787 in MA) fly from Hyannis year-round and offer charters. **Northwest Airlink** (tel. 800/225–2525) flies from Boston year-round, from Newark in season.

Ocean Wings (tel. 508/325–5548 or 800/253–5039) and **Coastal Air** (tel. 508/228–3350 or 203/448–1001) are year-round charter companies with island bases. **Westchester Air** (tel. 914/761–3000 or 800/759–2929) flies charters out of White Plains, New York.

Arriving and Departing by Ferry

From Hyannis   The **Steamship Authority** runs car-and-passenger ferries to the island from Hyannis year-round. (For policies and restrictions, *see* Arriving and Departing by Ferry in Chapter 4, Martha's Vineyard.) The trip takes 2¼ hours. *South St. dock, tel. 508/540–2022 for reservations or 508/771–4000; on Nantucket, 508/228–3274 for reservations or 508/228–0262; TTY/TDD 508/540–1394. Cost, one way: $9.75 adults, $4.90 children 5–12, $4.50 bicycles. Cars, one way: mid-May–mid-Oct., $83; mid-Mar.–mid-May and mid-Oct.–Nov. $65; Dec.–mid-Mar., $50.*

Hy-Line passenger ferries make the 1¾- to 2-hour trip from Hyannis mid-May–October. The MV *Great Point* offers a first-class section ($20 one way, adult or child) with a private lounge, rest rooms, upholstered seats, carpeting, a bar, and a snack bar. The "Around the Sound" cruise, a one-day round-trip from Hyannis with stops at Nantucket and Martha's Vineyard and six hours at sea, is available June–mid-September ($31 adults, $15.50 children 5–12, $13.50 bicycles). *Ocean St. dock, tel. 508/778–2602 for reservations or 508/778–2600; on Nantucket, 508/228–3949. Cost, one way: $10.75 adults, $5.25 children 5–12, $4.50 bicycles.*

From Martha's Vineyard **Hy-Line** makes 2¹/₄-hour runs to and from Nantucket from mid-June to mid-September—the only interisland passenger service. (To get a car from the Vineyard to Nantucket, you must return to the mainland and drive from Woods Hole to Hyannis.) *Tel. 508/778–2600 in Hyannis, 508/228–3949 on Nantucket, 508/693–0112 in Oak Bluffs. Cost, one way: $10.75 adults, $5.25 children 5–12, $4.50 bicycles.*

Arriving and Departing by Private Boat

Harbor facilities are available in town year-round at the **Town Pier** (tel. 508/228–7260) and at the **Boat Basin** (tel. 508/228–1333 or 800/626–2628), which has shower and laundry facilities, electric power, cable TV, phone hookups, fuel dock, and summer concierge service.

Madaket Marine (tel. 508/228–9086 or 800/564–9086), with electric hookups and fuel, has moorings May–October and slips year-round for boats up to 32 feet in Hither Creek.

Getting Around

One of the attractions of a Nantucket vacation is escape from the fast lane. Most visitors find themselves walking a lot more than they're used to and taking advantage of the island's miles of scenic bike paths. Even so, in high season the main streets are clogged with traffic (and the parking spaces filled), and residents beg you to leave your car at home.

If your visit will be short and spent mostly in town and on the beaches, taxis and beach shuttles can supplement foot power adequately. If, on the other hand, your focus will be on the farther-out beaches and nature preserves, or if you'll be staying a week or longer, a car may make life simpler. Renting a car on the island for a day or two is cheaper and less troublesome than bringing one over on the ferry (but do reserve well in advance).

Some of the island's most beautiful and least touristed beaches are accessible only by foot or four-wheel-drive vehicles. Permits are available for $5 for private vehicles, $25 for rental vehicles, at the police department (tel. 508/228–1212) on South Water Street. Coatue–Coskata–Great Point is open to Jeeps but requires a separate NCF permit (*see* Tour 2 in Exploring Nantucket, *below*).

By Car Cars and Jeeps are available at the airport desks of **Budget** (tel. 508/228–5666), **Hertz** (tel. 508/228–9421), and **Nantucket Windmill** (tel. 508/228–1227 or 800/228–1227). **Nantucket Jeep Rental** (tel. 508/228–1618) rents Jeep Wranglers and delivers. In high season, you will pay up to $60 a day for cars, up to $150 for Jeeps (reserve well ahead for Jeeps; they disappear quickly).

By Bus From mid-June to Labor Day, Barrett's Tours (20 Federal St., tel. 508/228–0174), across from the Information Bureau, runs beach shuttles to 'Sconset and Madaket ($5 round-trip, $3 one-way), Surfside ($3 round-trip, $2 one-way), and Jetties ($1 one-way) several times daily. Children pay half-fare to 'Sconset and Surfside.

By Taxi Taxis usually wait outside the airport or at the foot of Main Street by the ferry, or call **A-1 Taxi** (tel. 508/228–3330 or 508/228–4084), **Aardvark Cab** (tel. 508/228–2223), **All Point Taxi** (tel. 508/228–5779), or **Peterson's Taxi** (tel. 508/228–9227). Rates are flat fees, based on one person with two bags before 1 AM: $3 within town (1½-mile radius), $6 to the airport, $11 to 'Sconset, $12 to Wauwinet.

By Bicycle and Moped Mountain bikes are best if you plan to explore the dirt roads. To drive a moped you must have a driver's license and a helmet; you may not use the vehicle within the town historic district between 10 PM and 7 AM, and you may never drive it on the bike paths. Moped accidents happen often on the narrow or dirt roads—watch out for loose gravel.

Rentals are available at Steamboat Wharf from **Young's Bicycle Shop** (tel. 508/228–1151), which also rents cars and four-wheel-drive vehicles in season, and from **Nantucket Bike Shop** (tel. 508/228–1999; Apr.–Oct.). Both provide excellent touring maps. Daily rentals typically cost $10–$20 for a bicycle, $30–$50 for a moped, though half-, full-, and multiple-day rates are available.

By Horse-drawn Carriage **Carried Away** (tel. 508/228–0218) offers narrated carriage rides through the town historic district in season.

Guided Tours

Orientation **Barrett's Tours** (20 Federal St., tel. 508/228–0174) and **Nantucket Island Tours** (Straight Wharf, tel. 508/228–0334) give 75- to 90-minute narrated bus tours of the island from spring through fall; buses meet the ferries.

Gail's Tours (tel. 508/257–6557; Apr.–Dec.) are lively 1½-hour van tours narrated by seventh-generation Nantucketer Gail Johnson, who knows all the inside stories.

Walking Tours The Information Bureau has a free self-guided tour pamphlet, **"Historic Nantucket Walking Tours,"** published by the Nantucket Historical Association.

Nantucket Literary Walking Tours (tel. 508/228–6307) explore the island "homes and haunts" of Melville, Poe, and other literary greats.

Roger Young's historic walking tours (tel. 508/228–1062; in season) of the town center are entertaining and leisurely.

Special-Interest Cruises *Yachting* magazine named Nantucket's harbor one of the 10 most romantic in the world. Boats of all kinds leave from Straight Wharf for harbor sails throughout the summer; many are available for charter as well. The 31-foot Friendship sloop ***Endeavor*** (Slip 15, tel. 508/228–5585) offers harbor sails and sails to Coatue, where you are rowed ashore to spend a private morning beachcombing. The renovated lobster boat ***Anna W. II*** (Slip 12, tel. 508/228–1444) offers sunset and moonlight cruises, as well as lobstering demonstrations and winter seal cruises. The 40-foot sailing yacht *Sparrow* (Slip 18, tel. 508/228–6029), with a teak, brass, and stained-glass interior, offers 1½-hour sails for six guests, plus charters.

Great Point   **Beach Excursions Ltd.** (tel. 508/228–5800) offers Jeep trips to Great Point, with views of the spit's beaches, eagle nesting grounds, clamming and oyster ponds, and lighthouse. The Trustees of Reservations sponsor naturalist-led **Great Point Natural History Tours** (tel. 508/228–6799).

Nature   **Birding Adventures** (tel. 508/228–2703) offer tours led by a naturalist who knows his raptors from his oystercatchers. **The Maria Mitchell Association** (Vestal St., tel. 508/228–9198) organizes wildflower and bird walks from June to Labor Day (*see also* What to See and Do with Children, *below*).

Whale-watching   **Nantucket Whalewatch** offers naturalist-led full-day excursions every Tuesday mid-July–August. *Hy-Line dock, Straight Wharf, tel. 508/283–0313, 800/942–5464, or 800/322–0013 in MA. Cost: $65 adults, $45 children under 12. Reservations required.*

Exploring Nantucket

The 14- by 3-mile island of Nantucket has one town, also called Nantucket; the village of Siasconset (called 'Sconset), with a number of services, on the east coast; the village of Madaket, on the west, with a beach and harbor, great sunsets, a seasonal restaurant, and bluefishing off the point; and a number of residential areas with no commercial or tourist facilities. Although major roads will take you to most of these areas, exploring them must often be done on dirt roads. Bike paths lead east to 'Sconset, south to Surfside Beach, and west to Madaket.

Nantucket Town has a small commercial area of a few square blocks leading up from the waterfront; beyond it, quiet residential roads fan out. As you wander you may notice a small round plaque by some doorways. Issued by the Nantucket Historical Association, the plaques certify that the house dates from the 17th century (silver), 1700–1775 (red bronze), 1776–1812 (brass), 1813–1846 (green), or 1847–1900 (black). Unfortunately, they all seem to turn coppery green or black with age.

Highlights for First-time Visitors

Altar Rock (*see* Tour 2: Town–'Sconset–Polpis Loop)
Eel Point (*see* Nature Areas)
First Congregational Church, for the view (*see* Tour 1: Nantucket Town)
Madaket Bike Path (*see* Sports and the Outdoors)
Museum of Nantucket History (*see* Tour 1: Nantucket Town)
Siasconset (*see* Tour 2: Town–'Sconset–Polpis Loop)
"Three Bricks" (*see* Tour 1: Nantucket Town)
Whaling Museum (*see* Tour 1: Nantucket Town)

Tour 1: Nantucket Town

Numbers in the margin correspond to numbered points of interest on the Nantucket Town map.

NOTE: Fourteen historic properties along Nantucket Town's streets are operated as museums by the **Nantucket Historical**

Association (tel. 508/228–1894). At any property you can purchase an NHA Visitor Pass ($8 adults, $4 children 5–14), which entitles you to free entry at all 14 museums, or you can pay single admission to each. All the properties (except the one or two closed each year for maintenance) are open daily from Memorial Day to Columbus Day. The only exceptions are the Museum of Nantucket History (which reopens for Thanksgiving and Christmas Stroll weekends) and the Whaling Museum (which, while open year-round, is closed Christmas Day and on weekdays January through the April Daffodil Festival). NHA hours vary greatly from year to year, but 1993's schedule was as follows: Memorial Day–mid-June, daily 11–3; mid-June–Labor Day, daily 10–5; Labor Day–Columbus Day, daily 11–3. Most NHA properties close for winter sleep between Columbus Day and Memorial Day.

❶ The geologic and historical overview given by the **Museum of Nantucket History** helps put into perspective the sights you will see when touring the island. The brick building in which the museum is set was built by Thomas Macy after the Great Fire of 1846—which destroyed the wharves and 400 buildings, about a third of all those in the town—as a warehouse for the supplies needed to outfit whaling ships. It has been restored to be accurate historically, down to period doors, hatchways, and hoists. Inside, audio and visual displays include an early fire-fighting vehicle, ship models, blowups of old photographs, and a 13-foot diorama (with narration) showing the shops, ships, and activities of the bustling waterfront before the fire. The second floor features changing exhibits. Live demonstrations of such early island crafts as candle making are given daily from mid-June to Columbus Day. *Straight Wharf, tel. 508/228–1894. Admission: $3 adults, $2 children 5–14; or NHA pass. (See note above for opening times.)*

❷ Walking up Main Street, you'll come to the redbrick **Pacific Club** building, still housing the elite club of Pacific whaling masters for which it is named. Understandably, since the last whaling ship was seen here in 1870, the club now admits whalers' *descendants*, who gather for the odd cribbage game or a swapping of tales. The building began in 1772 as the counting house of William Rotch, owner of the *Dartmouth* and *Beaver*, two of the three ships that hosted a famous tea party in Boston. (According to the NHA, the plaque outside the Pacific Club identifying the third ship, the *Eleanor*, as Rotch's is incorrect.) Upstairs is the office of the **Chamber of Commerce** (*see* Important Addresses and Numbers in Essential Information, *above*), where you might want to stop for maps and other information.

From here you get the most photographed view of Main Street. The cobblestone square has a harmonious symmetry; at the foot it is anchored by the Pacific Club, and at the head, by the Pacific National Bank, another redbrick building. The only broad thoroughfare in town, Main Street was widened after the Great Fire leveled all its buildings except those made of brick, to safeguard against flames hopping across the street in the event of another fire. The cobblestones—brought to the island as ballast in returning ships—were laid to prevent the wheels of carts heavily laden with whale oil from sinking into the dirt on their passage from the waterfront to the factories.

At the center of Lower Main is an old horse trough, today overflowing with flowers. From here the street gently rises; at the

Nantucket Town

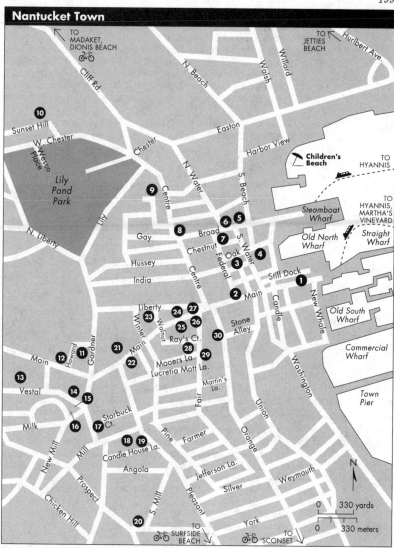

TO MADAKET, DIONIS BEACH

TO JETTIES BEACH

Hurlbert Ave.

Cliff Rd.

N. Beach

Walsh

Willard

Sunset Hill

W. Chester Place

Wesco Place

Chester

Easton

Harbor View

Children's Beach

TO HYANNIS

Lily Pond Park

N. Liberty

Lily

N. Water

Centre

First Congregational Church, **9**

S. Beach

Gay

Broad

Chestnut

Whaling Museum, **5**

Peter Foulger Museum, **6**

Nantucket Information Bureau, **7**

Jared Coffin House, **8**

Steamboat Wharf

TO HYANNIS, MARTHA'S VINEYARD

Old North Wharf

Straight Wharf

Hussey

India

Federal

Oak

S. Water

Atheneum, **3**

Pacific Club/Chamber of Commerce, **2**

Still Dock

Dreamland Theatre, **4**

Museum of Nantucket History, **1**

New Whale

Old South Wharf

Liberty

Macy-Christian House, **23**

Henry Coffin House, **24**

Pacific National Bank, **27**

Charles G. Coffin House, **25**

John Wendell Barrett House, **26**

Walnut

Winter

Main

Ray's Ct.

Unitarian Universalist Church, **30**

Stone Alley

Candle

Washington

Commercial Wharf

Howard

Gardner

Fire Hose Cart House, **11**

"Three Bricks," **21**

Hadwen House, **22**

Mooers La.

Lucretia Mott La.

Quaker Meeting House/Fair Street Museum, **28**

St. Paul's Episcopal Church, **29**

Greater Light, **12**

Main

Old Gaol, **13**

Vestal

Mitchell House, **14**

Maria Mitchell Science Library, **15**

Fair

Martin's La.

Union

Town Pier

Milk

New Mill

Hinchman House, **16**

Starbuck Refinery and Candle Works, **17**

Starbuck Ct.

Pine

Farmer

Orange

Mill

1800 House, **18**

Moors' End, **19**

Candle House La.

Jefferson La.

Weymouth

Prospect

Angola

Pleasant

Silver

Chicken Hill

S. Mill

Old Mill, **20**

TO SURFSIDE BEACH

York

TO 'SCONSET

N

0 330 yards

0 330 meters

Atheneum, **3**

Charles G. Coffin House, **25**

Dreamland Theatre, **4**

1800 House, **18**

Fire Hose Cart House, **11**

First Congregational Church, **9**

Greater Light, **12**

Hadwen House, **22**

Henry Coffin House, **24**

Hinchman House, **16**

Jared Coffin House, **8**

John Wendell Barrett House, **26**

Macy-Christian House, **23**

Maria Mitchell Science Library, **15**

Mitchell House, **14**

Moors' End, **19**

Museum of Nantucket History, **1**

Nantucket Information Bureau, **7**

Old Gaol, **13**

Old Mill, **20**

Oldest House, **10**

Pacific Club/Chamber of Commerce, **2**

Pacific National Bank, **27**

Peter Foulger Museum/Nantucket Historical Association Research Center, **6**

Quaker Meeting House/Fair Street Museum, **28**

St. Paul's Episcopal Church, **29**

Starbuck Refinery and Candle Works, **17**

"Three Bricks," **21**

Unitarian Universalist Church, **30**

Whaling Museum, **5**

bank it narrows to its pre-fire width and leaves the commercial district for an area of mansions that escaped the blaze. The simple shop buildings that replaced those lost are a pleasing hodgepodge of sizes, colors, and styles. Elm trees—thousands of which were planted in the 1850s by Henry and Charles Coffin—once formed a canopy over Main Street, but Dutch elm disease took most of them; 1991's Hurricane Bob took two dozen more.

Time Out   You can breakfast or lunch inexpensively at several soup-and-sandwich places, including **David's Soda Fountain** (Congdon's Pharmacy, 47 Main St., tel. 508/228–4549) and **Nantucket Pharmacy** (45 Main St., tel. 508/228–0180). The **Espresso Cafe** (40 Main St., tel. 508/228–6930) serves excellent coffee, espresso, cappuccino (try it iced), and desserts, as well as quick and satisfying lunches and dinners—pizza, chilis and soups, salads, and more. In a small indoor space or outside, **Off Centre Cafe** (29 Centre St., tel. 508/228–8470) serves delicious breakfasts, such as huevos rancheros or fruit popovers and pancakes; sandwiches made from its own breads; and homemade desserts.

Turning down Federal Street, you'll come to a huge white Greek Revival building with an odd windowless facade and fluted Ionic columns. This is the **Atheneum** (Lower India St., tel. 508/228–1110), Nantucket's town library, built in 1846 to replace a structure lost to the fire. The opening ceremonies featured a dedication by Ralph Waldo Emerson, who—along with Daniel Webster, Henry David Thoreau, and John James Audubon—later delivered lectures in the library's second-floor Great Hall (open Saturday morning and Thursday afternoon). In the 19th century the hall was the center of island culture, also hosting public meetings, suffrage rallies, and county fairs. Fundraising for a new wing is under way.

A right turn onto Oak Street brings you to South Water Street. Across the way is the **Dreamland Theatre,** a good illustration of early Nantucketers' penchant for multiple use of dwellings as well as for moving houses around. Trees (and therefore lumber) were so scarce that Herman Melville joked in *Moby-Dick* "that pieces of wood in Nantucket are carried about like bits of the true cross in Rome." Currently a summer cinema, the Dreamland was built on Main Street as a Quaker meeting house; became a straw factory, then an entertainment hall; was moved to Brant Point as part of the grand Nantucket Hotel in the late 19th century; and was floated across the harbor by barge about 1905 and installed in its present location.

From Oak Street, turn left on South Water; at the end is the **Whaling Museum,** set in an 1846 factory built for refining spermaceti and making candles. (Spermaceti candles, incidentally, which you'll see for sale at various shops, give off a clean, steady light and only a slight fragrance, which is why they became such popular replacements for smelly tallow candles.) This museum immerses you in Nantucket's whaling past with exhibits that include a fully rigged whaleboat, harpoons and other implements, portraits of sea captains, a large scrimshaw collection, a full-size tryworks (used to process whale oil aboard ship), the skeleton of a 43-foot finback whale, replicas of cooper and blacksmith shops, and the original 16-foot-high glass prism from the Sankaty Light. The knowledgeable and enthusiastic staff gives a 20- to 30-minute introductory talk peppered with tales of a whaling man's life at sea (call for tour times). Don't miss the museum's gift shop next door (*see* Shopping, *below*). *Broad St., tel. 508/228–1894. Admission: $4 adults, $2 children 5–14; or NHA pass. (See note above for opening times.)*

❻ The next building up on Broad Street houses the **Peter Foulger Museum** and the **Nantucket Historical Association Research Center.** The latter's extensive collection of manuscripts, photographs, ships' logs and charts, and genealogical records is open only to those doing research. The museum displays changing exhibits from the permanent collection, including portraits, textiles, porcelains, silver, furniture, and more; a 1994 China Trade exhibit will be supplemented by pieces from Nantucket private homes. *Museum: tel. 508/228–1894. Admission: $3 adults, $2 children; or NHA pass. (See note above for opening times.) Library: tel. 508/228–1655. Research permit: $10 (3 days). Open weekdays 10–5.*

Time Out Across the street, the **Juice Bar** (12 Broad St., tel. 508/228–5799; Apr.–mid-Oct.) offers homemade ice cream (with lots of toppings), waffle cones, and baked goods, plus fresh-squeezed juices, frozen yogurt, specialty coffees, and always a long line.

❼ Just around the corner on Federal Street is the **Nantucket Information Bureau** (*see* Tourist Information in Essential Information, *above*), with public phones, rest rooms, and a bulletin board posting events.

Most of the Greek Revival houses you will see as you continue up Broad Street were replacements for buildings lost in the **❽** Great Fire. Pause to admire the **Jared Coffin House,** which has operated as an inn since the mid-19th century. Coffin, a wealthy merchant, built this Georgian brick house with Ionic portico, parapet, hip roof, and cupola—then the only three-story structure on the island—for his wife, who wanted to live closer to town. They moved here in 1845 from their home on Pleasant Street, but (so the story goes) nothing would please the woman, and within two years they had left the island altogether for Boston.

❾ A right onto Centre Street takes you past the **First Congregational Church** (also known as the Old North Church), Nantucket's largest. Its tower—whose steeple is capped with a weathervane depicting a whale catch—rises 120 feet, providing the best view of Nantucket to be had. On a clear day the reward for climbing the 92 steps (many landings break the climb) is a panorama encompassing Great Point, Sankaty Light, Muskeget and Tuckernuck islands, moors, ponds, beaches, and the winding streets and rooftops of town. Peek in at the church's interior, with its old box pews, a chandelier seven feet in diameter, and a trompe-l'oeil ceiling done by an Italian painter in 1850 and since restored. The organ, installed in 1904, has 914 wood and metal pipes. (Organ aficionados may want to have a look at the 1831 Appleton organ—one of only four extant—at the United Methodist Church, next to the Pacific National Bank on Main Street.) The Old North Vestry in the rear, the oldest house of worship on the island, was built in 1725 about a mile north of its present site. The main church was built in 1834. *62 Centre St., tel. 508/228–0950. Admission: $1.50 adults,*

50¢ children. Open mid-June–mid-Oct., Mon.–Sat. 10–4. Closed mid-Oct.–mid-June.

A short walk along Centre Street (past lovely Lily Street) and West Chester Street leads to the **Oldest House,** also called the Jethro Coffin House, built in 1686 as a wedding gift for Jethro and Mary Gardner Coffin. The most striking feature of the salt-box—the oldest house on the island—is the massive central brick chimney with brick horseshoe adornment; other highlights are the enormous hearths and diamond-pane leaded-glass windows. Cutaway panels show 17th-century construction techniques. The interior's sparse furnishings include an antique loom. *Sunset Hill, tel. 508/228–1894. Admission: $3 adults, $2 children 5–14; or NHA pass. (See note above for opening times.)*

Turn left off West Chester Street onto North Liberty Street, where you'll see the entrance to **Lily Pond Park,** a 5-acre Land Bank conservation area. Its lawn and wetlands (there is a trail, but it's muddy) foster abundant wildlife, including birds, ducks, and deer. You can pick blackberries, raspberries, and grapes in season.

A bit farther on, you'll come to the **Fire Hose Cart House.** Built in 1886 as one of several neighborhood fire stations—Nantucketers had learned their lesson—the house displays a small collection of fire-fighting equipment used a century ago. *8 Gardner St., tel. 508/228–1894. Admission free. (See note above for opening times.)*

Turn into the little street just before the firehouse. At the end, on the right, is **Greater Light,** an example of the summer homes of the artists who flocked to Nantucket in its early resort days. In the 1930s two unusual Quaker sisters from Philadelphia—actress Hanna and artist Gertrude Monaghan—converted a barn into what looks like the lavish set for an old movie. The exotic decor includes Italian furniture, Native American artifacts and textiles, a wrought-iron balcony, bas reliefs, and a coat of arms. The sisters also remodeled the private house next door, called Lesser Light, for their parents. Greater Light is scheduled to be closed for the 1994 season, but get the latest scoop at the tourist office. *8 Howard St., tel. 508/228–1894.*

Continue on Howard Street to the end; turn right, then left on Bloom, then right; a sign on the right points the way to the **Old Gaol,** an 1805 jailhouse in use until 1933. Shingles mask the building's construction of massive square timbers, plainly visible inside; walls, ceilings, and floors are bolted with iron. The furnishings consist of rough plank bunks and open privies, but you needn't feel too much sympathy for the prisoners: Most of them were allowed out at night to sleep in their own beds. *15R Vestal St., tel. 508/228–1894. Admission free. (See note above for opening times.)*

Head left when you come out of the jail; at the beginning of Vestal Street is the **Mitchell House,** birthplace of astronomer and Vassar professor Maria (pronounced "Mah-RYE-ah") Mitchell, who in 1847, at age 29, discovered a comet while surveying the sky from the top of the Pacific National Bank. (Her family had moved to quarters over the bank, where her father—also an astronomer—worked as a cashier.) The restored 1790 house contains family possessions and Maria Mitchell memorabilia, including the telescope with which she spotted the comet. The kitchen, of authentic wide-board construction, retains the antique utensils, iron pump, and sink of the time. Tours of the house, the roof walk, and the wildflower garden are available; the adjacent observatory is used by researchers and is not open to the public. *1 Vestal St., tel. 508/228–2896. Admission: $3 adults, $1 children. Open mid-June–Aug., Tues.– Sat. 10–4. Closed Sept.–mid-June.*

⑮ Across the street is the **Maria Mitchell Science Library,** which has science books and periodicals, including field-identification guides and gardening books, as well as books on Nantucket history. *Tel. 508/228–9219. Admission free. Open mid-June– mid-Sept., Tues.–Sat. 10–4; mid-Sept.–mid-June, Mon.–Thurs. 1–4.*

⑯ Next door, at the corner, is the **Hinchman House**—a natural-science museum, with specimens of local birds, shells, insects, and plants. *7 Milk St., tel. 508/228–0898. Admission: $3 adults, $1 children under 13. Open mid-June–Aug., Tues.–Sat. 10–4. Closed Sept.–mid-June.*

The three previous properties—as well as the **Loines Observatory** (Milk St. Ext., tel. 508/228–9198), which offers Wednesday-night stargazing mid-July to mid-August; and an aquarium near Commercial Wharf (*see* What to See and Do with Children, *below*)—are administered by the Maria Mitchell Association, established in 1902 by Vassar students and Maria's family. A combination admission ticket to all sites is $4 adults, $1.50 children.

One of 10 children of Quaker parents, Mitchell attained many firsts in her day—first woman astronomy professor in the United States, first woman to discover a comet—and world fame to boot. It is not surprising that a Nantucket woman would do so, given the history of women on the island. During the whaling days men would be gone for up to five years at a time; the women learned to keep the town going. They became leaders in every arena, from religion to business. Mary Coffin Starbuck helped establish Quakerism on the island and was a celebrated preacher. Lucretia Coffin Mott was a powerful advocate of the antislavery and women's-rights movements. During the post–Civil War depression, Centre Street near Main Street became known as Petticoat Row, a reflection of the large number of women shopkeepers.

Cross Milk Street and walk down New Dollar Lane; on your
⑰ left, down a long driveway, are the remains of the **Starbuck refinery and candle works,** now used as apartments and ga-
⑱ rages. A left at the end of the street leads to the **1800 House,** typical of a Nantucket home—one not enriched by whaling money—of that time. Once the residence of the high sheriff, the house features locally made furniture and other household goods, a six-flue chimney with beehive oven, and a summer kitchen. *10 Mill St., tel. 508/228–1894. Scheduled to be closed for 1994 season.*

The massive brick structure at the corner, at 19 Pleasant
⑲ Street, is **Moors' End,** the handsome Federal brick house where Jared Coffin lived before building what is now the Jared Coffin House. (The proximity to the fumes from the Starbuck refinery was one of Mrs. Coffin's complaints.) It is a private home, but insiders tell of vast murals of the whaling era on the

walls, and of scrawled notes about shipwreck sightings in the cupola. Behind high brick walls is a lavish garden.

Make a right onto Pleasant Street and another onto South Mill Street for the **Old Mill,** a 1746 Dutch-style octagonal windmill ㉑ built with lumber from shipwrecks. Several such windmills sat on hills in Nantucket in the 1700s, but only this one remains. The Douglas-fir pivot pole used to turn the cap and sails into the wind is a replacement of the original pole, a ship's foremast. The mill is worked with wood gears and wind power (when the wind is strong enough) to grind corn into meal that is sold here. *South Mill St., tel. 508/228–1894. Admission: $3 adults, $2 children 5–14; or NHA pass. (See note above for opening times.)*

From here, return to town via Pleasant Street. At the end is Upper Main Street, where many of the mansions of the golden age of whaling were built. Facing you, at Nos. 93–97, are the ㉑ well-known **"Three Bricks,"** identical redbrick mansions with columned, Greek Revival porches at their front entrances. Similar in design to the Jared Coffin House but with only two stories, they were built between 1836 and 1838 by whaling merchant Joseph Starbuck for his three sons (one still belongs to a Starbuck descendant).

The two white, porticoed Greek Revival mansions across the street—referred to as the Two Greeks—were built in 1845 and 1846 by superrich factory owner William Hadwen, a Newport native. Number 94, built as a wedding gift for their adopted niece, was modeled on the Athenian Tower of the Winds, with Corinthian capitals on the entry columns, a domed stair hall with statuary niches, and an oculus. The Hadwens' own house, ㉒ at No. 96, is now a museum, called the **Hadwen House.** A two-year program to restore the house to its mid-19th-century origins—including the addition of classic Victorian gas chandeliers and furnishings, as well as reproduction wallpapers and window treatments—was completed in 1993. A guided tour points out such architectural details as the grand circular staircase, fine plasterwork, and carved Italian-marble fireplace mantels, as well as portraits, needlework, silver doorknobs, and other decorative objects. Behind the house are period gardens. *96 Main St., tel. 508/228–1894. Admission: $3 adults, $2 children 5–14; or NHA pass. (See note above for opening times.)*

㉓ A turn down Walnut Lane leads to the **Macy-Christian House.** The two-story lean-to, built c. 1740 for another Thomas Macy, features a great open hearth flanked by brick beehive ovens and old paneling. Part of the house reflects the late 19th-century Colonial Revival style of the 1934 renovation by the Christian family; the formal parlor and upstairs bedroom are in authentic Colonial style. *12 Liberty St., tel. 508/228–1894. Admission: $3 adults, $2 children 5–14; or NHA pass. (See note above for opening times.)*

Back on Main Street, facing each other, are two more attractive ㉔ brick houses built for brothers: the **Henry Coffin House** (at No. ㉕ 75) and the **Charles G. Coffin House** (No. 78). Wealthy shipping agents and whale-oil merchants, the Coffins used for these 1830s houses the same mason who later built the Three Bricks.

㉖ The last of the grand Main Street homes is the **John Wendell Barrett House,** on the right at No. 72. Legend has it that Lydia Mitchell Barrett stood on the steps and refused to move when, during the Great Fire, men tried to evacuate her so they could blow up the house to stop the spread of the fire; luckily, a shift in the wind settled the showdown.

㉗ Across the street is the 1818 **Pacific National Bank.** Like the Pacific Club it faces, the bank is a monument to the far-flung voyages of the Nantucket whaling ships it financed. Inside, above old-style teller cages, are murals of street and port scenes from the whaling days. Near the bank, at 62 Main Street, is Murray's Toggery, the site of R. H. Macy's first retail store.

㉘ A right on Fair Street will bring you to the **Quaker Meeting House,** built around 1838 as a Friends school and now a Quaker place of worship in summer. A small room of quiet simplicity— white-and-gray walls, 12-over-12 windows with antique glass, and unadorned wood benches—it is in keeping with these peaceful people, who believe that the divine spirit is within each person and that one does not require an intermediary to worship God.

Attached to the meeting house is an unattractive 1904 concrete building that houses the **Fair Street Museum.** In celebration of the NHA's centennial in 1994, the museum will showcase the association's collection of antique lightship baskets. *1 Fair St., tel. 508/228–1894. Admission: $3 adults, $2 children 5–14; or NHA pass. (See note above for opening times.)*

㉙ Across the street is the 1901 **St. Paul's Episcopal Church,** a massive granite structure adorned at the front and back by beautiful Tiffany windows. The interior is cool and white, with dark exposed beams. From here, you might take a minute to wander down one of the pretty side streets, such as Lucretia Mott Lane or Mooers Lane.

Continue along Fair Street to Martin's Lane and make a left onto Orange Street. On the left, past the only row houses ever **㉚** built on the island (in 1831), is the 1809 **Unitarian Universalist Church,** also known as South Church, with the gold-domed spire that soars above the town as the First Congregational Church's slender white steeple does. Also like First Congregational, South Church features a trompe-l'oeil ceiling painting, this one a false, intricately detailed dome, executed in 1840 by another European painter. Here, however, illusion is taken to greater lengths: The curved chancel and paneled walls you see are also creations in paint. The 1831 mahogany-cased Goodrich organ in the loft is played at services and concerts. In the octagonal belfry of the tower, which houses the town clock, is a bell cast in Portugal that has been ringing out the noon hour since it was hung in 1815.

Across the street is **Stone Alley,** a byway that's as pleasant a way of returning to town as any. A left onto Union Street brings you back to the foot of Main Street. On the wall of the last building on the left on Washington Street, notice the sign listing distances from Nantucket to various points of the globe (it's 14,650 miles to Tahiti).

Tour 2: Town–'Sconset–Polpis Loop

Siasconset, 7 miles from Nantucket Town, is reached by road or by a mostly level bike path and makes a lovely day trip; off-season there's not a lot to do in the village, but the ride still has its attractions. From town, take Orange Street to the rotary, where Milestone Road and its bike path begin.

Time Out The **Nantucket Bake Shop** (79 Orange St., tel. 508/228–2797; in season) is a great place to stop to fill a knapsack with Portuguese breads and pastries.

About 5½ miles east of the rotary (white stone mile-markers on your left tick out the distance to 'Sconset), signs on the left point to the **Milestone Bog**, more than 200 acres of working cranberry bog surrounded by conservation land. Cultivated since 1857, the bog was the world's largest contiguous natural cranberry bog until it was subdivided after 1959. The land was donated to the Nantucket Conservation Foundation in 1968; the bogs are leased to a grower, who harvests and sells the crops. (For a map of the foundation's properties, visit or write to NCF headquarters at 118 Cliff Rd., Box 13, Nantucket 02554, tel. 508/228–2884, weekdays 8–5. The map costs $3, or $4 by mail.)

The harvest begins in late September and continues for six weeks, during which time harvesters work every day from sunup to sunset in the flooded bog. The sight of the bright red berries floating on the surface while the moors turn the rich colors of autumn is not to be missed. At other times the color of the dry bog may be green, rust-red, or, in June and early July, the pale pink of cranberry blossoms, but always the bog and the moors have a quiet beauty that's worth the effort to get there.

Another half-mile on Milestone Road brings you to an intersection that marks the center of **Siasconset,** a charming village of pretty streets with tiny rose-covered cottages and driveways of crushed white shells. A community of cod and halibut fishermen and shore whalers from the 17th century, 'Sconset was already becoming a summer resort during whaling days, when people from Nantucket Town would come here to get away from the smells of burning whale oil in the refineries. In 1884 the narrow-gauge railway—built three years earlier to take spiffily clad folk from the New Bedford steamers to the beach at Surfside—came to 'Sconset, bringing ever more off-islanders. These included writers and artists from Boston in the 1890s, followed soon by Broadway actors and actresses on holiday during the theaters' summer hiatus. Attracted by the village's beauty, remoteness, sandy ocean beach, and cheap lodgings (converted one-room fishing shacks, and cottages built to look like them), they spread the word, and before long 'Sconset had become a thriving actors' colony.

Today the village is almost entirely a summer community—the local postmaster claims that about 150 families live here through the winter, but you'd never know it. At the central square are a post office, a liquor store, a bookstore, a market, and two restaurants (Claudette's makes box lunches for picnics—*see* Dining, *below*). The town is so small that you really can't go wrong no matter what route you take, but here's a suggestion.

Head back the way you came and turn left onto Morey Lane. Three side streets here—Evelyn, Lily, and Pochick—remain much as they were in the 1890s, when a development of rental

cottages in the fishing-shack style was built here. Turn left onto
Evelyn Street, then right and your first left onto Pochick Avenue, which ends at Ocean Avenue, the shore road. To the left
on Ocean is the **Summer House,** an upscale inn with a fine restaurant and a poolside café (*see* Dining *and* Lodging, *below*).
Walk on and you'll return to the square; here, turn onto Gulley
Road for 'Sconset Beach (or Codfish Park Beach), signaled by
a children's swing set. Head back up Gulley to return to town.

At the rotary, turn right and follow Broadway around; a left
just before the sign to Quidnet leads to a plaza and the 'Sconset
Pump, a preserved well marked with a plaque proclaiming it
"dug in 1776." Turn up New Street, which leads past an art
gallery on the right and, farther on, the much-photographed
entryway of the **Chanticleer** (*see* Dining, *below*): A trellis arch
topped by a sculpted hedge frames a rose garden with a flower-
bedecked carousel horse at its center. Opposite the restaurant
is the **Siasconset Casino,** built in 1899 as a tennis club and bowling alley and used during the actors'-colony heyday as a venue
for theater productions (never for gambling). Though some
theater is still seen here, the casino is mostly a summer tennis
club and cinema. Farther on the left is the 'Sconset Union
Chapel, the village's only church, which on summer Sundays
holds a Roman Catholic mass at 8:45 AM and Protestant services at 10:30.

Return to the Quidnet sign, which leads you out of 'Sconset by
a more scenic route. Outside town, turn right onto Bayberry
Lane, then left to reach the red-and-white-striped **Sankaty
Light.** Situated on a 90-foot-high bluff that has lost as much as
200 feet of shoreline in the past 75 years, the 1849 lighthouse
is in danger of being lost, as Great Point Light was in 1984, to
further erosion. A fragile piece of land, Nantucket loses more
of its shoreline every year, especially at Sankaty and on the
south shore, where no shoals break the ocean waves as they do
on the north shore. Several oceanfront houses at Cisco have
been lost or moved since 1990 because of massive bluff erosion
due to many unusually fierce winter storms.

The lighthouse is at a dead end; as you head back out, on your
right are the Scottish-looking greens of the private **Sankaty
Head Golf Club.** A right turn will bring you back to the Polpis
Road, alongside which hundreds of thousands of daffodils
bloom in spring. A million Dutch bulbs donated by an island
resident were planted along Nantucket's main roads in 1974,
and more have been planted every year since. A bike path is
forever being planned for the Polpis Road.

Turning right onto Polpis, you'll pass **Sesachacha Pond** (pronounced "Seh-SAH-kah-cha" or, more often here, where long
words seem to be too much trouble, just "SAH-kah-cha"). At
the intersection of Quidnet Road, take either a right (which will
bring you to an **Audubon wildlife area** a mile down the road [go
right at the stop sign], with a walking path around the pond
and a good view of Sankaty Light high above) or a left, remaining on Polpis Road. The entrance to the 205-acre **Windswept
Cranberry Bog** (part working bog, part conservation land),
with a parking area, is a bit farther on Polpis on the left. A map
of the bog, as well as the 30-page *Handbook for Visitors to the
Windswept Cranberry Bog,* is available for $4 ($5 by mail) from
the NCF (*see above*).

Continuing on Polpis, a right onto Wauwinet Road leads (after about 2 miles) to the gateway of **Coatue–Coskata–Great Point,** an unpopulated spit of sand comprising three cooperatively managed wildlife refuges. The area may be entered only on foot or by four-wheel-drive vehicle, for which a permit ($55 for a year; $10 a day for a rental vehicle; tel. 508/228–2884 for information) is required. Issued only for a vehicle that is properly registered and equipped—confirm this with the rental agent if you plan to enter the area—the permits are available at the gatehouse at Wauwinet (tel. 508/228–0006) June–September or, in the off-season, from a ranger patrolling the property. If you enter on foot, be aware that Great Point is a 5-mile walk from the entrance on soft, deep sand; Jeepless people often hitchhike here. Another alternative is a Jeep tour (*see* Guided Tours, *above*).

Coatue is open for many kinds of recreation—shellfishing for bay scallops, softshell clams, quahogs, and mussels (license required); surf casting for bluefish and striped bass (spring through fall); picnicking; or just enjoying the crowdless expanse. Its beaches, dunes, salt marshes, and stands of oak and cedar attract marsh hawks, oystercatchers, terns, herring gulls, and many other bird species.

Because of frequent dangerous currents and riptides and the lack of lifeguards, swimming is strongly discouraged, especially within 200 yards of the 70-foot stone tower that is the **Great Point Light.** A 1986 re-creation of one destroyed by a storm in 1984, the new light was built to withstand 20-foot waves and winds of up to 240 miles an hour.

Continue on Polpis for 1.7 miles, past large areas of open moorland technically called lowland heath, which is very rare in the United States. On the left, an unmarked dirt track leads to **Altar Rock,** a high spot in the midst of moor and bog land from which the view is spectacular. The entire area, of which the Milestone Bog is a part, is laced with trails leading in many directions, so if you want to find your way back to Polpis Road, watch how you come.

Half a mile farther along Polpis, on the right, is the **Nantucket Life Saving Museum,** housed in a re-creation of an 1874 Life Saving Service station. Exhibits include original rescue equipment and boats, as well as photos and accounts of daring rescues. *Polpis Rd., tel. 508/228–1885. Admission: $1. Open mid-June–mid-Oct., Tues.–Sun. 10–5. Closed Mon. and mid-Oct.–mid-June.*

After 2 more miles, Polpis meets the Milestone Road just before the rotary, where Orange Street leads back into town.

What to See and Do with Children

There are playgrounds at **Jetties and Children's beaches** (*see* Beaches, *below*), and the **Nantucket Community Pool** (*see* Sports and the Outdoors, *below*) has kids' swim time.

Actors Theatre of Nantucket (*see* The Arts and Nightlife, *below*) offers post-beach matinees for children in July and August.

The Atheneum (Lower India St., tel. 508/228–1110) has a morning story hour in its children's wing year-round, and a Saturday-morning children's film in the off-season.

J. J. Clammp's is an 18-hole minigolf course set in gardens, reached by a path connecting with the 'Sconset bike path. Other amusements include remote-control boats on two ponds and a splash-gun game with castle-and-dragon target shooting. There's also a restaurant and a free shuttle from downtown. *Nobadeer Farm and Sun Island Rds., off Milestone Rd., tel. 508/228–8977. Admission: $6 adults, $5 children. Open July–Aug., daily 10 AM–midnight; June and Sept., daily (hours vary widely). Closed Oct.–May.*

Maria Mitchell Aquarium displays local marine life in salt- and freshwater tanks. Family shell- and plant-collecting trips are given weekly in season. *28 Washington St., near Commercial Wharf, tel. 508/228–5387. Admission: $1. Open mid-June–Aug., Tues.–Sat. 10–4. Closed Sept.–mid-June.*

Maria Mitchell Association (tel. 508/228–9198), in July and August, offers nature classes and astronomy lectures for children, and separate astronomy lectures for adults.

Murray Camp of Nantucket (Box 3437, Nantucket 02584, tel. and fax 508/325–4600) offers four- or eight-week summer day camps for children 5–14. Activities include French instruction, water and other sports, arts and crafts, drama and music, and environmental-awareness classes.

Nantucket Babysitters' Service (tel. 508/228–4970) is offered by the South Suburban Nurses Registry.

Nantucket Island School of Design and the Arts (*see* The Arts and Nightlife, *below*) offers a year-round program of multicultural, environmental, nature, and arts and crafts classes, lectures, and slide shows for children.

Off the Beaten Track

At **Bartlett's Ocean View Farm & Greenhouses** (Bartlett Farm Rd., off Hummock Pond Rd., tel. 508/228–9403), a 100-acre farm run by eighth-generation Bartletts, a farm stand is open in season. In June you can pick your own strawberries.

Miacomet Pond. A right turn off Surfside Road onto Miacomet Road (which begins paved but turns to dirt) leads to a freshwater pond surrounded by grass and heath and separated from the ocean by a narrow strip of sandy Land Bank beach. The pond—in whose reedy fringes swans and snapping turtles are sometimes seen, along with the resident ducks—is a peaceful setting for a picnic or quiet time.

Nantucket Vineyard. Five varieties of vinifera grapes grow at this vineyard and winery 2½ miles south of town. Tastings of red, white, and rosé wines are available year-round, as are bottles for purchase. *3 Bartlett Farm Rd., tel. 508/228–9235. Admission free. Open Mon.–Sat. 10–6 (call first in winter).*

Shopping

The island specialty is Nantucket lightship baskets, woven of oak or cane, with woven covers adorned with scrimshaw or rosewood. First made in the 19th century by crew members passing time between chores on a lightship that stood off Sankaty Head, the baskets are now used as chic purses by those who can afford them (prices from $400 to well over $1,000).

Miniature versions of the baskets are made by plaiting fine threads of gold or silver wire. Some have working hinges and latches; some are decorated with plain or painted scrimshaw or small gems. Prices start at around $300 for gold versions.

Another signature island product is a pair of all-cotton pants called Nantucket Reds, which fade to pink with washing; they're sold only at Murray's Toggery Shop (*see* Clothing, *below*).

The majority of Nantucket's shops are seasonal, opening sometime after April and closing between Labor Day and November, though an active core stays open longer.

Shopping Districts Nantucket Town's commercial district—bounded approximately by the waterfront and Main, Broad, and Centre streets and continuing along South Beach Street—contains virtually all the island's shops.

Old South Wharf, built in 1770, hosts crafts, clothing, and antiques stores; a ship's chandlery; and art galleries in small, connected "shanties." Phones are at the end of the wharf.

Straight Wharf, where the Hy-Line ferry docks, is lined with T-shirt and other tourist-oriented shops, a gallery, a museum, and restaurants. Phones and rest rooms are at the end of the wharf; boats for sails and charters line up alongside.

Food Market Monday through Saturday in season, colorful farm stands are set up on Main Street to sell local produce and flowers.

Auctions Auctions of fine antiques are held by **Rafael Osona** (tel. 508/228–3942) from Memorial Day to early December in the American Legion Hall at 21 Washington Street. Items range from the 18th to the 20th century and include everything from furniture and art to Nantucket baskets and memorabilia. For a schedule, write to Box 2607, Nantucket 02584.

Specialty Stores The *Nantucket Guide to Antique Shops* is available at many of
Antiques the following shops. (*See also* Art *and* Crafts, *below.*)

Forager House Collection (20 Centre St., tel. 508/228–5977) specializes in folk art and Americana, including whirligigs, wood engravings, vintage postcards, Nantucket lightship baskets, and antique maps, charts, and prints.

Nina Hellman Antiques (48 Centre St., tel. 508/228–4677) carries scrimshaw, ship models, nautical instruments, and other marine antiques, plus folk art and Nantucket memorabilia.

19 Petticoat Row (19 Centre St., tel. 508/228–5900) carries French and English country china, needlework, lace, linens, pottery, and furniture.

Tonkin of Nantucket (33 Main St., tel. 508/228–9697) has two floors of fine English antiques, including furniture, china, art, silver, marine and scientific instruments, and Staffordshire miniatures; plus new sailors' valentines and lightship baskets.

Art **Janis Aldridge** (50 Main St., tel. 508/228–6673), in a new location, has beautifully framed antique engravings, including architectural and botanical prints, plus home furnishings.

Paul La Paglia (38 Centre St., tel. 508/228–8760) has moderately priced antique prints, including Nantucket and whaling scenes, botanicals, and game fish.

Robert Wilson Galleries (34 Main St., tel. 508/228–6246 or 508/228–2096) carries outstanding contemporary American marine, impressionist, and other art.

Sailor's Valentine Gallery (40 Centre St., tel. 508/228–2011) has contemporary fine and folk art (including international "outsider art") and exquisite sailor's valentines.

William Welch Gallery (14 Easy St., tel. 508/228–0687) exhibits Welch's signature watercolors, pastels, and oils of Nantucket scenes, as well as the Nantucket oil paintings of Jack Brown.

Books **Mitchell's Book Corner** (54 Main St., tel. 508/228–1080) has a room full of books on Nantucket and whaling, many ocean-related children's books, plus the usual bookstore fare.

Nantucket Bookworks (25 Broad St., tel. 508/228–4000) carries hardcover and paperback books, with an emphasis on literary works, plus a children's-book room and unusual gift and stationery items.

Clothing **Cordillera Imports** (18 Broad St., tel. 508/228–6140) sells exotic, affordable clothing, jewelry, and crafts from Latin America, Asia, and elsewhere.

Michelle's Romantic Clothing (7 Centre St., tel. 508/228–4409), new in 1993, offers lacy vintage dresses and lingerie, flower-bedecked hats, and more.

Murray's Toggery Shop (62 Main St., tel. 508/228–0437) is a provider of traditional clothing (much of it designer-label) and footwear for men, women, and children. An outlet store at 7 New Street (tel. 508/228–3584) offers discounts of up to 50%.

The Peanut Gallery (60 Main St., tel. 508/228–2010) has a discriminating collection of children's clothing, including Cary, Cottontail Originals, and island-made items.

Vis-a-Vis (34 Main St., tel. 508/228–5527) has unique funky and classic women's and children's clothing, accessories, and decorative objects, including hooked rugs, quilts, and collectibles.

Zero Main (0 Main St., tel. 508/228–4401) has stylishly classic women's clothing, shoes, and accessories.

Crafts **Artisans' Store at Nantucket** (18 Broad St., tel. 508/228–4631) sells fine American arts and crafts, featuring hand-stitched quilts, jewelry, and wall art.

Claire Murray (11 S. Water St., tel. 508/228–1913 or 800/252–4733) features the designer's Nantucket-theme and other hand-hooked rugs and kits, quilts, and knitting and needlework supplies.

Erica Wilson Needle Works (25 Main St., tel. 508/228–9881) sells the famed designer's kits, plus home decorative items.

Four Winds Craft Guild (6 Straight Wharf, tel. 508/228–9623) carries a large selection of antique and new scrimshaw and lightship baskets, as well as ship models, duck decoys, and a kit for making your own lightship basket.

Rosa Rugosa (18 Federal St., tel. 508/228–5597) has home decorative items, including furniture painted with roses.

Scrimshander Gallery (19 Old South Wharf, tel. 508/228–1004) deals in new and antique scrimshaw.

The Spectrum (26 Main St., tel. 508/228–4606) sells distinctive art glass, wood boxes, jewelry, kaleidoscopes, and more.

Nantucket lightship basket makers include **Michael Kane** (18½ Sparks Ave., tel. 508/228–1598) and **Bill and July Sayle** (112 Washington St., tel. 508/228–9876).

Food **Chanticleer to Go** (15 S. Beach St., tel. 508/325–5625) offers prepared gourmet foods from the 'Sconset French restaurant (*see* Dining, *below*), with instructions for home use, as well as pastries, salads, sandwiches, imported cheeses and pâtés, wine, and espresso and cappuccino.

Gifts **Museum Shop** (Broad St., next to the Whaling Museum, tel. 508/228–5785) has island-related books, antique whaling tools, spermaceti candles, reproduction furniture, and toys (including reproduction 18th- and 19th-century whirligigs).

Seven Seas Gifts (46 Centre St., tel. 508/228–0958) stocks all kinds of inexpensive gift and souvenir items, including shells, baskets, toys, and Nantucket jigsaw puzzles.

Jewelry **The Golden Basket** (44 Main St., tel. 508/228–4344) and its affiliated shop, **Golden Nugget** (Straight Wharf, tel. 508/228–1019), sell miniature gold and silver lightship baskets, pieces with starfish and shell motifs, and other fine jewelry.

Sports and the Outdoors

Bicycling The **Madaket Bike Path,** reached via Cliff Road, is a hilly but beautiful 6-mile route to the western tip of the island. There are picnic tables by Long Pond along the way. The 6-mile **'Sconset Bike Path** starts at the rotary east of town and parallels Milestone Road, ending at 'Sconset. It is mostly level, with some gentle hills (*see* Tour 2 in Exploring Nantucket, *above*). The easy 3-mile **Surfside Bike Path,** which begins on the Surfside Road (from Main Street take Pleasant Street, then turn right onto Atlantic Avenue), leads to the island's premier ocean beach. Benches and drinking fountains are placed at strategic locations along the paths.

Nantucket Cycling Club (tel. 508/228–1164) holds open races in summer.

Fishing Bluefish and bass are the main island catches (bluefishing is best at Great Point). **Barry Thurston's Fishing Tackle** (Harbor Sq., tel. 508/228–9595) and **Bill Fisher Tackle** (14 New La., tel. 508/228–2261) rent equipment and can point you in the direction of the best fishing spots. For guided surf-casting by four-wheel-drive, including gear rental, contact **Whitney Mitchell** (tel. 508/228–2331) or **Beach Excursions Ltd.** (tel. 508/228–5800). **Nantucket Boat Rentals** (Slip 1, Boat Basin, tel. 508/325–1001) rents powerboats. **Nantucket Harbor Sail** (Swain's Wharf, tel. 508/228–0424) rents sailboats and outboards.

Charters Leaving out of Straight Wharf in season are several fishing-charter boats, including the **_Herbert T_** (Slip 14, tel. 508/228–6655).

Golf   **Miacomet Golf Club** (off Somerset Rd., tel. 508/228–8987), a public course owned by the Land Bank and abutting Miacomet Pond and coastal heathland, has nine holes (expansion to 18 is in the works) on very flat terrain.

Sankaty Head Golf Club (Sankaty Rd., 'Sconset, tel. 508/257–6655), a private 18-hole course, is open to the public from late September to mid-June. This challenging Scottish-style links course cuts through the moors and offers spectacular views of the lighthouse and ocean from practically every hole.

Siasconset Golf Club (Milestone Rd., tel. 508/257–6596), begun in 1894, is an easy-walking nine-hole public course surrounded by conservation land.

Health and   **Club N.E.W.** (10 Young's Way, tel. 508/228–4750) offers Stair-
Fitness Club   Masters, Lifecycles, treadmills, rowers, Airdyne bikes, New Generation Nautilus, and free weights; aerobics, dance, and yoga classes; plus a nutritionist, personal trainers, and baby-sitting.

Rollerblading   **Nantucket Sports Locker** (14 Cambridge St., tel. 508/228–6610) offers rentals.

Sailing and   **Force 5 Watersports** (Jetties Beach, tel. 508/228–5358; 37 Main
Water Sports   St., tel. 508/228–0700) rents day sailers, Sunfish, Windsurfers, kayaks, surfboards, boogie boards, and other water gear; Sunfish and Windsurfer lessons are also available. **Nantucket Harbor Sail** (*see* Fishing, *above*) rents sailboats.

The Sunken Ship (Broad and S. Water Sts., tel. 508/228–9226) offers complete dive-shop services, including lessons, equipment rentals, and charters; it also rents water skis, tennis racquets, and fishing poles.

Shellfishing   The **shellfish warden** (38 Washington St., tel. 508/228–7260) issues digging permits for littleneck and cherrystone clams, quahogs, and mussels.

Swimming   Besides the island's many ponds and beaches (*see* Beaches, *below*), the **Summer House** in 'Sconset (*see* Dining, *below*) offers its pool, on the bluff above the ocean beach, to diners at its poolside café in season. Year-round, the Olympic-size, indoor **Nantucket Community Pool** (Nantucket High School, Atlantic Ave., tel. 508/228–7262) is open daily for lap swimming and lessons.

Tennis   There are six asphalt **town courts** (tel. 508/325–5334) at Jetties Beach; sign up at the Park and Recreation Commission building for one hour of court time (usually the limit), or for lessons or tennis clinics. **Brant Point Racquet Club** (N. Beach St., tel. 508/228–3700), a short walk from town, has nine fast-dry clay courts and a pro shop and offers lessons, rentals, playing programs, and round robins.

Siasconset Casino (New St., tel. 508/257–6661) is a private club with seven clay courts and one poor hard court. Infrequently the club has openings at 1 or 2 PM; call ahead to check.

Beaches

The water around Nantucket is warm from mid-June sometimes into October. The south and east shores have strong surf and undertow; those on the north and west side are calmer and warmer. Some beaches are accessible by bike path (*see* Bicycling, *above*), others by shuttle bus (*see* Getting Around in Essential Information, *above*), and others by foot or four-wheel-drive. A mobile food truck serves the Cisco, Dionis, and Madaket beaches.

Children's A calm area by the harbor, Children's Beach is an easy walk from town (along South Beach Street from Steamboat Wharf) and is good for small children. It offers a grassy park with benches, a playground, lifeguards, food service, picnic tables, showers, and rest rooms.

Cisco From the top of Main Street turn onto Milk Street, which turns into Hummock Pond Road; 4 miles beyond there's a long, sandy south-shore beach (popular with body and board surfers) with lifeguards and rest rooms.

Dionis To get to this north-shore beach, take the Madaket bike path to Eel Point Road and look for the white rock pointing to Dionis Beach—about 3 miles west of town. The narrow strip of beach at the entrance turns into a wider, more private strand with high dunes and fewer children. The beach has a rocky bottom and calm, rolling waters, lifeguards, and rest rooms.

Eel Point Six miles from town and accessible only by foot, Eel Point (*see* Nature Areas, *below*) boasts the island's most beautiful and interesting beaches for those who don't necessarily need to swim—a sandbar extends out 100 yards, keeping the water shallow, clear, and calm. There are no services, just lots of birds, wild berries and bushes, and solitude.

Jetties Jetties, a short bike or shuttle-bus ride from town, is the most popular beach for families because of its calm surf, lifeguards, bathhouse, rest rooms, and snack bar. It's a lively scene, especially with ferries passing, water-sports rentals (Windsurfer, sailboat, kayak) and a playground and volleyball nets on the beach, and tennis courts adjacent.

Madaket Known for great sunsets, this west-end surf beach is reached by shuttle bus or the Madaket bike path (6 miles) and offers lifeguards and rest rooms. The Westender restaurant (*see* Dining, *below*), a short walk away, has a takeout window, a bar, and a deck for drinks.

'Sconset Follow the 'Sconset bike path (or take the shuttle) 7 miles to
(Codfish Park) the village, then take your first right to this golden-sand beach with moderate to heavy surf, a lifeguard, showers, rest rooms, and a playground. Restaurants are a short walk away.

Surfside Three miles from town by the Surfside bike path or by shuttle bus, this is the premier surf beach, with lifeguards, rest rooms, a snack bar, and a wide strand of sand. It attracts college students as well as families.

Nature Areas

In addition to **Milestone Bog, Windswept Cranberry Bog,** and **Coatue–Coskata–Great Point** (*see* Tour 2: Town–'Sconset–Polpis Loop, *above*), the following nature areas are great to explore.

Eel Point Eel Point is an unspoiled conservation area covered in places with goldenrod, wild grapes, roses, bayberries, and other coastal plants. A spit of sand with harbor on one side and shoal-protected ocean on the other, the area is a nesting place for gulls and also attracts great numbers of other birds, which perch on small islands formed by a sandbar that extends out 100 yards or more. The water is shallow (*see* Beaches, *above*), and the surf fishing is good.

Take a right off the Madaket bike path onto Eel Point Road; cars will have to be left along the dirt road about a half-mile before the beach, 6 miles from town. (About 2 miles in on Eel Point Road, watch for a Land Bank marker for **40th Pole Beach,** accessed via sand roads across dunes sprinkled with roses, grasses, and heather.) Nature guides on Eel Point are available from the **Maria Mitchell Association** (2 Vestal St., Nantucket 02554, tel. 508/228–9198; $4.50) or the **Nantucket Conservation Foundation** (118 Cliff Rd., Box 13, Nantucket 02554, tel. 508/228–2884; $3, or $4 by mail).

Long Pond Long Pond is a 64-acre Land Bank property with a diversity of habitats and terrain that makes birding especially good. To reach a 1-mile walking path along the pond, past meadows and a natural cranberry bog, take a left off Madaket Road onto the dirt road across from the sign to Hither Creek (near Madaket); across the bridge is a parking area and the entrance to the trail.

Sanford Farm Sanford Farm, Ram Pasture, and The Woods comprise more
and Ram Pasture than 900 contiguous acres of wetlands, grasslands, forest, and former farmland off Madaket Road. Maps are available through the NCF (*see* Eel Point, *above*), which owns 767 acres, or the Land Bank (22 Broad St., Nantucket 02554, tel. 508/228–7240), which owns 165. Interpretive markers border the 6½-mile (round-trip) walking trail that leads to the shore via Hummock Pond and offers great ocean and heath views. It begins off the Madaket Road parking area near the intersection of Cliff Road, as do a 1.7-mile loop and a 3.1-mile round-trip to a barn on high ground with views of the south shore. In addition to these NCF trails, a ¾-mile Land Bank walking trail begins at the picnic tables on Madaket Road, a half-mile beyond the Eel Point Road intersection heading west. It wanders upland to an overview of a swamp, among a hawthorn grove and blueberry patches, and across meadows.

Dining

Dining in Nantucket's excellent restaurants is one of the island's greatest—and most expensive—pleasures. In the face of complaints about the expense, many establishments now offer lower-priced café menus in addition to their regular menus (the price categories below are based on the latter only). All the eating places are in town or in 'Sconset, except for Madaket's Westender (*see below*). **Nantucket Picnic Basket** (7 N. Beach St., tel. 508/228–5177), **Provisions** (Straight Wharf, tel. 508/228–3258), **Something Natural** (50 Cliff Rd., tel. 508/228–0504), and **Claudette's** ('Sconset center, tel. 508/257–6622) put up box lunches in season.

Category	Cost*
Very Expensive	over $40
Expensive	$30–$40
Moderate	$20–$30
Inexpensive	under $20

per person, excluding drinks, service, and 5% tax

Very Expensive

Based on reviews by Malcolm Wilson

★ **Chanticleer.** Within a rose-covered cottage in 'Sconset is what many consider the island's finest restaurant and what others deem overpriced and overly touted—you decide. For two decades owner-chef Jean-Charles Berruet has created classic French fare using fresh local ingredients and herbs. Characteristic dishes include roast spring lamb with rosemary, grilled sea bass with roasted peppers and aïoli, and lobster-and-truffle soup baked in puff pastry. Desserts may include a puff-pastry apple tart with Calvados custard or a chocolate marquis (fudgy cake) with espresso sauce. A four-course prix-fixe menu ($60) is offered at dinner (à la carte also available). The downstairs dining room is formal, with a low ceiling, pearl-gray and faux-marble walls, flickering candle-bulb sconces, a fireplace, and a view of the gardens through small-pane windows. The upstairs dining room is smaller and more casual, in pale pink. Lunch in the rose garden is the closest thing to heaven. Chanticleer's wine cellar, honored by the *Wine Spectator* with a Grand Award, offers more than 1,000 selections from California and France. *9 New St., Siasconset, tel. 508/257–6231. Reservations strongly advised. Jacket required at dinner. AE, MC, V. Closed Wed. and Columbus Day–Mother's Day.*

Expensive–Very Expensive

★ **Club Car.** The name comes from the railway car—one of those that ran from Steamboat Wharf to 'Sconset years ago—that houses the piano bar and where soup-and-sandwich lunches are served. The dining room, despite being rather noisy, is pleasantly decorated with hanging plants, cane-back chairs, soft lighting, and linen and silver. The Continental dinner menu, which often features seafood, changes with the season and includes game in fall. The signature rack of lamb is spectacular, glazed with honey mustard and herbs and served with a minted Madeira sauce. *1 Main St., tel. 508/228–1101. Reservations advised. Dress: smart casual. AE, D, DC, MC, V. Closed early Dec.–mid-May; mid-May–June and mid-Sept.–early Dec., closed Tues. and Wed.*

★ **Le Languedoc.** Housed in a refurbished building in the historic district, Le Languedoc consists of an upstairs, French country-style dining room, a bistro-style café downstairs, and the garden terrace. Favorites among the innovative menu of American and Continental cuisine are roast rack of lamb with a honey-mustard crust, softshell crabs, seasonal fish, and offal. The café menu (Inexpensive–Moderate) features a daily risotto and simply cooked seafood, as well as some more elaborate dishes. *24 Broad St., tel. 508/228–2552. Reservations and jacket advised* *upstairs. AE, MC, V. No lunch July–Aug. Closed Jan.–mid-Apr.; Sun. in shoulder seasons.*

Summer House. A prime location—in 'Sconset on a bluff overlooking the sea—as well as fine food attract a stylish clientele to this bastion of easygoing classiness. The bar/lounge is an informal area with piano music nightly in season. The dining room carries on the '30s and '40s beach look, with white painted furniture, rose and light-green linens, lots of flowers and hanging plants, and paintings of Nantucket scenes. The menu centers on fresh fish, such as nutmeg-pecan-crusted swordfish on radicchio, endive, and blue cheese salad. The poolside café lunches include grilled fish and Black Angus burgers, sandwiches, salads, and frozen drinks. *Ocean Ave., Siasconset, tel. 508/257–9976. Reservations advised. Dress: casual. AE, MC, V. No lunch in season in dining room. Closed Columbus Day–mid-May; some weekdays in shoulder seasons.*

★ **Topper's.** Far from town at the exclusive Wauwinet resort (complimentary jitney service is provided), Topper's serves new American cuisine based on fresh regional products, including such dishes as sautéed lobster with citrus, wild mushrooms, and roasted peppers in a Chardonnay beurre blanc; and grilled Arctic char with matchstick potatoes and fried capers. The list of mainly California and French wines has received the *Wine Spectator* Award of Excellence. The interior, a sophisticated yet relaxed setting with woodburning fireplace, reflects the quality of workmanship that is apparent throughout the inn: pickled pine floors, fine wood paneling, lovely oil paintings. The outdoor patio overlooking the water is a great place for lunch or drinks, especially at sunset. Also offered are an elegant Sunday brunch ($25) and an inexpensive bar menu featuring light fare. Weekdays, cruise from Straight Wharf for lunch or a shore dinner at Topper's, then jitney back to town. Or round off dinner with a sunset-and-dessert cruise. *Wauwinet Rd., tel. 508/228–8768. Reservations required at dinner; advised at lunch. Jacket advised at dinner. AE, DC, MC, V. Closed Nov.-mid-May.*

Expensive

Company of the Cauldron. The small-pane windows at the entrance of this romantic spot are framed with climbing ivy. Inside, a profusion of flowers and antique decorative items—hanging copper pans, a Colonial chandelier and pie-plate sconces, old rustic beams, and plaster walls—completes the mood. A single three- or four-course prix-fixe menu ($36–$42) is offered at one or two seatings each evening. A sample menu: fusilli with artichokes, pine nuts, smoked chicken, and sun-dried tomatoes; grilled saltimbocca with a sage–white wine sauce, scallion rice, and seared rapini; and crème caramel. Service is unhurried but impeccable; a harpist plays three nights a week. *7 India St., tel. 508/228–4016. Reservations required (sometimes days in advance). Dress: smart casual. MC, V. No smoking. No lunch. Closed Mon. and Columbus Day–Memorial Day.*

Moderate–Expensive

★ **American Seasons.** From a menu broken into regions—New England, Down South, Wild West, and Pacific Coast—come such creative entrées as fried Mississippi catfish with mustard greens, okra, and jalapeno butter, and such appetizers as a pancake of hickory-smoked lobster and wild mushrooms with American golden caviar. Presentations are elaborate and painterly. Folk-art murals and tables handpainted with decorative game boards are part of the relaxed decor. *80 Centre St., tel. 508/228–7111. Reservations strongly advised. Dress: casual. AE, MC, V. No smoking. No lunch. Closed mid-Dec.–early Apr.*

DeMarco. A chic, formal restaurant in a refurbished old home in the historic district, DeMarco serves healthfully lightened northern Italian cuisine, using homemade pastas, breads, and desserts, and local vegetables and seafood. Among the imaginative dishes produced here are poached lobster with a saffron-tomato broth and ragout of leek and Vidalia onion; and linguine with littlenecks, bell and hot peppers, onions, and marinated garlic. The overall look is refined rustic: Downstairs there's dark wood, brick walls, and lacy white curtains, while the upstairs is brighter, with white walls. The wine list is a regular *Wine Spectator* Grand Award winner. *9 India St., tel. 508/228–1836. Reservations advised. Dress: smart casual. AE, D, DC, MC, V. No lunch. Closed Nov.–Apr.*

The Hearth at the Harbor House. On an outdoor patio and in an attractive dining room with parquet floor, oversize steel-and-copper weathervane chandeliers, antique-red walls, and comfortable upholstered chairs, simply prepared New England fare is served. Surf-and-turf combinations (filet mignon, lamb chop, and baked stuffed shrimp, for example) are popular, as is crabmeat-stuffed baked flounder with parsley butter. A lavish Sunday brunch buffet includes a raw bar and a dessert table. The four-course "sunset special" helps beat the high cost of eating—it's served 5–6:30 year-round, and children under 13 dine free with parents. *S. Beach St., tel. 508/228–1500. Reservations advised; required for Sun. brunch. Dress: casual. AE, D, DC, MC, V. No breakfast or lunch in off-season.*

India House. This downtown inn, built as a private home in 1803, has two small dining rooms that reflect their origins, with low beamed ceilings, hardwood floors, and small-pane windows with white café curtains. In the blue room, walls are covered half in wainscoting and half in colonial-print wallpaper, with period paintings and petit-point lacework. The cuisine is nouvelle American. Appetizers like Indonesian pasta, callaloo, or baby-back ribs are all available in dinner portions; entrées are a mix of meats and such seafood dishes as pecan-cashew-glazed swordfish with carmelized Bermuda onions, lime, and thyme beurre blanc. There's also outdoor dining in summer. The popular Sunday brunch includes such temptations as three-berry French toast and poached eggs with smoked salmon and caviar. *37 India St., tel. 508/228–9043. Reservations advised for dinner; no reservations for brunch. Dress: casual. AE, D, MC, V. No lunch. Closed Jan.–Mar.*

Jared's. The formal restaurant of the Jared Coffin House is the island's most elegant dining room, with a high ceiling, salmon-colored walls, pale-green swag drapes, and Federal-period antique furnishings. The fare is equally elegant, typified by such dishes as herb-crusted tenderloin of beef with chianti glaze, or grilled swordfish on a bed of Greek salad with feta. Service is impressive and pleasant, and the wine list is large. *29 Broad St., tel. 508/228–2400. Reservations advised. Jacket advised. AE, D, DC, MC, V. No lunch; no dinner Jan.–Apr. (breakfast year-round).*

★ **Sconset Cafe.** In 'Sconset center one of the finest cooks on the island serves an imaginative American cuisine in a beach-café setting. Inexpensive lunch offerings include sandwiches and salads, such as the Café chicken salad: a grilled, marinated breast on spinach with toasted walnuts, Stilton cheese, and a cranberry vinaigrette. Save room for the homemade desserts. The evening menu, which changes daily, features fish and more elaborate dinners, such as confit of duck with lemon-caramel sauce. *Post Office Sq., Siasconset, tel. 508/257–4008. Reservations accepted for 6 PM seating. Dress: casual. No credit cards. BYOB (liquor store next door). Closed mid-Sept.–mid-May.*

21 Federal Street. The epitome of sophisticated island dining, this is a place to be seen, as well as to enjoy some of the best new and traditional American cuisine served north of Manhattan. An informal dining room extends into the dark-paneled bar. Beyond are two other dining rooms, with gray wainscoting, black-suede banquettes, and damask-covered tables; a curving staircase leads to a similar second floor. Lunch is served in the courtyard. Entrées include grilled halibut with potato cake and shiitake mushrooms, and a country grill sampler (steak, chops, chicken). *21 Federal St., tel. 508/228–2121. Reservations advised. Dress: smart casual. AE, MC, V. Closed Jan.–Mar.; may close Mon. in shoulder seasons.*

Woodbox. The three small dining rooms on the first floor of this inn a few blocks from town reflect their 1709 origins, with seasoned variable-width plank floors, exposed beams, and braided rugs. One room at the back looks like the kitchen it was in the inn's early days, with walls of aged brick and extra-wide "king's boards," antique kitchen implements, and Colonial-style furniture. Contemporary American and Continental dishes—crispy duck with three-berry cassis sauce, herb-crusted rack of lamb with cabernet sauce—and wonderful popovers are served by candlelight on English china and silverplate. *29 Fair St., tel. 508/228–0587. Reservations advised. Jacket requested. No credit cards. Breakfast and dinner only. Closed Mon. and Jan.–May.*

Moderate

★ **Beach Plum Cafe and Bakery.** Well outside town, with polished-wood floors and softly hued local artworks on white walls, this casual restaurant serves three delicious meals a day year-round. Lunches feature pastas, soups, and sandwiches like roast beef and Boursin on a choice of baguette, Portuguese sweet roll, or herbed whole-grain bread from the bakery (which moved next door in 1993). At dinner, there's a nightly ravioli special (like smoked salmon mousse) and entrées ranging from grilled duck breast with sun-dried cherry sauce to jerk-spiced pork tenderloin with orange-mango chutney sauce. *11 West Creek Rd., tel. 508/228–8893. No reservations. Dress: casual. AE, MC, V.*

The Tap Room. The downstairs tavern restaurant of the Jared Coffin House is a dark, woody, cozy room decorated with ship prints and whale models. The dinner menu features hearty meat and fish dishes, such as prime rib, fried clams, and baked stuffed shrimp; at lunch choose from a light menu, including several fish dishes, eaten on the outdoor patio, weather permitting. *29 Broad St., tel. 508/228–2400. No reservations. Dress: casual. AE, D, DC, MC, V.*

Westender. This spot 100 yards from Madaket Beach offers take-out burgers, salads, sandwiches, and fried fish; a bar with fireplace and old fishing photos; an outdoor cocktail terrace; the main dining room, with natural wood wainscoting and local art on white walls; and a second floor with views of the water and great sunsets. The menu features American grilled seafood, with nightly specials based on the day's catch, and always a lobster plate. A light menu includes nachos, quesadillas, popcorn shrimp, steamers, and a raw bar. *Madaket Rd., tel. 508/228–5197. No reservations. Dress: casual. MC, V. Closed Columbus Day–Memorial Day.*

Inexpensive–Moderate

Atlantic Cafe. This casual, sometimes noisy year-round place at the center of town offers an active bar, taped popular music, and a fun menu, with large portions at a good price. Finger foods include crisp, delicious zucchini sticks and crabmeat wontons. Entrées are a mix of simply prepared fish, steaks, chicken, burgers, Mexican items, salads and sandwiches, and more. There's a $2.95 kids' menu. *15 S. Water St., tel. 508/228–0570. No reservations. Dress: casual. AE, D, DC, MC, V.*

★ **The Brotherhood of Thieves.** Long lines are a fixture outside this English-style pub restaurant. Inside, lit by flickering candles, is a dark room with low ceilings, exposed brick and beams, and a fireplace that is especially welcoming on cold or rainy evenings. When the place gets busy, strangers are seated together at long tables; a section at the back has more intimate seating. A convivial atmosphere prevails—thanks partly to the live folk music at night and to the hundreds of coffee drinks and other alcoholic beverages on the menu. Dine happily on good chowder and soups, fried fish and seafood, burgers, jumbo sandwiches, and shoestring fries (long curls with the skins on). *23 Broad St., no phone. No reservations. Dress: casual. No credit cards.*

★ **Quaker House.** This storefront restaurant—two small, prettily decorated rooms whose small-pane windows framed in lace look out onto Centre Street—is the best bargain on the island. Prix-fixe four-course dinners ($16–$25; 20% off before 6:30) feature such entrées as Bombay chicken (a curry with apple, raisins, and coconut) and bay scallops with red-pepper puree over angelhair pasta. The owners take pride in the quality of their ingredients, which include meats and poultry raised humanely and free of chemicals, hormones, or additives. At breakfast try the baked-apple pancake, huge and sweet, with cinnamony apples and powdered sugar. *5 Chestnut St., tel. 508/228–9156. Reservations advised for parties of 5 or more. Dress: casual. AE, MC, V. No lunch. Closed Columbus Day–Memorial Day.*

Rose & Crown. A fun, lively place, the Rose & Crown is a barn-like room with beam ceiling, walls hung with old signs and musical instruments, a big bar, and a dance floor (*see* Nightlife, *below*). Choose from such appetizers as a zesty chowder, Buffalo chicken wings, and popcorn shrimp; for main courses, there are grilled pizzas, burgers, fried clams, fajitas, and such exotic choices as black bean beer chili or penne with sun-dried tomatoes and goat cheese in cream sauce. *23 S. Water St., tel. 508/228–2595. Reservations advised for parties of 6 or more.*

Dress: casual. AE, MC, V. Closed early Dec.–mid-Apr.; Tues. in shoulder seasons.

Lodging

Other than cottages (which are scattered throughout the island) and a few inns and hotels, all of Nantucket's lodging places are in town. Those in the center are convenient, but houses are close together and right on the street; in season there may be street noise until midnight. Inns a five- or 10-minute walk from the center, as on Cliff Road or Fair Street, are quieter. 'Sconset is quieter still and has the rose-covered cottages and less crowded beach, but those looking for action may be frustrated by the 7-mile commute to town.

Nantucket Accommodations (Box 217, Nantucket 02554, tel. 508/228–9559) and **Martha's Vineyard and Nantucket Reservations** (Box 1322, Lagoon Pond Rd., Vineyard Haven 02568, tel. 508/693–7200 or 800/649–5671 in MA) book inns, hotels, bed-and-breakfasts, and cottages. **House Guests Cape Cod and the Islands** (Box 1881, Orleans 02653, tel. 508/896–7053 or 800/666–4678, fax 508/896–7054) books B&Bs, cottages, and efficiencies. **Heaven Can Wait—Accommodations** (Box 622, Siasconset 02564, tel. 508/257–4000) also plans island honeymoons. **Dest-INNations** (tel. 800/333–4667) handles a limited number of Nantucket hotels and B&Bs but will arrange any and all details of a visit.

A number of realtors (complete lists are provided by the chamber and the Information Bureau) offer rentals ranging from in-town apartments in antique houses to new waterfront houses. **Congdon & Coleman** (57 Main St., Nantucket 02554, tel. 508/325–5000, fax 508/325–5025) has properties islandwide; **'Sconset Real Estate** (Box 122, Siasconset 02564, tel. 508/257–6335 summer, 508/228–1815 winter), in the 'Sconset and Tom Nevers areas.

The **Nantucket Information Bureau** (*see* Important Addresses and Numbers in Essential Information, *above*) maintains a list of room availability in season and at holidays for last-minute bookings; at night, check the lighted board outside for available rooms. In the off-season, places that remain open drop their prices dramatically, by as much as 50%. No camping is allowed on the island.

The **Star of the Sea AYH-Hostel,** a 49-bed facility in a former lifesaving station, is a 3-mile ride on a bike path from town, at Surfside Beach. Planned for 1994 are four "family rooms" sleeping four. Reservations are essential in July and August, recommended always. *31 Western Ave., Nantucket 02554 (in off-season, 465 Falmouth Rd., Hyannis 02601), tel. 508/228–0433. Facilities: kitchen, common room, piano, volleyball court, picnic tables, grill. Closed Columbus Day–Apr.*

Category	Cost*
Very Expensive	over $200
Expensive	$150–$200
Moderate	$110–$150
Inexpensive	under $110

all prices are for a standard double room in high season, excluding 5.7% state tax and 4% local tax

Very Expensive

★ **Cliffside Beach Club.** Although the cedar-shingle exterior, landscaped with climbing roses and hydrangeas, and the pavilion on the private sandy beach a mile from town reflect the club's 1920s origins, the interiors are done in summery contemporary style, with white walls, fine woodwork, white or natural wood furniture, cathedral ceilings, and local art. All rooms have minifridges, cable TV/HBO, phones, and air-conditioning. Some have kitchenettes, fireplaces, wet bars, or private decks. Two big "town-house suites" have full kitchens and decks overlooking dunes, moors, and Nantucket Sound. *Jefferson Ave., Box 449, Nantucket 02554, tel. 508/228–0618, fax 508/325–4735. 19 rooms, 8 apartments, 1 cottage. Facilities: Continental breakfast, restaurant, piano bar, beach, playground, exercise room, day sails (fee). AE. Closed mid-Oct.–late May.*

Summer House. Here, across from 'Sconset Beach and clustered around a flower-filled lawn, are the rose-covered cottages we associate with Nantucket summers. Each one- or two-bedroom cottage is furnished in a blend of unfussy, breezy beach style and romantic English country—trompe-l'oeil-bordered white walls, white lace and eyelet curtains and spreads, Laura Ashley floral accents, and stripped English-pine antique furnishings. Some cottages have fireplaces or kitchens; most have marble baths with whirlpools. *Ocean Ave., Box 313, Siasconset 02564, tel. 508/257–4577, fax 508/257–4590. 8 cottages. Facilities: large Continental breakfast, 2 restaurants, piano bar, oceanfront outdoor pool, water aerobics, poolside bar, private beach, concierge; golf and tennis arranged at private clubs. AE, MC, V. Closed Nov.–late Apr.*

★ **Wauwinet.** An exquisite location, impeccable furnishings, a first-rate restaurant, and extensive services and amenities make this historic inn, which was completely renovated in 1988, a most luxurious perch. A sweeping lawn with white chaise longues leads to a pebbly private harbor beach (where you can play with a life-size wooden chess set). A minute's walk through dunes brings you to sandy Atlantic Ocean beach stretching for miles in relative isolation—there is little else here, at the gateway to Coatue. Jitney service to and from town 8 miles away, plus Steamship pickup, make the location convenient for those without cars. Each guest room—individually decorated in country/beach style, with pine antiques—has a phone, air-conditioning, and cable TV with VCR; the most expensive have spectacular views of the sunset over the water. *Wauwinet Rd., Box 2580, Nantucket 02584, tel. 508/228–0145 or 800/426–8718, fax 508/228–6712. 25 rooms, 5 cottages. Facilities: full breakfast, afternoon port or sherry and cheese, restaurant, bar, room service, 2 Har-Tru tennis courts, Sunfish and lessons, Great Point*

Jeep tours, island tours, boat shuttle to beach, mountain bikes, croquet, concierge, videocassette library, business services. AE, DC, MC, V. Closed Dec.–May.

Wharf Cottages. These weathered-shingle cottages sit on a wharf in Nantucket harbor, with yachts tied up just steps away. Each unit is pretty snug but well fitted out, with a little garden and sitting area, a telephone, cable TV with VCR, a fully equipped kitchen, and attractive modern decor with a nautical flavor: white walls, navy-blue rugs, light-wood floors and furniture. Studios have a sofa bed for sleeping; other cottages have one to three bedrooms. Some have large water-view windows; all have water views. There's a three-night minimum in high season; monthly and seasonal rates are available. *New Whale St., Box 359, Nantucket 02554, tel. 508/228–4620; for reservations, 800/475–2637, fax 508/228–7197. 27 cottages. Facilities: daily maid service, docking facilities. AE, D, DC, MC, V. Closed mid-Oct.–Memorial Day.*

★ **White Elephant.** Long a hallmark of service and style on the island, the White Elephant offers above all a choice location—right on Nantucket harbor, separated only by a wide lawn. The main hotel, wrapped by a deck with a fine view of the bobbing boats, has a formal restaurant with waterside outdoor café, a lounge with entertainment, and a large new harborfront pool and Jacuzzi, beautifully landscaped with pink roses. Rooms have an English country look, with stenciled pine armoires, sponge-painted walls, and floral fabrics. A similar decor characterizes the one- to three-bedroom cottages (some with full kitchens); the waterfront cottages are especially handsome, rimmed in roses. The Breakers, a separate unit, offers more luxurious accommodations that include minibars and minifridges. The entire property has been renovated since 1989, and everything is fresh and new. All rooms have phones and cable TV; some have VCRs and air-conditioning. *Easton St., Box 359, Nantucket 02554, tel. 508/228–2500; for reservations, tel. 800/475–2637, fax 508/228–7197. 48 rooms, 32 cottages. Facilities: restaurant, lounge with entertainment, room service, poolside food and bar service, concierge, heated outdoor pool (with lift for disabled), croquet court, putting green, reduced rate at local health and tennis clubs, fully disabled-accessible rooms, meeting rooms, audiovisual equipment, fax, boat slips. AE, D, DC, MC, V. Closed mid-Sept.–Memorial Day.*

Expensive–Very Expensive

★ **Harbor House.** This family-oriented complex, like its more up-scale sibling, the White Elephant, has been extensively renovated and prides itself on service. The 1886 main inn and several "town houses" are set on a flower-filled quadrangle steps from the town center. Standard rooms are done in English-country style, with bright floral fabrics and queen-size canopy beds; some have French doors that open onto decks. The generally larger town house rooms, in buildings grouped around the pool, have a more traditional look, with upscale pine and pastels; some have whirlpools, cathedral ceilings, sofa beds, and decks. All rooms have phones and TVs with VCR. The Garden Cottage has its own garden and a private-house feel, but its rooms (some with pressed-tin ceilings) are smaller. *S. Beach St., Box 359, Nantucket 02554, tel. 508/228–1500; for reservations, tel. 800/475–2637, fax 508/228–7197. 111 rooms. Fa-*

cilities: restaurant, lounge with entertainment, poolside bar, room service, concierge, heated outdoor pool, putting green, fully disabled-accessible rooms, business services, reduced rate at local health and tennis clubs. AE, D, DC, MC, V.

Wade Cottages. On a bluff overlooking the ocean, this complex of guest rooms, apartments, and cottages in 'Sconset couldn't be better located for beach lovers. The buildings, in the same family since the 1920s, are arranged around a central lawn with a great ocean view; the prize catch is a newer cottage nearer the water. Most inn rooms and cottages have sea views; all have phones. Furnishings are generally in somewhat worn beach style, with some antique pieces. *Shell St., Box 211, Siasconset 02564, tel. 508/257–6308; off-season, 212/989–6423. 8 rooms (3-night min), 3 with private bath; 5 apartments (1-wk min); 3 cottages (2-wk min). Facilities: Continental breakfast (inn rooms only), ping-pong, badminton, swing set, common refrigerator, coin laundry, beach. MC, V. Closed mid-Oct.–late May.*

Expensive

Beachside Resort. Those who prefer rooms-around-a-pool motels with all the creature comforts will find a very nice one here, a bit of a walk from town center. Each unit in the one- and two-story buildings is furnished in white wicker and florals and has a queen-size or two double beds, tiled bath, minifridge, cable TV, phone, and air-conditioning. Some rooms have pool-view decks; some have French doors opening onto them. *N. Beach St., Nantucket 02554, tel. 508/228–2241 or 800/322–4433, fax 508/228–8901. 86 rooms, 3 2-bedroom suites. Facilities: Continental breakfast, heated and disabled-accessible outdoor pool; tennis club adjacent. Children under 16 stay free with parents. AE, D, DC, MC, V. Closed mid-Oct.–mid-Apr.*

Seven Sea Street. This inn on a quiet side street in the center of town was built in 1987 by the owners, also publishers of *Nantucket Journal* magazine. Though the furnishings are in the Colonial style and colors, the place has a somewhat Scandinavian look, with tongue-in-groove light pine and red oak, exposed-beam ceilings, stenciled white walls with pine trim, and highly polished wide-board floors. Each room has a braided rug, a queen-size bed with fishnet canopy and quilt, a rocking chair, a modern bath with large fiberglass stall shower and brass fittings, air-conditioning, a phone, cable TV, minifridge, hairdryer, and desk area. Guests can relax in the garden patio or on the harbor-view widow's walk. *7 Sea St., Nantucket 02554, tel. 508/228–3577. 8 rooms. Facilities: Continental breakfast, (group-size) Jacuzzi room, library of leather-bound classics. No smoking. AE, MC, V.*

Moderate–Expensive

18 Gardner Street. Set in two antique buildings, including the 1835 main house with 9-foot ceilings, this B&B offers good-size rooms—10 with working fireplaces—and a number of thoughtful amenities, like fresh-baked cookies always at the ready. Rooms are done in mauve and pale green, with satin wallcoverings, wide-board floors, mostly queen-size beds (some canopy or four-poster) with eyelet sheets and handmade quilts, some nice antique pieces, and brass lamps. Most have cable TV with remote. One common room has a TV, another a fireplace. Winter and holiday packages are available; summer holiday weekends feature a backyard barbecue. *18 Gardner St., Nantucket 02554, tel. 508/228–1155 or 800/435–1450. 14 rooms (2 share bath), 3 suites. Facilities: full breakfast, guest fridges, beach towels, honor bar for sodas and snacks, 40 bikes, parking; picnic baskets available. No smoking. AE, MC, V.*

Jared Coffin House. This complex of six buildings is a longtime favorite of many visitors to Nantucket for its dependability and class. The main building, a three-story brick mansion built in 1845 by a wealthy shipowner and topped by a cupola, has a historic tone that the others don't. The public and guest rooms are furnished with period antiques (the other buildings, with reproductions), Oriental carpets, and lace curtains. The Harrison Gray House, an 1842 Greek Revival mansion across the street, offers larger guest rooms with large baths and queen-size canopy beds. All rooms have phones and, except in the main house, cable TV; some have minifridges. Small, inexpensive single rooms are available. *29 Broad St., Box 1580, Nantucket 02554, tel. 508/228–2400 or 800/248–2405, fax 508/228–8549. 60 rooms. Facilities: full breakfast, restaurant, tavern, outdoor café, concierge, some accommodation for pets. AE, D, DC, MC, V.*

Manor House. From the screened and open porches or the little front yard, you can watch the town go by at this spot at the dead center of the action. Rooms in this 1846 house are spacious, with reproduction rice-carved beds (king or queen), Waverly or Schumacher wallpapers, coffeemakers, and air conditioning. Seven rooms (a steal in winter, at $75) have king canopy beds, working fireplaces, and minifridges. In winter, a guest room is converted into a common room with fireplace. A small cottage next door, done in wicker and chintz, has two bedrooms, two TVs, a phone, and a kitchen. Rates include a voucher for a muffin and coffee at the café next door. Packages are available. *11 India St., Box 1436, Nantucket 02554–1436, tel. 508/228–9009, 800/992–2899, or 800/673–4559, fax 508/325–4046. 15 rooms. AE, D, MC, V.*

★ **Westmoor Inn.** Built in 1917 as a Vanderbilt summer house, this yellow Federal-style mansion with widow's walk and portico is a short walk to a quiet ocean beach, just off the Madaket bike path, and a mile from town. The many common areas include the wide lawn, set with Adirondack chairs, and the garden patio, secluded behind 11-foot hedges. Beyond the entry hall and grand staircase is a large, gracious living room with piano and game table, where guests meet at an early evening wine and cheese reception; and a wicker-filled sun room with the inn's only TV. A high point of a stay is breakfast in the dining room, with glass walls and ceiling. Guest rooms are bright and white; one first-floor "suite" has a giant bath with extra-large Jacuzzi and French doors opening onto the lawn. Three apartments in a separate building were redone with new kitchens in 1991. *Cliff Rd., Nantucket 02554, tel. 508/228–0877. 14 rooms, 3 apartments. Facilities: Continental breakfast, bicycles, beach towels. AE, MC, V. No smoking. Closed early Dec.–Apr.*

Moderate

Centerboard Guest House. The look of this inn, a few blocks from the center of town, is different from any other. The white walls (some with murals of moors and sky in soft pastels), blond-wood floors, and natural woodwork create a cool, spare, dreamy atmosphere. There is yet more white, in the lacy linens and puffy comforters on the feather beds. Touches of color are added by stained-glass lamps, antique quilts, and fresh flowers. The first-floor suite (right off the entry hall) is a stunner, with 11-foot ceilings, a Victorian living room with fireplace and wet bar, parquet floors, superb furnishings and decor, and a green-marble bath with Jacuzzi. Each room has a TV with VCR access (you rent tapes in town), a phone, and a minifridge. *8 Chester St., Box 456, Nantucket 02554, tel. 508/228–9696. 4 rooms, 1 suite, 1 apartment. Facilities: Continental breakfast. AE, MC, V.*

★ **Cliff Lodge.** Guest rooms at this B&B are big, bright, and airy, with lots of sky blue and crisp white, pastel hooked rugs on spatter-painted floors, country curtains and furnishings, down comforters, and phones and small TVs. Built in 1771, the lodge preserves lots of old-house flavor, in moldings, wainscoting, and wide-board floors. Some baths are very small. The very pleasant apartment has a fireplaced living room, a private deck and entrance, and a large eat-in kitchen. In addition to the attractive common rooms, guests may take afternoon tea or cocktails (setups and snacks provided) on the wicker sun porch, the garden terrace, or the roofwalk patio, with a great view of the harbor. Also available are apartments on Old North Wharf, including a four-bedroom with fireplace and cathedral ceiling. *9 Cliff Rd., Nantucket 02554, tel. 508/228–9480. 11 rooms, 1 apt. Facilities: Continental breakfast, afternoon tea in season, common refrigerator and coffeemaker, barbecue grill, beach towels, parking. No smoking in rooms. AE, MC, V. Closed Jan.; weekdays in Feb.*

Nantucket Settlements. These attractively decorated properties consist of three apartment houses and a complex of seven cottages, all with kitchens, TVs, phones, and access to free laundry facilities. Right in town are the Nantucket Whaler (8 N. Water St.), an 1846 Greek Revival with pilastered white clapboard facade and a large deck, and the 1822 Grey Goose (24 Hussey St.), with high ceilings, old moldings, and antique-looking furnishings. Within a half-mile of town center are the Orange Suites (95 Orange St.), in a late 18th-century house renovated in 1987 with all new kitchens and baths and a brick patio with barbecue grill. Also a half-mile out are the gray-shingled Brush Lane Cottages, in a quiet compound with lots of flowers and greenery; the newest cottages are spacious and bright, with cathedral ceilings, lots of white and light wood, oak cabinets in big kitchens, and French doors that open onto decks. There's daily maid service, and baby-sitting is available. *Office: 8 N. Water St., Box 1337, Nantucket 02554, tel. 508/228–6597 or 800/462–6882, fax 508/228–6291. 24 units (studios to 3-bedroom cottages). MC, V.*

76 Main Street. Built in 1883 by a sea captain, just above the bustle of the shops, this B&B carefully blends antiques and reproductions, Oriental rugs, handmade quilts, and lots of fine woods. The Victorian entrance hall is of cherry and is dominated by a long, elaborately carved staircase. Room No. 3, originally the dining room, also has wonderful woodwork, a carved-wood armoire, and twin four-posters; spacious No. 1, once the front parlor, has three large windows, massive redwood pocket doors, and a bed with eyelet spread and canopy. Both are on the first floor. The motel-like rooms in the 1955 annex out back have low ceilings and are a bit dark but are large and good for families: They have cable TV and a minifridge. *76 Main St., Nantucket 02554, tel. 508/228–2533. 18 rooms. Facilities: Continental breakfast, common refrigerator. No smoking. AE, MC, V.*

Ten Lyon Street Inn. A five-minute walk from the town center, this mostly new house has been rebuilt with historical architectural touches such as variable-width plank floors, salvaged Colonial mantels on the nonworking fireplaces, and hefty ceiling beams of antiqued red oak. The white walls and blond woodwork provide a clean stage for exquisite antique Oriental rugs in deep, rich colors; choice antiques, such as Room No. 1's French tester bed draped in white mosquito netting; and English floral fabrics, down comforters, and big pillows. Bathrooms are white and bright; several have separate shower and antique tub, and all have antique porcelain pedestal sinks and brass fixtures. The garden is pleasant for sitting, but there's little common space indoors. *10 Lyon St., Nantucket 02554, tel. 508/228–5040. 7 rooms. Facilities: health-conscious Continental breakfast. AE, MC, V. Closed mid-Dec.–mid-Apr.*

Inexpensive–Moderate

Century House. This 1833 house, a few blocks from the town center, was built to serve guests, and innkeeper Jean Heron continues to do so with enthusiasm. The decor is casual: wallpapers and fabrics (including down comforters) in the Laura Ashley light-floral style, homey furnishings (some canopy beds) on spatter-painted wide-board floors. A lavish breakfast buffet highlighted by homemade granola is served in the country kitchen or on the wide veranda. In the afternoon guests gather for tea or cocktails; setups and snacks are provided. The innkeepers also rent two cottages, one in 'Sconset across from the beach and one on Nantucket harbor. *10 Cliff Rd., Box 603, Nantucket 02554, tel. 508/228–0530. 12 rooms, 8 with private bath. Facilities: Continental breakfast, common TV (hours very limited). MC, V.*

Chestnut House. At this centrally located guest house, the innkeepers' hand-hooked rugs and paintings, along with their son's Tiffany-style lamps, are everywhere, creating homey guest rooms. All rooms have minifridges; each suite has a sitting room with sofa and TV. The guest parlor reflects the Arts and Crafts style, and some rooms have William Morris–theme wallpapers. The cheery, newly redone cottage sleeps four (queen-size bed and sofa bed) and has a full kitchen and bath and a small deck—a convenient option for a family here in the center of town. *3 Chestnut St., Nantucket 02554, tel. 508/228–0049. 3 rooms, 3 suites, 1 cottage. Facilities: morning coffee in season, common TV. AE, MC, V.*

★ **Corner House.** Accommodations at this B&B a block or two from the town center range from small, rustic third-floor rooms with tiny baths in the main house (a 1790 gem with lots of old-house flavor) to rooms with cathedral ceilings in a new building nearby. Some rooms have separate sitting or extra sleeping areas, TVs, or refrigerators; all have interesting beds (antique, reproduction, canopy, brass, tall-post) on firm mattresses, topped with down pillows and comforters. The main house's original keeping room, where guests gather for tea, and a large living room with fireplace and TV both feature richly detailed Colonial woodwork, as do some rooms. There's also a wicker-filled screened porch and a garden terrace. Golf, tennis, and sailing packages are available. *49 Centre St., Box 1828, Nantucket 02554, tel. 508/228–1530. 14 rooms, 1 suite. Facilities: Continental breakfast, afternoon tea, common TV, fax. No smoking in rooms. MC, V. Closed mid-Jan.–mid-Feb.*

Hawthorn House. Not only did innkeeper Mitch Carl continue the family business when he opened his guest house; he opened his inn just down the street from his folks' place, the Chestnut House (*see above*). Mitch and his wife, Diane, have filled their 1850 house with art, hooked rugs, and stained glass; each room has a minifridge. The small rooms are decorated with antiques, William Morris–style wallpapers, and Diane's handmade quilts. A dark but conveniently located cottage sleeps two and has air-conditioning and TV. *2 Chestnut St., Nantucket 02554, tel. 508/228–1468. 9 rooms, 7 with private bath; 1 cottage. Facilities: morning coffee, common TV. MC, V.*

★ **Martin House Inn.** This nicely refurbished B&B in an 1803 house off the main drag offers mostly spacious rooms with four-poster beds or canopies, pretty linens, and fresh flowers; several have queen-size beds and couches. Room No. 21, on the second floor, has a queen-size canopy bed, a fireplace, a minifridge, and a private porch overlooking the backyard. The large living room with a fireplace and the wide porch with hammock invite lingering. Third-floor shared-bath rooms are sunny and bright, with a quirky under-eaves feel. *61 Centre St., Box 743, Nantucket 02554, tel. 508/228–0678. 13 rooms, 9 with private bath (4 rooms share 1 bath). Facilities: large Continental breakfast, sherry in rooms, common TV, piano. No smoking. AE, MC, V.*

Inexpensive

Nesbitt Inn. This family-run guest house in the center of town offers comfortable, shared-bath rooms (including cheap singles) sweetly done in authentically Victorian style, with lace curtains, some marble-top and brass antiques, and a sink in each room. Some beds are not as firm as they should be, and the location (next door to a popular bar-restaurant) means it gets noisy (ask for a room on the quieter side), but the Nesbitt is still a very good buy. The backyard's good for children. *21 Broad St., Box 1019, Nantucket 02554, tel. 508/228–0156 or 508/228–2446. 10 doubles and 3 singles share 3 baths. Pets allowed. Facilities: Continental breakfast, common refrigerator, swing set, backyard deck and grill, beach towels and blankets. MC, V. No smoking in rooms.*

The Arts and Nightlife

For listings of events, see the free seasonal weekly *Nantucket Map & Legend*, the ferry companion paper *Yesterday's Island*, and both island newspapers. All venues listed below are located in Nantucket Town, unless otherwise indicated.

The Arts

Nantucket Filmworks presents a different slide show on Nantucket each year, created by one of the island's best photographers, Cary Hazlegrove. Shows are given at the Methodist Church (Centre and Main Sts., tel. 508/228–3783) mid-June–mid-September.

Nantucket Island School of Design and the Arts (Wauwinet Rd., tel. 508/228–9248; for schedule, write to Box 958, Nantucket 02554) offers a year-round program of classes, lectures, and slide shows for adults and children.

Theater **Actors Theatre of Nantucket** (Methodist Church, Centre and Main Sts., tel. 508/228–6325) presents several Broadway-style plays Memorial Day–Columbus Day, plus children's post-beach matinees, comedy nights, late-night productions, and readings.

Theatre Workshop of Nantucket (Bennett Hall, 62 Centre St., tel. 508/228–4305), a community theater since 1956, offers plays, musicals, and staged readings year-round.

Music **Nantucket Arts Council** (tel. 508/228–2227) sponsors a music series (jazz, country, classical) at the Methodist Church on Centre Street September–June.

Nantucket Chamber Music Center (Coffin School, Winter St., tel. 508/228–3352) offers year-round choral and instrumental concerts as well as instruction.

In July and August, **Nantucket Musical Arts Society** (Box 897, Nantucket 02554, tel. 508/228–3735) holds Tuesday-evening concerts featuring internationally acclaimed musicians (past participants include Virgil Thomson and Ned Rorem) at the First Congregational Church (62 Centre St.), and free informal "Meet the Artists" gatherings the previous evening elsewhere.

Also in July and August, **Noonday Concerts** on an 1831 Goodrich organ are given Thursdays at noon at the Unitarian Church (11 Orange St., tel. 508/228–5466).

Band concerts (tel. 508/228–1700) are held on Sundays in July and August at 7 PM at the Straight Wharf bandstand.

Film **Dreamland Theatre** (19 S. Water St., tel. 508/228–5356) and **Gaslight Theatre** (1 N. Union St., tel. 508/228–4435) are the island's two first-run theaters. The **Siasconset Casino** (New St., Siasconset, tel. 508/257–6661) shows first-run films in season—bring a pillow for the metal folding chairs.

Nightlife

If you're in the mood for something a little different during the off season, the **Hearth at the Harbor House** (*see* Dining, *above*) hosts concerts, children's events, and auctions with wine-reception previews either individually or as part of early-dinner packages.

Tavern Restaurants **The Brotherhood of Thieves** (*see* Dining, *above*) has live folk music year-round. The well-stocked bar offers an interesting selection of beers and ales, plus dozens of cordials and liqueurs.

The Tap Room (*see* Dining, *above*) has live easy-listening piano or guitar, and sometimes Irish folk music, year-round.

Piano Lounges **The Hearth at the Harbor House** (*see* Dining, *above*) has dancing to live music (country to folk) in its attractive, fireplaced lounge on weekends year-round and to Top 40 tunes by a piano-and-vocal duo most nights in season. Also available are darts, backgammon, cribbage, sports on four large-screen TVs, and a fun light menu.

The Regatta at the White Elephant (Easton St., tel. 508/228–2500) has a formal, harbor-view lounge with a pianist playing show tunes most nights from Memorial Day to mid-September. Proper dress is suggested. It's also a good place to sit and watch the boats over afternoon drinks and hors d'oeuvres.

Dance Clubs   Open daily year-round are **The Box** (aka Chicken Box; 6 Dave St., off Lower Orange St., tel. 508/228–9717) and **The Muse** (44 Atlantic Ave., tel. 508/228–6873 or 508/228–8801), where all ages dance to rock, reggae (especially popular on the island), and other music, live or recorded. The Box has live music every night in season, weekends off-season. The Muse also has a take-out pizza shop (tel. 508/228–1471).

The **Rose & Crown** (*see* Dining, *above*) is a friendly, noisy seasonal restaurant with a big bar, a small dance floor, live bands, DJs, and karaoke nights.

Index

Personal Itinerary

Departure *Date*

Time

Transportation

Arrival *Date*   *Time*

Departure *Date*   *Time*

Transportation

Accommodations

Arrival *Date*   *Time*

Departure *Date*   *Time*

Transportation

Accommodations

Arrival *Date*   *Time*

Departure *Date*   *Time*

Transportation

Accommodations

Personal Itinerary

Arrival *Date*   *Time*

Departure *Date*   *Time*

Transportation

Accommodations

Arrival *Date*   *Time*

Departure *Date*   *Time*

Transportation

Accommodations

Arrival *Date*   *Time*

Departure *Date*   *Time*

Transportation

Accommodations

Arrival *Date*   *Time*

Departure *Date*   *Time*

Transportation

Accommodations

Addresses

Name _____ | *Name* _____

Address _____ | *Address* _____

Telephone _____ | *Telephone* _____

Name _____ | *Name* _____

Address _____ | *Address* _____

Telephone _____ | *Telephone* _____

Name _____ | *Name* _____

Address _____ | *Address* _____

Telephone _____ | *Telephone* _____

Name _____ | *Name* _____

Address _____ | *Address* _____

Telephone _____ | *Telephone* _____

Name _____ | *Name* _____

Address _____ | *Address* _____

Telephone _____ | *Telephone* _____

Name _____ | *Name* _____

Address _____ | *Address* _____

Telephone _____ | *Telephone* _____

Name _____ | *Name* _____

Address _____ | *Address* _____

Telephone _____ | *Telephone* _____

Name _____ | *Name* _____

Address _____ | *Address* _____

Telephone _____ | *Telephone* _____

Discover New England all over again this year

HALLIDAY'S NEW ENGLAND FOOD EXPLORER
Tours for Food Lovers

Now — a guidebook to New England for food lovers. In 12 tours through 6 states, discover the region's best markets, restaurants, farms, inns, even road-side stands in the literate, opinionated company of veteran food writer Fred Halliday. Packed full of culinary lore, food sources, and recipes, here's the best place to start the most delicious vacation of your life.

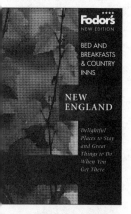

FODOR'S BED & BREAKFASTS AND COUNTRY INNS — NEW ENGLAND

This meticulously honest and thoroughly up-to-date guide includes critical reviews of more than 280 inns and B&Bs, plus everything you need to know about what to see and do and where to eat when you get there. The guide has 109 illustrations and its 36 pages of maps and charts instantly locate B&Bs with pools, golf, gourmet dining, and facilities for children, nonsmokers, and pets.

FODOR'S NEW ENGLAND '94
A Four Season Guide with the Best of the B&Bs and Ski Resorts

Nobody knows New England better than Fodor's, and in this discriminating, accurate, and up-to-the-minute guide you'll find all the best of New England — its top hotels, resorts, inns, and B&Bs in every category, great restaurants, cafes, and diners, wonderful shops for antiques and crafts, where to stay at 50 ski resorts, festivals and seasonal events, fishing, camping, and other outdoor sports, and 51 pages of maps.

At bookstores everywhere, or call 1-800-533-6478   **Fodor's**

Fodor's Travel Guides

Available at bookstores everywhere, or call 1-800-533-6478, 24 hours a day.

U.S. Guides

Alaska

Arizona

Boston

California

Cape Cod, Martha's Vineyard, Nantucket

The Carolinas & the Georgia Coast

Chicago

Colorado

Florida

Hawaii

Las Vegas, Reno, Tahoe

Los Angeles

Maine, Vermont, New Hampshire

Maui

Miami & the Keys

New England

New Orleans

New York City

Pacific North Coast

Philadelphia & the Pennsylvania Dutch Country

The Rockies

San Diego

San Francisco

Santa Fe, Taos, Albuquerque

Seattle & Vancouver

The South

The U.S. & British Virgin Islands

The Upper Great Lakes Region

USA

Vacations in New York State

Vacations on the Jersey Shore

Virginia & Maryland

Waikiki

Walt Disney World and the Orlando Area

Washington, D.C.

Foreign Guides

Acapulco, Ixtapa, Zihuatanejo

Australia & New Zealand

Austria

The Bahamas

Baja & Mexico's Pacific Coast Resorts

Barbados

Berlin

Bermuda

Brazil

Brittany & Normandy

Budapest

Canada

Cancun, Cozumel, Yucatan Peninsula

Caribbean

China

Costa Rica, Belize, Guatemala

The Czech Republic & Slovakia

Eastern Europe

Egypt

Euro Disney

Europe

Europe's Great Cities

Florence & Tuscany

France

Germany

Great Britain

Greece

The Himalayan Countries

Hong Kong

India

Ireland

Israel

Italy

Japan

Kenya & Tanzania

Korea

London

Madrid & Barcelona

Mexico

Montreal & Quebec City

Morocco

Moscow & St. Petersburg

The Netherlands, Belgium & Luxembourg

New Zealand

Norway

Nova Scotia, Prince Edward Island & New Brunswick

Paris

Portugal

Provence & the Riviera

Rome

Russia & the Baltic Countries

Scandinavia

Scotland

Singapore

South America

Southeast Asia

Spain

Sweden

Switzerland

Thailand

Tokyo

Toronto

Turkey

Vienna & the Danube Valley

Yugoslavia

Special Series

Fodor's Affordables

Caribbean

Europe

Florida

France

Germany

Great Britain

London

Italy

Paris

Fodor's Bed & Breakfast and Country Inns Guides

Canada's Great Country Inns

California

Cottages, B&Bs and Country Inns of England and Wales

Mid-Atlantic Region

New England

The Pacific Northwest

The South

The Southwest

The Upper Great Lakes Region

The West Coast

The Berkeley Guides

California

Central America

Eastern Europe

France

Germany

Great Britain & Ireland

Mexico

Pacific Northwest & Alaska

San Francisco

Fodor's Exploring Guides

Australia

Britain

California

The Caribbean

Florida

France

Germany

Ireland

Italy

London

New York City

Paris

Rome

Singapore & Malaysia

Spain

Thailand

Fodor's Flashmaps

New York

Washington, D.C.

Fodor's Pocket Guides

Bahamas

Barbados

Jamaica

London

New York City

Paris

Puerto Rico

San Francisco

Washington, D.C.

Fodor's Sports

Cycling

Hiking

Running

Sailing

The Insider's Guide to the Best Canadian Skiing

Skiing in the USA & Canada

Fodor's Three-In-Ones (guidebook, language cassette, and phrase book)

France

Germany

Italy

Mexico

Spain

Fodor's Special-Interest Guides

Accessible USA

Cruises and Ports of Call

Euro Disney

Halliday's New England Food Explorer

Healthy Escapes

London Companion

Shadow Traffic's New York Shortcuts and Traffic Tips

Sunday in New York

Walt Disney World and the Orlando Area

Walt Disney World for Adults

Fodor's Touring Guides

Touring Europe

Touring USA: Eastern Edition

Fodor's Vacation Planners

Great American Vacations

National Parks of the East

National Parks of the West

The Wall Street Journal Guides to Business Travel

Europe

International Cities

Pacific Rim

USA & Canada

WHEREVER YOU TRAVEL, *H*ELP IS NEVER FAR AWAY.

From planning your trip to providing travel assistance along the way, American Express® Travel Service Offices* are always there to help.

Boston/Cape Cod

American Express Travel Service
One Court Street
Boston
(617) 723-8400

For the office nearest you, call
1-800-YES-AMEX